HISTORICAL COLLECTIONS
of the Georgia Chapters
Daughters of the
American Revolution
Volume I

I0130432

SEVENTEEN
Georgia Counties

With an Index by
Lelia Thornton Gentry

CLEARFIELD

Historical Collections
of the Georgia Chapters
Daughters of the American Revolution
Volume I
was originally published
Atlanta, Georgia, 1926.
Reprinted with permission of
The Georgia State DAR.

Index to Volume I
was originally published
Atlanta, Georgia, 1931.
Reprinted with permission of
The Georgia State DAR.

Reprinted, two volumes in one, for
Clearfield Company, Inc. by
Genealogical Publishing Co., Inc.
Baltimore, Maryland
1995, 2002

International Standard Book Number: 0-8063-4580-2

Made in the United States of America

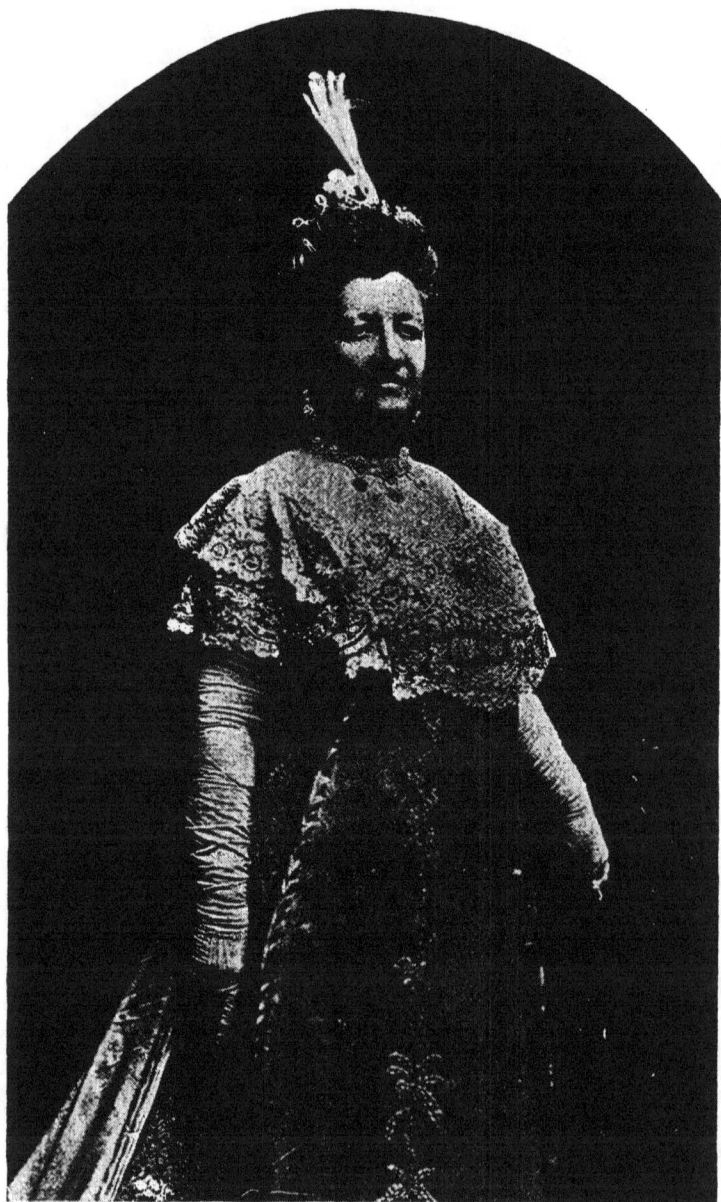

MRS. WILLIAM LAWSON PEEL

A GREAT GEORGIAN

(Tribute to Mrs. William Lawson Peel)

By AGNES NEVILLE DAVIS

———

The deeds of men live after them:
Their greatness measures by their deeds—
And glory crowneth all.

We should live so that when we die
The world would say with parting sigh
A useful life has passed away,
That with the closing of the day,
In memory can not die.

For deeds and glory measure far—
They live and show just what we are—
And so we live for aye!

Just so she lived in deed and thought:
Her greatness measured in each heart—
Her glory crowning all.

A daughter of the Empire State—
Whose name shall be among the great:
And we shall know and understand
Just how she gave her heart and hand
For dear old Georgia's fame—
Nor from her glory take!

The deeds of men live after them:
They show the greatness of their lives—
And glory crowneth all.

As the sun at even when it goes to rest—
Shows in its golden glory best—
Her useful life has reached the end:
We say with a sigh we have lost a friend
We never can forget.

Her greatness measures to the height
Of Glory's star in heaven's light:
Her deeds are with us yet!

PREFACE

In offering this volume of Historical Collections, the Georgia Daughters of the American Revolution concludes its labor of love for one whom they will ever hold in reverent memory, Mrs. William Lawson Peel, Founder and first Regent of the Joseph Habersham Chapter of Atlanta, Ga., Honorary State Regent of Georgia, Originator of and first chairman of the National Committee of Real Daughters, and former Vice President General of the National Society Daughters of the American Revolution.

This book is one of great value to historical and genealogical students, giving as it does, in convenient form, many facts gleaned from many sources of the early history of Georgia, and the names of many Revolutionary heroes buried in North Carolina.

It represents many days of careful and painstaking study, and contains considerable matter never before published. We hereby express our thanks to all who have so kindly contributed to this work.

The State Conference of 1923, established the Lucy Cook Peel Memorial Fund for the preservation of records, as a tribute to Mrs. William Lawson Peel. She was the first to lead the Georgia D. A. R. into definite lines of historical work.

In presenting this volume to the public, we wish to thank Miss Helen M. Prescott, genealogist of the Joseph Habersham Chapter, and member of Executive Board, Ga. D. A. R., for requesting that the Chapter donate the valuable county records, which she had collected years ago, for volume 4, Joseph Habersham Historical Collections; Mrs. W. B. Daniel for the Telfair County marriage records; Mrs. B. C. Wall for the very interesting history of St. Paul's church, which she had presented to Mrs.

Peel for this volume; Mrs. Walter S. Wilson, and Mrs. Jno. L. Davidson for the careful and painstaking work they did in compiling the Franklin County records; Miss Anna Blair and Mrs. Charles W. Tillet for the list of North Carolina revolutionary soldiers; Mrs. Eugene E. Smith for the genealogies of the Christian and Russell families; and Governor Peter Early Chapter for copies of land grants.

MRS. W. F. DYKES, Chairman,
MRS. HOWARD H. McCALL,
MISS HELEN PRESCOTT,
MRS. CHRISTIAN CLARK,
MRS. FORT LAND,
MRS. C. H. LEAVY,
MRS. J. H. REDDING,
MRS. DI INGRAM,
Lucy Cook Peel Memorial Committee.

DEDICATED TO A GREAT GEORGIAN

Mrs. William Lawson Peel

Founder and Life Regent Joseph Habersham Chapter D. A. R.,
Honorary State Regent Ga. D. A. R., Vice-president
General National Society D. A. R.

———

"As the sun at even when it goes to rest
Shows in its golden glory best,
Her useful life has reached the end.
We say with a sigh, we have lost a friend
We never can forget.
Her greatness measures to the height
Of glory's star in heaven's light."

———

Lucy Cook Peel was born Nov. 13th, 1849, in Schley
County, Georgia, on the plantation of her father, Gen.
Philip Cook, who rendered distinguished service in the
Confederate Army, afterwards serving for many years
as Secretary of State.

She graduated from Wesleyan Female College at
Macon, Ga. Following her graduation she served many
years as president of the Alumnae Association.

On April 22nd, 1874, she was married to William Lawson Peel. Coming to Atlanta to live in 1876, until her
passing, Feb. 16, 1923, she was always to be found a distinguished leader and ardent co-worker in every project
looking toward the development of her home city, State
and the Southland, she loved with such patriotic devotion.

A patron of the fine arts, there was no field of culture in
which she lacked interest. Her home for many years a
center of art and music, in which hundreds of prominent
visitors, artists, musicians, writers, and men and women

of affairs were entertained, true Southern Hospitality reigning supreme.

A brilliant writer, her forceful articles on topics of interest and the City Beautiful, an organization of which she was president, served to stimulate much thought and interest, and the movement for beautifying streets, parks, and establishing play grounds was greatly influenced by these contributions from her facile pen.

An accomplished musician and ardent lover of music, to her and her husband Col. William Lawson Peel, president of the Atlanta Music Festival Association, is due the renaissance in music which has made possible the production of Grand Opera in Atlanta annually, an outstanding event of the greatest artistic and cultural value. To put the varied material resources of her beloved Georgia before the public, a Georgia Products dinner was organized and with the assistance of the Joseph Habersham Chapter D. A. R., a Georgia Products dinner was served to a thousand guests, serving as an inspiration for similar dinners throughout the state, emphasizing the possibilities of Georgia's resources.

The necessary legislation for the celebration of Georgia Day was also initiated and successfully inaugurated by her with the co-operation of the Joseph Habersham Chapter. During the World War, as president of the National League for Women's Service, chairman for the Fatherless Children of France, directing activities for the comfort of the soldiers at Camp Gordon, no task was too large or too small for her to render the best service possible, giving generously of her wealth, time, and executive ability.

As a charter member of the Atlanta Chapter D. A. R., second oldest chapter by a few hours in the United States, untold assistance was rendered Georgia, and the National Society by collecting the records and presenting to the State a roster of five thousand Revolutionary soldiers. For this conspicuous service she was made Honorary State Regent of Georgia. She was honored by the National Society by being elected Vice-president General and appointed National Chairman of Real daughters. Through her efforts the legislation necessary for the pensions given Real daughters was secured.

The Joseph Habersham Chapter D. A. R. was organized at her home Feb. 10th, 1900. Her genius, untiring devotion and splendid leadership, coupled with a deep devotion to the organization, and the principle upon which it is founded were concentrated upon the building of a Memorial Hall to American heroes of all wars.

Today, crowning those efforts, her memory is enshrined in the hearts of the membership of one of the largest chapters in the National Society.

The membership gather together in a beautiful and stately building, where rare historical records, compiled and published by the chapter under her guidance are of untold value. Priceless Revolutionary relics and relics of other wars and times will preserve the history of past and present, and from this memorial building the influence of her Idealism and Patriotism will be felt for years to come. In truth, "Her deeds are with us yet."

With affectionate appreciation,

MRS. WARREN D. WHITE, Ex-Regent.

Historian Joseph Habersham Chapter D. A. R.

CONTENTS

BALDWIN COUNTY.

Baldwin County was formed in 1803 from Hancock, and Milledgeville made the County Seat. The Court House was burned in 1861 and all the early deeds were destroyed, but the old wills were saved and they are now well cared for in a good fireproof vault. They are recorded in two books "1806 to 1819" and "1819 to 1864." These are well indexed and in neat condition.

The Marriage records are in books "A," 1819 to 1833, and "B," 1833 to 1851, all indexed. In the back of book "A" are nearly 300 marriages, from 1807 to 1818, which were made up from original papers after the first book was accidentally lost in the burning of the Court House. A list of these is given.

First Book of Wills, 1806-1819.

Allen, John	Buchannan, Robert	Bedingfield, John
Benson, Mary	Beckcom, Charlotte	Baker, Joseph
Brimfield, James	Brown, John	Buchannan, Sarah
Barrow, Nancy	Barrow, James	Bass, Martha
Chewing, Samuel	Cocks, Henry	Coleman, Elliott
Carter, Francis	Cooper, Edmund	Cooper, James
Calhoun, Philip	Curry, Cary	Digby, Joseph
Devereaux, A. M.	Du Bose, Peter, Sr.	Delannay, James A.
Doles, Jesse	Ellis, William	Edmundson, James
Freeney, Robert	Flewellen, Abner	Freeman, Frederick
Fourd, Braxton	Fair, Peter	Gray, Zachariah
Greenlee, Samuel	Goodwin, "Ru B"	Gray, Pricilla
Gholston, Eggleston	Harvey, James	Hammett, James
Howard, Benjamin, Sr.	Harvey, Michael	Horton, Stephen
Holt, Simon	Hepburn, Joseph S.	Harris, Thomas
Hines, John B.	Haws, Claiborne	Holt, Thaddeus
Jones, John	Jemison, Henry	Jackson, Drury
Jackson, Peter	Jenkins, Jesse	Justice, Dempsey
Jenkins, Polly W.	Kirkley, Charlotte	King, John
Kirkpatrick, Samuel	Lewis, John	Lester, James
Lewis, Elizabeth	Moss, Henry, Sr.	Martin, William
Matthews, Jeremiah	M'Cormick, James	Moore, Luke
Morris, Obediah	M'Cormick (Agreement)	Miles, John
Manderson, John H.	M'Gehee, William	M'Millan, John
Neaves, James	Neaves, John	Owens, Elijah
Peterson, John	Parham, Stith	Parker, Jacob
Pickett, William	Pitts, John	Payne, Thomas
Pine, Tamsey T.	Pryor, Martin L.	Pickett, Betsy
Parham, Haddon	Rowlet, Peter	Ready, John

Redding, Charles
Reynolds, James
Sims, William
Stephens, Thomas
Slaughter, Samuel
Sanford, Jesse
Tipton, James
Trice, Benjamin
Wiley, Moses
Wilson, William
Wynn, Robert
White, Edward

Redding, William
Smith, Peyton S.
Scott, James
Smith, Marshall
Scurlock, Joshua
Smith, John H.
Tomlinson, John
Vickers, Nancy
Walker, Elizabeth
Waller, Joseph, Jr.
Worsham, Archer
Williamson, Charles

Rutherford, Nancy
Sayre, Francis
Sheppard, Charles
Smith, Griffin
Scoggin, Smith
Smith, Richard J.
Tiller, Joseph
Williamson, William
Weaver, Henry
Waller, Joseph, Sr.
Wright, John S.

Will Book 1819 to 1864.

Anderson, Elizabeth
Bower, Benaniel
Blount, R. A.
Butts, Lewis
Bass, Martha
Babb, Martha
Clayton, George R. Sr.
Campbell, D. C.
Doyle, Dennis
Du Bourg, Andrew
Ellington, Martha
Fort, Tomlinson
Gill, Days
Geddes, Ann E.
Grantland, Seaton
Huff, Polly
Hodge, John
Johnson, Samuel
Jordan, E. T.
King, Margaret
Lewis, William Jr.
Tamar, Thomas B.
M'Murray, James
Malone, Charles
Moran, John
Meacham, Angelina
Mahon, Zilpha
Moore, Pricilla J. M.
Myrick, Martha
M'Donald, Catherine
Park, Susan
Rowell, Richard
Root, Eveline
Smith, Mansell I.
Smith, L. L.
Speights, John
Tompkins, Wiley J.

Anderson, William
Bonner, James
Buchannan, B.
Blizzard, Brinkley
Brown, Henry
Chapman, Milly
Clements, Stephen
Conn, John
Dyer, Ann
Delannay, Maud S.
Foard, Jane S.
Forard, A. J.
Graybill, Michael
Gladdin, James
Hammond, Abner
Humphries, William C.
Haas, John
Jarratt, Alexander
Jarratt, Ann
Lamar, Zachariah
Lynch, Drucilla
Murphy, Cornelius
Malone, Henry W.
Murray, George W.
Meacham, Henry
Marler, Ann
M'Neil, John S.
Murph, George
M'Crary, Francis M.
M'Donald, Maria
Rutherford, John
Rice, Susan
Robinson, John C.
Stovall, Joseph
Shoeinbein, Frederick
Torrence, William
Tucker, Sarah B.

Brown, George A.
Banks, Solomon
Buchannan, Mary Ann
Banks, Jane
Bowers, Matilda
Crowder, Thomas S.
Carter, Farish
Davies, William
Dolee, Thomas
Daniel, Augustus
Foard, Thomas
Fitzgerald, Catherine
Greene, Elizabeth
Grimes, John
Hall, Benjamin
Howard, Penelope
Ivey, Robert
Jordan, Green H.
King, Elijah
Lewis, William
Leeves, George
Myrick, John
Murphy, Drury
Moore, Whittington
Mitchell, William S.
M'Geehee, Catherine
Mitchell, J. J.
Moore, Mary
Murph, Mary
Park, Joseph
Robinson, John R.
Russell, Martin
Steel, Elizabeth
Stubbs, James W.
Sanford, William
Tucker, Mrs. Ann
Turner, Stephen C.

Thomas, Mary
Vinson, E. C.
West, Joseph
Williams, Peter J.
Wooten, Josiah M.
White, Benjamin A.

Tinsley, William B.
Welburn, Robert
Washington, Robert B.
Walker, Joel
Ward, John
Young, Thomas

Veasey, Thomas
Whitaker, William
West, Moses S.
Ward, Ridley
Ward, Peyton

Marriages, 1807 to 1818.

Adams, Anthony, and Rutha Rutledge.
Aveventon, James, and Nancy Griffin.
Allen, William, and Polly Davis.
Acridge, Abel, and Polly Clark.
Allumus, James, and Sarah Jackson.
Alexander, John, and Sally Bridges.
Abercrombie, Willie, and Eliza M. Carson.
Anderson, Abram and Elizabeth McMullan.
Allum, John, and Pamelia Scoggin.
Belding, William, and Jenny Gaw.
Brookins, Ben, and Prissa Sawyer.
Beckham, Daniel, and Fanny Hawkins.
Bateman, Bryant, and Charity McCrary.
Boggs, James, and Polly Simmons.
Borland, William, and Sally Thompson.
Brown, Hollinger, and Sally Marcus.
Brown, Mark, and Sally Waller.
Barksdale, Terrell, and Sarah Harvey.
Brooks, Wm., and Elizabeth Lavane.
Berryhill, James, and Elizabeth Clemons.
Brown, John, and Sally Taliaferro.
Barrow, James, and Lucy Miles.
Bostwick, Stephen, and Polly Wells.
Bernard, John, and Elizabeth Smith.
Bivins, John, and Cidney Davidson.
Brown, Luke, and Delilah Lacy.
Bivins, William, and Eliza W. Harris.
Buchannan, James, and Nancy Herrington.
Byington, Amos F., and Nancy Freeny.
Bruen, Timothy, and Mary Louisa Downer.
Bivins, Wm., and Polly Hall.

Beasley, James C., and Temperance Jackson.
Brown, Hugh, and Elizabeth Deane.
Boon, John, and Alcey Selby.
Boreland, Wm., and Sarah King.
Baker, Charles, and Celia Clarke.
Baxter, Thomas W., and Mary Ann Wiley.
Copeland, Wm., and Agnes Triplett.
Cox, Ephraim, and Lotty Crawford.
Carnes, Thomas P., and Susanna Crews.
Clark, Drury, and Susanna Hammond.
Calhoun, Irwin, and Martha Lawrence.
Chappell, Benjamin, and Betsy Bass.
Collins, James, and Elizabeth Benson.
Chapman, Isaiah, and Frances Buchannan.
Cobb, Jacob, and Susan Allen.
Childs, Daniel, and Sarah Andrews.
Callaway, Elisha Hall, and Delilah Proctor.
Chaines, Benjamin, and Sarah Powell.
Curry, Carvey, and Nelly Moore.
Cooper, Josiah, and Elizabeth Jones.
Chapman, Ambrose, and Elizabeth Andrews.
Carter, Francis, and Polly Holly.
Campbell, John D., and Martha Gates.
Chapman, Isaiah, and Prudence P. Slaughter.
Crenshaw, Wm. H., and Susan N. Wallace.
Crews, Francis, and Nelly Marks.
Chapman, J. D., and Martha Chapman.
Chavis, Wm., and Rhoda Miflin.
Coyne, Phineas, and Nancy D. Franklin.
Denham, Nathaniel, and Milly Periman.
Davis, Ichabod, and Patsy Brooks.
Darnell, John, and Mary Lord.
Dawson, John, and Ann McDonald.
De La Huff, G. W. F., and Mary Pruet.
Disbrou, Wm., and Edy Lineth.
Dukes, Wm., and Polly Harris.
Douglas, Stephen, and Polly Rice.

Davis, Abner, and Nancy Williams.
Dupree, Jesse, and Polly Moore.
Doles, Benjamin, and Rebecca Stevens.
Davis, William, and Sarah Grantland.
Easties, David, and Fany Parker.
Edwards, William, and Sally Cox.
Etheridge, John, and Frances Rainey.
Etheridge, John, and Susanna Langford.
Evans, John, and Cinthia Kelley.
English, James, and Rebecca Bankston.
Etheridge, Samuel, and Sally Raines.
Etheridge, Lewis, and Sarah Chambliss.
Evans, Anselm L., and Jane Waggoner.
Freeman, Frederick, and Patsy Moss.
Foster, Absalom, and Elizabeth Sturdevant.
Fort, Moses, and Eudocia W. Moore.
Flewellen, Wm., and Mary Thweatt.
Green, Daniel, and Fanny Garrat.
Green, Myles, and Nancy Bass.
Gallman, Silas, and Patsy Fairchild.
Gleen, Otway, and Patience Smith.
Gallier, John, and Mary Ann Davis.
Gates, Elisha, and Ann B. Muzzell.
Hayes, Wm., and Janet Wilson.
Howe, Robert, and Susan Gray.
Holder, Wm., and Sally McCormick.
Heming, Micajah, and Rebecca Cox.
Head, Thomas, and Rebecca Haddaway.
Hill, Robert, and Lucy Wilkinson.
Hill, Jeptha, and Temperance Chapman.
Harden, Thomas and Behethland Pruett.
Harvey, Thomas, and Frances Coleman.
Herring, George, and Charlotte Wilson.
Horton, James, Jr., and Sarah Hilliard.
Hansel, Wm. Y., and Susan Harris.
Huff, Edmund, and Milly Harrison.
Haws, Clayburn, and Sally Pickett.

Hardee, John, and Peggy Mitchell.
Horton, Elijah, and Nancy Holcomb.
Hardwick, Wm. H., and Winifred A. Richardson.
Horton, Edmund, and Martha Freeny.
Hammond, Daniel J., and Louisa Brown.
Howard, John, and Harriet Smith.
Hickman, John, and Elizabeth McDade.
Hilliard, James, and Polly Carter.
Hill, Robert H., and Elizabeth Spencer.
Hutchinson, Wm., and Elizabeth Wooten. (1817)
Hoy, James, and Phebe Sims.
Lebbetter, James, and Peggy Baker.
Loughren, Joseph, and Polly Barzill.
Leonard, John, and Rebecca Nobles.
Lamar, Jeremiah, and Joanna Troutman.
Long, Lunsford, and Nancy Jackson.
Long, Evans, and Lovoice Pritchard.
Lord, Wm., and Margaret Durden.
Lesueur, Drury M., and Mahala Beckcom.
Magriff, John, and Ann Green.
Mullins, Thomas, and Ruthy Cohorn.
Martin, Benjamin, and Martha Lester.
Melton, Joseph, and Selah Dukes.
Magnan, Charles, and Eliza M. Halstead.
Martin, Jesse, and Betsy Harrison.
Moran, Henry, and Theny Bailey.
Moseley, Isaiah, and Sarah Hunt.
Miles, Gillian, and Cynthia Irwin.
Miles, Thomas, and Rachel McKenzie.
Moran, John, and Martha Russell.
Moore, Newbell, and Mary Matthews.
Matthews, Josiah, and Jane Brown.
McGuire, Richard Lewis, and Julia Beanbridge.
Moore, Wm., and Rachel Beauchamp.
Matthews, Elijah, and Mary Cobb.
Moore, Miss Eudocia, and Moses Fort.
McCrary, Bartley, and Rebecca McCrary.

McCrary, John, and Jenny McCrary.
McGinty, Washington, and Tabitha Moore.
Maddox, Benjamin, and Nancy Chambless.
McCrary, Isaac, and Hannah Hoy.
Moore, John, and Nancy Currey.
Moreland, Jesse, and Elizabeth Coleman.
Methvin, Richard, and Martha Perdue.
McGinty, Isaac, and Sarah Samples.
Middleton, Owen, and Nancy Raines.
Mash, Eli, and Sarah Johnson.
Morrow, Arthur, and Elizabeth Tooly.
Mills, Thomas, and Nancy Coulter.
Martin, Maurice, and Salathea Dismukes.
Nelson, George, and Polly Sturdevant.
Neves, John, and Catherine Jewell.
Norman, James, and Candy Wood.
Olmstead, Roger, and Elizabeth Navy.
Owens, John J., and Lucinda Long.
Parham, Thomas T., and Amey Myrick.
Phillips, John, and Olive Hunt.
Perdue, George, and Lucinda Darden.
Partee, Benjamin, and Eleanor Cone.
Pullen, Sanford, and Darkis Willis.
Perdue, John D., and Hetty White.
Pride, John, and Mrs. Sally Mills.
Parrish, John, and Sally Barnes.
Prepwood, Robert, and Mary Pierce.
Patterson, Robert M., and Mary Currey.
Parker, John, and Winney Hunt.
Pulley, Benjamin, and Sarah Callaway.
Pratt, John, and Mary Ann Wommack.
Persons, Josiah, and Sarah Babcock.
Parker, Elisha, and Sarah Wilson.
Pryor, Wm., and Charity Holliday.
Parish, Green, and Parthenia Parish.
Quinally, Archibald, and Susanna Read.
Roper, George, and Elizabeth Owen.

Russell, Wm., and Mary Andrews.
Rutherford, Robert, and Eliza Howard.
Robinson, Nathaniel, and Serene Ragan.
Robinson, Allen, and Sarah Chapman.
Ready, Spotswood, and Polly Beckcom.
Rogers, Willie, and Sally Johnston.
Rhew, Wm., and Jancy Tucker.
Reeves, John T., and Mrs. Harriet E. Beddingfield.
Reagan, Simson, and Bethina Veasey.
Russell, Wm., and Dianna Roberts.
Rogers, George W., and Caroline Worsham.
Reddick, John, and Sally Hitson.
Rogers, Timothy L., and Mary Miles.
Redding, Ezekiel, and Winny Scurlock.
Rogers, Wiley, and Elizabeth H. Smith.
Sawyer, Simpson, and Mary Lester.
Stephens, Price, and Elizabeth Wilson.
Smith, John, and Celia Lester.
Sanders, Jesse, and Mary Ann Malone.
Sturdevant, James, and Polly McBride .
Simmons, Jesse, and Jenny Green.
Sampson, Wm., and Sally Digby.
Smith, Charles, and Eliza D. Jackson.
Scurry, Richardson Owen, and Catherine Jinny Goff.
Simpson, George, and Milly Coleman.
Strickland, Allen, and Polly Dillard.
Shiver, John, and Sarah Swilley.
Sanford, Frederick, and Mary S. Stanton.
Slaughter, John, and Ann Brown.
Sledge, Alexander, and Martha Waller.
Sims, Frederick, and Susan Jackson.
Sims, Wm., and Tamar Lowe.
Sheppard, Wm., and Jane Oliver.
Shaw, John, and Elizabeth Page.
Stovall, Joseph, and Mary P. Bonner.
Sanford, Thornton, and Elizabeth Brown.
Smith, Ben B., and Nancy Hoskins.

Stanford, Thomas, and Elizabeth Reynolds.
Stewart, John, and Lydia Cone.
Sanders, Stephen, and Mary P. Greene.
Thompson, Charlton, and Ann Castleberry.
Tracy, Levi, and Rachel Walker.
Thompson, Henry, and Drucilla Jackson.
Turner, Isham, and Charity Buffington.
Taylor, Ward, and Nancy Matthews.
Trappe, Thomas, and Rachel Wootten (1814).
Taliaferro, John, and Lydia Howard.
Thweatt, James and Frances Moore.
Taliaferro, Richard, and Mary Chapman.
Underwood, Wm., and Sally Robertson.
Underwood, Enoch, and Mrs. Elizabeth Buckner.
Vann, Edward, and Tacy Downing.
Watley, James, and Anna Jones.
Williams, Floyd, and Loosey Weeks.
Wilder, Nathaniel, and Patsey Greene.
Woolsey, Benjamin, and Elizabeth Pedigrew.
Williams, Nathaniel, and Laviney Smith.
Watson, James C. and Elizabeth H. Woodward.
Williams, Wm., and Hannah Thomas.
Webb, James, and Nancy Etheridge.
West, Isham, and Elizabeth H. McKenzie.
Wiggins, Osburn, and Sarah H. Redding.
Williams, Jesse, and Betsy Brooks.
Woodall, Archibald, and Celiel Matthews.
Wright, Amos, and Mary Jordan.
Waller, Wm., and Elizabeth Waller.
Whitehead, Wm., and Catherine Clemm.
Williamson, Charles, and Sarah P. Jones.
Wood, Willis, and Margaret Travers.
Wallace, James, and Elizabeth Bernier.
White, John, and Mary Etheridge.
Waller, Levi, and Elizabeth Simmons.
Wallace, Wm., and Elizabeth Sexton.
Wood, John, and Susan Evans.

Woodall, John, and Emelia Cooper.
Zachery, James, and Polly Flournoy.
(About 300 Marriages.)

BULLOCH COUNTY.

This county was formed in 1796 from Scriven and Bryan Counties, and has a good Court House at Statesboro. In the Office of the Ordinary little care has been taken of the very old records. The first book of Wills could not be found at all, and Will Book "B" 1816 to 1840, has no index. Another Book "B," 1813 to 1846, contains Administrators and Guardian's Returns; also Book "C," 1836 to 1845, and Book "D," 1830 to 1850. These are indexed.

An old book of marriage licenses, 1816 to 1856, containing 200 pages, is not indexed or alphabetically arranged.

In the clerk's office the records are in much better shape, and all Deeds, from 1796 to date, are well indexed, and a lady being in charge, everything is clean and orderly.

Book "B" returns and administrators and guardians 1813 to 1846.

Hannah Lanier, Ad. of John Lanier.
Sarah Gigger, Ad. of Austin Sheffield.
Hesom Monk, Guar. of Benjamin Miller.
Mary Pittman, Ad. of Benjamin Morris.
Allen Brown, Ad. of Isham Elerbee.
William Richardson, Ad. of John Lane.
James Williams, Ad. of Richard Kirkland.
Mary Lowther, Ad. of John Lowther.
Simeon Travis, Ad. of Jacob Huffman.
James Williams, Ad. of John Roberts.
John & Dilsey Williams, Ad. of Samuel Williams.
Malichi Denmark, Ad. of Redding Denmark.
Luke Mizell, Ad. of David Hendrix.
David Williams, Ad. of Rebecca Ryals.

Francis Akins, Ad. of Elijah Stanford.
Henry Clifton, Guar. of Drury Jones, Jr.
Allen Denmark, Guar. of Richard A. Lane.
Garrett Williams, Ad. of William Milles.
Allen Denmark, Ad. of Stephen Denmark.
Thomas Rawls, Guar. of Rebecca and Zachariah
Rawls.
Jehu Everitt, Guar. of Bazell and Buckner Jones.
Samuel Williams, Guar. of Samuel Williams.
Samuel Williams, Guar. of Philip Green.
Garret Williams, Guar. of David and John G. Williams.
Richard Cooper, Guar. of Nancy Jones.
William Brown, Guar. of Allen Ellerbee.
Aaron Cone, Guar. of James Goodman.
Sarah Gigger, Guar. of Simeon and William Sheffield.
Henry Parrish, Ad. of James Williams.
Hezekiah Parrish, Ad. of John Roberts.
Jeremiah Pittman, Ad. of Benjamin Morris.
R. T. Stanland, Guar. of Jesse Ellerbee.
Henry Parrish, Guar. of E. I. Williams.
David Lastinger, Guar. of Allen Ellerbee.
John Wise, Guar. of Nancy Jones.
William A. Coursey, Guar. of William Milles.
Margery Semmons, Ad. of Brice Semmons.
James Hendrix, Guar. of Griffin Hendrix.
Henry Parrish, Guar. of Sampson Williams.
Henry Parrish, Guar. of Richard Kirkland.
Levicy Jones, Ad. of Benjamin Jones.
James Wilkenson, Ad. of Benny Jones.
Samuel Lockhart, Ad. of David Conklin.
John Grimes, Guar. Minor Heirs of B. Morris.
William Deloatch, Ad. of Jacob Futch.
Shep Williams, Guar. of Child of Drury Jones.
Aaron Cone, Ad. of William Cone.
John E. McCall, Guar. of Thomas Baker.

Betsy Jones, Ad. of William Jones.
Francis Jones, Guar. of Elizabeth and Hannah Jones.
A. Richardson, Ad. of Samuel Stone.
Nathaniel Long, Guar. of V. G. Hall.
James Wilkerson, Guar. of Heirs of B. Jones.
Francis Jones, Ad. of John Stanford.
John Wise, Guar. of Margaret Jones.
Lucy Sheffield, Ad. of Isham Sheffield.
Sarah A. Bain, Ad. of A. Bain.
John C. Evereff, Ad. of Philip Miney.
Robert Cone, Ad. of Thomas Hylton.
James Mikell, Ad. of John E. M'Call.
Jacob Minchew, Ad. of Philip Minchew.
William Moore, Ad. of Penelope Davis.
William B. Williams, Ad. of Seth Williams.
James Burnside, Ad. of John Dukes.
John Waters, Ad. of Isaac Waters.
Solomon Brannon, Guar. of James Monford.
Cullen Barrow, Guar. for his Children Bennett, William, James, David, Polly, and Elizabeth B.
A. Rawls and Sarah Wilson, Ad. of Thomas Rawls.
John Waters, Ad. of Isaac Waters.
Susannah French, Ad. of Allen French.
Aaron Cone, Ad. of William Cone.
Ely Kennedy, Ad. of David Kennedy.
Malachi Denmark, Ad. of James Denmark.
Margaret Hogan, Ad. of Ethelred Hogan.
Anderson Wilson, Guar. of John S. and W. H. Rawls.
James Nesmith, Guar. of Heirs of Hendley.
Nathan Jones, Guar. of Heirs of Charley Groover.
Joseph Fletcher, Guar. of Eliza Fletcher.
James Mikel, Ad. of John E. M'Call.
A. Brannan, Ad. of Daniel Hendrix.
Mary Slater, Ad. of W. Slater.
Sheppard Williams, Ad. of Samuel J. and Dorcas Lines.
Susannah Burnside, Ad. of Edmund Burnside.

Preston Wise, Ad. of James Wise.
Allen Rawls, Guar. of John and W. H. Rawls.
James Cone, Ad. of Aaron Cone.
Margaret, Ad. of John Allen.
Peter Cone, Ad. of Joseph Cone.
Sarah Goodman, Guar. of John Goodman.
Simon and Vicy Smith, Ad. of M. Smith.
Wilson H. White, Guar. of Heirs of Isham Sheffield.
Francis and Josiah Collins, Ad. of James Collins.
Rachel Wise, Ad. of John Wise.
Solomon Futch, Ad. of Solomon Futch, Sr.
John Hobbs, Ad. of Edward Hobbs.
John Hobbs, Ad. of Henry Hobbs.
James and Wiley Hendrix, Ad. of Ben. Pearson.
James Cone, Ad. of Aaron Cone.
Benjamin Ellis, Ad. of John C. Everett.
William Purvis, Ad. of James Purvis.
James B. Newman, Ad. of Daniel Newman.
Thomas Jones, Guar. of James J. Miller.
Elizabeth Clanton, Ad. of Daniel Clanton.
Margaret Hagan, Ad. of Soloman Hagin.
Frances Collins, Guar. of Heirs of James C. Collins.
William Little, Guar. of Jane Little.
Reddick Thornton, Guar. of Edwin Hobbs.
Allen Mikell, Ad. of Seaborn Mikell.
John Lockhart, Ad. of S. S. Lockhart.
Mitchell Brown, Guar. of Edward Hobbs.
Andrew Wilson, and H. Dutton, Ad. of A. Hagan.
James G. Kerby, Ad. of Arthur Kerby.
Sarah Stewart, Ad. of Alexander Stewart.
Benjamin Aycock, Ad. of Jesse Aycock.
Susan Davis (Cogdell), Ad. of Levy Davis.
James Hagan, Ad. of Simeon Sheffield.
Isom Ellerbee, Ad. of Elisha Bragg.
Barber Cone, Ad. of W. Slater.
Jemima Hendrix, Ad. of John Hendrix.
Patrick Lanier, Guar. of Lena Slater.

Roanna Kirby, Guar. of Mary and Hannah Kirby.
Richard Lane, Executor of W. Wright.
Jesse Ellerbee, Guar. of Heirs of W. Bragg.
Susannah Bragg, Ad. of W. Bragg.
James G. Kirby, Ad. of Arthur Kirby.
James Young, Ad. of Thomas Womack.
Peter Strickland, Guar. of Heirs of E. Burnside.
William M'Elvin, Ad. of William M'Elvin.
James and William Lee, Executors of James Lee.
Erastus Waters, Guar. of Thomas W. Davis.
Nathan Jones, Guar. of James Miller.
Haskell Simmons, Guar. of Jasper Sims.
Dicy Donaldson, Ad. of Jane Donaldson.
David Beasley, Ad. of Levi Davis.
Moses L. Hodges, Ad. of Joshua Hodges.
Nancy Brannon, Ad. of William Brannon.
J. G. and Asher Rogers, Ad. of John Everitt.
John Green, Guar. of Michael Collins.
James Young, Ad. of Thomas Womack.
Silas Scarborough, Guar. of John Smith.
William Lee, Guar. of Thomas Lee.
Allen Waters, Guar. of Matthew Griner.
Nathaniel Hodges, Ad. of G. Jackson.
Philip I. Dell, Ad. of E. J. Dell.
John Brown, Ad. of Jesse Brown.
Susannah Brack, Ad. of W. Brack.
James Cone, Guar. of Levy Davis.
John Lee, Guar. of Freeman Hendley.
James Lee, Guar. of Thomas Lee.
A. L. Kirkland, Ad. of John Kirkland.
Solomon Futch, Guar. of Heirs of Solomon Futch.
John D. Clanton, Guar. of Heirs of Daniel Clanton.
Augustus Lanier, Guar. of Thomas Lee.
Hardy B. Hodges, Ad. of Ely Kennedy.
Sarah R. Jones, Guar. of S. E. and D. R. Groover.
Wm. H. McLeon and David Mikell, Ad. of Donaldson.

Malachi Mercer, Guar. of Bryant and Mitchell Collins.
William Wright, Guar. of John M. Wright.
William Lester, Ad. of Mary Lester.
Robert Williams and Sarah, A. Hall, Ad. of N. G. Hall.
Robert Williams, Guar. of John D. Lester.
Adam Jones, Guar. of James J. Miller.
Allen A. Williams, Guar. of Martha A. Lewis.
William H. McLean, Ad. of James J. Kirby.

CLARKE COUNTY

First Book Minutes of Superior Court, 22 March, 1801.
Judge, Thomas Peter Carnes
Grand Jury.

Absalom, Rainey, For'mn	Willoby Hammock	John M'Falls
John Cunningham	John Smith (R. H)	Robert Day
David Stuart	William Dukes	Jeremiah Brown
Samuel Kellough	Handley Brewer	Absalom Autry
George Gray	William Wortham	Joseph Clarkson
John Strong	Rolen Taylor	John Malone
John Smith	Richard Woods	Thomas M-Coy.
William Kilgore	Richard Wood	

Grand Jury 1802.

Richard Whitehead	James Hitchcock	Johnson Strong
Martin Nalls	James Greer	John Chisholm
James Hill	David Shay	Harmon Runnells
Robert Day, Sr.	Isaac Underwood	Benjamin Bazil
Francis Truett	Henry Trent	William Tolbert
Chatton Scroggin	William Sparks	Joel Martin
John Blair	Randolph Burn	Benjamin Hogwood
Mial Barnett	Jonathan Melton	Burkett Dean.
Horatio Walker	Daniel Bankston	
Thomas Hill	John Wallace, Sr.	

Petit Jurors 1802.

Berry Thompson	Thomas Trammell	Thomas Hinton
Nathan Gann	Vining Cooper	Joel Freeman
Benjamin M'Cree	Thomas Yarborough	Jesse Sparks
David Coward	William Nobles	Thomas Greer

Elijah Hopkins
Richard Bankston
Archibald Cathey
John Sparks
John Jolly

James Strawther
Lewis Crane
John Price
Joseph Hickman
William Finley

Abraham Bowden
Greenhugh Adamson
James Cunningham
Benjamin Crawley
Willlam Benge.

Clark County Petit Jurors.

Jonathan Nobles
George Ewing
John Holder
Andrew Maddox
Jeremiah Milton
Thomas Wood
Jeremiah Matthews
Richard Cole

John Armstrong
John Clements
James Ewing
Samuel Head
David Luckie
Solomon Burfood
James Armstrong
John Bankston

Thomas Webb
Stephen Price
Levi Bankston
William Thurman
Daniel Thewatt
Isaac Middlebrooks

Will Book "A" 1802-1822.

Akin, James
Brown, Thomas
Britton, Thomas
Brown, Bedford
Cary, Dudley
Cocke, Jack F.
Evans, George
Finley, Robert
Gresham, Young
Hopkins, Lambeth
Hays, Richard
Harper, George
Hogue, Jacob
Hodge, John
Hicks, Daniel
Malone, John
Maxey, John
Mitchell, William, Sr.
Nail, Elisha
Powell, Charles
Purkins, Robert
Boberson, William
Browning, Joshua
Broach, Jonas
Brown, Betsy Ann
Born, Daniel
Castlebury, Henry
Clements, John

Finch, William
Fulwood, Robert
Gray, Anna
Hagan, Edward
Hannah, Thomas
Harvey, William
Humphreys, Uriah
Howard, Hiram
Kilgore, Peter
McCartey, Hannah
Milton, Jonathan
Nuth, William
Nixon, John
Patton, Jane
Radford, Henry
Randolph, Peter
Bankston, William
Billups, William
Braswell, George
Camron, John
Davidson, Charles
Fambrough, Anderson
Gentry, Elisha
Holowell, Asa
Hendon, Isham
Herring, William
Hayes, Edmund
Harris, Rebecca

Hutson, Caty
Ligon, James
McCoy, Henry
Martin, Hugh
Nall, Richard
Oliver, Joseph
Perry, Peter
Runnells, Dudley
Royston, Robert
Robertson, John S. M.
Spur, John
Strong, John
Stone, Uriah
Wallace, Oliver
Wright, William,
          Preacher.
Stroud, John
Stewart, Charles
Simmons, John
Simonton, Theophilus
Waggoner, Susanna
Stokes, George
Strong, William, Jr.
Strong, William, Sr.
Thompson, John
Wright, William, Dr.
Wells, Edward

Will Book "B" 1822-1842

Alred, Jonathan	Durham, Abram	Hester, Samuel
Beal, Zephaniah	Doran, Andrew	Jackson, Henry
Brightwell, John	Elder, Sterling	Lumpkin, George W.
Bones, William H.	Flint, Ira H.	Ligon, Mary
Cary, Lucy	Garner, Jail	Meriwether, David
Croxton, James	Harvey, John	Meriwether, David
Clayton, Augustine S.	Hambleton, Barton	Moore, William
Davenport, Francis	Holt, Cicero	Nunnally, John
Durham, Samuel D.	Jarrell, James S.	Osburn, John
Echols, James	Lumpkin, George W.	Pope, Burwell
Foster, John	Lee, John	Spullock, Owin
Greer, James	Lamar, Zachariah	Strong, Montford
Holder, John	Malone, Elizabeth	Sibbald, Jane
Harvey, Judith	M'Cullock, William	Stephens, David, Sr.
Hill, Isaac	Morton, Joel	Sims, Charley
Haile, Hosea	Nisbet, James S.	Tindall, William
Lambert, Thomas	Price, James	Taylor, Joseph
Laird, Robert	Stewart, Susanna	Wright, John
Linton, Alexander B.	Atkinson, A. C.	Strong, Frances
Malone, William	Bostick, Rebecca	Sheats, Nicholas
Moon, Francis	Barnett, Anna	Smith, John, Sr.
Maddox, Joseph	Cabbell, Robert J.	Sims, Robert
Newton, Clary	Crow, Stephen	Thomas, Stephen
Preston, _nomas	Cole, James D.	Williby, William
Ransom, Reuben	Coats, John G.	Wise, Patterson
Adams, John	Doughety, Rebecca	Strong, William J.
Bearden, Richard	Daniel, William, Sr.	Smith, William
Billups, Robert T.	Early, Jacob	Smith, Joseph, Sr.
Carnes, Thomas P.	Freeman, John	Turner, James
Crews, John	Garner, Peggy	Treadwell, Isaac, Sr.
Cox, Richard	Hester, Stephen	Wright, Mary
Clifton, George	Harper, John W., Sr.	Williamson, Ann E.

Clarke County was formed in 1801, and the condition of the Records in the Court House at Athens is what you might expect at this seat of learning. A "gentleman of the old school" has charge of the Ordinary's office, and the books are neat and well cared for.

The old wills are in two books, "A" and "B," from

1802 to 1849. The marriage records are all alphabetically arranged and easy to refer to.

In the Clerk's office the same order and cleanliness prevail. All the old minutes of Superior Court, and other books of Court records as well as Deeds are in good condition and indexed.

Marriages—Book "A," 1805 to 1814.

Aquilla Phelps and Jenny Hinson.
Asa Garrett and Nancy Brown.
Amos Crow and Elizabeth Stephens.
Allen Thornton and Ann Heard.
Allen Trawick and Salley Kinney.
Asa Goodwin and Peggy Sawers.
Aaron Parker and Margaret Browning.
Andrew Pettifice and Fanny Thompson.
Arthur Smith and Elizabeth Sanders.
Aaron Hopkins and Sally Strong.
Alexander Kennady and Darcus Walker.
Aaron Crow and Nancy Walden.
Abram Johnston and Margaret Ray.
Alexander Mash and Sarah Strawn.
Anderson Fambrough and Elizabeth Hester.
Alexander Baker and Sarah Wilson.
Bollin Cox and Rebecca Cabiniss.
Burwell Matthews and Sally Smith.
Buckner Earley and Polly Meredith.
Benjamin Thurman and Polly Brownfield.
Briant Rushin and Charity Obear.
Baily George and Delila Greer.
Christopher Bowen and Elizabeth McCoy.
Charles Burger and Malinda Garner.
Charles Sayers and Mary Hopkins.
Champion Davis and Joanah Bradsha.
Coleman Reynolds and Betsy Durham.
Charles Smith and Nancy Hays.
Charles Horton and Sarah Thompson.

Charles E. Hayns and Martha H. Harrison.
Charles Broach and Polly Smith.
Charles C. Jackson and W. Connally.
Charles A. Redd and Elizabeth Gresham.
David Day and Mary Johnston.
Durham Kelly and Miriam Orare.
Daniel West and Polly Middleton.
Daniel Tramel and Polly Boyd.
David Neely and Sarah Smith.
David Elder and Elizabeth Allen.
Duvil Simmons and Patsy Harper.
Daniel Hagins and Elizabeth Newsom.
Edward Paine and Matilda Brinton.
Eli Stroud and Betsy Durby.
Edmond W. Taylor and Sally Stuart.
Elijah Wilkeson and Polly Holt.
Elijah Strong and Polly Matthews.
Edmond Duke and Clary Fannon.
Edward Loyd and Sarah Anderson Halekit.
Edmund Elder and Nancy Tigner.
Ezekiel Bassett and Sarah Thomas.
Edward Akin and Patsy Parr.
Elbert Matthews and Sally Hails.
Edward Hagan and Hearly Powl.
Edward Cary and Lucinda Clayton.
Edmond Green and Frances Hodnett.
Edward Conner and Rebecca Cook.
Edmund Rainey and Jane S. Haynes.
Ezekiel Stanley and Elizabeth Rutledge.
Edward Johnston and Lyna McCartney.
Edward Craft and Whinney Tankersley.
Elijah Loving and Elizabeth Robertson.
Francis Roberts and Highly Carter.
Francis Arnold and Epsebeth Arondale.
Felix McGee and Elizabeth Walls.
Fred Hays and Elizabeth Lambert.
Fountain Tankersley and Chaney Kinney.

Green Lea and Peggy Muffit.
George Cliftin and Milley Brown.
George Johnston and Susanna Clifton.
Gadiel Fambro and Nancy Elder.
George A. Dilworth and Catherine A. Jones.
Gabriel Mathis and Leaticia Billups.
George Martin and Ann Ramsey.
George Cagle and Izabelle Ray.
Gideon Kimbal and Ann Maxey.
Henry Cannon and Polly Martin.
Henry Langford and Nancy Patterson.
Henry Lane and Martha Herring.
Henry McWhorter and Heleny Ligon.
Hawood Harper and Elizabeth Smith.
Harris Trammel and Sally Hagood.
Henry N. Pope and Elizabeth Hinton.
Henry Johnson and Elizabeth Hodnett.
Henry Phillips and Nell Ward.
Henry Funderburg and Patsy Connor.
John Simmons and Betsy Whalley.
James Pruet and Polly Lord.
John M. Dobbins and Asena Sayres.
Joel Lamberth and Mary Morgin.
John Pace and Sally Anderson.
John Jackson and Susanna Hicks.
Joshua Tilyery and Sally Fussell.
John Huston and Betsy Maddox.
James Daniel and Sarah Nixon.
Jacob Bankston and Nancy Brown.
Jonathan Adams and Rachel McClendon.
Josiah Taylor and Elizabeth Looker.
James Black and Sally Dean.
John McCarty and Burchet Cook.
John Black and Nancy Herring.
Jack F. Cock and Sally Strong.
John Trammel ad Polly Dickerson.
John McGee and Esther Hutson.

Jeremiah Yarborough and Elizabeth Simmons.
James McCullough and Elizabeth McCullough.
Jeremiah Pace and Betsy Hails.
James Hagood and Sally Strand.
Joseph Lane and Elizabeth Hill.
John Holofield and Elizabeth Kilgore.
James Hambrick and Polly Bankston.
John Hagler and Nancy Dodson.
James Tomoson and Elizabeth Hindon.
James Reppy and Mary McCune.
John Phillips and Sally Kirkwood.
James Briant and Raney Hamock.
James Blakeley and Susanna Strong.
Jesse Fann and Nancy Bagget.
James Smith and Eady Arendale.
John Powel and Sally Waters.
James Yarborough and Elizabeth Harris.
Isaac Martin and Polly Caldwell.
John Clement and Patience Hendon.
John Sansom and Elizabeth Dun.
John Loyd and Sarah Harris.
John Skean and Eady Hancock.
John Butler and Jincy Hurd.
John Kelly and Hannah Cagnet.
John Loyd and Betsy Holt.
John Nutt and Polly East.
Isaac Middlebrooks and Betsy Thompson.
James Apperson and Betsy Magbee.
John Parker and Fanny East.
Joseph Dunaway and Cathrin McCullough.
James Wheeler and Betsy McCune.
John Kent and Lousey Hambrick.
John H. Lowe and Kiddy Hill.
John Hodnett and Elizabeth Tigner.
James Cunningham and Lucy Holmes.
John Payne and Lucy Smith.
Isaac Newton and Clary Stewart.

John Finch and Elizabeth Easley.
Joseph Albright and Elizabeth Maddox.
Jack Welborn and Betsy Jackson.
James McCarty and Elizabeth McCarty.
Joseph Bridges and Sally Lovin.
James N. Brown and Patsy McCoy.
John Rainey and Penina Manning.
John Tweedle and Salley Rice.
Josiah Bonner and Nancy Hubert.
Joseph Self and Rachel Bearden.
James Robeson and Sally Haynes.
James S. Boyle and Miss E. Tanney.
Joseph Pickering and Marion Cook.
John Harris and Frankey Loyd.
Josiah Daniel and Sally Burrow.
Jesse Freeman and Katrin Jackson.
Joshua Elder and Ann Gray.
James Robeson and Margaret Simonton.
Joseph Rasberry and Polly Shaw.
John McAlpin and Sucky Smith.
Jordan Bonner and Polly Adam.
James Prophet and Louisa Runnels.
John Webb and Faithy Alford.
James Simons and Pricilla Smith.
John M. Edwards and Suckey Harris.
John McAlpin and Jiney Hicks.
John Bankston and Elizabeth Maho.
Isham Cagle and Malinda Rea.
Jesse Jinnings and Mary Adams.
Jeremiah Earley and Ann Billups.
John Henning and Judith Meriwether.
Jeremiah Hill and Virginia Phillips.
James Harney and Alia Smith.
John Tyner and Nancy Briant.
James Kunum and Polly Kunum.
John Hinsley and Mary Huff.
John Allen and Elizabeth Davis.

John Durham and Matilda Reynolds.
Joseph Cotton and Mary Greenwood.
Joseph Prinning and Rebecca Belcher.
Joseph Ewing and Elizabeth Newton.
John Shaw and Patsy Grimes.
Jesse Levans and Whiny Levans.
Josaph Moss and Sophia Easley.
Jesse Kinney and Fanny Dogget.
James Nicholson and Polly Stone.
Joseph Jolly and Polly Freeman.
John Cagle and Barbary Cagle.
Jesse Hammock and Polly Jones.
Jonathan Hardigree and Polly Giles.
John J. Cox and Betsy Herring.
John Parker and Milly East.
Levy Stroud and Fanny Hagood.
Louis Baldin and Jiny Tait.
Lesley Bankston and Elizabeth Brewer.
Lewis Powel and Frances Bradbury.
Lewis McKee and Ann Atkinson.
Laban Shepperd and Agnes Smith.
Leroy McCoy and Nancy Hicks.
Lemuel Brown and Betsy Mitchell.
Martin Crow and Rachel Parker.
Micajah Thomas and Eliza Turner.
Matthew Kilgore and Rebecca Beasley.
Martin Hines and Elizabeth Wood.
Mark Dogget and Fetna Nall.
Moses W. Dobbins and Edith Smith.
Moses Watkins and Elizabeth Angle.
Noris Hendon and Aly Clement.
Nimrod Smith and Patsy Baker.
Nathan Gann and Nancy Summers.
Nathan B. Barnett and Sally Lumsden.
Nimrod Dickens and Nancy Roberts.
Nathaniel Twinny and Sally Hunter.
Osborn Rogers and Mary Thorn.

Obediah Ward and Susan Fambrough.
Philemon Thompson and Sarah Hester.
Peter Williamson and Betsy Spurlock.
Preston Runnels and Dicy Cannon.
Philip Jones and Peggy Johnston.
Paul Satterwhite and Katherine Powell.
Robert Trawick and Elizabeth Powell.
Richard Lovin and Sally Kinney.
Robert Mitchell and Jamima Ponder.
Reason Whitehead and Celia Bole.
Ralph Smith and Susanna Turner.
Richard Hilton and Milly Davis.
Robert Trimble and Ruth Thrasher.
Robert Stewart and Pricilla Greer.
Robert Middleton and Pricilla Findley.
Richard Lewis and Betsy Jiels.
Richard Jeils and Della Dean.
Robert Marable and Catherine Vickers.
Robert Conner and Nancy Stewart.
Robert Minter and Sarah S. Puryear.
Robert J. Cabell and Ann Billups.
Robert Morris and Dinah Atkins.
Richard Stewart and Polly Culbertson.
Richard Thompson and Fanne Middlebrooks.
Robert Polley and Polly Darnald.
Samuel Lard and Linda Lineacum.
Samuel Echols and Elizabeth Wood.
Stephen Thomas and Eliza P. Cary.
Samuel Hamby and Barshaba Haydin.
Samuel Lawrence and Florow Cameron.
Sanford Rainey and Nancy Heard.
Samuel Wallace and Lida Beazley.
Solomon Kilgore and Ann Heard.
Shoanans Doolittle and Mary Glawson.

Sterling Elder and Polly Herring.
Sterling Aince and Susanna Meddis.
Samuel H. Swinny and Nancy Laseter.
Samuel Wier and Ann Wheeler.
Samuel Brown and Martha McKigney.
Stephen Dukes and Sucky Kunam.
Samuel Briant and Polley Barber.
Samuel Laurence and Ruthy B. Finley.
Thomas Worsham and Sally Herrin.
Thomas Leeg and Olivia McFalls.
Thomas Dicken and Elizabeth Ramsey.
Thomas McBurnett and Sarah Smith.
Thomas Bowlin and Milly Dean.
Thomas Hester and Sarah Boyd.
Thomas Daniel and Pattsy Smith.
Thomas Chaney and Lucy Middlebrooks.
Thomas Baecus and Lucy Gilbert.
Thomas Cousins and Patsy Tye.
Thomas Laurence and Mary Bushin.
Tucker Whitfield and Elizabeth Croxon.
Thomas Anderson and Polly Barnett.
Tapley Shahan and Nancy Shahan.
Thomas Roberts and Amey Eastridge.
Thomas Norton and Elizabeth Gill.
Thomas Scalez and Prudence Peavey.
Thyas Lord and Renchy Whitehead.
Travis Stranger and Nancy Parker.
Thomas Allen and Polly Cole.
Wm. Broadnix and Polly N. Gleeson.
Wm. Kimbro and Martha Gann.
Wm. Hester and Elizabeth Stone.
Wm. Gamble and Jinny Laurence.
Wm. Wright and Nancy McCoy.
Walter Johnston and Ruthy Stephens.
Wm. Barber and Rachel Daniel (1810).
Wm. Hinyard and Mary Spinks.
Wm. Stroud and Serena Battles.

Wm. H. Dismukes and Mary Cook.
Wm. Hagood and Polly Stroud.
Wm. Tigner and Jenny McAlpin.
Wm. H. Walden and Betsy Mercer.
Wm. Simons and Polly Wood.
Wm. Curtis and Nancy Jones.
Wm. Powell and Clary Estridge.
Wm. Clement and Patsy Stedman.
Wm. Thompson and Patsy Kunum.
Wm. East and Rachel Castlebury.
Wm. Collins and Betsy Caldwell.
Wm. Wright and Susanna Herring.
Wm. Edwards and Katy Cole.
Wm. Dobbins and Nancy Stanley.
Wm. Fears and Nancy Thrasher.
Wm. Saunders and Ann Gilmore.
Wm. H. Hunt and Nancy Stewart.
Wm. McMichael and Lucy Poettett.
Wm. Finch and Lidda Davis.
Wm. Gann and Elizabeth Summers.
Wm. Weathersby and Elizabeth Smith.
Wm. Beavers and Sucky Talbot.
Wm. Wood and Betsy Sims.
Wm. Hardigne and Leah Moore.
Wm. Herring and Elizabeth Wilson.
Wm. Mitchell and Judith Brown.
Wm. Beasley and Charity Cook.
Wm. Dickins and Nancy P. Earnest.
Willis Richards and Harriet Lee.
Wm. Hall and Delilah Wheeler.
Willoughby Thomas and Agnes Hays.
Zachariah Jordan and Tabitha Stokes.
Zebediah Lewis and Nielky Gill.

JACKSON COUNTY.

Jackson County was formed in 1796 from Franklin, and consequently was the home of many Revolutionary soldiers. There is a nice new Court House at Jefferson and in the office of the Ordinary the presence of a lady with a dust brush is very evident. The old book of wills, beginning 1802, is well preserved and cared for.

The old marriage records, 1806 to 1860, are in three books that are not indexed, and the writing in the first one is so faded it ought to be transcribed.

In the Clerk's Office all deeds are included in the Duplex Index and the books, containing unbroken records from 1796, are neat and clean.

Marriages.

Hosea Camp and Elizabeth Kennedy.
Sharwood Dean and Delphia Young.
Wm. Johnson and Betsy Dedrick.
Charles Edwards and Susanna Barber.
Nathan Simon and Lucritia Dean.
Redman Hutchins and Isabel Betts.
Solomon Gilmore and Polly Dean.
James Smith and Milly Garrett.
Patrick Glaze and Alsey Fulcher.
Thomas Norris and Elizabeth Whaley.
Leonard Maddox and Jane Beauchamp.
Wm. Ellison and Smitha Coker.
Wm. Windham and Polly Williams.
Sharwood Lyles and Rebecca Smith.
Ebenezer Miller and Elizabeth Miller.
George Oliver and Ruth Peck.
Morrel Collin and Patsy Burton.
Thomas Harris and Sally Watson.
Wm. Bohannon and Patsy Ivy.
David Shelton and Nancy Hendrix.

Thomas Cain and Nancy McClung.
Wm. Sample and Kiddy Alexander.
Boley Emery and Winney Key.
Stephen Lewis and Milly Watkins.
James Wilson and Peggy Green.
Richard Jones and Rebecca Watson.
Thomas Banks and Sally Graves.
Vincent Flannigan and Susanna Wade.
Andrew Thompson and Cynthia Reed.
Irwin Strickland and Patsy Crow.
Daniel Murdock and Anny Wates.
Wm. Harper and Matty Caven.
Jacob Hickman and Nancy Robertson.
Charles Edwards and Polly Pool.
Joseph J. Scott and Nancy Wood..
Wiley Langley and Sally Langley.
Robert D. Johnston and Milly McKinny.
Nathaniel Legg and Lucy Hampton.
John Tarrants and Sally McGuire.
Patton Gardner and Rachel Patterson.
Moren Moon and Elizabeth Snow.
George Moore and Polly Cowan.
John Rainey and Nancy Haynie.
Wm. Jones and Polly Tillman.
Forges Cavin and Susanna Harrison.
Alexander Cavin and Sally Wright.
James McClure and Nancy Whitfield.
Benjamin Johnston and Rhody Jones.
John Thomas and Hannah Walker.
Wm. Hancock and Eliza Smith.
Wm. Noblett and Ann Hughs.
Samuel Montgomery and Hannah Pattrick.
Richard Wilson and Molly Espy.
Isham Philips and Polly Smith.
Joseph Adare and Elizabeth McCord.
David Rutherford and Alsy Myers.
Wm. Fondren and Penny Efridge (1808).

John Brown and Sally Fondren.
James McClung and Rebecca Reed.
James Blackstock and Susanna Higgins.
James Carryan and Rhody McClesky.
Jacob Bushby and Mariah Mitchell.
Thomas Mullins and Eliza Kirkley.
Daniel Wofford and Tempy McGehee.
Drury Shields and Elizabeth Beavers.
James Kirbo and Sarey Reed.
Joseph Boggs and Mary Ellis.
John Leper and Frida McCord.
Thomas Espy and Eleanor Witherspoon.
Moses Cowan and Eliza Malone.
James McClure and Nancy Whitfield.
Thomas McAdams and Polly Clements.
James Haggard and Rebecca Ellison.
Asa Hearn and Eliza McKinney.
James Shepherd and Patsy Morgan.
Stephen Borders and Polly Moore.
Wm. Thompson and Unity Rogers.
Samuel Hawkins and Nancy Davis.
John McElhannon and Nancy Hodge.
Wm. Flannigan and Sally Williams.
Wm. Dobbs and Rhoda Miller.
Thomas Dukes and Nancy Morgan.
John Stapler and Anny Norman.
Valentine Harlin and Malinda Snow.
Wm. Campbell and —— —— Wurms.
Thompson Wallace and Eady Collins.
Isaac Gordon and Elizabeth Cain.
Adair Cox and Nelly Whitehead.
Sir James Pittman and Nancy Benton.
David Tuttle and Polly Harris.
Alexander Boyd and Peggy McCarrel.
David Smith and Nancy Williams.
John Picket and Elizabeth Jones.
Alexander McCulloch and Margaret Russel.

Edward Doss and Jinny Williamson.
Simeon More and Eliza Branham.
Gideon Bohannan and Nancy Williams.
Thomas Koel and Elizabeth Laurence.
Rowland Thurmond and Eliza Harrison.
James Wilson and Patsy Bowles.
Peyton Chapman and Susanna Anderson.
Richard J. Watts and Sally Clements.
David H. Miller and Patsy Bradford.
Benjamin Hawthorn and Elizabeth Sharp.
Wm. Gardner and Milley Hampton.
James Kennedy and Zilpha Lindsay.
Wm. Byford and Polly Sellers.
Wm. Watkins and Jerusha Jennings.
Washington Allen and Patsy Horton.
Wm. Cavin and Polly Holland.
Wm. Nisbet and Polly Lawless.
Jesse Grizzle and Mary Wilson.
John Hampton and Sally Lane.
James Barron and Delia Smith.
Vincent Hudgins and Betsy Williamson.
Thomas Jones and Sally Stanley.
John Blackforks and Anny Whorton.
James Parker and Mary Carn.
Elijah Williams and Judith Adare.
James Wright and Nancy Park.
Enoch Rogers and Rachel Pettigrue.
Samuel Knox and Polly Montgomery.
James Mitchell and Dorcas Benton.
Oswell Langley and Polly Lorey.
Alexander Crawford and Christiana Crumby.
Isaac Pierce and Hannah Backus.
Aldredge Bailey and Peggy Brown.
Wm. Carrigan and Patience Rogers.
John Jetton and Judith Higgins.
Wm. Moon and Nancy Sparks.
John Haynes and Sarah Magby.

Wm. Lawless and Rachel Atwell.
John Johnson and Martha Adams.
Stephen Briant and Mary Ann Green.
Moren Moore and Anny Waits.
Hope Watts and Polly McConnel.
Thomas Morris and Peggy Wilson.
John Brown and Nancy Camp.
Alexander Bachelor and Ruth Borders.
Wm. Arnold and Polly Thomason.
Isaac Ivy and Caty Curry.
Charles Smith and Elizabeth Hardeman.
Adam Williamson and Betty Horton.
John Short and Sally Garrett.
Early Harris and Polly Harrison.
Peter Wallace and Sally Short.
Robert D. Carter and Sally C. Jarrell.
Alexander Robertson and Ruthy Boon.
Charles Eads and .. .. Williams.
Peter T——l and Polly Cornelson.
Nimrod Hambrick and Sally Wardlaw.
James Shields and Charity Beavers.
John Blankenship and Betsy Kinney.
Lewis Barker and Nancy Chandler.
James McCreight and Patsy Harris.
Jacob Awbrey and Nancy Hill.
Henry Hutson and Rosey Rowland.
Samuel Cleaton and Peggy Hill.
Wm. Legg and Polly Hampton.
Ephraim Prescot and Patsy Dennis.
Andrew Armor and Rachel Griggs.
Mark Hayse and Elizabeth Foster.
John Jetton and Judith Higgins.
John Wadsworth and Anny Hancock.
Joseph McEver and Polly —— ——
Bobert Reed and Polly Parks.
John Orr and Polly Bradford.
Wm. Nowlin and Anny Bostwick.

Peter Haynie and Sally Wheeler.
— — Holmes and — Payne.
Gad Pierce and Betsy Blankenship.
James Todd and Charlotte Bennett.
Eldridge Barker and Matilda Polk.
Hugh Polk and Pricilla Barker.
Evan Polk and Sally Barker.
Benjamin Stockton and Sally Hall.
Richard Charles and Patsy Byford.
Solomon Strickland and Julia Windham.
Murdock Martin and Nancy Smith.
Robert Patton and — — Wilson.
Francis Patton and Malinda Thurmond.
Edward Adams and Tabitha Stovall.
Charles Dunston and Milly Rogers.
Isaac R. Dyche and Kitty Echols.
Charles Pate and Jemima Barnes.
David B. Driskel and Sally Tallent.
James Cash and Agnes Kolb.
David Dixon, Jr., and Letitia Harris.
James R. McCleskey and Fanny Wood.
John Bishop and Sally McCune.
David McCleskey and Lucy Bird.
Nathan Aldridge and Aley Hanson.
Ephraim Barker and Rachel Brown.
Robert McDowell and Betsy Magby.
Colyer Johnston and Olive Futcher.
David Owen and Elizabeth Wiley.
Robert Camp and Polly Pierce.
Michael Dickson and Rebecca Awbrey.
Wm. Thompson and Nancy Tillman.
Willis Pope and Agnes Hobson.
Robert Ober and Liley Bearden.
David Jackson and Rachel — —
James Montgomery and Hulda Dobson.
Wm. Dowdy and Sarah Harden.
Lary Smith and Nelly Cornelson.

Harrison Ezel and Nancy W. Gilbert.
David Thompson and Drucilla Camp.
Thomas Awbrey and Tempey Chapman.
John Borders and Cynthia Knox.
Wm. Sailors and Betsy Beard.
Thomas Thurmond and Jane Shields.
Robert Taylor and Sally Alcorn.
Wm. Garrett and Sally Martin.
Stephen Key and Elizabeth Jordan.
Abram Scott and Polly Robertson.
George N. Lyles and Matilda Green.
Samuel McKinney and Beddy Rowden.
Dennis Hopkins and Jane Ray.
John Bennett and Elizabeth Tilsworth.
Wm. H. Terrell and Cynthia Eddy.
Benjamin Griffith and Polly Albert.
Wm. Adams and Betsy Stone.
Wiley Brogdon and Sally Lawless.
Littleton Crabtree and Rebecca Cox.
Calham Carter and Eliza Cleaton.
Joseph Williamson and Peggy McDowel.
James Ellison and Eleanor Wilson.
Thomas Stapler and Elizabeth Walker.
Martin H. Pittman and Nancy Smith.
John F. Bowen and Polly Grizzle.
Wm. Nicholson and Polly Kingston.
Gideon Gunter and Polly Jones.
Larkin Green and Betsy Bennett.
Abram Scott and Polly Robertson.
Wood Hinton and Sarah Burson.
Gordon McClendon and Betsy Yord.
Samuel Street and Sally Spurlock.
John Davis and Abia Cromby.
Mark Doss and Elizabeth Taylor.
James Eakin and Nelly Paine.
Elisha Norris and Polly Hogan.
Zachariah Morris and Rachel Jones.

Andrew Boy and Fanny Reeves.
Thomas Jordan and Polly Brown.
John Lyles and Sally Ady.
John Beavers and Polly Shields.
Benjamin Mitchell and Patience Powell.
Wm. Reed and Jane Wharton.
Warner Young and Sally Reed.
Wm. Blackstick and Hannah Right.
Jesse Harris and Lavinia Adams.
Francis Montgomery and Hetty E. Bell.
Stephen Arnold and Carry Camp.
Aaron Glaze and Eazealy Oneal.
John Adams and Aditha Medkiff.
James Cunningham and Polly McWier.
Robert Beall and Betsy Green.
James Hood and Peggy Hill.

Some of the Ministers of the Gospel and Justices of the Peace who performed above marriages were:

James Riley, M. G.
Wm. Spruce, J. P.
John S. Watkins, J. P.
James McClesky, J. P.
James Rogers, M. G.
James Hindren, J. I. C.
Wm. Norman, J. P.
John Doss, D. D. & P. G.
Elisha Winn, J. P.
Levi Lowry, J. P.
Isaac Boring, J. P.
Thomas Johnson, M. G.
Bartlet Walker, J. P.
B. Harris, J. I. C.
James Hine, J. P.
John King, J. P.
David Will, J. P.
B. Adams, J. P.

George Cowan, J. I. C.
James Hendrix, J. I. C.
Ephraim Lindsay, J. P.
Robert Johnston, J. P.
Williamson Robey, J. P.
Jonathan Hearn, J. P.
David Witt, J. P.
Edward Pharr, V. D. M.
Wm. Moore, J. P.
M. S. Montgomery, J. P.
James Thurmond, J. P.
John Hemphill, J. P.
Thomas B. Sample, J. P.
C. T. Traylor, J. P.
Agrippa Atkinson, J. P.
Arnold Atkinson, J. P.
Edmund Gresham, J. P.
Elijah Pugh, J. P.

Thomas Hughs, J. P.   B. Watts, P. G. (Preacher
Ezekiel Darrigan, J. P.   of Gospel).

JASPER COUNTY.

This County, formed in 1812, comprised part of old
Randolph County, which was formed in 1808, and afterwards divided up into Jasper and Baldwin Counties. In
the basement of the new Court House at Monticello, are
many volumes and scraps of volumes of the records of
that defunct county. While the room they are in may be
fireproof, it is not mould and dust proof, and it will not
take long in such quarters to completely ruin these valuable relics. They should be carefully sorted out and
either transcribed or put in better shape for reference.

The First Book of Marriages, a thin one of 27 pages,
1808 to 1810, has no index, and contains about 1,000 marriage records. The Second Book, 1810 to 1821, and the
later ones are indexed.

In the Clerk's office there are seven old books of deeds
that are not included in the General Index, which begins
1818, and there are also several old books of minutes of
the Superior Court that contain interesting history.

First Book of Wills and Appraisements, 1812 to 1817.

Antony, James	M'Michel, William	Mitchell, Daniel
Boon, Exum	Phillips, Isaac	Parks, John B.
Bender, John	Armstrong, John	Reeves, Abner
Culverson, Samuel	Croll, James	Singleton, John
Goode, William	Hill, William	Tripp, William
Holloway, Isom	Landrum, Thomas	Whatley, John B.
Jones, Edward	Pinson, James	Ivey, Lot
Landrum, Thomas	Armor, James	M'Afee, Greene
Maghee, Edward	Broughton, Belitha	Wise, Barney
Powell, Zacheus	Butts, Samuel	Ballard, William
Ramsey, Henry	Evans, Henry W.	Cochran, John
Stephens, James	Gunn, Gabril	Hill, William
Singleton, Henry	Lassetter, Elisha	Moses, John
Walton, Robert J.	Hood, Wiley	Bass, Allen
Holt, James	Lanier, William	Burrow, John

Burroughs, — —
Folly, Thomas
Hamilton, Winny
Jones, James
Lockwood, James
Morris, John
Platt, George

Reid, Alexander
Rice, John
Whattley, Willis
Respass, Churchwell
Sansom, Archibald
Fitzpatrick, William
Laws, Joseph

Powell, William
Waits, John
Byars, John
Hill, Isaac
Loyd, Thomas, Jr.
Moses, Samuel.

Will Book "C" 1813 to 1819.

Appling, Otho H.
Bullard, Jesse
Butler, Thomas
Daggett, John
Freeman, Timothy
Heard, Thomas
Boon, Jacob
Byers, John
Chapman, Edward
Ellis, Radford
Goode, William
Hill, William
Brown, Jeremiah
Briers, Lawrence
Chapman, Edmond

Flournoy, Gibson
Hill, Theophilus
Huff, Thomas
Hoadley, Thomas
King, John M.
Mims, William
Moses, John
Pinson, James
Ramsey, Alexander
Sheffield, Barnaby
Weathersby, Owen
Jones, Hugh
Loyd, Thomas, Jr.
Mapp, Jeremiah
Messer, Joseph

Paschal, Samuel
Ray, Solomon
White, Samuel
Wise, Isaiah (minor)
Jackson, John
Melton, Timothy
M'Michel, William
Nall, Nathan
Parham, Polly and
    Tamsy.
Respass, Churchwill
Wise, Patton
White, Solomon.

Will Book "G" 1820 to 1823.

Brownfield, John
Brown, James
Bass, William A.
Cargill, Thomas
Flowers, Edward
Goode, Starling
Harville, Mason
Henderson, John
Hines, Robert
Jenkins, Cyrus R.
M'Michael, Zachariah
M'Cune, Thimas B.
Powell, Moses
Robey, Robert
Smart, F. B.
Sabin, Resolved

Bonner, Whitmel
Buchanan, Benjamin
Byrom, Seymour
Darden, John
Gardner, Ethelred
Goolsby, William
Hodnett, Benjamin, Sr.
Harwell, Mason
Hale, Josey
Jackson, Thomas
M'Lemore, John
M'Clendon, Wiley
Robinson, Elizabeth
Rodden, Abner
Slappy, Henry
Tucker, Thomas

Broughton, Charles
Beal, Elizabeth
Compton, John, Sr.
Edmondson, Mary
Gay, Martha
George, James
Henderson, John (minor)
Hicks, Joseph
Johnson, Walter
Loyd, Edmund
M'Elroy, James
Parrot, Henry
Rodgers, John
Robinson, Thomas
Slaughter, Henry
Wisener, Thomas

Will Book 1823 to 1833.

Appling, Otho H.	Alexander, Jane	Boyd, Richard
Brown, George	Boyd, Richard	Brown, James
Butt, Willis	Beall, James	Cross, John
Cargile, John	Chekler, Jacob	Cox, Jesse
Cross, George	Carden, William	Crenshaw, Jarrel W.
Edmonds, Rachel	Eagerton, Charles	Echols, Philip H.
Freeman, Josiah	Gardner, Ethelred	Gardner, William
Gregory, Lewis	Hall, John	Hill, James
Holland, Henry I.	Higgenbotham, Robert	Heard, John
Higgenbotham, Jacob	Johnson, Benjamin	Kennedy, Jane
Kelly, Daniel	Lloyd, Edmund	Lindsay, Samuel
M'Clendon, Isaac	M'Clendon, Jonathan	M'Kemie, John
M'Dowell, William	Newton, James	Porter, Elizabeth
Perkins, Moses	Pollard, Richard	Phelps, Lucinda
Rogers, Dred	Ragan, Asa	Robinson, John
Richardson, George	Stanley, Martin	Shaw, Eli D.
Stephens, George	Towns, John G.	White, John
Wade, Benjamin	Usher, Abner	Usher, Oliver

Will Book "H" 1822 to 1826.

Alexander, Robert	Moseley, Henry	Taylor, Anna
Binns, Burwell	Boykin, William P.	Ware, Henry
Chapman, John	Compton, Pleasant	Martin, Isaac N. D.
Dabney, Hannah	Deal, Thirza and	M'Michael, Green
Foster, John	Joseph J.	Phelps, Washington
Higgenbotham, Joseph	Edwards, Susan	Starnes, Elizabeth
Hines, Elias	Good, Theophilus	Slaughter, Henry
Hobson, Christopher	Holloway, Jesse	Williamson, Isaac
Lunsford, Leonard L.	Harris, Brittain	Wisson, George
Boykin, Francis	Kilgore, Simeon	M'Dowell, William
Cole, Duks	M'Michael, Green L.	Parks, John B.
Dabney, Anderson	M'Lemore, Catherine	Russell, David
Dabney, Elizabeth	Morris, John	Saunders, Mary A.
Folly, Thomas	Prickett, John	Truett, Riley
Harral, James	Stephens, Henry	Wilson, Joseph
Hicks, Joseph	Spencer, E. T. & L. &	Walthal, Edward
Johnson, William	M. E.	

Will Book "J" 1825 to 1831.

Alexander, Mary Ann	Collin, John	Hayes, James
Banks, John T.	Chickler, Jacob	Holloway, Mary
Brown, Bartlett	Edmondson, Crawford	Johnson, Alexander
Betts, Abraham	Farley, James	Kilby, William

Mitchell, William
Perry, William
Rivers, John
Stephens, Jane
Thompson, William G.
Andrews, Robert
Benton, Jeremiah
Brown, Edward
Byrom, Seymour
Clay, Jesse, Sr.
Davis, Thomas B.
Farley, John
Flournoy, William F.
Harris, Isham

Holloway, Jesse
Johnson, William
Lewis, Thomas
M'Clendon, Francis
Porter, Catherine
Stephens, James
Thurmond, Fountain M.
Wilkinson, Hammon
Arnold, William
Bryant, John, Sr.
Brewer, E.
Boynton, Stewart
Cole, William
Daniel, Levi

Flournoy, Josiah
Goolsby, John
Halloway, William
Hill, Isaac
Hobson, John
Johnson, Samuel
Lewis, Agnes M. (minor)
Pennington, Thomas
Purifoy, Arington
Smith, Charles
Tinsley, Lucy
Willson, John
Willis, Arthur
Walker, Henry

Will Book "K" 1826 to 1831

Allen, David
Alexander, Abden
Avery, William
Avery, Herbert
Armour, James
Andrews, Green
Blount, John
Brown, John W.
Bradford, Edward
Boykin, Jesse W.
Ballard, Wiley
Bender, John S.
Collin, William L.
Clay, Mariam
Cardin, William
Cross, Ann
Cross, Rhoda
Compton, Polly
Cornwell, Elijah
Daniel, Moses
Dingler, William

Edmondson, Samuel
Freeman, Mildred
Grimmet, William
Greene, Burril
Garlington, James
Hitchcock, Jesse
Houghton, Josiah
Heath, Richard
Holloway, William
Johnson, William, Sr.
Lyon, John
Lawson, David
Morris, Henry
M'Dowell, William, Sr.
M'Dowell, Martha
Mulkey, James
Owens, Jacob
Perkins, Archibald
Peacock, John
Phillip, Hilery
Pinchard, James

Peacock, Daniel
Potts, Stephen
Purifoy, S. M.
Pain, William
Pace, James
Pennington, William B.
Robinson, William
Stewart, Mary
Sistrunk, Samuel
Starnes, Samuel
Scott, William
Sharp, James
Traylor, William
Turner, John G.
Thomas, H. S.
Twilly, Joseph
Willard, Roswell
Wade, James
Wisdom, Frank
Wade, William
Cargile, George

Will Book "N" 1831 to 1839

Adams, Jonathan
Alexander, Adam
Abbott, Ezekiel
Armstrong, William
Adams, David

Bullard, James
Bender, John S.
Banks, John
Bullard, Sarah
Buchannan, James

Brooks, Walker, Jr.
Boswell, Henry
Bealley, Robert C.
Brantley, Green
Clay, Jesse C.

Cox, Wiley J.
Cox, Sarah C.
Cargile, John
Dean, Thomas
Dogby, John
Ezell, John
Egnew, William
Estes, Catherine
Guinn, Franklin
Gaston, Thomas
Goode, Jesse
Glenn, Thornton T.
Gaston, George M.
Holifield, Wiley
Harvey, Zepheniah
Holland, Lavinia
Jinkins, Francis
Johnson, Annis (minor)
Knight, James
Loyd, Edmund
Ledbetter, Henry
M'Daniel, Benjamin W.
Mapp, Jeremiah
Meriwether, George M.

Montgomery, David
Malone, Sherrard
Miller, William
Maize, Abney
M'Michael, David
M'Clendon, Ethelred
Montgomery, Benj. H.
M'Eneroe, William
Moreland, Francis
Morgan, Stokeley
M'Daniel, Jacob
Morgan, William
Phillips, James
Potts, Stephen
Pou, James
Payne, John
Phelps, Thomas
Rivers, James
Rucker, Mastin
Rainey, Absalom
Robinson, Cornelius
Roby, Nathan
Roby, Williamson
Ross, James J.

Smith, Abraham
Smith, Sarah
Smith, Alexander
Studevant, John
Sharp, James
Smith, Thomas
Smith, Eliza P.
Smith, Harrison J.
Thompson, Hannah
Turner, John G.
Wilson, Achilles
White, William H.
Wildon, Isaac
Wisdom, Frances
Wooten, Elizabeth
Walker, Moses
Wilson, Elijah
Wilkins, Drury
Whitaker, Ensign
Whitaker, John B.
Waldrope, Solomon
Wilson, Sarah

Jurors in Old Randolph Now Jasper Co., 1808.
Grand Jury.

Richard Carter
Jorden Baker
Adam Glazier
Spencer Laws
Jethrew Mobley
Stephen Lacey
Henry Haynes
Solomon Stricklin
Micajah Fretwell
Boling Smith
Jesse Evans, Sr.
John Margin
Wm. Pate.
Thomas Ramsey, Sr.
Joshua Hagerty
John H. Whatley
Thomas Gamage
Solomon Patrick

Wm. Lord
Thomas Hooks
Samuel Townsend
John C. Patrick
George Morgin
Jarel Beasley
Jacob Mercer
James Richards
Robert Germany
Thomas Gaston
Thomas Gammage
Larkin Clark
Wm. Scott
David Neel
Thomas Robinson
Robert Richards
Jacob Loughridge

Isaac Phillips
Matthew Duncan
Royal Clay
Wm. Hammett
Wm. Germany
John Cargil
John Martin
Thomas Carter
Stokely Morgan
Isaac Hill
Edmond Chapman
John Robinson, Jr.
Patton Wise, Esq.
Alexander McKey
Jesse Evans
James Simmons
Thomas Bass

Petit Jurors

Jacob Brazel	James Sansome	John Brooks
Benjamin Carrel	Edward Chapman	Malleciah Gulledge
Jeremiah Harrison	Presley Sanford	Elias Spencer
Levi Martin	Benjamin Irwin	Philip Thambson
Wm. Germany	Edward Wester	Joel Wise
John Bishop	Robert Sansum	Thomas Jones
Absalom Awtrey	John Powell	Wm. Wallace
Wm. Leveret	Elijah Martin	John Armstrong
Royal Clay	Wm. Brazel	Joseph Fitz Patrick
Matthew Duncan	James Lanear	Elisha Hall
Allen Cotton	Robert Edwards	Silas Barren
Isaac Morris	Joseph Dickinson	Washington Phelps
Absalom Hamby	Jesse Harris	John Morris
James Stanley	John Welcher	Christopher Baker
Wm. Stanley	Radford Ellis	Abyhugh Sowel
Elijah Cornwell	George Ramsey	Isaac Philips

Marriages, 1808 to 1810.

John Wardrope and Elizabeth Barnes.
Waid H. Turner and Elizabeth Mosley.
James Hicks and Elizabeth Northcut.
Samuel Flanagan and Elizabeth Bradley.
Gilford Whitehead and Sally Laws.
John Allen and Sarah Hendrick.
Elijah Lumsden and Nancy White.
John Edwards and Margaret Whitehead.
Samuel Harwell and Rebecca Walker.
Britan Starne and Patsy Passons.
John Moore and Susanna Findley.
David Bishop and Elizabeth Ogle.
Zacheus Powell and Polly Sansom.
Elias Carden and Elizabeth Williams.
Belitha Broughton and Polly Jones.
Lucy Martin and Jeremiah Harris.
Samuel Wyatt and Sally Sheffield.
Joel Haynes and Patsy Cargill.
Frederick Scarborough and Patsy Stinson.
Jesse George and Clarissa Ann Glazier.

Alexander Urquhart and Elizabeth Smith.
Joshua Moore and Mary Findley.
Jacob Moore and Patsy Sheffield.
Wm. Magouirk and Polly Pratt.
Shadrack McMichel and Polly Corterlou.
James Sansom and Lucy Wright.
Wm. Germany and Nancy Hardwick.
Robert Melear and Matilda Wilkinson.
Cary W. Pope and Nancy Thornton.
Thomas Coulson and Barbara Woffington.
Daniel Ackins and Unity Yancey.
Thomas Hickson and Laney Daniel.
John Ayles and Lydy Howell.
Echols Daniel and Elizabeth King.
Samuel Flanigan and Rachel Bradley.
Waid H. Turner and Elizabeth Massey.
Edward Lovejoy and Rachel Spears (1809).
Henry Blankenshire and Eady Barnes.
Wm. Reid and Anna Holt.
Richard Ivy Loyd and Rachel Pugh.
Absalom Kenedy and Jane Steadman.
Aaron Williams and Mary Hays.
Jeremiah Mosley and Sally Sansom.
John Jones and Polly Ivy.
Jesse Williams and Cinthia Hays.
John Spence and Hetty Downs.
Parker Knowles and Polly Nichols.
Gillis Gray Adams and Elizabeth Moases.
Wm. Bullard and Tempy Head.
George Ramsey and Sally Cornwell.
Wm. Powell and Elizabeth Persons.
Joseph Hicks and Jenny Russell.
Robert Westmoreland and Ann Foreman.
Wm. Nicholson and Mary Findley.
George Hardwick and Elizabeth Reed.
Allen Hood and Sarah Grimmen.
Edmond Bradford and Aley Richardson.

Wm. Holeman and Rachel West.
Joshua Bailey and Elizabeth Morrow.
David Dukes and Rebecca Bonner.
Hilley Pippin and Nancy Morris.
Elisha Mosley and Susanna Wilson.
Hiram Ryan and Sally Wilson.
Wm. Poor and Sally Hearn.
Martin Kinard and Sally Webb.
Dennis Knowles and Elizabeth Mercer.
Thomas Merritt and Sally Bias.
Stokely Morgan and Polly Evans.
Needham Bryant and Polly Bryant.
Robert C. Dunham and Sarah Lewis.
Elhannon Gibbs and Fanny Williams.
Joshua Stafford and Judy Morgan.
Chesley Burks and Lydia Robinson.
Redman Rix and Polly Williams.
John Jones and Polly Stewart.
Wm. Thornton and Debby Shattuck.
James Lanier and Polly Smith.
Fred Mies and Sarah Shaddock.
Joshua Evans and Rebecca Smith.
Philip Fitchpatrick and Fanny Tranum.
Elias Reed and Clary Newton.
James Burges and Sally Fowler.
Caleb Willingham and Elizabeth Glass.
Thomas Ramsey and Susannah Lyon.
Radford Ellis and Jinny Phillips.
John Beshop and Rebecca Cassett.
Enoch Hays and Rebecca Clark.
Richard Braswell and Polly Jintrey.
Simon Byrum and Polly Billingsley.
Wm. Daws and Mary Blankenship.
Thomas Ward and Sarah Ross.
Burwell Almond and Polley Mashburn.
John Hodge and Pheby Lumsden.
Lang Rix and Ellender Mays.

James Downs and Ruthea Wilson.
Moor Bagley and Jane Graves.
Isaac Williams and Sally Ezell.
Minor Tidwell and Peggy Bean.
Sion Fields and Salley Carrel.
Alexander Bean and Dorothy Tidwell.
John Mitchell and Ann Woods.
Daniel Nelson and Joannah Townsend.
Joseph Howard and Elizabeth Gray.
Matthew Hicks and Cola Leverett.
John Ivy and Armine Leverett.
Charles Broughton and Nancy Briton.
John Waits and Patsey Washington.
Robert Hudson and Candis Crow.
Samuel Crawford and Nancy H. Long.
John C. Patrick and Olive Stewart.
John Jones and Sarah Patterson.
John McMichel and Ghita Griffin.
James Bartrom and Elizabeth Kates.
George Ray and Mary Darney.
James Cartner and Ann Burton.
John Stewart and Vincy White.
Joseph Baly and Faby Gray.

JEFFERSON COUNTY.

Jefferson County formed in 1796, was one of the unfortunate counties that lay in the wake of Sherman's army. All records of deeds were burned at that time, and many valuable books in the office of the Ordinary, but, by some streak of luck, most of the original wills were saved, and are now preserved in tin files, alphabetically arranged, as are also all marriage licenses, administrators' returns, etc.

There is no index in the office to these estates, so one has to go patiently through the files to find out what is there. The records begin 1796, and no doubt there are many valuable items hidden away in those pigeon holes. The papers are getting too tender to be handled and, in a few more years, they will be lost to Georgia historians. To be in keeping with the beautiful new Court House that has recently been finished at Louisville, these old papers should now be transcribed and indexed for ready reference.

The best list of early inhabitants that could be secured, was a Tax List for 1802. A glance over this list will show that many of our most prominent citizens lived in Louisville, which was then the Seat of Government and bid fair to be a great city. An old map of the place shows many streets that are now in the surrounding woods. Among the wills noted were Howell Cobb, 1817, and Governors Herschel V. Johnston and Charles J. Jenkins.

WILLS (300)
(Miss Helen Prescott—May 1910).

James Anderson, 1817
John Akridge, 1806
Thomas Alexander, 1778
Samuel Andrews, 1802
John Allen, 1805
Harris Austin, 1826
Thomas Askew, 1798
John Arrington, 1827
Joseph Allen, Sr., 1817
Sarah Alexander, 1842
Noah Alexander, 1830
Jane Andrew, 1816
Charles McAlester, 1808
James Arrington, 1813
Silas Arrington, 1847
John Boutin, 1835
John Wm. Balls, 1847, of Burke Co.
Littleberry Bostick, Sr., 1823
Elizabeth Beal, 1843
Selma Beal, 1852
Samuel Bothwell, 1828
Thomas McBride, 1844
William Batts, 1832
Cath. McBride, 1826

Robert Boyd, 1811
Thomas Berryhill, 1816
Russel Brown, 1813
Nathan Brassell, 1817
James Bigham, 1810
Agathy Beal, 1835
James Braly, Sr., 1815
Joseph Beatty, 1796
Nathan Barr, 1815
William Brown, 1807
John Berrien, 1811
Samuel C. Boyd, 1833
Rachel Blair, 1802
Jane McBride, 1805
John Bigham, 1835
Sarah Bothwell, 1828
Nathan Bostick, Sr., 1817
John Bostick, 1840
William Calhoun, 1849
Mary McCuller, 1803
John Cowart, 1821
Howell Cobb, 1818
R. E. Cunningham, 1841
Robert Crook, 1836
George Cox, 1814

Robert Eve Cunningham, 1838 and 1841—codicil.

Elizabeth Causey, 1832

James H. Carr, 1816

Nathan Christie, 1835

William Clarke, 1827

Sylvia Chisholm, 1829

Adam Calhoun, 1813

Margaret Cuddy, 1815—Probate, but will gone.

David Marion McConkey, 1820

Samuel Clements, 1831

Nicholas Cavenah, 1794—of Burke Co.

Silvey Chisholm, 1838

William Clements, 1828

L. B. Cavanah, 1848

Lydia Crofton, 1839

Mary Clements, 1826

Henry George Caldwell, 1802

James A. Carswell,1841

Frederick Clem, 1806

Henry Cox, 1807

John Coleman, 1836

David Bothwell, 1801

Thomas Drake, 1794—1808, of Warren Co., blacksmith

John Dupree, 1807

William Dawkins, Sr., 1800

James McDaniel, 1811, of Burke Co.

Andrew Dillon, Jr., 1824

Daniel Dees, 1802

Henry W. Dodge, 1839

Stevens Doreauzeaux, 1833

James McDonald, 1800

William McDowell, 1801—Clk. of Court—father and uncle of Killarney, Ireland.

John Dupree, 1807

Samuel Denny, 1848

Isham Evans, 1842

John D. R. Figg, 1818

John Freeman, 1857

Samuel Fleming, 1834

Richard Fleeting, 1817

Roger L. Gamble, 1838

Owen Fort, 1818

J. Fountain, 1803, Jonathan.

Zacharias Fenn, 1799

Robert Fleming, 1826

Henry Fountain, 1826

William Fokes, Sr., 1807

George Fowler, 1832

Margaret Fleeting, 1836

John Fleming, 1837

William Fountain, 1814 "very old."

Martin Foreman, 1815

Alexander Gordon, of Burke Co.

George Granberry, 1804

Samuel Gordon, 1805

Barnabas Gay, 1810

Ann Ganeway, 1810

John McGowan, 1828

Sarah Granberry, 1817

David McGowan, 1796

Rachel Green, 1816

Jesse Hatcher, 1815

James Ingram, Sr., 1827

William Hadden, 1813

David Holloway, 1825

Charles Hudspeth, 1811

Blassingame Harvey, Sr., 1799

Valentine Hatcher, 1812

Richard Hudson, Sr., 1834

Martha, widow of Richard Hudson, Sr., 1844

John P. Harvey, 1812

Dr. Bennett Harris, 1843—property in Charleston, S.C.

Mrs. Prissy Hatcher, 1833

Willis Howard, Sr., 1826

Pleasant Wall Hargrove

William Hudeston, 1828

Richard Hodges, 1824

Thomas Hannah, 1817

Eli Hudson, 1833

Elias Hodges, 1821

Charles Harvey, 1800

Jesse Hatcher, 1815

Pool Hall, 1800

John D. Holder, 1852

Isaac Harris, 1812

Elizabeth Hutchins, 1836

Samuel Irwin, 1822

Silas Herrington, 1849

Elizabeth Hadden, 1830

Anthony Hancock, 1806

Ben. James, 1800

John Ingram, 1817

George Ingram, 1820

William Ingram 1807

Charles J. Jenkins, 1828

Joseph Jackson, 1800

Elizabeth Jarvis, 1818

William Jenkins, 1777—father
James J. in Penna., of Learn
Co., Antrim, Ireland

Jesse Jackson, 1812

John Kennedy, 1822

Sion C. Kirkland, 1842

Charles King, 1811—father
Thos. D. King, of Sampson
Co., N. C.

Godfrey Keller, 1838

Dr. Alexander Lowrey, 1845

Jesse Lofety, 1804

William Lowry, 1815

Robert Lowry, 1820

Roger Lawson, 1803

Abraham Lafaver, 1814

Isaac Lamb, 1827

Jesse Lock, 1802

Ruth Mulkey, 1816—of Burke
Co., wid. of Philip M.

Jane Mountain, 1830

Fredk. Morris, 1835

Matthew Marshall, 1849

James Meriwether, 1817

Thomas Meriwether, 1802

Sarah Moye, 1845

Dr. John H. Mason, 1831

William Marshall, 1839

Joseph Marshall, 1839

John Moore, 1815

Mary Deborah Marbury, 1817—
wife of Horatio Marbury.

John Mountains, 1821

Aquilla Matthews, Sr., 1826

Henry Mears, 1812

John McMahan, 1809

Elizabeth Milton, 1836

Stephen Morgan, Sr., 1825

Meshack Matthews, Sr., 1818

Hugh McNeely, 1816—bounty
of land I drew in 23rd Dist.
Wilkinson Co.

Edward More, 1805

Samuel Marshburn, 1808

Ann Marshall, 1846

John Morgan, 1845

Samuel Mayo, 1804

William Matthews, 1798

James Matthews, 1849

Anne Montgomery, 1835

Hardy Morgan, 1840

William Manson, 1828

Mrs. Sarah Murphy, 1837

Morris Murphy, 1828

Ulrich Neidlinger, 1781—of St.
Mat. Pa., Tanner

John Neely, 1822

Andrew McNeely, 1809

Patrick McNeely, 1801

Margaret McNeely, 1816

Samuel McNeelys, 1797

Ephraim Ponder, 1836

Nathaniel Polhill, 1844

Thomas Pierce, 1845

John Peel, Sr., 1816

Robert Prior, 1820

David Paulett, 1810

William Perdue, 1823

Sion Pennington, 1822

Mary Paulett, 1800

Rebecca Polhill, 1838

Thos. M. Patterson, 1840

Elijah Pagett, 1805

Robert Patterson, 1822

Mildred Palmer (no date)

Ann Parsons, 1826

John Padgett, 1815

Stephen Powell, 1802

Dr. John Powell, 1826

Reuben Powell, 1823

Theophilus Powell, 1824

Elizabeth Pool, 1847

James Powell, 1803

John Parsons, 1800

Thomas Parsons, 1800

Elizabeth Paulett, 1799

Joseph Gabriel Posner, 1812

Richard Peel, 1793-1806

Jason Powell, no date.

William Parsons, 1813—Prob. from Wake Co., N. C.

Aaron Pool, 1803

Major James Patillo, 1804

Dr. David Robison, 1842

Walter Robinson, 1808

Jane Robinson, 1813

John Reese, 1816

Isabella Reed, 1803

John Raiford, 1812

Morris Raiford, 1826

J. B. Raines, 1802

Jethro Rogers, 1839

William Spiers, 1831

Marble Stone, 1788

Philip Scott, 1804

Mary Scott, 1832

Brittain Smith, 1802

John Sandifer, 1821

Priscilla Sandefer, 1830

Thomas Street, 1846

James Stone, 1841

Ethelred Smith, 1844

James Smith, 1801

Mary Smith, 1799, of Lincoln Co.

William Tarver,

Noah Turner, 1822

Samuel B. Tarver, 1846

Daniel Thomas, 1812

John F. M. Tarver, 1836

John Tomkins, 1836

John Vining, 1801

Shadrack Vining, 1805

Nancy Vining, 1827

John Whigham, 1823

Elias Wiggins, 1837

Elijah Warner, 1822

William Wilson, 1801

Reason Whitehead, 1780—of St. George, Pa.

William Wright, 1814

James Warnock, 1804

Joshua Watson, 1825

Elizabeth Walker, 1834

Benjamin Whitaker, 1820

Job Woodman, 1822

David E. Whitaker, 1833

Dennis Williams, 1822

Thomas B. Wells, 1836

John Wilson, 1801

John Wells, 1805

Jefferson B. Wells, 1823

James L. Willson, 1807—of Richmond Co.

William Whigham, 1848

Samuel Waldon, 1809

John Warren, 1797

Caleb Welch, 1826

Benjamin Warner, 1820

Nancy Wright, 1843

Solomon Willey, 1823.

End of Wills.

LIST OF PERSONS ENTITLED TO DRAWS IN LOTTERY.

List taken December. Only Revolutionary Soldiers and Widows of Revolutionary Soldiers were copied.

John Boutin, Rev. Soldier.
Jane Bostwick, Widow R. S. (Nathan).
Ann D. Powell, Widow R. S.
Cloey Pate, Widow R. S.
Mary Scott, Widow R. S.
John Arrington, R. S. (d. 1827).
Hugh Alexander, R. S.
Rhoda Barber, widow and daughter of Rev. Soldier. (Joseph).
Ezekiel Causey, Sr., R. S.
James Cotter, R. S.
William Clements, Sr., R. S. (d. 1828).
Elizabeth Causey, W. R. S. (dau. Matilda).
Benjamin Green, R. S.
Rebecca Garvin, W. and Dau. Rev. Sold. (Thomas Garvin).
Mary Haddin, W. R. S. (William Haddin).
Ann Montgomery, W. R. S.
Elinor McNeely, W. R. S. (Hugh McNeely).
Mary Patterson, W. R. S.
Esther Brett, W. and Dau. Rev. Soldier.
Michal Cowart, Rev. Soldier.
Elizabeth Durougeaux, W. and Dau. Rev. Soldier. (Peter D.)
Stephen Durougeaux, R. S. (d. 1833).
George Fowler, Sr., R. S.
Sarah Fountain, W. R. S.
Catherine Goitman, W. R. S.
Dempsey Hall, Sr., R. S.
John S. Holder, R. S.
Mrs.. Ann Hall, W. R. S.
Mary Spivey, W. R. S. (James Spivey).
John Thompson, R. S.

Sarah Thompson, W. R. S. (by son Jere).
Joshua Watson, R. S.
Lucretia Alford, W. R. S.
John Boutin, R. S.
William Lions, R. S.
Morris Murphy, R. S.
Martha D. Moss, W. R. S.
Moses Newton, R. S.
Nancy Sammons, W. R. S.
Caleb Welch, R. S.
Jere Wilsher, R. S.
Catherine Warner, W. & Dau. R. S.
James Cook, R. S.
Elizabeth Fort, W. & D. R. S.
Norman McCloud, R. S.
Seth Pierce, R. S.
James Johnston, R. S. (wounded).
Hudson Hall, Sr., R. S.
John Darby, Sr., R. S.
William Thompson, R. S.

Jefferson County Tax List 1802.

Moses Brinson	John Newman	Jonathan Matthews
Brice Bratcher	Shadrack Lee	James Hogans
Mary McNair	Jesse Horn	Prior Stone
Abraham Mott	John Martin	Frederick Evans
Abraham Coursey	Michael Matthew	Henry Bloodworth
Robert Tillman	Petenah Wilson	Silas Bailey
William Pervis	William Donaldson	Jesse Pervis
William Peel	John Cummerford	James Temples
James Buchanan	David Brinson	Daniel Richardson
Richard Corbett	John Mock	George Young
Masheck Matthews	Hugh Montgomery	John Lee
Micajah Paulk, Sr. & Jr.	Elkanah Lofton	Isaac Horn
Mary Yerby	James Johnston	Ephraim Peobies
John Beggs	Jeremiah Lofton	John Spring
Samuel Slocumb	Robert Patterson	John Van Winkle
Thomas Bloodworth	Richard Peel	John Caldwell
Jacob Young	Mary Peel	Godfrey Lee
Matthew Bailey	Gilson Joiner	Needham Bryant
George Stapleton	David Hart	George Mock

David Montgomery
Daniel Conoly
Henry Beatty
Elisha Gove
John Peel, Jr.
Francis Wren
William Tilley
Frederick Clem
Francis Brown
John Tilley
John Musgrove
Samuel Bloodworth
Needham Pervis
Charrich Tharpe
William Perdew
Aaron Pool
John Rozier
Joseph King
Margaret Horn
Presley Tharpe
Jacob Matthew
Thomas Matthews
Joel Darcy
Barwell Evans
Thomas Gay
Barnaby Gay
William Thomas
James Isham
Samuel Little
Thomas Little
Foster Little
John Brackenridge
Robert Mountain
William Thompson
George Meron
Willis Howard
John Bails
John Cumming
Alexander Whigham
Hugh Wilkinson
John Whitehead
Thomas Whitehead
James Young
Thomas Moseley

Major Collins
Elias Barrow
Stiring Brinson
Samuel Bothwell
John Neely
Jane Neely
Thomas Neely
James Neely
Benjamin Harper
William Matthews
Orandatus Watson
George Spieres
William Donaldson
Hugh Donaldson
John McAnally
Absolom Prior
Aquilla Matthews
Jonathon Minton
George Wright
Joseph Wise
William Hair
James Smith
David Young
John Turner
Demsey Barnes
Alexander Love
James Henry
Benjamin Darcey
Reuben Beckham
Haden Tillman
Samuel Slater
Absolom Wells
Stephen Thompson
Strander Crawford
David Crawford
William Spieres
David Terry
Robert Prior
Stephen Johnston
Arthur Cheatham
Andrew Hampton
Isaac Benton
Joseph Hampton
Jacob Farmer

Jesse Brown
William Pennington
John Mannen
Jane Bothwell
Joseph Pool
Reason Cawley
James Tillman
Abraham Roberts
Henry Churchwell
James Benton
John Cook
Chloe Hunt
John Wells
Gideon Thompson
Thomas Mellville
William Darcey
James Minton
Hall Hutson
David Brown
Jesse Hollingsworth
William McGlocklin
John Anderson
Abraham Lafever
Caleb Wright
Hugh Wilson
Samuel Wilson
William Wilson
Jacob Godown
William Boykin
James Arrington
Berry Hughs
William Lowrey,
   trustee
Robert Lowrey
Richard Young
James Trowell
Thomas Parsons
John Donaldson
John Gamble
Alexander Douglas
John Douglas
Thomas Douglas
Benjamin Thompson
Joseph Harp

Alexander Berryhill	Mecum McCullers	David Paulett, agt.
John Murry	William Womack	Jeremiah Welcher
Jesse Jump	William Hardwick	Caleb Welch
Pitman Lofley	George Hardwick	Richard Walden
Jesse Lofley	Francis Coleman	Reuben Walden
Joseph Brannan	Hardy Harrell	Henry Walden
Simon Barden	James Manson	Adam Calhoun
John Vining	Jane McNeil	Abraham Yerby
Thomas Rogers	William Clark	John Smith
James Rogers	Edmund Bailey	Joseph Smith
John Irwin	David Desuell	William Dawkins
John Rowland	John Rogers	George Dawkins
Thomas Hannah	Russell Brown	James Coats
William Hannah	Thomas McWally	James Chastain
Kedar Vining	Samuel Stephen	Charles Hudgepeth
Henry Tommey	Jesse Glover, Sr. & Jr.	Thomas Hudgepeth
Robert Broddy	Richard Brown	William Vining
Simon McCullers	John Reese	Jethro Weaver
Lemuel Hickman	Nathaniel Swansey	Nathaniel Weaver
Richard Clark	James Brigham	John Morgan
William Clark	Isaac Jones	Dr. Moses Newton, Tr.
Nathaniel Sample	Garland Hardwick	Benjamin Sammons
William Duncan	Peter McCartney	William Craig
William Allen	William Brown	Nathaniel McMicken
James Allen	George R. Brown	Nancy Fenn
Joseph Allen	Adam Tapley	Mary Prince
Richard Wingate	Andrew Thompson	John Davies
Sarah Jump	Derixon Wootton	Samuel Walden
John Martin, Sr. & Jr.	William Allen	George Smith
William Hadden	John Hartsfield	Shadrack Vining
Thomas Summerfield	Henry Wall	William Davis
(Free negro)	John Lewis	Hardy Harrell
James McKigney	William Lewis	Nathaniel Brassell
Abner Womack	John Goodgame	Richard Davies
David Showers	Daniel McNeil	William Smith
Sanders Bush	Benjamin Bryan	Joseph Tommy
David Ingram	Burrell Cammel	Thomas Warden, Sr.
William Ingram	John Cammel	William Lions
James Williams	Isaac Robinson	William Warden
Hugh N. Ingram	John Morehead	Hardy Morgan
James Brannen	Jesse Moreland	Stephen Morgan
George McMullen	Abraham Bush	Matthew Caudie
Loved Harrell	Robert Wood (dec'd)	Robert French
John Little	William Lasser	Ann Coats

Isaac DuBose
Benjamin Janus
William Coats
Edward Ryan
William Pendleton
Benjamin Warner
Daniel D. Moss
Micajah Dawkins
Elijah Chrisae
John Walden
William Wood
George Pierce
William Wood, Jr.
Nathaniel Williams
Samuel Walden, Jr.
John Banton, Jr.
William Andrew
Lewis Naule
Solomon Willey, Jr.
Isaac Coleman
James Pattillo
Hezekiah Gates
Morris Murphy
Elizabeth Terry
Drury Harris
Elias Hodges
John Hodges
Jeremiah Dubank
John Coleman
William Leaven
George Jones
John Darby
James Darbey
Peter Farr
Valantine Hatcher
John Jones
Isaac Rawls
Jane Andrews
James McDonald, Sr.
Bartholomew Barnes
Thomas Harvey
Jesse Hatcher
Jeramiah Flougnoy
William Freeman

Jesse Jones
John Morris
Jeptha Duboise
Isaac Lockhart
Samuel Lockhart
Joseph Lockhart
William Lockhart
Daniel Eubanks
Horatio Gates
Daniel Cole
Adam Jones
Francis May
Henry Cox
Simpson Chance
Ephraim Chance
George Eubanks
John Eubanks
John Harvey
William McGeehee
Robert Ried
Thaker Ninion, Jr.
John Herrington
Jesse Hammock
Martha Boone
Meldy Bozeman
Jesse Webb
Stephen Stephens
Abraham Pierce
Darling Lanier
William Pierce
Nathan Herod
John Herrod
Daniel McMillan
David King
Jesse Bowden
Willis Williams
James Smith
Thomas Wooden
Druet Dees
Owen Farr
William Porch
Isaac Coleman
James Dees
Drury Dees

Elizabeth Dees
Rice Webb
Elijah Padgett
Edward Moore
Solomon Crawford
Simon Smith
Nicholas Braggett
Aquilla Lowe
Willis Williams
Steven Matthews
Robert Manwell
William Folks, Sr. & Jr.
John Sandiford
Abraham Peacock
Seth Pierce
Levi Jackson
Herod Dupree
John Dupree, Jr.
Eli Peacock
Arthur Peacock
Reuben Powell
John Dupree, Sr.
William Walker
George Granberry
Gabril Parker
Elizabeth Smith
Millebee Fullford
John Cattle
Joseph Boseman
Nathaniel Knolls
John Powell
Stephen Webb
John Fleming, Jr.
Hugh Triven
William Fleming
Richard Kessel
John Joiner
Harvy Herrington
Arthur Dupree
Thacker Ninion, Sr.
Elisha Ward
David Ward
Felix Maxwell
John Woods

Phebee Grant
Richard Powell
John Bryant
Peter Durouzeaux
John Trueluck
Charles North
John Hammock
William Cawthron
William Wilson
John Hicks
Samuel Hammock
Jonas Mays
John Denton
Solomon Wood
Joab Horn, Jr.
John Burton
Willey Horn
Isham Ross
John Ingram
John Tinsley
Joseph Hall
Robert Craig
William England
Mourning Horn
David Wood
Zachariah Albutton
Andrew Berryhill, Jr.
John Evers
Daniel Gutman
Bartholomew Gutman
David Gutman
Bartholomew Gutman
Michael Fields
Thomas Sandford
John Ricks
Joseph Truecluck
Steven Durouzeaux
John Hendricks
James Roach
Benjamin Mays
Jonas Mays, Jr.
John Cowart
John Shoemake Holden
John Thomson

John Bryant, Jr.
James Mills
Esaias Fountain
Culver Horn
Joab Horn, Sr.
John Land
James Hall, Sr.
James Hall, Jr.
Dempsey Hall
Redding Hall
William Askew
Thomas Askew
John Bats
Jonathan Fountain
Wm. Fountain, Sr. & Jr.
Seth Fountain
Thomas Davis
Samuel Mays
Spiers Cannon
William Cannon
Harmon Mays
Gabriel Pickering
Zachariah Brown
William Legate
James Warner
Joseph Jackson
Jacob Sutton
Morris Raiford
Stephen Powell
Asa Brown
Henry Senterfilt
Samuel Sanford
Caswell Sanford
John Sanford
Benjamin Sanford
Lemuel Page
William Spivey
George Ingram
Samuel Smith
Dorcas Smith
Wilson Warren
Bird Tarver
Thomas Kenedy
Thomas McBride

George Tanin
Richard Summer
Berry Mack
Peter Moss
Benjamin Jones
Benjamin Green
Jesse Caney
John Green
Joseph Chairs
David Jamison
John Gandy
John Marshall
Ann Hargrove
Mary Wilson
William Baker
Rachel Crossley
George Brewer
William Mills
Joseph B. Spencer
Jonathan Archer
George W. Chisolm
Noah Minton
Joseph Barker
John Raiford
Thomas Street
Peter Moss
William Moss
William Calhoun
William Ronaldson
John Tompkins
Henry Shephard
Jacob Page
Daniel Merrian
Thomas Gauley
Ashley Wood
Isaac Simms
Thomas Allen
John Lowe
James Kennedy
Alexander Goodgame
Whitus Brinson
William Kenedy
John Parker
Isaac Mathers

Andrew Boyd
Jane Wier
Robert Boyd
Samuel Boyd
Isaac Wood
Samuel Clements
Saint Marian
Elisha Baker
William Morrison
Peter Ray
John Gibson
McNeely (William)
John Clements
Samuel Carter
Joseph Marshall, Jr.
Agnes Whitaker
Hugh Alexander
Samuel Gibson
William Gillam
Josiah McCarty
Charles C. Jenkins
William Thompson
Robert Greives
Samuel McBride
John McBride
Thomas Garvin
Joseph Kenedy
William Craig
Joseph Breckenridge
Benjamin Howard
Robert Montgomery
Benjamin Davis
Nicholas Baker
Joseph Marshall
Joseph Sumner
Mary Chestnut
Andrew Berryhill, Sr.
Archibald Little
Richard Barker
William Burdock
Margaret McNeely
Page Tally
Hugh McNeely
Irwin Calhoun

Moses Horn
John Greer
James Mathres
Samuel Barber
Thomas Schley
Benjamin Gobert, Sr.
Zachariah Lamar
Phillips Scott
Elizabeth Palmer
William Herring
Michael Schley
William Wright
Frances McMurray
Leon H. Marks
George Johnston
George Micklejohn
Job Townsley
Joseph White
John Downs
John Pugsley
Jonathan Sawyer
Howell Hargrove
Ambrose Day
John Bostwick
Thomas Collier
John Shellman
David Sturges
John Allen
Thomas Peebies
Zachariah Gray
John Manson
Simmons' Fowler
William Hughs
Thomas Fulton
Thomas Mountian
Matthew Hughs
Henry G. Caldwell
Matthew Casswell
Anthony Handcock
David Fairess
Thomas Handcock
Richard Warnock
Benjamin Bowring
Alexander Carswell

William Parsons
John Parsons
John Rodgers
Rodger Lawson
William Baron
Benjamin Whitaker
Richard Fleeting
Thompson Lawson
Robert Fagil
William Battey
Samuel Battey
Robert Warnock
John McMahan
Douglas Hancock
Robert Fleming
Blassinghame Thomas
Thomas Walker
John Whigham
William Whigham
William Kenedy
James Warnock
John Bigham
Robert Stone
John Fleming
John Stephevson
John Moore
John Paulett
Harvey Paulett
William Blackmar
Daniel Thomas
Patrick McCullough
William Manson
James Wilson
Agnes Mountain
John Hughs
Blassinghame Harvey
Hugh Gilmore
John Lowrey
Robert Flournoy
Thomas Merriwether
William Hadden
James Stubbs
David Emanuel, Jr.

JONES COUNTY.

Jones County was formed in 1807, and Clinton made the County Seat. Recently a fine new Court House has been built at Grays, on the railroad and two miles from old Clinton. Here the records of the county are all in safe quarters and in a fairly good condition. In the office of the Ordinary there are four Will Books, before 1850, and several old books of Minutes of the Inferior Court that contain much interest to middle Georgia families. Book "A" of Marriage Licenses begins 1812, and has an index, and also those that follow it.

In the Clerk's office all deeds are in good condition and well indexed.

First Book of Wills, 1810 to 1828.

Allen, Jesse	Eilands, Absalom	M'Clendon, Joel
Allen, William R.	Flowers, John	Newman, Allison
Boswell, Susannah	Garrett, John	Oxford, Jonathan
Blalock, Allidea	Grizzle, Grigsby	Partain, Peter
Bedell, Abner	Halstead, Jonathan	Piggs, William
Cary, Ann	Hines, John	Stone, William
Chapman, William	King, Littleberry	Trammel, Daniel
Castleberry, Richard	Long, Mary	Trice, John
Dickens, Ephraim	M'Gill, Susannah	Williams, Joshua

Will Book "B" 1812 to 1823

Adkerson, John	Calhoun, John	Hawkins, Samuel
Allen, William W.	Carson, Elizabeth	Hassell, William
Ballard, John	Cary, Robert	Hobson, John
Bond, Seth	Carson, John	Hood, Elizabeth
Buckner, John	Finnie, John	Hawkins, Benjamin P.
Barron, John	Feagin, Richardson	Hamlin, John, Sr.
Baldwin, Robert	Fryes, Richard	Hamlin, Richard, Sr.
Birdsong, B.	Finney, Benjamin	Horn, Simeon
Davidson, William	Edwards, Ambrose	Jones, Jacob R.
Dennis, Jacob	Gorden, Gaven	Lacey, Nancy
Davis, Gardner	Grigsby, Bathsheba	Ledbetter, Samuel
Denson, James	Gafford, Stephen	Ledbetter, Benjamin
Dent, Samuel	Harris, Edwin	M'Lamore, Charles
Dunn, Nehemiah	Harris, Joshua, Sr.	Magee, Davis
Davis, William	Hansford, Benoni	Martin, Elijah

M'Daniel, Benjamin W.
McDougal, Andrew
M'Farlin, Peter
Morris, Elizabeth
Morgan, David
Newberry, William
Oliver, Caleb
Owens, Spencer
Peirson, John
Pettway, H. B.
Pitts, Aaron
Phillips, Mary

Rease, Alexander
Rees, Isham, Sr.
Rogers, Collin
Rimes, Jesse Janet
Smith, Samuel
Spencer, Charity
Stubbs, James
Smith, John
Smith, John C.
Slatter, Solomon
Taylor, Joseph G.
Trice, James

Trice, Elisha
Thompson, Henry
Walden, Richard
Wynn, Green
Williams, James
Walden, Lewis
Ward, John
Willis, Joel
Wheless, Hardy
Wall, Elizabeth
Wyche, Peter

Will Book "C" 1826 to 1850.

Adams, James
Allen, Boler
Bray, Elizabeth
Barrow, Samuel
Bell, Samuel
Blount, James
Bowin, Charles S. B.
Bourgwin, Benedics
Blalock, James
Billingslea, James
Breedlove, Nathan
Blount, Elizabeth
Barron, Joannah
Bazemore, Thomas
Barker, Burwell
Bridges, Jonathan F.
Blunt, Thomas
Bayne, John
Bostick, David D.
Bryant, Wiley
Bradley, Dennis
Broach, George
Brantley, Joseph
Blow, John
Bennett, Elizabeth
Blow, Miriam
Blandford, Francis

Brown, Abraham
Blount, Henry N. S.
Brantly, Edmund
Brown, Robert
Cruthers, Robert
Childs, John, Sr.
Comer, Nancy
Cook, Samuel
Childs, Nathan
Cook, James
Cox, Jesse, Sr.
Comer, James
Chappell, Wiley
Capel, Sterling
Comer, Ann
Carson, Adam
Childs, John
Clark, Joshua B.
Clower, Stephen
Cabaniss, Sarah
Chapman, Grace
Clower, Peter
Caruthers, Jane
Chiles, Joseph
Driver, Giles
Damson, Washington N.
Duckworth, Joseph

Duke, John
Dennis, John
Dumas, Jeremiah
Dismukes, Garland T.
Deadwilder, Martin
Dixon, Hickman
Davison, James
Duncan, George, Sr.
Denning, Nathan
Duncan, Edmund
Emmerson, William
Eilands, Nancy
Emmerson, Zachariah
Eiland, Ruth
Flewellen, William
Finney, Henry
Fitzjames, Blake
Goodwin, Shadrack
Gordon, Nancy
Green, Allen
Godard, Simon
Gilsum, Francis
Heltan, Sarah
Harris, Richard
Harrison, Joseph
Haws, C.

Hoskins, John
Hester, Zachariah
Hart, Warren
Holladay, John
Harrass, Arthur
Hart, Robert
Harper, George
Hodges, Susannah
Hutchings, Robert
Healy, Michael M.
Hunt, Alexander I.
Jordan, Robert
Johnson, Thomas
Justice, Eliza H.
Jones, Elizabeth
Johnson, William
Jackson, Wilkins
Jones, John
Ivey, Bythan
Jarrel, Blake
Kirk, John
Kitchens, William
Ledbetter, Silas
Lowther, Samuel
Lamar, John
Locketts, James
Lowe, John
Middlebrooks, Thomas
Manning, Levi
M'Farland, Dugal

Mainyard, John
Monghan, William
Morris, Thomas
Moorē, Ebenezer H.
Mathis, Nathaniel
Messer, Noah
Moore, Green B.
Miller, George
Mitchell, Robert M. I.
Messer, Sarah
Morris, Nathaniel
Mason, Gideon
Mullens, Jeremiah
Mackay, Hugh
M'Gehee, Robert
Moore, John
Moore, Bishop
Mills, Jacob
Moore, Matthew
Moore, Mary
Marshall, William
Middlebrooks, William S.
Monghan, Thomas
Paramore, James
Pippins, Clayton
Patterson, Willie
Pitts, John
Richardson, Sarah
Robertson, James C.

Reynolds, James
Rose, Susannah
Roberts, Reuben
Roberts, Luke
Simmons, John
Stephenson, Nancy
Smith, John
Spinks, Rolley
Slatter, Nancy
Spinks, Henry M.
Stewart, Thomas
Smith, Sterling W., Sr.
Tooley, William
Tye, Daniel
Tuffs, Francis
Todd, Benjamin, Sr.
Ussery, John
Vanzant, Garrot
Walker, George
Weathers, Jenkins
Wimberly, Lewis
Watson, Tabitha
Wells, William
Wilder, William
Woodall, John
Williams, Howell F.
Williams, John, Sr.
White, E. H.
Zachray, John S.

LAURENS COUNTY.

This county was formed in 1807 and included much of the rich lands that were given to Revolutionary soldiers in the earlier Washington County grants. The new Court House in Dublin is surrounded by one of the best kept green lawns in the State, and the offices inside are in keeping with the lovely grounds.

The records in the office of the Ordinary are all indexed, except the early marriage records in two small books, from 1807 to 1820. All deeds are in good condition and recorded in a duplex index. A very fine history of this county was compiled by various county officials, and published in the Centennial Edition of the Dublin Courier Dispatch of December, 1907. It is to be hoped that it will be put in book form and placed in our public libraries as an inspiration for other counties to do likewise.

Index to Will Book No. 1, 1809 to 1840.

Anderson, H.
Allen, Rachel A.
Allen, Benjamin
Allen, Elizabeth
Albritton, Avarilla
Askew, Frederick
Beddingfield, Solomon
Bacon, John B.
Blackshear, Elijah
Barlow, Mary
Beaty, Mary
Blackshear, Joseph
Cook, Thomas
Coleman, Theophilus
Carey, Jesse
Culpepper, Sampson
Collier, John
Collier, Thomas
Coats, Robert
Coats, J. G.
Daniel, Benjamin
Duncan, Thomas
Dorsey, Benjamin
Daniel, Lucretia
Duncan, Ellis
Farmer, Thomas

Fulwood, John
Goodman, Henry
Gibbon, Ann
Holley, Jonathan
Hester, Rebecca
Hollensworth, George
Hampton, Andrew
Hudson, John
Joiner, Burwell
Jones, Adam
Jones, Jonathan
Joiner, Jesse
Kirkland, Samuel
Livingston, John
Livingston, Joseph
Long, Nicholas
Lely, Edward
Manning, John S.
Maddux, Alexander
Manning, Williby
Montford, Thomas
Moore, Sinthy
M'Bane, John
M'Cormick, Elizabeth
M'Caul, Eliza M. A.
Oliver, William

Oliver, William
O'Neal, William
Phillips, Mark
Pope, Fleet
Pullen, Thomas
Payne, George
Ramsey Burwell
Roberts, Frederick
Rowland, John
Ryals, Siphia
Solomon, Willis L.
Smith, Bennet
Smith, Isham
Sparks, Samuel
Spear, David
Stewart, John
Spivey, Jethro Benton
Spivey, G. A.
Todd, John
Usery, Elizabeth
Weaver, Jethro
Whitehead, William
Whitehead, Beason
Woodard, Young
Young, Owen W.

Marriages.

Noel Lambert and Polly Willis, 1817.
John Tucker and Easter Nobles, 1817.
Thomas Vickers and Piety Beaty, 1817.
Thomas Smith and Abigail Faircloth, 1814.
John Bryan and Gracy Tuttle, 1816.
John Hutto and Polly Usry, 1816.

Henry Hutto and Catherine Bullock, 1816.
Joseph Jernagan and Zany Lindsay, 1817.
William Ennels and Susanna Albritton, 1817.
Jesse Centerfeit and Polly Faircloth, 1817.
David Brooks and Mary Peal, 1817.
Elijah M. Daniels and Polly Batson, 1815.
Meridy Usry and Jane Watson, 1817.
Josiah Warren and Margaret Ann Martin, 1817.
John Dean and Jane Albritton, 1817.
Robert Holton and Miss Margaret Holton, 1814.
Elas Hutto and Milly Ussary, 1814.
Samuel Perkins and Betsy Alexander, 1813.
Dennis Batson and Martha J. Corker, 1814.
Asa L. Cook and Betsy Kent, 1814.
Owen Fields and Anna Griffin, 1814.
William Miller, Jr., and Sally Miller, 1814.
William Roberts and Nancy Tucker, 1814.
Emry Stringer of Burke Co. and Miss Polly Horn.
William Ward and Nancy Hutchins, 1811.
Owen W. Young and Patsy Howell, 1814.
Jacob Careker and Lucy Griffin, 1814.
Robert Higdon, Jr., and Elizabeth Green, 1814.
John Varnedore and Jennet Carson, 1813.
Henry Montford and Agey Stokes, 1813.
David Register and Bethany Faulk, 1813.
John Dale and Sarah Wright, 1813.
Fleet Pope and Sally Mines, 1816.
Joseph Flowers and Charity Spurlock.
William Hendrick and Susanna Webster.
John Love and Betsy Hall, 1814.
Nathan Grantham and Susanna Strickland, 1817.
Mark Roberts and Mitty Smith, 1817.
Daniel Trammel and Elizabeth Knight, 1817.
Edwin Dudley and Catherine Kellum, 1817.
John Yeates and Patsy Hinson, 1817.
Ebenezer Folsom and Nancy Montford, 1817.
James Salter and Polly Shearby, 1817.

Willis Wood and Mary Anderson, 1817.
James Yates and Agnes Rolings, 1817.
James Thompson and Mary Joiner, 1814.
William Hollinger and Rachel Hester, 1814.
John Register and Vancey Lane, 1817.
Joseph Atkins and Polly Grimes, 1817.
William P. Duke and Eliza Fenn, 1817.
Noah Creach and Sally Trammel, 1817.
Andrew M. Carson and Mrs. Charity Horn, 1814.
Thomas Swinson and Mrs. Sarah Robinson, 1816.
Matthew Smith and Unity Register, 1809.
John Varendo and Honor Hagan, 1809.
Irwin Stringer and Nelly Green, 1809.
Abner Hicks and Mary Beatty, 1809.
James Johnston and Mrs. Sarah Norton, 1809.
Daniel McNair and Celia Yarbrough, 1811.
Lock Boyet and Nancy Fort, 1811.
Nathan Sheffield and Permelia Phillips, 1811.
John Davis and Sophia Lomax, 1809.
James W. Shine and Elizabeth Taylor, 1810.
Joseph J. Battle and Rody Whitehead, 1810.
William Cawthorn, Jr., and Sarah Smith, 1809.
Burrel Philips and Sally Philips, 1809.
William Beatty and Polly Drew, 1810.
Lewis Johnson and Betsy Carter, 1810.
Thomas Manning and Patsy Hart, 1810.
Elias Vickers and Elizabeth Gibbs, 1811.
Green Wallace and Levina Rowland, 1811.
Alfred Thompson and Mary Roberts, 1811.
Samuel Way and Rachel Hampton, 1816.
Burrel McClendon and Feriby Joiner, 1816.
Philemon Coneby and Hannah Winston, 1816.
William Perkins and Penina Anderson, 1816.
John Hogan and Luisa Russell, 1816.
Edward Moore and Elvy Newby, 1816.
John Wynne and Peggy Clements, 1816.
Michael Connelley and Edney Green, 1816.

Naman Pickering and Smitty Smith, 1817.
David Smith and Hannah Tuttle, 1816.
David Scott and Ann Hutto, 1817.
Jonathan Morris and Nancy Loften, 1817.
William Roberts and Tabitha Faulk, 1816.
Isaac Smith and Milberry Smith, 1817.
Raiford Hare and Polly Darby, 1817.

LINCOLN COUNTY.

Lincoln was formed 1796 from Wilkes County and in its faraway Court House at Lincolnton, are to be found many items concerning the early settlers of Wilkes. In the old brick Court House the records are better preserved than in many of the up-to-date fire-proof buildings, where they are handled oftener and with less care. About half a dozen of the *oldest* books are kept in a safe while the others are on shelves in the office. The deeds are intact from 1796 to 1812, then two books ''G'' and ''J'' are missing. All are recorded in a Duplex Index.

The old wills are in three books, from 1796 to 1869, each having a separate index and the writing is very good.

The first book of marriage records, 1806 to 1829, is alphabetical as to names of the men, and later ones are indexed.

Index to First Book of Wills and Estates 1796 to 1805.

Ayres, William	Clayton, Alexander	Grove, Jared
Adcock, Emanuel	Clark, Elijah	Glaze, Thomas
Avera, Isaac	Cameron, Alexander	Gamble, John
Adcock, Edmund	Carter, William	Griffin, Richard
Bussey, Hezekiah	Crawford, Robert	Hammock, Samuel
Brown, Robert	Conner, Henry	Harris, James
Blanton, Christopher	Davis, Samuel	Hester, James
Bostick, John	Edger, Hugh	Hunter, Job
Bradley, Abraham	Florence, William	Hunter, Samuel
Blanton, Charles	Graves, James	House, William
Blalock, David	Griffin, Richard	Hammons, Jacob

Hambrick, John
Hambrick, Charles
Hughs, Thomas
Hogan, Shadrack
Hughs, James
Hammock, Samuel
Hix, John
Hogan, William
Jones, Henry
Jones, William
Johnson, Alexander
Jeter, Oliver
Jemison, Robert
Ingram, Isaac
Jones, Henry W.
Hughs, James
Jourdan, Henry
Jones, Aaron
Jeter, Garland
Jones, Henry
Kelly, William
Kinnon, William
Kinnebrew, William
Lankford, John
Loften, Daniel
Leverett, Robert
Lay, Emanuel
Lott, Reuben
Lankford, Milly

Lankford, Amelia
Lamar, Basil
Loflin, George
Lamar, Jacob
Lancaster, William
Lay, Vincent
Lyon, John
Mosely, Benjamin
Mann, John
M'Kenny, Travis
M'Cord, John
Matthews, Moses
Mahoney, George
M'Donald, Agnes
Maddox, Jane
M'Cormick, Joseph
Mitchell, John D.
Nail, Aquilla
Owens, Thomas
Pendall, Sarah
Perkins, David
Ratliff, Robert
Reed, Jesse
Russell, William
Ratliff, Robert
Sudduth, John
Sanders, Robert
Stovall, Josiah

Steel, John
Spires, Zachariah
Spinks, John
Sudduth, James
Sturdevant, Matthew
Standard, Kimbro
Sudduth, James
Tatum, Abel
Tomlinson, David
Towler, James
Thurmond, Felix
Tatum, Isaac
Tatum, Jane
Tatum, John
Warren, Lott
West, Andrew
Webb, Leonard
Ware, Henry
Wallace, William
Walker, John
West, Henry
Wyatt, Peyton
Winn, John
Williams, William
Ware, Henry
Webb, Leonard
Walton, Thomas, Sr.
Zimmerman, Philip

Book "B" 1808 to 1832.

Ansley, William
Ashley, Stephen
Aycock, Richard
Ammons, Jacob
Bohannon, Duncan P.
Bentley, Balaam
Bibb, William
Branch, Thomas
Bostic, Wade
Barnett, Jacob
Bussey, Thomas
Bennett, James
Bradford, John

Curry, James
Dowsing, William
Dooley, John M.
Davie, William
Evans, William
Florence, John
Florence, Jenny
Frazin, Samuel
Florence, Juda
Frazor, Arthur
Gillum, Peter
Grimage, Joshua
Groce, Shepherd

Harrington, Drury
Harves, Bennett
Huguley, George
Hemphill, Thomas
Harves, Isaac
Harves, Spencer
Hardy, Sarah
Hardy, Jesse, Sr.
Harnesberger, Mary
Harper, William
Hawes, N.
Howard, Thomas
Hancock, John, Sr.

Clarke, Edward
Covington, William
Curry, Thomas
Gray, James
Gatrell, Francis
Highs, Fielding
Harper, Martha
Jones, Henry
Lancaster, Sarah
Loflin, Elijah
Landers, Elizabeth
Lyon, Edmund
Lyon, Thomas
Lockhart, Britain
Moseley, William
Moss, Charity
Moncrief, Austin
Nolan, William, Sr.
O'Neal, William
Paradise, William
Price, John
Phipps, Joseph

Palmore, Elisha
Russell, James
Reynolds, William F.
Russell, Clariann
Roberts, Arthur
Ragan, Nathaniel
Samuel, Edmund
Stokes, William, Sr.
Stokes, Richard H.
Stinson, Alexander
Stokes, Lucretia
Suddoth, Elijah
Shepherd, John A.
Slatham, William
Stewart, Sarah
Sharpe, John
Stovall, Lewis
Seale, Robert
Stokes, William
Sims, Leonard
Suddoth, Lawrence
Simmons, Stern

Sharmon, William
Turman, John
Trammell, Thomas
Tatom, John
Ware, Henry
Walker, Lankford
Wright, Susan
Wallace, Thomas
Wright, John
Weathers, Samuel
Wadsworth, Thomas
Wilson, Sarah
Walton, John H.
Walton, Newell
Wright, William
Walton, Noah
Walker, David
Wallace, James
Wheeler, James B.
Zellers, Jacob
Zelner, George, Sr.
Zelner, George, Jr.

Will Book "H" 1831 to 1869.

Averett, Thomas
Ammons, James
Ashmore, John
Albea, Amanda
Brimson, Josiah
Bussey, Joshua
Bennett, William, Sr.
Benson, Elizabeth
Curry, Nathaniel
Cantilou, Alice
Curry, Thomas
Cliatt, Isaac
Cole, John, Sr.
Cartledge, James
Crawford, William H.
Collars, Elizabeth
Cartledge, Francis G.
Cantilou, William B.
Collars, Isaiah

Cantilou, Lucinda M.
Carnelison, Sarah
Cameron, George S.
Dill, Philip
Dallas, Thomas, Jr.
Dallas, Thomas, Sr.
Dallas, Dennis B.
Davis, Ransom
Dickson, Michael
Davie, Randolph
Davie, Sarah
Dunn, John L.
Dallis, Lavina
Elliott, Thomas
Fraser, John
Fleming, Francis F.
Farrow, Mary
Foulk, Jared
Ferguson, John

Florence, Thomas
Grover, L. H.
Garnet, Elizabeth
Gresham, Jeremiah
Goldman, Francis
Gray, Isaac
Guice, Peter
Garnet, Elia
Glaze, Susannah
Gunby, William
Glaze, Mary
Glaze, Thomas G.
Hogan, James
Haws, Laton
Haws, John
Harper, Nancy
Houghton, Elizabeth
Harris, Henry P.
House, Lott

House, Lewis
Jones, Thomas
Ivy, Marion
Johnson, John
Knox, John G.
Kinda, David
Landers, John
Linvill, Mary
Lamar, LaFayette
Little, John H.
Lansdale, Luke
M'Cridie, David
Matthews, John
Mahoney, George
Moss, Lydia
Mumford, Robert
Mercier, Henry F.
Moss, David M.
M'Cord, Johns
Moncrief, Wiley
M'Corkle, Archibald, Sr.
Murry, Elizabeth S.
Matthews, Joseph F., Sr.
Nocholson, James

Norman, P. W.
Pealmon, Elizabeth
Parks, William
Pitman, James N.
Paschal, William
Parks, Lewis
Parks, Lewis G.
Quinn, William
Remson, Rem P.
Reed, James
Rhodes, Eustice H.
Reid, Robert J.
Samuel, Benjamin
Sistrunk, John
Spires, Martha
Stovall, Stephen
Shipp, Mark, Sr.
Samuel, Elizabeth
Stokes, William W.
Stokes, Nancy H.
Sybert, John H.
Smally, Michael, Sr.
Sutton, Francis S.

Spires, William S.
Sistrunk, Green B.
Sale, Peyton W.
Strother, William F.
Turner, Lewis
Turner, William
Tyler, Francis
Tillory, Thomas
Tutt, Benjamin
Wheat, Mary
Wright, John
Wright, Nathan, Sr.
Walton, John S.
Wallace, William
Wright, Elizabeth
Walton, Robert
Wright, Mary F.
Woods, William, Sr.
Willingham, Reuben S.
Wheat, Harvey
Wright, Nathan
Weathers, Elisha
Wright, Charlotte

Marriages, 1806 to 1818.

Edmund Adcock and Sally Malcolm.
Wm. Ansley and Amy Edmunds.
Abram Ayers and Mary McCord.
Peter Averett, Jr., and Jinny Gant.
John Averett and Sally Harris.
Cornelius Averett and Liny Chamberlain.
Warren W. Athey and Susan Swords.
Wm. Ashley and Nancy Walton.
Henry Black and Polly Tanner.
Luton Brady and Hephzibah Mason.
James Barnes and Sally McKinny.
Isaiah Bohannon and Polly Guigle.
Wm. Bond and Nancy Florence.
Austin Bunch and Pamelia Jones.
Dennis Bussey and Frances Chrozer.

Robert Brown and Sally Bennett.
John Briscoe and Mary Hughes.
John Bell and Rhoda Bates.
Jesse Bates and Delilah Aran.
John Carter and Zilpha Benson.
Elisha Crawford and Nancy Turner.
Thomas Covington and Elizabeth May.
Thomas Curry and Nancy Walton.
John Colson and Franky Lockhart.
John Culbreath and Margaret Bragg.
Wm. T. Clemonds and Sarah Jordan.
John Cartledge and Elizabeth Ellis.
Lemuel McLorde and Elizabeth Moss.
Lewis Crosson and Susanna Steward.
Wm. Dennis and Milly Agoo.
Wm. Dent and Caty Dallis (1810).
Jonathan Douglas and Susan Jarred.
Jesse Dennis and Tabitha Posey.
Allen Dennis and Elizabeth Lott.
Thomas Dallis and Rebecca Miller.
Hiram Dennis and Nancy Howard.
Jeter Davis and Rutha Gilmore.
Dennis Dallis and Elinor Grimsley.
John Edmunds and Avarilla Tatum.
Adam Edgar and Elizabeth Hardy.
Frizell Edington and Winny Nelson.
James Edwards and Sarah Little.
Henry Evans and Rosy Mosely.
Benjamin Ford and Liza Schofield.
Wm. Elliott anl Elizabeth Gray.
John Eddy and Catherine Brunson.
Thomas Florence and Lucy Blalock.
Anderson Foster and Agnes Suddeth.
David Florence and Polly Hicks.
Wm. Fraser and Martha Perryman.
Samuel Fraser and Nancy Guice.
Shadrach Floyd and Martha Lyon.

James Ferrer and Jane Jennings.
Wm. Fleming and Elinor Johnson.
Richardson Ford and Nancy Killgore.
Seaborn Florence and Eveline Blalock.
George Gudder and Phebe Pate.
John Grayson and Martha Butler.
Buckner Griffin and Pattsy Foreman.
Wm. Gillam and Fanny Walton.
Benjamin Golden and Sarah Langford.
Wm. Gambell and Elizabeth Loften.
Drewry Griffin and Polly Gullatt.
Samuel Gilmore and Nancy Hardy.
John Gibbs and Parrey Smart.
Joseph Gant and Charlotte Smith.
Allen Goulden and Polly Bohannan.
Jesse Holder and Sarah Hunter.
John Hammond and Polly Harrington.
Hardy Hunter and Mary McGill.
Jeremiah Hardy and Susanna Hardy.
John Hammock and Sarah Thornton.
Cornelius Hardy and Sally Parks.
Peyton Harris and Catherine Matthews.
Allen Holliday and Nancy Oneal.
Edward Hardy and Martha Standard.
Aquilla Hardy and Polly Steward.
Joseph Harris and Nancy Tatum.
Bartley Hudgins and Hetty Harris.
Tolliver Harris and Susan Fleming.
Charles Jurdon and Elizabeth Lockett.
Wm. Jeter and Mary Lamar.
Thomas Jeter and Mary Walton.
Henry Jenning and Mrs. Rachel Mosley.
Wm. Jewell and Polly McKinny.
Thomas Jarred and Elizabeth Wright.
John Jarred and Elizabeth Towns.
Clark Johnston and Margaret Bowler.
Presley Jeter and Mary Florence.

Edmund Kilcreas and Nancy Cafry.
John Kelly and Agnes Hooks.
Robert Kilgore and Hannah Bussey.
Jacob Kinnebrew and Elizabeth Swisher.
Travis McKinney and Patsy Leverett.
Henry Kerby and Sally Harper.
James Kenney and Sally Dennis.
Edmund King and Nancy Ragan.
Silvanus Kendrick and Elizabeth Parks.
John Laramore and Polly Killgore.
Daniel Loflin and Edith Trammell.
Andrew Lee and Peggy Harper.
John Lockhart and Molly Simpson.
Joel Lockhart and Mary Parks.
Micajah Lane and Lucinda Hester.
John Little and Polly Moncrief.
Wm. Loflin and Eady Walker.
John McKorkle and Martha M'Son.
John Malcom and Joanna Adcock.
John McCord and Nancy McKinny.
Wm. Miles and Natty Reynolds.
John Morgan and Jane Stinson.
George Miller and Abby Covington.
Absalom Maldin and Cynthia Seale.
Benjamin Mosely and Sally Paradise.
Allen Mabry and Nancy Sherer.
Alexander Moss and Gracy Truthson.
Wm. Nolan and Jean Hatton.
Wm. B. Norman and Mary B. Wiseman.
John D. Overstreet and Cynthia Bohannon.
Andrew Owens and Mariah Mills.
George Owens and Mrs. Rebecca Goulsby.
James Olive and Mrs. Alcy Walton.
Wm. Oneal and Aney Bussey.
Martin Pickett and Sally Runnels.
Francis Powell and Nancy Ratliff.
Moses Paul and Mary Hargroves.

Wilson Palmer and Sally Flourence.
Oliver H. Prince and Mary R. Norman.
Gilford Pullin and Mrs. Susanna Willis.
Lewis Peters and Elizabeth Linders.
Wm. Prather and Cidney N. Glaze.
John Pead and Peggy Ayres.
David Prickett and Amanda Ferrington.
John M. Quinn and Lucy Samuel.
Daniel Rickley and Sarah Bennett.
Benjamin R. Raglan and Mary A. C. Stokes.
Hezekiah Ratliff and Anna Paradice.
Asa Roe and Charity Moss.
Isham Rosier and Elizabeth Cresson.
Hamilton Remson and Polly Murray.
Washington Russell and Malinda Blalock.
Richard Rook and Peggy Gouldman.
James Ratliff and Mary Gouldman.
John Smith and Nancy Parkinson (1806).
Spencer Suddeth and Elizabeth Mosley.
John Sanders and Eleander Hunter.
Stephen Stovall and Polly Ratliff.
Willis Sudduth and Edith Mosley.
Wm. Starks and Elizabeth Lancaster.
James Edmunds and Polly Statham.
Taliaferro Stribling and Lettice Sudduth.
John Simmons and Frances Hester.
Thomas K. Sandwich and Burthy Blalock.
Robert Smiley and Mary Laydon.
Philip Thomas and Lucy Pickett.
Abram Tanner and Amey Butler.
James F. Turner and Sally Turner.
John Little and Hannah C. Wyatt.
James Tatum and Elizabeth Bibb.
Shadrack Turner and Unity Gillam.
James Thompson and Mary Booth.
Meshack Turner and Fanny Tatum.
Absalom Tatum and Eliza Gresham.

Dennis Trammel and Elizabeth Howard.
Dennis Trammel and Elizabeth Goulding.
George Taylor and Elizabeth Walton.
Jere Thomson and Elizabeth ——
Martin Willis and Elizabeth Russell.
John Wright and Elizabeth Walker.
Ennis Willis and Sally Pullen.
Wm. Willingham and Ann Samuel.
Samuel Walker and Linney House.
Benjamin Waid and Malinda Hill.
John Vasser and Jane Oneal.
Solomon White and Rachel Ray.
Timothy Walton and Ruhama Phibbs.
George Whitler and Nancy Hicks.
Abel Wheatley and Nancy Benson.
Stephen Withers and Elizabeth McCormick.
John Walton and Polly Walker.
Wm. Wilkins and Catherine Weldon.
Timothy Walton and Sally Norman.
James Wadsworth and Jenny Mays.
James York and Jenny Flourence.
Singleton York and Rebecca Palmer.

MADISON COUNTY.

Madison County formed 1811 from Franklin and Elbert, has a splendid new Court House at Danielsville and all records are kept with neatness and order. The wills begin in 1811 and are indexed up to date. Marriage records are alphabetically arranged and easy of reference, and all deeds can be found by a Duplex Index.

Will Book "A" 1811 to 1840.

Aaron, Daniel
Arnold, William P.
Allen, Fanny
Bird, Lee
Berryman, Charles
Bird, James

Bullock, John G.
Burroughs, Bazel
Christian, Edward L.
Clements, Sarah M.
Colbert, Philip P.
Caile, James

David, William
David, Isaac
Gardner, Thomas
Grimes, Thomas M.
Gholston, Dabney
Graham, James

Graham, William
Griffith, Robert
Hall, Jeremiah
Hopkins, Josiah
Hodge, William
Hodge, Ann
Humphrey, John
Long, Samuel
Millican, Charles
Millican, John
M'elrath, Jacob

Montgomery, John
Mannen, Henry
O'Kelly, Thomas
Power, Francis
Power, William
Power, James
Power, David
Stokes, Sarah
Simmons, William
Smith, William

Shields, Littleberry
Strickland, Tolbert
Sims, Charles
Smith, Stephen
Simmons, Harry M.
Thompson, John
Williford, Lucy
Ware, Edward
Woods, Robert
Wilhite, John.

Will Book "B" 1840 to 1893.
(Extract from Index to 1860)

Allen, Gray
Berry, Bridges J.
Bolton, Leonard
Black, Thomas J.
Bragg, Joseph
Bragg, George
Burroughs, James
Barnett, David
Carithers, Mary
Cellum, Samue.
Carithers, William C.
Collins, John
Embry, John
David, Berry
Dobbs, John
Eberhart, George
Eberhart, Adam
Griffith, James
Groves, Samuel

Hart, Archibald
Human, Susannah
Hart, Harris J.
Jordan, Thomas
Johnson, Jane
King, Carson
Kellum, Samuel
Long, James
Lawless, James
Moon, Archelaus
M'Leroy, John
Madox, Berry J.
Morris, Stephen
Montgomery, Mrs.
 Elizabeth
Nash, William
Norris, Archer
Nuth, Mrs. Jane
Power, William W.

Porterfield, James
Sanders, James
Spratling, Francina
Strickland, Solomon
Scarborough, Fredrick,
 Sr.
Shields, William G.
Smith, Elizabeth
Strickland, Nancy
Towns, James
Tait, Robert L.
Thompson, Wm.
Thompson, Jas., Sr.
Vaughan, Wm.
White, Henry
Ware, Elisha
Williams, John.
White, Stephen

Index to Marriages—1813 to 1834 (Men only).

Anderson, Maxwell
Adare, Whitmell H.
Albright, Christian (1816)
Allen, Benjamin
Albright, Jeremiah
Albright, Jacob, Jr.
Allen, Nathaniel
Adare, William
Anderson, Jacob

Anderson, Terrell
Anderson, William
Atcheson, John
Anderson, Philip
Albright, Jacob (1825)
Allen, Gray W.
Arnold, James
Anderson, Tillman T.
Adare, James L.

Adare, John B.
Aaron, James
Allen, Stephen
Anthony, David
Ashley, Moses
Bruce, James
Barnet, Samuel
Barron, James
Boman, Moses
Berton, Nathaniel
Bradberry, Joseph
Bradberry, Robert
Brooch, Littleberry
Blocker, Michael B.
Baily, John
Blackburn, Thomas
Britt, Hugh
Britt, William
Bullock, Alexander G.
Bone, James
Britt, Ephraim
Brazel, David
Borum, Benjamin
Baker, Joseph
Bone, William
Brown, Lewis
Britt, Joseph
Bond, Joel
Beard, Samuel
Beasley, John H.
Brown, William
Baxter, Wm.
Braswell, Wesley
Brand, Jonas
Barnett, David
Bone, John
Burks, James

Bone, Matthew
Burks, Jonathan
Bone, George
Brassel, Wm.
Bowen, Drewry W.
Burks, Nathan
Bragg, Humphrey A.
Blare, Powell
Bird, Wilson
Bone, Bailey
Bondy, Lindsay
Bird, Wm. D.
Brannon, James A.
Beard, Thomas
Bradley, James
David, John
Daniel, Allen C.
Downs, Thomas
Dean, Jeptha
Dobbs, James
Dean, John
Evans, David
Elzey, Charles
Elder, Littleberry
Evans, Thomas
Eberhart, Jacob
Eberhart, James
Estes, John T.
Eberhart, Robert
Eckles, Joel
Eberhart, Samuel
Embry, Wiley
Eberhart, George
Eberhart, David B.
Floyd, Jabez
Forrester, George
Forrester, Moses

Folkner, John
Fortune, Richard
Floyd, Jabez
Ford, Joel
Floyd, Turner
Floyd, John
Fitzpatrick, Thomas
Gilbert, Isaac
Graham, Josiah
Gee, Drury
Griffith, John
Gholston, Zachary
Goolsby, Job
Graham, Josiah
Gilbert, James (1818)
Gholston, Benjamin
Gower, Reuben
Goolsby, Jeremiah
Griffith, Thomas D.
Gillum, Wm.
Galleher, James
Graham, James
Griffith, James R.
Griffith, James L.

Graham, Joseph
Gholston, Nathaniel B.
Glenn, John A.
Gossett, John W.
Graham, Henry
Gardner, Daniel
Grimes, Washington
Gholston, James S.
Graham, Jabez
Gordon, Vincent
Grimes, John P.
Harrison, Colmore
Hales, John
Hannah, Wm.
Harris, Henry
Hopkins, Dennis
Hicks, Stephen F.
Hodge, James
Hales, Jonas
Higginbotham, Samuel
House, Willis
Higginbotham, Nelson
Holland, James H.

MARRIAGES

Burks, Isaiah
Bradwell, Henry L.
Bone, William
Baxter, Nathaniel
Bullock, Wm. G.
Butler, Peter P.
Bradley, Abden
Bonds, James B.
Bird, James W.
Bond, John R.
Bell, Matthew
Bullock, Hawkins, S.

Bray, Banister R.
Bone, Barney
Butler, Patrick R.
Barber, Reas
Bryant, John P.
Baxter, John
Carithers, James
Cox, Joseph
Cartledge, Samuel
Cox, James
Cooper, Jonathan
Christian, Simon

Christian, Edward L.
Cotton, Joseph
Colly, John
Cox, John
Culbreath, Anguish
Cox, Abijah
Chick, James
Catlett, Alsa
Christian, Elijah W.
Carrington, Wm.
Cunningham, David
Clark, Sanford
Connelly, Thomas
Cooper, James
Carruth, Iredell
Carruth, Josiah
Clements, Noble
Chandler, James
Castleberry, Wm.
Christian, George A.
Crittenton, Wm. H.
Cooper, Milton
Caldwell, John E.
Colbert, John
Check, James
Crawford, Augustus
Cash, Benjamin W.
Calvery, John H.
Culbertson, Isaac M.
Carruth, Alexander L.
Carroll, John G.
Cobb, Benjamin
Carruth, James E.
Christian, Washington
Carithers, Wm.
Cummings, James
Donald, Alexander

Davis, John
Daniel, Wm.
Drake, Meridy
Dudley, Anderson
Dudley, Joseph C.
Daniel, James
Dudley, James L.
David, Berry M.
Daby, James
Holland, Linsy
Hays, John
Hartsfield, Wm.
House, Thomas
Haynie, Joseph
Howet, Jackson
Hamlet, John
Hannah, James
Hales, Saletheal M.
Haynie, Irvin B.
Hunt, Wm.
House, Sihon
Hampton, Hubbard
Hanley, Drury B.
Hailey, Joel
Harris, Tinsley
Hudson, John
Hodge, Allen L.
Hemphill, Thomas
Hampton, Hiram
Hemphill, Robert I.
Hemphill, Pleasant
Handcock, Richardson
Ham, Theophilus
Hall, John
Hunt, Joel
Hall, Robert P.
Hardeman, Larkin P.

Hawks, Edward
Jones, Dabney P.
Jones, Wm. A. (1816).
Jones, Dudley M.
Ingram, Wm.
Jones, Wiley
Johnson, Lee
Jarrel, John
Johnson, Joshua
Johnson, Lindsay
Johnson, Alexander
Johnson, Wm. S.
Jarrel, Willis
Jarvis, Nathan
Jenkins, Abner G.
Johnson, James
Jordon, Radford
Jordan, Britton
Jolley, Wm.
Kennedy, J. C.
King, John B.
Leeper, Hugh B.
Long, James
Lawless, Wm.
Landers, James
Landers, Samuel
Lawrence, John
Landers, Wm.
Landers, Lewis
Lester, Pleasant
Lay, Sampson
Lumpkin, George (1821).
Lawrence, Richard
Lane, Wm. M.
Lawrence, Jacob
Lassure, James M.

Millican, John
Muckleroy, John
Mudd, John
Merony, Wm.
McDaniel, Charles
Montegue, Philip
Morgan, Bethel
Murrow, Valentine
McCurdy, James
Martin, James B.
Manes, Thomas
Matthew, Phineas
Moon, John M.
Manley, Edward
Martin, Wm.
McGinnis, John
Macdonor, James
Mase, Henry M.
Mickleroy, Thompson
Millican, John
McDonough, Ransom
Manning, Henry
Morris, Wm.
McCurdy, Samuel
Martin, Nephthaline
McDurment, Joseph
Morgan, James
Manning, Redrick
Morrow, James
Mitch, John T.
Matthews, Lewis
Merony, John
Murrow, Woodson
Millican, Andrew
Morgan, Wilson
Mitchell, Samuel
Moore, Joseph

Maxwell, James
McGrady, Silas M.
McDuff, Alford
McCurdy, Wm. A.
McGrady, Wm. B.
Meadows, Berry G.
Meadows, Duren H.
McGinnis, Levi Q. C.
McKey, Samuel
Meadows, Noah W.
Milham, Henry
New, Jesse
Nash, Thomas
Nunn, Samuel
Nash, Henry E.
Nunn, Seaborn
Nunn, James
Nunn, Peyton
Old, Joshua J.
Ogilvie, Artenias W.
Powell, Oliver C.
Page, Benjamin
Patten, James
Payton, Howard
Patton, John
Patton, Elijah
Potter, Plummer
Payton, Randolph
rower, John M.
Patterson, John
Penn, Richard T.
Polk, James
Pitts, Coleman
Patton, John
Pitts, John
Parks, Wilson
Patton, Samuel

Pye, Edward
Pearce, Green
Pritchett, Jacob
Power, Wm.
Parks, Jenkins
Pittman, James F.
Pickett, Jephthah
Power, David
Palmer, James S.
Power, James M.
Polk, Levi
Pittman, Noah W.
Power, Charles T.
Power, Wm. W.
Power, Wm. G.
Pickett, Reuben B.
Porter, Bartholomew
Russell, John
Ray, John
Richard, Thomas
Rowe, Martin
Reeves, John B.
Richards, Royal
Reed, Reuben
Richie, Samuel
Richards, Wm.
Sims, Isham (1814)
Shoemaker, Samuel
Sanders, John
Shields, Wm.
Stevens, Stephen B.
Shepard, John
Sanders, James H.
Stevens, George
Spicer, James
Strickland, Thompson C.

Scott, James
Sanders, Jonathan
Sims, Barkley
Shoemaker, Fleming
Smith, Samuel
Sorrow, Joshua M.
Sorrells, Bennett
Strickland, Solomon
Simmons, Thomas
Smith, Jordan
Smith, Malcolm
Scarborough, Fred
Sanders, Jonathan
Scarborough, Wm.
Smith, Drewry
Smith, Aaron
Sims, Charles
Strickland, Milza
Sims, Richard R.
Sims, Murry
Simmons, Reuben
Sims, Wm.
Saye, Wm. H.
Strickland, Hardy
Sorrells, Charles S.
Sanders, Silas
Streetman, John W.
Streetman, Wm. R.
Strong, Samuel
Swendle, Thomas
Strickland, Willis
Strickland, Willis H.
Smith, Elijah
Streetman, John
Strickland, Jacob
Smith, Wm.
Scott, Andrew

Simmons, John
Stephens, Hailey
Streetman, Wm. R.
Sorrells, Richard T.
Stephens, Stephen W.
Sewell, Wm.
Spurlock, John
Smith, Wm.
Sorrells, Charles
Streetman, Pearson L.
Swendle, Solomon
Smith, Augustus C.
Sanders, Simeon
Sorrells, Richard W.
Simmons, Harvey M.
Smith, Martin
Stephens, Shadrack
Scott, Patrick
Stephens, Elisha
Strickland, Wilson
Sorrells, Wm. L.
Stewart, John (1831)
Strickland, Peter H.
Simmons, David
Stovall, John
Smith, James
Stamps, Britton
Strickland, Richard
Sanders, Hardy T.
aSnders, Tully
Sims, Charley
Stephens, Wm. A.
Smith, James M.
Seagraves, Alford
Smith, Wm.
Seagraves, Noah
Smith, Porter E.

Taylor, Grant R.

Towers, James

Tollison, John

Towns, Willis

Tollison, Hitson

Tolbert, Allen

Thompson, Bridges

Thompson, Andrew

Thompson, Berry

Teaver, James

Tolbert, Osborn

Trible, Spillsby

Tolbert, Harman

Taylor, Daniel

Trible, James L.

Thompson, Wm.

Tims, Samuel

Thompson, Obediah

Trible, John T.

Thompson, Obediah

Vineyard, Isaiah

Vineyard, James

Vineyard, Samuel

Vineyard, Wm.

Vandeford, Barzella

Vineyard, John

Vaughn, Isaac D.

Vandeford, Josiah

Vaughn, James M.

Ware, Col. Edward (1814).

White, Stephen

Whitehead, Samuel.

Whitworth, Winston.

Williams, James.

Williford, Jeptha V.

Wilhite, Meshack T.

Waters, Wm.

Wright, Asa.

Whitworth, Samuel.

Williford, John.

Ware, Elisha.

Williams, Robert.

Woods, Robert.

Welsh, Benjamin.

Williford, Samuel.

Webb, Wm.

White, John.

Wilson, Thomas.

Whitaker, Abram.

Witcher, Benjamin.

Woods, Abram D.

Williford, Stephen

Watson, Gilford D.

Watson, Gideon

Ware, Edward

Whitworth, Wm. S.

Wynn, John.

Wiley, John

Wilder, Jonathan

Wood, John

Williams, Martin

Williams, Elijah

Ware, George

Ware, Hamilton

Webb, Archie

White, Anderson

Ware, Burrel

Williams, John

Williams, Pleasant

Williams, Robert, Jr.

Williams, John E.

White, Luke

Wortham, George

Ware, James M.

White, James R.
Ware, Augustus G.
Woods, Robert
Wilson, Andrew
Whitehead, Samuel
Williams, Isam
Wood, Israel R.
Williams, Button S.

Williams, Wm. B.
Wynn, Hezekiah
Witcher, Charles T.
Wynn, Daniel
Ware, Asa I.
Young, Wm.
Yerby, Wm.

MORGAN COUNTY.

Morgan County was formed in 1807, and is now rejoicing in a fine new Court House at Madison. In the office of the Ordinary the wills, from 1808 to 1860, are in three books, and each book has an index for the wills, but the first book, 1808 to 1818, has about 500 marriages, scattered through it, that are not indexed.

The records in the Clerk's office are in good condition and all deeds are included in the Duplex Index.

First Will Book 1808 to 1818.

Allen, James
Bryant, Patrick
Bailey, William
Buchannan, Joseph
Bankston, Daniel
Carlton, Henry
Davis, Thomas

Davis, John
Fielder, John
Hambleton, Robert
Hanson, Edward
Jones, John
Mitchell, William

M'Murray, William
Pattillo, David
Stroud, John
Snellings, Peter
Wooten, Jeremiah
Whatley, Elizabeth

Will Book 1814 to 1830.

Allen, William
Anderson, William
Allen, Elizabeth I.
Aiken, Bartley
Brown, Robert
Betty, Joseph
Bailey, Joseph
Brewer, Nathan
Browning, William
Bailey, John

Barton, Presley
Burge, Willie
Barnes, John
Barnes, Nathan
Braswell, Benjamin
Barnett, Zadock
Barfield, William
Battle, Lazarus
Buckhoun, William F.
Beasley, William S.

Billingslea, Cyrus
Beasley, Robertson
Bandy, Lewis
Benton, William
Bellah, Samuel
Ball, Isaiah
Boon, Sion
Bandy, William
Butler, John M.
Boon, Rebecca F.

Butts, Eldridge	Hemphill, Samuel	O'Neal, Warren
Ball, Joel	Hughs, James	Nutts, Andrew
Cochron, Benjamin	Harris, William	Nelson, Taylor
Carlton, Thomas, Jr.	Hanson, Samuel	Perkins, Constantine
Chappell, Robert	Hackny, Nathan	Prator, Jennet
Cox, John	Harriss, Graves	Phillips, Benjamin
Campbell, Charles	Hicks, John J.	Prior, John
Clements, Austen	Hail, James	Baskil, Samuel
Crayne, Benjamin	Harris, Agnes	Porter, Douglas M.
Campbell, Sarah D.	Howard, Joseph	Penick, Robert
Corbet, Hansford	Heard, Faukner	Pickett, Nancy
Carlisle, Edmund	Ison, Christian	Reese, Eaton
Davis, Richard	Irwins, James	Radford, Reuben
Davis, Polly	Jinning, Pricilla	Robinson, Littleberry
Downs, William	Jordan, Hezekiah	Reaves, Simon
Davis, Isabel	Johnson, William	Roberts, John
Drummond, Edwin C.	Jones, Isaac	Russell, Burnett
Davenport, William	Jackson, Peter	Stamper, Robert
Evans, John	Jenkins, Peyton R.	Smith, Elizabeth
Edmundson, William	Lawrence, Claborn	Spratlin, William
Fayil, John	Larde, Samuel	Simpson, James
Fielder, William L.	Langston, Moses	Sidwell, David
Foster, Kimme	Lewis, William, Sr.	Scott, Joseph
Franklin, Bedney	Leviritt, Anna	Swift, William
Fannin, Isham S.	Liggon, Willis	Starr, Henry
Franklin, John	Lucas, Barbery	Shaw, Robert
Fitzpatrick, Benjamin	Mathews, James	Shields, William
Fielder, Samuel	Moore, Benjamin	Simmons, William
Fayil, Mary	Mooney, Betsy	Swift, Elias
Flinthon, Clement	Myhan, James	Simmons, Hugh F.
Fitzpatrick, Sarah	Middlebrooks, Isaac	Smiths, Richard
Grier, Thomas	Mulkey, James	Shackleford, John
Gillam, Ann	Mann, Catherine	Thompson, George
Gillam, Charles	M'Courn, William	Terry, Thomas
Gatlin, Zacheriah	Morgan, John, Sr.	Taylor, John
Gilson, David	Miers, Margaret	Turner, Boswell
Garner, Benjamin	Maquer, Louis	Taylor, Walter
Gaar, Joel	M'Intosh, David	Tillery, Joshua
Gaar, Lewis	Malcolm, James	Thrasher, Zeney
Gatling, Levi	Neal, William	Turner, James
Heard, Stephen	Noble, William	Walker, David
Harris, Ralph	Neal, Demaris	Warburton, Thomas

Weavers, Othniel
Walkers, Enoch
West, James
Wade, John

Ware, James
Ware, Lemuel
Warren, Henry

Warren, Stephen
Ware, Nicholas
West, William

Will Book 1830 to 1860

Askins, Aley
Akins, John
Atkinson, Thomas
Awtrey, Absalom
Allen, Charles
Arnold, F. W.
Bradley, Drury
Beman, Thomas
Bowder, Isham
Butt, John E.
Boon, Benjamin H.
Barton, Elizabeth
Bradley, Sarah
Boon, Gilly
Bird, George L.
Broughton, William
Barkley, William
Brewer, Drury
Brown, Fanny C.
Binford, Betsy
Brawner, Plyny
Binner, Frankling G.
Baldwin, Thomas B.
Brawner, Lucius W.
Barnett, Josiah
Bostwick, Azariah B.
Ballard, Benjamin F.
Bonner, Thomas
Baldwin, John R.
Chaffin, Lemuel
Campbell, Charter
Colbert, John G.
Campbell, George
Cochran, Matthew
Crowley, Charles, Sr.
Collin, William

Cardwell, John W.
Crowley, Charles, Jr.
Cochran, Banister
Campbell, Porter F.
Crawley, John
Davis, Grant
Daniel, William
Daniel, John M.
Davis, Thomas
Davis, Arthur L.
Dickerson, Calvin
Evans, Elvira J. H.
Evans, William T.
Edmondson, Thomas
Elliott, Alexander
Feagin, William, Sr.
Fox, Francis C.
Floyd, John
Fitzpatrick, C. Perkins
Fielder, Thomas
Fuller, George W.
Fitzpatrick, Mary
Fears, James
Fears, Zachariah
Gill, John
Garland, Sarah F.
Gardner, Elizabeth
Gordon, John
Head, Martha Virginia
Hanson, William
Hemphill, Elizabeth
High, John
Hubbard, James
Hewston, James
Haralson, Bradley
Hanson, James

Howard, Starling
Head, Baldwin B.
Hardaway, Levi
Hilsabeck, Henry
Heard, Joseph
Harris, John
Head, James, Sr.
Hammond, Thomas
Harwell, Littleton T. P.
Jenkins, Elijah
Johnston, Bartholomew
Johnson, John
Johnston, William
Johnston, Woodford A.
Johnston, Mary
Jones, Stephen B.
Kirby, Jesse
Kolb, Wilds
Love, David
Lane, William
Low, Thomas
Lock, Elizabeth
Lane, William T.
Lanier, John
Lambert, William
Mulkey, Eliza
M'Intosh, Martha
Malcolm, James
M'Gahun, James
Malcolm, Gomonay
McCoy, John
Mead, Edward
M'Coy, Ewell
Mann, Reuben
Mattox, Hardage

Milburn, John I.
M'Neil, John T.
M'Alpin, Ellis
M'Allister, James C.
M'Kenzie, James
Nisbet, James
Northington, James
Nolan, Thomas
Porter, John
Peters, Edmund
Puckett, Martin
Peck, David
Porter, Elizabeth
Pope, Wiley H.
Peoples, Mary
Prior, Elizabeth H. C.
Penick, Joseph P.
Perkins, William
Park, Betsy Ann
Ponder, John H.
Randle, William
Robinson, James F.
Radford, John
Rutledge, Kioh
Rhymes, Elizabeth
Rhymes, Willis J.
Robertson, Wiley
Russell, Mary Jane
Robertson, Hilliard W.
Radford, Elijah
Robertson, Wilson L.
Smith, Charles
Shepherd, Talmon W.

Snellings, John
Snellings, Tabitha
Snellings, John 2nd
Skidmore, Jett T.
Sparks, Jeremiah
Swift, John D.
Sidwell, John
Shields, Samuel
Smith, Sarah
Seats, Thomas
Swanson, John, Sr.
Saffold, Adam G.
Sheriff, Charles
Springer, Martha
Skidmore, Samuel
Swift, Katherine
Smith, Guy
Streeter, Willey
Shepherd, Carter
Stallings, William
Saffold, Seaborn J.
Swift, Thomas
Slade, Jane
Speed, Terrell
Shepherd, Mary A.
Slack, Joseph B.
Snellings, Virginia B.
Smith, George W.
Thomas, Jesse
Towler, Martha
Terrell, Henry
Thompson, Charles W.
Turner, William

Thomas, Henry S.
Trimble, Ruth
Vasan, John
Vasan, Rebecca
Wood, James
Wood, Catherine
Wright, Pleasant
Walker, John, Sr.,
Walton, Joseph W.
Williams, William H.
Wade, Hudson
Wyatt, Thomas H.
Wallace, James
Watts, Elizabeth
Wittich, Ernes', L.
Walton, Peter W.
Wellborn, Josiah
Wilson, William
Walker, Isaac
Wittich, Lucius L.
Whiting, Charles
Walton, Joseph W.
Wingfield, John
Wellborn, Curtis
Wellborn, Burkit
Wade, William F.
Walton, Bryant
Walker, Jonathan A.
Wittich, Ernest L., Jr.
Zachray, Abner
Zachray, Clementina R.
Zachray, Asa C.

Marriages—1808.

James Garret and Tabitha Tarver.
James Taylor and Rebecca L. Harris.
John Raburn and Polly Barren.
Thomas Dixon and Charity Gilbert.
Tyre Kelly and Elizabeth Jenkins.

James Ashley and Judith Foster.
Jordan Harris and Polly Fletcher.
Daniel Shaw and Sally Shaw.
Daniel Sessions and Euphamy Perryman.
Amos Wheeless and Nancy Cooper.
Coleman Brown and Unicy Atkins.
Lodowick Pullins and Rachel Megouirt.
Mark McClusky and Catherine Waits.
Benjamin Harrison and Jean Matthews.
Wm. Harkins and Nancy Still.
Thomas Wyatt and Nancy Wooten.
Stephen Jones and Caty Head.
Thomas Maberry and Rebecca Bailey.
Robert Penicks and Jane Buchanan.
Charles Lee and Nancy West.
Wm. Gilmore and Catherine Bentley.
Lemuel Fannin and Susanna Montford.
John Dingler and Mary Tucker.
Jeremiah Tucker and Milly Dingler.
Henry Askew and Polly Noble.
Wm. Williams and Betsy Sanders.
— — Whaley and — — Kinman.
Joseph Morrow and Matilda Hamner.
John P. Ryan and Polly Hansford.
Lewis Autery and Rebecca Young.
Ludwell Watts and Eliza Matthews.
Laburn Mosely and Elizabeth Lucas.
John Myhan and Barsheba Hicumbotum.
Isham Laws and Jane Ward.
George Medford and Sally Burges.
John Berryhill and Mary Rutledge.
Joseph White and Patsy Wall (P. 16).
Young Wilkinson and Lucy Head (P. 21).
John Jones and Aggy Ready.
Joshua Brantley and Tempey Radford.
Daniel Maberry and Betsy Robertson.
James Malcolm and Peggy Patterson.

Thomas Summerlin and Polly Daniel.
Joel Tapley and Elizabeth Durham.
Daniel Mosely and Sally Copeland.
James Wright and Mary Davis.
John Bentley and Catherine Pearce.
Lewis Spear and Fanny Rogers.
Wm. Garmain and Nancy Wilkinson.
Joseph Baker and Agnes Kenedy.
Joseph Still and Elizabeth Armstrong.
Bartholomew Johnson and Holland Warren.
Tandy W. Key and Nancy J. Bettey.
James Edwards and Betsy Ward.
Wm. Mitchell and Ann Clark.
Wm. Almond and Nelly Torrey.
John Middleton and Sarah Childers.
Wm. Hambleton and Cinthia Luckey.
Lundy Walker and Peggy Richerson.
Henry Rogers and Kirza Jackson.
Robert F. Sessions and Patience Patillo.
Richard Dorgett and Agga Spillars.
Brinkley Boyce and Sarah Thompson.
Philip Tinsley and Chaza Lapley.
George Harris and Sucky Allen.
John Houghton and Betsy Rogers.
Henry Carter and — — Kelly.
Edwin Lamber and Sally Henson.
George Malcom and Susanna Allen.
Matthew Philips and Polly Evans.
James West and Jane Adcock.

Index to Wills of Pulaski County from April 18th, 1816 to 1850.

Daniel, John
Dilliard, Phillip
Dykes, James
Deshazo, Richard
Daniel, John
Faircloth, Jonathan
Fitzgerald, David
Fleming, John
Gatlin, John
Graham, Green G.
Gilstrap, Jeremiah
Hendley, William
Hough, A. B. C.
Hamilton, William
Hayles, Margaret J.
Harrell, Miles
Hathaway, Henry B.
Harrison, Henry
Harrison, William
Hands, Richard
Harvey, John H.
Isler, William
Jones, John
Jones, Mary

Jelks, William
Kornegay, George
McGehee, W. B.
Mayo, Temperance
Mayo, William
Maddocks, Nathan
McComb, Samuel B.
McGriff, Thomas
McComb, Samuel
Mitchell, Stephen
Mitchell, John V.
Phillips, Tom
Pitts, George
Roberts, Elizabeth
Reeves, Joseph
Roach, James
Ragan, Daniel
Rozar, John
Snell, Daniel P.
Snell, David
Sutton, Moses
Sparrow, Daniel
Scarborough, Allen
Smith, Thomas

Stevens, Needham
Stephens, Needham
Thomas, Mary
Sanders, Jas. M.
Shiver, Abraham
Traywick, Jasper
Truluck, Sutton
Taylor, James M.
Tooke, Arthur
Tooke, Allen
Trull, John
Thomas, Mary
Tripp, James
Vickers, Edmun
Wood, Abraham
Wallace, Epps
Walden, Reubin
Walker, Thos. D.
Weeks, John W.
Whitfield, Wm. S.
With Compliments of
    P. T. McGRIFF,
        Ordinary.

PUTNAM COUNTY.

Putnam County, formed in 1807, has, at Eatonton, a nice new Court House, with beautiful grounds surrounding it, which gives courage to the hope that soon all the records inside will be as neat as the outside. In the office of the Ordinary all the will books are in very good condition and indexed, as are also the Marriage records, but there are many boxes of old records and papers that need sorting and arranging. (These have probably been attended to by now.)

The deed books in the Clerk's office are all in good condition and indexed in each volume, but there is no general index in the office.

Will Book "A" 1808 to 1822.

Allen, James	Heath, Stirling	Reese, Joel
Ashfield, Frederick	Hill, George	Read, Joseph
Burford, Amelia	Henderson, James	Rosser, George
Brewer, George	Harvey, Evan	Rutledge, James
Baugh, Daniel	Howard, Francis	Rousseau, William
Boling, Manning	Hardy, Edward	Roquemore, Thomas
Buckner, Charles	Hearn, Seth	Singleton, James
Bird, Job	Irwin, Sally	Stinson, Catherine
Bradford, John	Jackson, David	Spivey, William
Bailey, Simon	Jackson, David W.	Slaughter, Martin
Coleman, Daniel	Jones, Reuben	Stubbs, Peter
Cheevs, Thomas	Jones, Allen	Turner, Susannah
Cooper, Joseph	Johnson, Cornelius	Turner, Joseph
Clements, Jesse	Kelly, John	Tillery, Henry
Dennis, Joseph	Leverett, William	Turknett, Jacob
Dynnatte, Reuben	Low, Sarah	Thrash, Jacob
Dishazo, Lewis	Lee, John	Todd, John
Eakin, Samuel	M'Gehee, John	Turner, Susannah
Ector, Hugh	M'Kissack, John	Terrell, Richmond
Flournoy, John F.	M'Donald, Roderick	Williams, William
Felps, David D.	Morrison, Daniel	Whitehead, Thomas
Fannin, Joseph D.	Mathis, William	Whitaker, Thomas
Fretwell, Leonard	Oneal, Sarah	Wallace, Balim
Giles, Thomas	Perryman, Robert	Walton, Robert J.
Goodson, Arthur	Peterson, William	Wright, Parson
Gordon, Kenneth	Phillips, William	Whitaker, Elizabeth
Gains, Gustavus	Parker, Stephen	Williams, George
Garret, Jacob	Rhymes, John R.	Watkins, John
Haver, Timothy	Roger, John	Zuber, Jacob

Will Book "B" 1823 to 1856.

Avrea, Arthur	Bradley, Charles	Ballard, Ransom
Ashurst, Robert	Bigbee, James	Barrow, Nancy
Allen, John	Burt, Jesse	Bass, John H.
Allen, William	Bryant, Mary	Butler, Massey R.
Abercrombie, Wiley	Burgess, Josiah	Bledsoe, Robert
Allen, Chloe	Brantley, Mary	Badger, Levin
Adams, James M.	Butler, Zacheus	Batchelor, Jesse
Alford, Henry	Black, Richardson	Crews, Ethelred
Alexander, Matilda	Buckner, John	Copeland, Richard
Blunt, Edmund	Branham, Isham	Curry, Polly
Bird, Pue	Burt, James	Cullafer, Henry
Bailey, Green	Biscoe, Ann B.	Crouch, Shadrack

Cooper, Martha	Hill, John	Little, Robert
Collinsworth, John	Harwell, James R.	Little, Jesse
Cornett, George	Hearn, Jonathan	Madox, Joseph
Coleman, Willis	Hudson, Charles	Manning, Adam
Conine, Richard	Holland, Elizabeth	M'Coy, Arcgibald
Cooper, Thomas	Harden, Adam	Moreland, John, Sr.
Cole, Grovey	Howard, Henry	M'Ghee, James
Cooper, Henry	Hearn, Asa	M'Lendon, Frances
Crittenden, Lemuel	Hudson, William	Myrick, Polly C.
Duncan, Matthew	Hawkins, Nicholas	Marus, Andrew
Dickey, Patrick	Hudson, L. W.	Mason, Abical
Dixon, Nicholas	Holton, Thomas	M'Kinley, William
Denham, Charles	Hudson, Irby	Maddox, William
Dismukes, Finney	Hearn, Lot	M'Kee, F. A.
Dismukes, Garland T.	Harrison, Nathaniel	Napier, Tabitha Dixon
Denham, Nancy	Hagan, William	Newsom, John
Davis, James	Hurt, Charles S.	Oneal, Edmund
Dennis, William, Jr.	Head, Thomas	Pace, Stephen
Dennis, William, Sr.	Head, Thomas	Posey, John H.
Edmondson, Patience	Hearn, Benjamin	Park, Thomas
Espey, James	Holt, Peyton	Price, Zemulia
Edmondson, John	Hurt, Sarah	Perry, Green
Fretwell, John	Hudson, John	Prichard, Presley
Flournoy, William	Howard, John	Purifoy, Sarah
Faver, Isaiah	Ingram, Thomas	Pye, Jesse
Flournoy, Josiah	Ingram, John	Pye, Mary H.
Felts, John	Johnson, Margaret	Pound, Merryman
Flanders, Mandania	James, Elias	Parham, Susanna
Farrer, Abel	Jordan, Williamson	Park, Sarah D.
Gaither, Brice	Johnson, Green	Robey, Timothy
Gray, Thomas	Johnson, Joseph	Read, Asa
Gee, Peter	Johnston, Thomas	Rees, William
Gant, Brittain	Kendrick, Martha	Richard, William
Griggs, John	Kimbrough, Thomas	Rosser, David
Gordon, C. F.	Keeton, Jesse	Rees, Eliner
Gilbert, Frances	Killebrew, Robert	Rosser, Sarah
Goode, John C.	Kendrick, Jane	Reid, Alexander
Graves, John	King, Margaret	Ralls, Robinson
Green, Mary	Lunsford, Nancy	Smith, Joel
Griggs, Robert	Lawson, Leatha	Stembridge, William
Gregory, Hardy	Little, William	Stewart, James
Harris, Stephen W.	Lee, John	Stephens, Abram
Holt, Singleton	Lumsden, John G.	Sturdevant, John
Harris, Eli	Ledbetter, Sarah	Skaggs, Charles
Hearn, Phebe	Lumsden, Malinda	

Singleton, Hezekiah
Smith, Dorothy
Scott, Francis
Spivey, Henry
Stone, William
Sutton, Sarah
Smith, Banister
Smith, Ann
Sanford, Sarah S.
Seymour, R. A.
Stow, B. E.
Swanson, Francis
Spivey, William
Turner, John

Thrash, Andrew
Turner, Henry
Tomlinson, Elizabeth
Thompkins, Giles
Tomlinson, Nathan
Turner, Jehu
Turner, Joseph
Thomas, Juda Ann
Tunison, George M.
Underwood, Isaac
Williams, Stephen
Wolridge, Absalom
White, Micajah
Wynn, Jones

Wilborn, Thomas
Williams, Mabel
Wynn, John
Watkins, Charity
Wornum, William
Wallace, William
Whitfield, Benjamin
Wells, John
Ward, Amos
Walker, Samuel
Waller, Handy
Wilson, James
Ward, Mary

Marriages—Book "A," 1808 to 1816.

Ashurst, Robert and Patsy Moreland.
Anderson, Elijah and Celia White.
Allen, John and Ellender McMurry.
Alford, Henry and Sally Clemons.
Angling, Wm. and Lovey Maddox.
Averett, Ingram and Elizabeth Scaggs.
Adams, Reuben and Fanny Ware.
Berry, Jesse and Mildred Faver.
Barnes, John and Sally Stores.
Bazemore, Thomas and Sally Row.
Benton, Hardy and Nancy Jones.
Brown, Sampson and Nanny Gordon.
Bundles, James and Rachel Phelps.
Brown, Wm. and Polly Brown.
Brown, Charles and Candas Wooten.
Brooks, Isham and Serena Gordon.
Ballard, Ransom and Elizabeth Marshall.
Biscoe, Basil and Chloe Williams.
Barry, Bartlett and Nancy Pollard.
Boswell, Josiah and Harriet E. Gregory.
Bruce, Thomas M. and Sarah Crane.
Brooks, Robert and Frances Baugh.
Barker, Thomas and Susanna Babb.

Benson, Wm. and Polly Silvey.
Brannam, Richard and Mary Turkinet.
Bird, John and Nancy Jourmany.
Brooks, Jordan and Mary Jackson.
Bird, Robert and Polly Giles.
Bullock, Shadrack and Jinny Ewins.
Banks, Wm. and Elizabeth Jackson.
Brodnax, John H. and Catherine B. Whitaker.
Brakely, Richard and Minna Giles.
Bearden, Thomas and Mary Cole.
Branham, Henry and Valinda Harris.
Briant, Wm. and Mary Flournoy.
Barker, Edward and Susanna Osburn.
Barren, James and Polly Dossand.
Banks, Robert and Anny Gayton.
Benson, Eli and Polly Hall.
Bury, Green and Polly Coleman.
Berry, Gideon and Bally Whately.
Broadnax, Robert and Olive Whitaker.
Blacksher, Dandle and Caty Hungling.
Brooks, Elisha and Taney Mosely.
Brown, Hubbard and Elizabeth Wallace.
Baker, Drury and Elizabeth Parham.
Boswell, John and Susanna Baley.
Chapman, Wm. and Frances Fillups.
Clayclerk, John and Lucy Robertson.
Cooper, Jeremiah and Kitty Scurlock.
Cooper, Willis and Lany Ross.
Caster, Thomas and Sally Hawkins.
Carrel, John and Sally Garner.
Channel, Harmon and Delilah Coleman.
Cook, Julius and Patsy Winnand.
Cates, John and Celia Hopson.
Clopton, James B. and Mary J. Reas.
Nathaniel Coats and Penelope Hawes.
Cox, Jeremiah and Jinny Height.
Cotton, Wm. and Cinthia Smith.

Clements, Archibald and Polly Linesy.
Curry, Thomas and Rebecca Perry.
Causey, John and Rebecca Robertson.
Cotton, Wm. G. and Cinthia Smith.
Clopton, Alfred and Sally Kendrick.
Colb, Nathan and ——
Crowder, Frank and Phebe Hill.
Clark, John and Elizabeth Wells.
Chatham, George and Ceana Gholson.
Crane, Ezekiel and Minna Lambert.
Campbell, James and Creasy Murry.
Cox, Acy and Margaret McDaniel.
Conley, Val and Rhody Vert.
Chatham, Derias and Elizabeth Clackler.
Crawford, James and Martha Lynch.
Dismuke, James and Gilsy Cooper.
Denson, Wm. and Catherine Phillips.
Dixon, Bryan and Betsy Warren.
Darnell, Isaac and Hannah Mattucks.
Derham, Abner and Fanny Cooper.
Daniel, Stith and Mourning Pass.
Duberry, Thomas and Lydia Walker.
Jeptha, M. Daniel and Tabitha Self.
Duffie, Frederick and Nancy Willborn.
Daniel, Amos and Sophia Cox.
Dennis, John and Peggy McMurry.
Duke, Charles and Martha Milton.
Dunn, James and Sally Terry.
Echols, Obediah and Elizabeth Flournoy.
Edwards, John and Elizabeth Barnes.
Echols, Obediah and Elizabeth Jones.
Flournoy, Josiah and Martha D. Manley.
Favor, Wm. and Polly Lee.
Finley, Henry and Mary Barrett.
Fuller, James and Phebey Fuller.
Furlow, John and Cinthia Hill.
Favour, Hillsman and Polly Hawkins.

Fleming, James and Mildred Stubbs.
Favor, Christian and Catherine Pierce.
Garner, Ralph and Elizabeth Hickenbotham.
Grig, Jerry and Nelly Dejournett.
Giles, James and Sally Griffin.
Garner, Wm. and Mary Henderson.
Grampell, Israel and Nancy Smith.
Gammell, John and Rachel Smith.
Griffin, Nathan and Nancy Wright.
Gilmore, James and Nancy Langley.
Garrett, Wm. and Elizabeth Harrison.
Griffin, Wm. and Charlotte Phelps.
Glover, John and Drucilla Evans.
Griffin, James and Phalbuy Tuber.
Gilmore, John and Nancy West.
Groom, Council and Elizabeth Lopton.
Joseph Gray and Sally Miller.
Gibbs, Zachra and Esther Williams.
Groos, Elison and Sally Davough.
Green, Basley and Elender Turner.
Griffin, Charles and Elizabeth Wells.
Hooks, Henry and Lucy Wright.
Hill, Joseph and Elizabeth Clecker.
Harvey, Isaac and Sally Napper.
Howard, Henry and Sally Reed.
Hopson, Caswell and Polly Keeton.
Hill, Manning D. and Elizabeth Johnston.
Hearn, Wm. and Patsy Stephens.
Harper, Edward and Polly McDonald.
Harper, John and Leah Maddox.
Heath, John and Ann Pereman.
Holloway, Anthony and Elizabeth Williams.
Hunt, John and Polly Stovall.
Holland, John and Elizabeth Walker.
Harden, Seth and Salley Parker.
Hunt, John and Rutha Stowvall.
Hooks, Charles and Polly Cullifer.

Hurtard, Henry and Ema Sledge.
Harden, Hudson and Poley Nevis.
Holland, Samuel and Tabitha Kendrick.
Henderson, John and Sally Hearn.
Honycut Wm. and (torn off).
Holland, Dixon and Milly Gruzzard.
Howel, Samuel and Polly Cook.
Henderson, John and Hannah Davis.
Hill, Robert and Elizabeth Morgan.
Harper, Wm. T. and Sally Perdue.
Hawkins, John and Pricilla Smith.
Honeycut, Elisha and Fanny Whatley.
Harrison, Wm. and Jinny Henry.
Hudspeth, James and Jiney Junior.
Harrison, Wm. and Susan Kendrick.
Henderson, Wm. and Celia Thompson.
Hearn, Lott and Frances McLendon.
Hoxey, Thomas and Polly Gaither.
Harvey, Richard and Rebecca Reid.
Lewis, John and Nancy Sanders.
Irwin, John and Cidney Peters.
Jackson, Joel and Sarah Brooks.
Jones, Joseph and Rebecca Hightower.
Jackson, Peter and Lucinda Gray.
Jackson, Isaac and Kitty Thompson.
Kimbrough, Bradley and Polly Pace.
Jernergan, Wm. and Elizabeth Neeves.
James, ... and Jamima Folds.
Kellsey, Adam and Celey Napper.
Kenon, Charles and Lucy H. Cotton.
Knight, John and Frankey Goodson.
Killgo, Wm. and Celia M. Roney.
King, John and Winny Irby.
Kendrick, Drury and Amy Holland.
King, Lewis and Martha Flournoy.
Kinman, Thomas and Jane Avery.
Kith, Jeremiah and Louiza H. Doster.

Kendrick, Muda and Charity Harvey.
Killpatrick, Thomas and Martha Scott.
Lawson, Thompson and Marah Akens.
Loften, Thomas and Abigail Millirons.
Low, John and Susannah Sturdevant.
Lewis, John and Tempy Smith.
Lawter, Matthew and Hannah Taylor.
Langham, Wm. and Anny Acre.
Lampkin, Robert and Nanny Drewgton.
Lochorn, Simeon and Sally Nugin.
Long, Solomon and Sally Dunham.
Lane, Benjamin and Polly Word.
Lewis Thomas and Julia Foster.
Lunsford, John and Margaret Walser.
Lapread, John and Rachel Sanders.
Lamberth, Wm. and Polly Parker.
Lynch, Benjamin and Peggy Davidson.
Lane, Benjamin and Sally Garrett.
Leverett, Jeremiah and Nancy Williams.
Leverett, Boberee and Nancy Cody.
Lions, Nathan and Ann B. Reid.
Magee, Robert and Elizabeth Moreland.
McClendon, Dennis and Elizabeth Sawyers.
Mangham, Willis and Tempy Brewer.
McGormick, John and Polly Gray.
McCoy, Norman and Lydia Holoway.
Mahone, Thomas and Nancy I. Martial.
Maddox, Zach and Sally Smith.
Miller, James and Sarah Milton.
Maddox, Wm. and Sally Slavours.
Mirick, Dennis and Patsy Cosley.
Moreland, Colson and Sally Wouldridge.
McYaddin, Wm. and Catherine Holloway.
Musshead, Hiram and Nancy Phillips.
Moody, Benjamin and Silvey Warburton.
Mandy, Reuben and Polly Andrews.
Mapp, John A. and Sally Brothers.

Matthews, Wm. and Sally Orrick.
Mackay, John and Elizabeth Barns.
McConnell, Budwell and Stacy Lane.
Manley, Wm. and Ruth Brooks.
Murph, Richard and Fanny Davidson.
—— and Polly Hearn.
Marshall, John and Elizabeth Wright.
Mize, James and Elizabeth Dusmary.
Mitchell, John and Sarah Stubbs.
Maran, Wm. and Sarah Bass.
Mosley, Thomas and Nancy Smedley.
Morrow, James and Sally Wright.
Mahone, Gooding and Eliza Rogers.
Nentures, Stephen and Nancy Wilkerson.
Nesser, Jesse and Mariah K. Gregory.
Nowis, Wm. B. and Nancy Dishazo.
Naugent, Matthew and Martha Bazemore.
Owens, George and Susannah Wortley.
Ousley, Jesse C. and Sally Matta.
Owens, Lemuel and Mary Moreland.
Presley, Wm. and Elizabeth Goldsmith.
Pendleton, Coleman and Patsy Gilbert.
Philips, Reuben and Fanny Mosley.
Parker, John and Sarah H. Gilmore.
Perryman, David and Elizabeth Perryman.
Parker, Isaac and Elizabeth Rowel.
Palmor, John and Polly Cooper.
Posey, Chester and Milly Matheks.
Parker, Joseph and Nancy Bingham.
Porch, Henry and Patience Hargroves.
Pate, Peterson and Rebecca Huth.
Philips, David and Nancy Kelly.
Powel, Millenton and Polly Wooton.
Pitts, Archibald and Elizabeth Wallace.
Philips, Lewis and Sally Wilkins.
Porter, Lawson and Amelia Rees.
Peters, Robert and Elizabeth Davis.

Posey, John and Polly Flournoy.
Puckett, Edmund and Betsy Gray.
Perry, Elisha and — —
Robertson, John and Nancy Collins.
Reed, Thomas and Middy Ward.
Robertson, Thomas and Rebecca Cleakles.
Reed, John and Sally White.
Shiley, Moses and Betsy Groom.
Seal, Thomas and Binay Mosley.
Rausan, George and Polly Matthews.
Rogers, John and Eliza H. Dixon.
Robertson, James I. and Martha Rakin.
Robertson, Joseph and Catherine Sanders.
Rogers, Isaiah and Sally Wilson.
Rees, David and Polly Little.
Barbera, Bury and Elizabeth Hopkins.
Ridley, Robert and Sarah Cooper.
Ruson, James and Rebecca Smith.
Raburn, Richard and Thirsa Mantry.
Rill, Joshua and Sally Downing.
Richardson, Gatewood and Betsy Johnson.
Richards, Thomas and — —
Simmons, Henry and Lizzy Gouad.
Stephens, Solomon and Sally Barren.
Shepherd, Bennet and Elizabeth Webb.
Standafer, Skelton and Lydia Echols.
Smith, Thomas and Susanna Whitfield.
Smith, Arther and Betsy Keeton.
Stone, Michael and Polly Wells.
Shields, John and Sally Jones.
Smith, Henry and Sally Ousley.
Sanders, John and Elizabeth Hathorn.
Sealway, Thomas and Sarah Holloman.
Sanders, Daniel and Martha Brewer.
Stubbs, Thomas and and Catharine Stubbs.
Smith, John and Nancy Simons.
Scags, John and Polly Avey.

Singleton, Thomas C. and Tabitha Low.
Sturdevant, Denny and Matilda Porter.
Sessions, John and Polly Thompson.
Stone, Thomas and Nancy Tuchstone.
Sparkes, Wm. and Patsy Dixon.
Singleton, James and Polly Bullock.
Todd, Moses and Hetty Parker.
Thrash, Lander and Peggy Parrott.
Thrash, Martin and Jincy Sturdevant.
Todd, Adam and Elizabeth Parker.
Tuchstone, Solomon and Eve Meroney.
Tralor, Wm. B. and Molsey Whitfield.
Turkinett, Henry and Catherine Branham.
Turkinett, Jacob and Edia Brannam.
Thompson, David and Sally Watkins.
Thrash, Val and Lucinda Peavy.
Thrash, Jacob and Sally Puckett.
Teat, Henry and Rebecca Prual.
Turner, John and Peggy Garner.
Thomas, John and Eliza Smith.
Thomas, Wm. and Ellender Smith.
Tobin, John and Emily Felps.
Veal, John and Rebecca Jones.
Varner, Edward and Emma Dent.
Williams, Wm. and Elizabeth Gray.
Wright, Randle and Jincy Presley.
West, Uriah and Patsy Whitny.
White, John and Clarissy Mason.
Wilmer, Simeon and Elizabeth Hall.
Word, Albrittan and Easter Atkinson.
Wilkerson, Reuben and Winny Colverhouse.
Wilson, Hugh and Jinny Brooks.
White, David S. L. and Eizabeth S. Cannon.
Woodard, John and Polly Skinner.
Walton, John and Mary Rymes.
Williams, Joseph and Jinny Whatley.
Winn, John and Polly Thomas.

Williams, Benjamin and Cealy Rymes.
Woodroff, Ludikin and Morning Mitchell.
Williams, Hezekiah and Sally Richardson.
Weddington, Vino and Elizabeth Pace.
Wright, Jacob and Catherine Price.
Williams, Wm. and Rebecca Harvey.
Wells, Wm. and Nancy Cully.
Webb, Wm. and Polly Jackson.
Williamson, Henry and Polly Simons.
Williams, Hezekiah and Prisilla Tidwell.
Waid, Ira and Polly Mitchell.
Wall, Joseph and Lucy Riley.
Whiturst, Peletiah and Sally Pounds.
Wills, Benjamin and Nancy Faunce.
Weakes, Jeptha and Sally Jones.
Wilson, Joseph and Elizabeth Orrack.
Webb, Wm. and Nancy Williamson.
Winter, Henry and Charlotte Tuchstone.
Wheeler, Carrington and Polly Henry.
Wilkerson, Lemuel and Nancy Bouling.
Whitfield, Benjamin and Matilda Smith.
Wallace, Benjamin and Catherine Leverette.
Yarborough, James and Mary Dixon.
Zara, Williamson and Patsy Dennis.
Zuber, John and Mehaly Rose.
Zachry, Jesse and Elizabeth Cooper.

TATNALL COUNTY.

Tatnall County was formed in 1801, and has fine new Court House at Reidsville, but the *old* records are very scarce.

In the ordinary's office no wills could be found previous to 1863, and the first book of marriage records begins 1832. These are not indexed and are in several small books of about 100 pages each. There are several old books of Inferior Court records, that contain administrations and accounts of estates, that are in bad condition and should be copied. A few wills are scattered through the early books of deeds, but are not indexed with them. The Clerk of the Court has a lady now employed in copying all deeds with a book-typewriter, and those records bid fair to be in good shape eventually.

First Book of Inferior Court Records.
March Term of Court 1805. Held at Ohoopee Saw Mills.

Justices:—
Ezekiel Stafford
Batt Wyche
James Thomas
Henry Carter
William Hall.

Jurors:—
Daniel Highsmith
Thomas Vince
John Sharpp
Elijah Payne
Gabriel Cason
John Morris
Aaron Barber
Moses Adams

John Gilford
Joshua Latton
Samuel Pinkham
John Wood
Jonathan Willis
Needham Walker
Lewis Hall
John Higgs
Major Tyre
David Mims
Mack Pridgen
John Blake
John Swilley, Sr.
William Smith

Levi Whitehurst
George Browning
Daniel Highsmith
Gabriel Cason
Robert Standley
Frederick Cason
Colson Adams
Samuel Kitchen
Cornelius English
John Marshall
Radford Browning
John Joyce
Moses Gernagan
John Sands

Wills in Books "A, B, C, D," of Deeds 1800 to 1835.

Browning, George, Sr.
Baldree, Isaac K.
Collins, Jacob
Foy, George
Hodges, Mary
Havigal, Sarah

Joyce, James
Mattox, Michael
    M'Kenzie
McLeod, Alexander
Payne, Daniel
Staten, Solomon

Smith, Simon
Sharp, John
Sauls, Abram
Todd, William
Travis, Asa
Woods, Martha

Index to Deeds 1805 to 1810.

Ayers, Thomas
Adams, Colson
Acord, John
Avent, Ransom
Anderson, Thomas
Abbott, Bennett
Bostick, L. Perry
Bugg, Jacob

Bazemore, Thomas
Burnaman, Benjamin
Bird, Jesse & John
Beven, James
Brinson, Daniel & David
Buie, Agnes
Browning, Radford
Burney, David

Bowen, Stephen
Blackman, John P.
Cobbs, John & Absalom
Crumley, Anthony & E.
Coleman, John
Cooper, Nancy
Cooper, Richard
Cooper, P.

Conner, Wilson
Carter, Jacob
Carter, Sarah
Dunn, Nehemiah
Davis, Abner
Daughtry, David
Daughtry, Daniel
Dukes, Hansel
Dukes, John
Dukes, E.
Drigors, Matthew
Durrance, William
Durrance, C.
Dickson, John
Embree, Jesse
Easley, R.
Easley, E.
English, James
English, Nancy
Embree, Jonathan
English, Jane
Eason, William
Foreman, David
Ford, Jas.
Ford, John
Ford, Wm.
Fulcher, James
Foy, Thomas
Flournoy, Robert
Five-Ash, Elias
Glenn, William
Green, M'Keen
Green, Thos.
Ganey, Reddick
Gittuis, Richard
Gaston, Henry
Grace, John
Grace, James
Griner, Phil.
Griner, Esther
Griffin, Asa
Griffin, Lewis
Gilford, Isaac
Holleman, Mark

Hollinger, Wm.
Hollinger, Thos.
Hardin, Martin
Horn, Richard
Hutchinson, James
Hattey, Sherrod
Harris, Lewis
Harris, Sarah
Hancock, James
Hughes, Thomas
Hix, John
Henderson, M.
Henderson, J.
Hooker, Stephen
Johnson, Allen
Jones, Francis
Jones, Matthew
Jackson, James
Jackson, Frederick
Joyce, James
Jones, Drury
Killbee, Christopher
Kirksey, Isaac
Kelley, Moris
Kemp, Joshua
Lord, Loderick
Lott, Jno., Jr.
Lott, Robert
Linn, Jacob
Love, Amos
Longino, Bartholomew
Leigh, Ben.
Leigh, Mary
Lott, Arthur
Leonard, Calvin
Lightfoot, Jesse
Lankford, John
Large, William
Lewis, George
Marshall, Daniel
Mobley, John
Mobley, Wm.
Mallet, Abram
Mitchel, James

Mikel, James
Mikel, M.
Mixon, Reuben
Mobley, Solomon
Moore, Caswell
M'Tyiere, Holland
M'Leod, John
M'Leod, Kenneth
M'Leod, Angus
M'Rae, Daniel
M'Leland, Andrew
Nutt, John
Newman, Daniel
Nottage, Thomas
Phillips, Mark
Phillips, R. B.
Parker, Hubbard
Payne, Daniel
Payne, Absalom E.
Perry, Isaac
Perry, James
Peterson, John
Parten, Robert
Parish, Samuel
Payne, Zachariah
Prevatt, Peter
Rowell, Edward
Rowell, G.
Sibbald, George
Suilly, John
Suilly, Nicholas
Sharpe, Grover
Sharpe, Jno.
Suilly, Samuel
Striplign, Benjamin
Stradley, Nimrod
Smith, Samuel
Smith, Jno., Jr.
Span, George
Sykes, Arthur
Sykes, Josiah
Sellers, Samuel
Sellers, Mary
Spann, William

Smith, James G.	Townsend, Thomas	Wyche, Batt
Stanley, Shadrack	Turner, James, Sr.	Willeary, Solomon
Stanley, Robert	Underwood, Thomas	Wood, Thomas
Stafford, Ezekiel	Vasser, Micajah	Wood, Martha
Stansil, William	Valley, George	Williams, William
Sasser, Howell	Valley, Frances	West, Peter
Staten, P.	Warner, James	Wilson, John
Staten, B.	Wester, Elias	Whithurst, Simon
Stanfield, John	Walton, Newel, Sr.	Wylds, C. D.
Tennille, Francis	Wingate, Jeremiah	Wesberry, Moses
Thomas, James	Watt, Jacob	Wesberry, E.
Tennille, Benjamin	Wiggins, Michel	Watson, James
Tillman, Jeremiah	Wood, Demsy	White, Robert
Tison, William	Wilford, Lewis	Warner, John D.
Tippens, George W.	Williams, David	Watson, Jonathan
Tippens, James A.	Williams, Phebe	Williams, James

Marriages—1831 to 1839.

Josiah Everett and Harriet A. Archer.
Uriah Rogers and Martha Brewton.
Simon P. Smith and Clarissa Brewton.
Alexander Kennedy and Caroline Tippins.
John Grooms and Sarah Stephens.
Henry Mann and Winny Sapp.
Moses Taylor and Sarah Simms.
Peter Anderson and Mary Linn.
James Cheney and Sarah Brinson.
William T. Smith and Rebecca Newman.
Allen Johnson and Martha Gause.
John Douglas and Lydia Thompson.
Jacob Surrency and Zilpha Douglas.
John Thomas and Elizabeth Partin.
Edward Duke and Nancy Hodges.
Duncan McArthur and Elizabeth McLeod.
John Anderson and Cynthia Powell.
James Highsmith and Elizabeth Willis.
Wm. McClelland and Jane Anderson.
Jacob Anderson and Elizabeth Connor.
John Douglas and Lydia Thompson.
Joseph W. Smith and Matilda Durrance.

John Little and Elizabeth Gordon.
Samuel Hodges and Elizabeth Daniel, 1833.
James B. Archer and Penelope Stubbs.
Cornelius Joyce and Sarah Newmans.
Samuel Brewton and Mary Smith.
Albert Duke and Permelia Smith.
Anson Williams and Keziah Alexander.
George W. Collins and Temperance Collins.
Samuel D. Smith and Mary Ann Barnard.
William Newmans and Mary Davis.
John Vinzant and Nancy Youmans, 1834.
George Anderson and Susan Bowen.
James Underwood and Eleanor Anderson.
Robert Odam and Rebecca Smith.
Wm. M. Boggs and Louisa Johnson.
Daniel J. Curry and Susan A. Johnson.
Samuel Davis and Arceana Smith.
William O'Neal and Ann Cameron.
Edward Kennedy, Jr., and Mary Mattox.
George Smith and Sarah Ann Wilson.
George T. Gray and Mary J. Johnson, 1835.
Solomon Evers and Zilpha Mann.
Lionel Leigh and Nancy Brown.
Shadrack Standley and Laveny Smith.
Elijah H. Mattox and Sarah M. Eason.
Wm. Grice and Evalina Vastia Stuart.
Francis N. Cawswell and Harriet Coursey.
James Surrency and and Mary McClenin.
Wm. McCall and Amanda L. F. Mobley.
John Mattox, Jr., and Louisa A. Matlock.
Daniel W. Johnson and Holly Ann Knight.
Benjamin Alexander and Mary E. Tippens.
Maning Collins and Nancy Collins.
Godfrey Williams and Emaly Pittman.
Thomas Strickland and Winearey Holman.
Henry Rials and Mary Ann Dinkins.
Hugh G. Partin and Nancy Smith.

Benjamin F. Dowdy and Emaly Mattox.
Aaron Mattox and Harriet Julian Bacon, 1836.
Isaac K. Courter and Rachel Philips.
Aaron B. Everet and Sarah Tillman.
Wm. P. Guest and Elviney Tanner.
Jacob Anderson and Barbary Odam.
Wm. R. Townsend and Dorinda Stafford.
Josiah Collins and Wiltha Kennedy.
Martin H. Handcock and Elizabeth Arnold.
Clement Eckels and Margaret Wright.
Wm. Clifton, Jr., and Susan Sharpe.
John W. Todd and Elizabeth Deloatch.
Dacan Curry and Margaret Sharpe.
John Duberly and Nancy Grice.
Charles Anderson and Anna C. Daniel.
Elijah E. Stafford and Penelope Surrency.
Joseph Deloatch and Sarah Barnard.
John E. F. Bacon and Rose Ann Blocker.
Samuel S. Wester and Rebecca Sharpe.
Wm. Strickland and Miriam Kennedy.
Zachariah Daniel and Alby Duberley.
Isham Braddley and Honor Branch.
John G. Partin and Mary Harden.
Jacob Blocker and Mary Durrance.
Peter Groomes and Mary Warnell.
Wm. D. Rogers and Catherine Ann Tillman.
Allen Strickland and Nancy C. Kennedy.
Robert Surrency and Polly Ann Kennedy.
William Sapp and Dyca Lynn.
David J. Durrence and Mary Douglas, 1837.
Jesse Dukes and Rebecca Tedder.
Edward Kennedy, Sr. and Charlotte Sykes.
Joseph Tillman, Jr. and Penelope Strickland.
John C. Smith and Mary Jones.
Benjamin Weathers, Jr. and Easther Dyess.
Daniel H. Edwards and Elizabeth Jane Archer.
James J. Sands and Lydia Stephens, 1838.

John A. Mattox and Rebecca Smith.
John Daniel and Pearcy Waters.
Abram Powell and Sarah Sapp.
Wm. Lynn and Winnefred Green.
Jeremiah Jerod and Sarah Smith.
James Copeland and Harriet Chesser.
Wm. Findley and Martha Wilks.
Gade S. Miller and Sarah M. Tippins.
Edward Busch and Isabel McLeod.
Jackson Oquin and Delia McCall.
James McKnabb and Susanna Carpenter.
Jeremiah McSweeney and Rebecca Willis.
Wm. Hardin and Mary Ann Clifton.
Obadiah Strickland and Sarah Easterling.
James P. Daniel and Elizabeth Glisson.
John Rogers and Mary Grace.
David Millikin and Lucy C. Hedgcock.
Littleton Hammock and Elizabeth Riggs.
Godfrey Williams and Mary McCall.
Samuel Thomas and Cynthia Douglas.
Jackson Sapp and Susan Standley.
Stephen Mattock and Mary Copeland.
Shadrack Handcock and Cynthia Alexander.
Wright W. Alexander and Sarah Blocker.
John B. Moody and Bathsheba Prevatt.
Thomas W. Dinwoody and Katherine Underwood.
John N. Tatum and Nancy Copeland.
Franklin Williams and Rachel B. McDaniel.
John Collins and Mary Ann Kennedy.
Calvin Lovett and Celia Parramore.
Urias Anderson and Sarah Holland.
Pleasant W. W. Mattox and Caroline Warnell.
John Cobb and Ann Eliza Bunkley.
Wm. F. M. Grubbs and Susan Augusta Curry.
Abraham Strickland and Mary Duke.
Joshua Dinkins and Rebecca Rials.
Samuel Stephens and Cynthia Deloatch.

Hezekiah Lewis and Sarah Ann Poppel.
Daniel Barnard and Julia A. H. Mattox.
John W. Strickland and Anna Spears.
Shadrack Standley and Caroline Delbos.
James M. Smart and Lucy C. Milligan.
Isham Deloatch and Elizabeth Stephens.

JACKSON COUNTY.
Will Book "A" 1802-1860.

Allen, William	Brooks, Middleton	Dalton, John
Avery, Philip	Bowen, Thomas C.	Davis, Pelina
Angil, Ann	Blalock, J. L.	Elmore, James
Alexander, Hooper	Borders, Isaac	Embry, Boly
Adams, John	Cureton, William	Fowler, Nathan
Allison, James	Clarke, Johnston	Flag, Chandler
Adams, Thomas R. G.	Cowan, Elijah	Few, Leonidas
Adair, William M.	Curdon, Martha	Finley, Mary
Anthony, Mary	Carrell, James	Freeman, Jonathan
Beavers, Robert	Culpepper, Joseph	Flournoy, Eliza
Berry, John	Castleberry, William	Green, John
Borders, Michael	Coleman, John	Gideon, James
Bagby, George	Carmichael, John	Gilbert, John
Beard, Jean	Collins, Zachariah	Glenn, James
Bradford, George	Cash, Patrick	Gowen, James M.
Bayle, Peter	Crawford, John M.	Goodman, John T.
Barnett, Samuel	Cunningham, Andrew	Gathwright, William M.
Barker, Lewis	Cunningham, Elizabeth	Hayden, William
Ball, Josiah H.	Cochran, James	Hayden, George
Boshan, Matthew	Chandler, Tabitha	Hobson, N.
Bennett, Micajah	Cunningham, Ansel	Humphreys, Joseph
Braziel, Frederick	Cash, John	Haggard, Samuel
Bowen, Owen J.	Carter, Jno. M.	Hanson, Thomas
Beavers, James	Cunningham, J. T.	Hickman, William
Burson, Isaac	Cunningham, Mary	Heard, Richard
Brazil, Elizabeth	Chrisler, Absalom	Henderson, David
Bennett, William	Craft, Hannah	Horton, Prosser
Bailey, William	Chandler, Sterling	Heard, William
Baine, Isaac	Craft, Polly	Henderson, Josiah
Brazleton, Jacob	Deal, William	Harris, Jesse
Borders, Stephen L.	Dixon, David	Hiner, Lewis
Beavers, William	Dean, Shadrick	Henderson, Samuel
Barr, James	Dammon, Charles	Harrison, Joseph
Brown, Lemuel	Dougherty, Charles	Henderson, Samuel R.
Boothe, James	Davis, Joseph	Howard, Sarah

Henderson, John G.
Harris, Joseph
Heard, Eliza
Hays, George
Harvie, Frederick
Harrison, John
Hendrix, Finnel
Holladay, Robert M.
Holmes, David
Harrison, Tillman
Henderson, James D.
Henderson, A. H.
Hugby, J. A.
Hargrove, James
Hodge, James
Harrison, Coleman
Howard, Hardy
Johnson, Thomas
Justice, John
Jones, Russell
Justice, David
Jones, Jane
Johnson, Thomas
Jarrett, Martha
Johnson, Sanford W.
Kolbe, Jonathan
Knox, Samuel
Key, Tandy
King, John
King, John
Kerbow, Solomon
Lambert, John
Langston, Samuel
Legg, Nathaniel
Loft, William
Lay, William N.
Lowery, Vevi
Landrum, Joseph
Lowery, Martha
Lay, Eliza
M'Gehee, Nathan
Morgan, William
Morris, John
M'Dowell, Michael

Moon, Robert
Mays, Benjamin
McDowell, Margaret
Moore, William
Miller, John
Millsap, Thomas
Martin, John
M'Kinney, Charles
M'Kinney, Charles
M'Elhannon, John
M'Carty, John
Morrison, Alexander
Morris, Henry C.
Minnish, Isaac
M'Lester, Joseph
Martin, W. D.
Matthews, William
Minnish, John
Minnish, Elizabeth
M'Leskey, James R.
M'Lester, W. M.
Newton, William
Neil, Thomas
Nixon, Travis
Nash, James
Nicholson, Ann
Niblack, Thomas
Nash, Margaret
Orr, James
Orr, John
Oliver, Elizabeth
Pettijohn, Jacob
Patton, Samuel Y.
Pool, Samuel
Pickens, John
Pharr, Francis
Phillips, Thomas
Potts, William
Park, Hannah
Petty, Adah
Potts, Henry
Park, William
Pendergrass, Edwin
Ryan, Philip

Reynolds, William
Ratchford, Joseph
Rodgers, Rhoda
Roberson, John
Roberson, Alcy
Ryan, Obedience
Ryan, Philip
Ratchford, Robert
Rodgers, John
Rider, Benjamin
Rodgers, James
Ray, William
Randolph, W. L.
Snow, Henry
Smith, James
Stoneham, Henry
Scott, Joseph
Shields, Joseph
Scisson, John
Storey, Thomas
Stapler, Thomas
Shaw, William
Stapler, Ruth
Street, Samuel
Smith, James
Stovall, John
Stapler, Robert
Smith, Mary
Shankle, James W.
Sexon, Solomon
Sharp, Nathan J.
Stockton, Benjamin
Strickland, Elizabeth
Shankee, Eli
Stewart, Mary
Shotwell, N.
Slaton, Uriah
Sharp, Noah C.
Thurmond, James
Trout, Nathaniel
Trout, Sarah
Tait, James
Titsworth, Isaac
Thompson, Sherrod

Thurmond, Harrison
Thornton, Mark
Thurmond, William
Venable, Robert
Wright, John
Walker, Henry
Whitworth, Jacob
Wetherford, Charles
Wilson, Samuel
Watson, Obediah
Wallace, Levi
Walling, Michael

Winters, Richard
Wilson, Thomas M.
Winters, J.
Wilson, George
Williamson, Micajah
Wilson, Lucy
Wallace, Rachael
Wafford, Absalom
Williamson, William
Willingham, Harriet
Walker, Elizabeth

Worsham, Lud
White, Jesse
Winters, W. M.
Wheeler, James
Witt, Thomas
Wilson, Michael
Wood, Milton B.
Wood, William M.
Willborne, James
Witt, Middleton
Watkins, J. C.

JACKSON COUNTY MARRIAGES.

1805 to 1811.

James Jones and Esther Holmes.
John Purcell and Sally Casson.
Willis Jinks and Rebecca Wilson.
Humphrey Wates and Elizabeth Langford.
James Montgomery and Polly Hendrix.
Joseph Hughs and Elizabeth Jarrett.
Isaac House and Sally Headen.
John Russell and Sarah Carson.
Tandy Key and Ann Cochran.
Emeline Pruitt and Susannah Thompson.
Sion Pierce and Elizabeth Jones.
John Ewbanks and Susannah Shelton.
Bradley Thomas and Patsy Key.
Christopher Mucklehannon and Margaret Bell.
Wm. Dale and Rachel Rowden.
Isaac Oaks and Nancy Adair.
Richard Hill and Sally Elliott.
James Anglin and Martha Tyner.
Wm. Jarrett and Anny Knox.
Thomas Brown and Sally Elwell.
Wm. Powers and Sarah Elmore.
Regin Pugh and Elizabeth Jackson.
Adam Phillips and Tempy Pierce.
Samuel Shields and Peggy Arthur.

Thomas Nicholas and Susannah Travis.
George Moon and Drucilla Awtry.
Benjamin O'Neal and Polly Diamond.
Thomas Conan and Polly Williamson.
Robert Kelly and Martha Magee.
Jesse Kelly and Sally Pierce.
Haden Watts and Lou Wadsworth.
James Boggs and Viley Ward.
Wiley Ross and Jinny Holliday.
John Cash and Patsy Medkeff.
Bennett Ware and Jinny Holmes.
Jet Harrel and Abi Moore.
Hezekiah Gates and Polly Hampton.
R. Jones, Jr., and Sophia Harris.
John Cone and Anny Turner.
Jeremiah Travis and Peggy Peak.
John Ramsey and S. Anderson.
Needham Boon and Elizabeth Robertson.
Jervis Dale and Barbara Banks.
Stuart Cowan and Mary Stuart.
Reuben McClung and Polly Williamson.
John Thomas and Elinor Gregg.
Allen Adams and Susanna Boring.
Hiram Hodges and Hannah Henderson.
Abram Pennington and Susanna Procter.
Amos Pipkins and Prudy McKenzie.
Peyton Hardy and Frances Haggard.
David S. White and Hannah Holt.
Henry Duke and Mary Stephens.
James Clark and Sally Ross.
Sampson Harris and Rebecca Jones.
John Witcher and Elizabeth Smith.
Jesse Adams and Casy Posey.
Benedick Jetton and Elizabeth Campbell.
Abram Chandler and Polly Johnson.
Robert Wilson and Rebecca Orr.
Jacob Wommock and Elizabeth Hopkins.

David Mitchell and Dolly Wommock.
Hardeman Willingham and Anny Scott.
Samuel Montgomery and Hannah Patrick.
Thomas Espey and Eleanor Witherspoon.
John Leper and Fredy McCord.
James Moore and Phebe Borders.
David Moore and Polly Williams.
John J. Phipps and Sarah Kennedy.
James Cox and Elizabeth Martin.
Wm. Montgomery and Caty Boyle.
Richard Cleaton and Jane Carter.
Mark Hayse and Elizabeth Foster.
Michael Carney and Patsy Holley.
Clinton Joyce and Polly Cureton.
Wm. Blake and Sally Maddox.
Alexander Crawford and Christian Crumby.
Isaac McDonald and Mary Joyce.
Samuel Haggard and Ruth Ayres.
Peter Langford and Nancy Borough.
John Bryant and Elizabeth Crochet.
Samuel Carlisle and Sally Roach.
J. Cunningham and Agnes Montgomery.
George Brogdon and Sary Jackson.
Isaac Jackson and Miriam Peugh.
Andrew Hamilton and Nancy Hogg.
Washington Montgomery and Rebecca Hall.
Lewis Hynes and Nancy Myers.
Benjamin Camp and Rachel Hogg.
Ansel Bearden and Abigail Jourdan.
Wm. Cornish and Sarah Farrow.
John Farrow and Elizabeth Grier.
John Ship and Sally Watson.
Michael Bingham and Sally Williams.
Charles Kelley and Elizabeth Howard.
Wm. Blalock and Tempey Bailey.
John Sparks and Sary Brooks.
James Dukes and Polly Morris.

Andrew Foster and Sally Nichols.
Joseph Atkins and Polly Camp.
Archibald Wetherford and Sally Stroud.
Gideon Turner and Sally Osten.
John Pennington and Mourning Smith.
Burwell Hutchins and Peggy Kelly.
Solomon Townsend and Nancy Lyles.
John Campbell and Caty Patton.
John Hamilton and Posey Hearn.
Wm. Justin and Mary Carrigan.
John Phillips and Frances Sykes.
Sterling White and Sally Harlin.
Wm. Jack and Elizabeth Wardlaw.
John Barton and Patsy Harden.
John Williamson and Rachel Jones.
Elijah Shaw and Delilah Buggin.
Wm. Webster and Jane Waits.
Isham McBee and Susanna Wilson.
Benjamin Jackson and Betsy Harris.
John Smith and Esther Gillespie.
John Winters and Charity Patton.
Wm. Petty John and Lucy Bailey.
Isaac Reed and Betsy Swain.
John Lindsay and Polly Kennedy.
Joseph Wharton and Sally Moore.
Jarrett Bass and Patsy House.
James Trammel and Rachel Stocks.
Robert Langford and Rhody Barrow.
Wm. Johnson and Louisa Gardner.
John Cash and Zilpha Strickland.
James Anglin and Patsy Hancock.
Gibson Moore and Eliza Curry.
Eben Miller and Elizabeth Miller.
Miles Langley and Nancy Jetton.
Joseph Harrison and Sally Moore.
Josaph Barnett and Jane McDonald.
John Hanson and Maria Billups.

James Bairet and Nancy Blankenship.
Hugh Jackson and Kelly Reed.
David Fales and Elizabeth Jones.
Thomas Eakins and Polly Payne.
John Cates and Elinor Fondren.

MARRIAGES IN TELFAIR COUNTY.

Prior to 1850.

Hiram Ellis and Catherine Hatten, October 27, 1831.

James Parker and Anna Jane White, December 22, 1831.

Willis Newman and Sallie Sheffield, March 17, 1832.

Michael Pope and Mary Ann Posey, August 17, 1831.

James C. Fussell and Sallie Parker, August 21, 1832.

John Gaskins and Fanny Lott, June 18, 1832.

James Dunance and Elizabeth Friar, July 28, 1832.

Simon Whitehearst and Mrs. Christina Buckhaller, November 7, 1832.

Lazarus Williams and Catherine Parker, October 2, 1832.

William Burket and Rhoda Burket, January 28, 1832.

William Smith and Emmaline White, March 13, 1833.

Abraham Crim and Mary Fussell, April 3, 1833.

Alfred Burnham and Mary Ann Davis, January 28, 1833.

William Martin and Keziah Davis, April 17, 1832.

James Chaney and Rhoda Passmore, March 11, 1833.

Hugh McAlister and Sallie Gregory, May 27, 1833.

John Posey, Jr. and Laura Taylor, April 18, 1833.

Godwin Solomon and Jane Guskins, June 3, 1833.

Shepherd N. Phelps and Rebecca Ann Everitt, August 16, 1833.

Angus Finlayson and Martha E. Rogers, August 10, 1833.

Henry Brickell and Elizabeth Girtman, September 25, 1832.

Wright Parker and Elizabeth Ann Williams, November 1, 1832.

Jacob A. Bradford and Sarah Marsh, November 10, 1832.

Ashley P. Weaks and Catherine Shaw, November 9, 1833.

Owen Ryals and Frances Emely Amelia Sanders, November 13, 1833.

Wiley Cumming and Providence Sharber, October 15, 1833.

Samuel Denton and Priscilla Ward, December 5, 1833.

John Cravey and Effie Graham, January 27, 1834.

Alexander Mobley and Margaret McEachern, June 9, 1834.

Robert O. Catoe and Viney Sheffield, June 12, 1834.

Benazoe Pearson and Mary Lott, September 4, 1834.

Samuel Sikes and Elizabeth Smith, October 17, 1834.

William P. Knowles and Lucretia M. Fussell, September 16, 1833.

Rev. George W. Pournall and Amey Hall, January 20, 1834.

Henry S. Silvester and Jane Hancock, May 9, 1835.

George Paulk and Margaret Cook, April 30, 1835.

Henry L. Wells and Molsy Williams, June 4, 1835.

Abraham Powell and Mary Martha Buckhalter, June 15, 1835.

Jacob Marchant and Nancy Studstell, June 27, 1835.

John Reaves and Mahelia Burnham, February 10, 1835.

Joseph Asbell and Rebecca Willcox, February 6, 1835.

John B. Coffee and Rebecca Willcox, March 7, 1835.

Thomas Hinson and Eliza Cannady, April 13, 1835.

Curtiss Deal and Fanny Gill, July 4, 1835.

Daniel McRae and Sarah S. Livington, August 7, 1835.

John Nolen and Sealey Mullin, August 7, 1835.

Byrd Noles and Charity Jackson, August 13, 1835.

John McKinnon and Casandra Mizell, October 7, 1835.

Samuel Johnson and Mrs. Margaret Powel, October 23, 1835.

Neal Dillard and Miss Phereby Burket, October 27, 1835.

Jordan I. Harper and Fanny Gaskins, September 28, 1835.

Green Brewer and Mary Gaskins, December 5, 1835.

John Ellis and Bashaba Hatten, December 15, 1835.

John Barrow and Harriett McLendon, January 6, 1836.

Napolion Bonaparte Burke and Mary Merritt, March 7, 1836.

Simon White and Margaret Hutchins, January 2, 1836.

Alfred Barnadoe and Dusilla Gill, June 29, 1836.

Robert W. Jones and Mary Crem, June 5, 1836.

Martin Douglas and Mary Ann Stewart, May 6, 1836.

Parish Langford and Lupina Hall, May 18, 1836.

Ezekiel Thomas and Mehesa Ward, August 25, 1836.

Hustus Studstill and Mary B. Graham, October 18, 1836.

Ira Knowles and Rachael Graham, October 15, 1835.

William Mizelle and Flora Graham, November 27, 1836.

John M. Innes and Margaret Shall, January 3, 1837.

William Ham and Nancy Roe, April 18, 1837.

Henry Jackson Campbell and Mrs. Melza Miria Cook, August 24, 1837.

Ignatius B. Anderson and Rebecca Sharber, May 10, 1837.

James McAlister and Martha Sharber, June 14, 1837.

John J. Carmichael and Mary Livingston, June 20, 1837.

Aaron Brantly and Nancy Rae, August 12, 1837.

Peter Harrison Coffee and Susan Ann Baily Rogers, March 27, 1837.

William Smith and Elizabeth Stewart, November 7, 1837.

Joshua Cravey and Mary Jane Bony, October 17, 1837.

Alb Hatten and Sarah Fletcher, Nov. 4, 1837.

Henderson Frevy and Mrs. Hester Multer, November 10, 1837.

John Anderson and Nancy Sharber, September 7, 1839.

Mitchell G. Willcox and Martha Swain, December 13, 1839.

Tarlton Jones and Miss Ibaline, April 13, 1839.

John I. Carmichael and Mary Livingston, June 28, 1837.

David Gill and Sarah Ann Johnson, February 23, 1838.

Edmund Whiting and Mary McLean, June 3, 1838.

James W. Rollins and Mrs. Elizabeth Barramore, September 18, 1838.

Jas. McLeoa and Caroline Ruskin, August 18, 1839.

Archabald McKinnon and Mary Fenlayson, December 13, 1837.

Henry Jackson Campbell and Mrs. Miliza Maria Cook, August 24, 1837.

Joseph T. Rawlins and Catherine Harrell, December 28, 1839.

Samuel Thomas and Nancy Ward, November 22, 1837.

Amos Johnson and Nancy Wilson, December 22, 1840.

Henry Peterson and Martha Caskens, December 14, 1840.

Thomas Wilson and Martha Brewer, April 27, 1839.

Hiram Booth and Mary Cald, May 16, 1839.

James Henson and Selena Hall, June 2, 1840.

John Brooker and Nancy Sheffield, March 2, 1840.

John Yancey and Elizabeth Cravey, February 5, 1840.

Philip Reaves and Ann Eliza Bony, November 6, 1840.

Christopher Smith and Annie McEachen, May 31, 1840.

Josiah Reaves and Eliza Roundton, March 12, 1844.

William Buckhannon and Martha May, June 19, 1844.

William Harry and Lurary Owen, July 31, 1844.

Jno. J. Clements and Elizabeth Ann Wooten, August 19, 1844.

Benj. F. Girtman and Mary I. Luemary, October 8, 1844.

Jesse Lankford and Mary Metts, July 30, 1844.

Wm. Harrell and Winniford Williams, January 1, 1845.

Daniel Morrison and Henrietta Genson, July 6, 1844.

Joseph L. L. Clements and Sarah N. Smith, January 25, 1845.

Leonard C. Peek and Julia Ashley, October 28, 1844.

John Vickers and Abegail Boring, November 13, 1845.

Zachariah Studstill and Isabel B. Malay, January 16, 1845.

Jno. Van Taylor and Matilda Bohn, January 30, 1845.

Allen L. Dobson and Mary Daskins, November 12, 1845.

Wm. L. Rogers and Sarah H. Bryant, November 8, 1845.

Jno. F. McRae and Elvena Dobson, Dec. 25, 1845.

Jno. Cravey and Elizabeth Campbell, February 27, 1845.

Duncan Mims and Harriet Ray, April 6, 1846.

Archabald McLean and Margaret A. McRae, April 22, 1845.

Hugh McLean and Clementine C. Dasher, July 21, 1846.

Jno. Larkey and Isabella Graham, January 17, 1848.

Jno. Hill and Rebecca Young, February 13, 1847.

Thomas T. Jones and Susan T. Mizell, April 27, 1847.

Wm. B. Highsmith and Mary E. Taylor, September 27, 1847.

James N. Green and Vina Gant, September 18, 1847.

Wm. Asbell and Sarah Garrett, April 3, 1847.

Jacob C. Clements and Eliza Wooten, August 18, 1845.

Jacob Fussell and Lucretia Cummings, May 10, 1847.

Allen Hulett and Margaret Lucenda Gaskin, September 23, 1846.

Daniel Lott and Fanny Gaskens, October 24, 1848.

Wm. Ryals and Martha Knowling, April 27, 1846.

Jno. N. Douglas and Mary Ann Quincy Ellis, September 1, 1846.

Henry Fleetwood and Louisa Posey, June 25, 1845.

Daniel Atkinson and Patsy Pitts, November 20, 1847.

Jepthy H. Buckhalter and Elander Purvis, January 4, 1847.

Wm. Matchett and Nancy Collins, March, 1848.

Daniel McEntire and Elizabeth Studstill, November 23, 1847.

Eziekel J. Watson and Sarah Ann J. Towns, December 22, 1847.

Alexander Love and Christian McRae, January 25, 1847.

Benjamin T. Hunter and Sarah Smith, May 10, 1847.

Simon Wooten and Catherine J. Lastir, September 15, 1846.

James Humphreys and Sarah P. Willcox, November 7, 1846.

Josiah Friar and Narcessa Ashley, March 3, 1846.

Tillman R. Taylor and Mary Ann Smith, January 11, 1847.

William Cravey and Elizabeth Rainey, September 16, 1848.

Shadreck Young and Delia Gant, July 20, 1847.

Henry Telfair and Martha Hersey, January 10, 1849.

John Wooten and Hulda Clements, November 16, 1848.

Horace Johnson and Emely Hays, January 15, 1847.

Alfred Smith and Tobitha Wooten, November 18, 1846.

Calvin A. Ward and Precilla Ward, February 2, 1847.

Stephen Bony and Martha Williams, October 6, 1847.

Duncan B. Graham and Sarah Ann McLauchlin, August 3, 1848.

James A. Walker and Wenifred Howard, August 17, 1847.

James R. Dowdy and Mary Ann Ryals ,October 20, 1847.

Jacob W. Clements and Margaret McRae, January 20, 1848.

George W. Yancey and Mary Cravey, February 12, 1848.

David Cravy and Lydia Studstill, July 3, 1848.

Aaron G. Friar and Elizabeth McDuffie, December 20, 1848.

David D. Dyal and Elizabeth Mobley, November 28, 1848.

Felix Fussell and Martha E. Cravey, January 1, 1848.

Wm. Brewer and Amanda M. Hall, March 20, 1849.

Robert C. Anderson and Nancy McDuffie, March 22, 1849.

William M. Johnson and Rachael Pickren, August 8, 1849.

Martin Howard and Elizabeth Jane McDuffie, August 10, 1849.

Lemuel Sapp and Susie Ann McEachen, May 28, 1849.

Bryant M. Williams and Angel C. R. Guinn, December 29, 1849.

Jno. A. Clements and Maria L. Ryals, April 16, 1849.

Henry Brewer and Martha Ann Hatten, February 4, 1850.

Wright Collins and Jane P. Willcox, November 15, 1849.

167 Marriages.

Only will before 1850 in Telfair County is Alexander Watson *in a Bond book.*

ST. PAUL'S CHURCH, AUGUSTA, GEORGIA.

From Mrs. Annie McIntosh Wall.

Augusta declared for "Liberty" soon after the idea was born. At that time Fort Augusta and St. Paul's Church were the central points of interest in the place. The small Provincial force that garrisoned the Fort, which was then in a decayed condition and unfit for defensive purposes, knew that resistance was useless, when

Col. Campbell of the British army came with a thousand men, to take the town, in January, 1779. With the English in possession, Col. Brown was left in command, the fortifications improved and strengthened, and the name of the Fort changed to "Fort Cornwallis."

The Americans, encouraged by victory in the up country, made efforts to reach Fort Cornwallis in 1780; but were repulsed, with great loss of life and serious disaster to the country. The British commander, Col. Brown, was dangerously wounded—his second grievance from the patriots, for which he took ample revenge.

The Americans made a second effort to take Augusta and were successful. Fort Grierson, which was a short distance above and in sight, was first captured, and, after a short siege, Fort Cornwallis was taken.

It was early in June, 1781, when the reign of Col. Brown came to an end, and the starving prisoners, confined in the Fort, were released.

Patriots of the American Revolution, who died in the siege of Augusta, are said to have been buried in this churchyard, near where they fell. Some are supposed to lie beneath the walk which leads to the church.

I have been told that the piling, which supported the Fort on the river front, can still be seen when the water is low.

Once, when the river overflowed its banks and swept the street back of St. Paul's, graves were uncovered. Doubtless, soldiers of the Revolution were there laid to rest.

All this ground is hallowed ground. For the brave and true are here.

Within the church are numerous memorials, altars, tablets, windows, pictures, statuary, and many other tokens, in remembrance of those who have passed away. Tablets in memory of Edward Fenwick Campbell, his wife and children, form a link to the churchyard, where their remains rest.

Sacred

to the memory of

MARIA CAMPBELL,

wife of Edward Fenwick Campbell and

daughter of

General William Hull,

a native of Newton, Massachusetts, who died

in the City of Augusta,

May 24, 1845,

after a residence of 31 years in Richmond County, and
was buried in the cemetery of St. Paul's Church.

TOMBSTONE INSCRIPTIONS.

St. Paul's Church, Augusta, Ga.

There is an importance and beauty in this old historic
Church in Augusta, Ga. A most imposing monument
stands near the north wall and is of granite from Oglethorpe County. A beautiful cross of heavy blocks of
hewn stone, facing northward to the river, marks the
spot where the historic fort stood and an old cannon once
used in the fort, rests at its base. This was erected by
the Georgia Society Colonial Dames, and marks the site
of the Colonial Fort built by order of General Oglethorpe
and the trustees in 1736, and known during the Revolution as Fort Cornwallis. St. Paul's Church was built in
1750, under a curtain of this Fort.

The church as it now stands, is a little west of where it
was in 1750. It has been enlarged two or three times,
which necessitated the covering of some of the graves,
and the tombs of noted men and women are beneath the
edifice. The oldest tombs, on which the descriptions are
now decipherable are oblong, box-shaped. The sides are

bricked in and each has its slab of marble lettered in old English. Unfortunately, many of the slabs are broken, owing to the efforts of the Union soldiers, who hunted for treasure in the old church-yard in 1865.

The inscriptions on some of these tombs are all the histories we have of those who sleep in this old church-yard. There are no dates back of 1787.

Inscriptions on Tomb-stones.

To the memory of Dr. James Lander, and Francis, his brother, who both died suddenly at Augusta, Ga. James died December 28, 1789, age 20, Francis died December 26, 1787, age 19.

Martha Wallace, wife of William Wallace, died October 23, 1789, age 20.

Rachel Longstreet, daughter of Hannah and William Longstreet, died January 12, 1790, age 2 years and 4 months.

From the broken tombstone of Mrs. Jackson. In memory of *Mrs. Anne Jackson*, wife of —— Jackson, born June 25, 1765, died March 2, 1793.

Also their son James Lander Jackson, who died October 13, 1791, age 6 months.

In memory of *Mrs. Kitty Jack,* wife of Captain Samuel Jack. Died July 15, 1792, age 37.

To the memory of *Robert Forsythe,* Federal Marshal of Georgia, who in the discharge of the duties of his office fell a victim to his respect to the laws of his country, January 11, 1794. His virtues as an officer of rank, and unusual confidence in the war which gave Independence to the United States and in all the tender and endearing relations of social life have left impressions on his country.

Robert Forsyth was the father of John Forsyth, the Statesman. Robert Forsyth and Beverly Allen were both patriots of 1776, both determined, both unflinching in courage. They met and one died. There is nothing, with this exception, to mar the memory of Beverly Allen or the character of a man whose usefulness can now hardly be estimated. His eloquence and purity of living won for him the love and respect of the people of Elbert County and many stood ready to protect him with their lives. He had chosen the ministry, as his calling but after the trouble with Forsythe he went to Kentucky and devoted himself to the study of medicine. He became one of the best beloved physicians of his section.

William Thompson, Esq., is the next tomb. His grave is near that of Robert Forsythe. He was a member of the Order of the Cincinati, and a Colonel in the Revolution. The inscription on tomb is: Ewer and sword, in upper left hand corner, naked arm and hand, with broad sword, on upper right hand corner. Order of the Cincinnati carved in script; between a spread eagle, beneath holding laurel branches.

William Thompson, Esq., was an officer in the 9th Penn. Regiment. From its formation in 1776 to the end and from his American Brethren. He died March 19, 1794. His widow survived him.

Isabella Spencer. Spouse to Alex. Spencer who died July 11, 1797.

Miss Rosa Bowie, daughter Major John and Mrs. Rose Bowie, South Carolina. Age 11 years.

Commodore Oliver Bowen, a native of Rhode Island, where he sprang from honorable stock. Died July 11, 1815, age 56. A patriot of 1775. He was among the first in the State who stepped forth in vindication of our rights. His life equally with his property were often required in the cause. His widow survived him.

There are Bowens buried in one of the Buckersville semeteries in Elbert County said to be relatives.

II.

The tombs of the unknown dead are in the southwest corner of the church-yard.

On two of the oldest tombs can be seen the names of *Young* and *Moore*.

This monument was erected by *William Young* and *John Moore* to perpetuate the memory of *Mr. David Young*, who departed this life September 5, 1801, age 73 years.

Dinah Shepard Moore, daughter of John and Elizabeth Moore (daughter of Mr. David Young), age 2 months.

Mrs. Elizabeth Moore, wife of John Moore, who departed this life October 12, 1808. Age 40.

Mr. William Young, a native of Cumberland County, in England, who departed this life February 11, 1818. Age 58.

The monument of *Patrick Moore* is crumbling away. The urn-shaped figure that forms the apex, shows the work of a master hand and the delicate ivy-wreath, traced there, is more beautiful in the soft grey of age, than when the marble was new. This inscription to his memory is on the east side of the monument, while those in memory of his near relatives appear on the north and south sides.

Erected to the memory of *Patrick Moore,* a native of Ireland, born in the Parish of Bangor, and County of Down on the 25th of November, 1751, and died in Augusta August 23, 1803, age 52 years.

———

Thomas Moore, nephew of Patrick Moore, born July 1, 177—, died September 1, 1803.

———

Eleanor Moore, daughter of Thomas and Fannie Moore, born November 5, 1799, died August 20, 1800.

———

Frances Moore ———

———

William Moore, nephew of Patrick Moore, born September 22, 1788, died August 28, 1803. Age 25.

———

Another monument of fine marble, similar in form to that of Patrick Moore, is near the church, a little to the east, and is in memory of the wife of *Augustus Moore.* West side. Sacred to the memory of *Keziah Louisa Moore,* consort of Augustus Moore, born April 9, 1789, and died March 1, 1818.

———

In memory of *Mrs. Sarah H. Gardner,* wife of *James Gardner,* of Augusta, Ga., who departed this life July 22, 1801. Age 29 years.

———

James and Sarah H. Gardner had two children; a son who has descendants in Augusta, Ga., and a daughter, first Joseph McKinne and had a son Felix McKinne, who died young. After the death of Mr. McKinne, she married a Gould and they have descendants in Augusta.

———

In memory of *James Clark,* who departed this life December 21, 1797. He was in Killead, Kingdom of Ireland. Age 21.

In memory of *James Campbell,* merchant of Augusta, Ga. Died September 14, 1820. Age 37. He was a native of Randalstown, Antrim Co., Ireland.

In memory of *Mary Nesbitt,* wife of Hugh Nesbitt who departed this life December 8, 1802. Age 25.

Also their son, *James Wilson Nesbitt.* Died January 7, 1803. Age 7 weeks.

To the memory of *William Henry White,* who departed this life August 30, 1802. Age 7 months.

Sacred to the memory of *Colonel Ambrose Gordon,* born in the State of New Jersey, June 28, 1751, and departed this life in Augusta, Ga., June 28, 1804. Age 53 years.

In memory of *Julian Gordon,* daughter of Ambrose and Elizabeth Gordon, who died September 14, 1805. Age 3 years.

In memory of *Rev. Washington McKnight,* who departed this life September 5, 1805. Age 26. He was the first minister of the Presbyterian Church of Augusta. It was first organized by Rev. Washington McKnight in 1801. John Taylor, William Few, and George Watkins were ordained elders, and the sacraments were regularly administered from that time.

In memory of *Nicholas Danforth,* son of Jacob and Mary Danforth who died November 6, 1805. Age 2 years.

Sacred to the memory of *Mrs. Sarah Ballard,* wife of Mr. Frederick Ballard, who departed this life January 9, 1806. Age 48 years.

The tomb of Joseph G. Cormick seems to have been the first monument of imposing consequence erected in the church-yard.

The inscription on this tomb: "This tomb encloses the mortal remains of Joseph G. Cormick; he was a native of Ireland and in common with the majority of his country men, felt the varied wrongs which afflict that devoted land. In an attempt, prompted by patriotism, guided by honor, supported by courage, failing to redress these wrongs, he turned from the enslaved shores of Europe to America the only asylum of Liberty." He died August 19, 1806. Age 26.

As captain he commanded the "Irish Volunteers," an organization still in existence.

———

Ann, wife of *Doc. John Murray,* who departed this life December 21st, 1806. Age 49 years. Descendants of Doctor John and Mrs. Ann Murray, of Augusta, Ga. A line that can be traced, "Murray," "Bryson," "Davison," "Fargo."

———

Ann Howard, daughter of Rhesa and Hannah Howard, who departed this life January 5th, 1807. 18 years.

———

Thaddeus Phelps Howard, infant son of John and Louisa Howard, who departed this life December 23d, 1817. Age 3 years, 4 months and 10 days.

———

Amos Newton, who departed this life January 21st, 1813.

———

James Newton, son of Amos and Harriet Newton, who departed this life June 6th, 1807. Age 13 days. Near the resting place of Mrs. Ann Murray are several tombs that have Scotch names: "Blair," Mackintosh," "McKinne."

Alexander Blair, who was a native of Scotland and early in life became a citizen of the United States. Died 16th day of September, 1804, in the 36th year of his age.

Here also lie the remains of his son, James, who died at the age of 13 months, on 3rd of September, 1802. Erected by his mother, Eliza Blair.

Sons of *Major Alexander Blair* by whose side they lie. *Thomas Alexander Blair* died 11th October, 1805. Age 2 years and 6 months. *Alexander Blair,* died 18th November, 1805, aged 6 years and 2 days.

Mrs. Elizabeth McKinne, who died September 15th, 1809. Age 61, was a Miss Pope of North Carolina. Her husband and brothers were active patriots of the American Revolution. One of the descendants of Mrs. McKinne has given the name of her husband as John McKinne. Before the war between the states and for some years after, nearly every family in Summerville, a suburban town of Augusta, could trace relationship by birth or marriage, back to these McKinne ancestors. This family has no male representative of the name now living. Mr. Barna McKinne, a son of Mrs. Elizabeth McKinne, has descendants: Mrs. Winter, of Summerville; Mrs. C. A. Rowland, of Augusta; Mr. J. P. C. Whitehead, of Dallas, Texas; Mrs. Richard Wilde, of San Francisco; Mr. John Winter and Mrs. Robt. Robertson, of New Orleans; Mrs. Geo. Hardwick, Mrs. J. Hardwick Jackson, and many others in this and other sections of the South. The line, that connects the Montgomery family of Summerville, came through the daughter of Alexander Blair and his wife. Eliza McKinne, Mrs. Blair, became the second wife of James Gardner, of Augusta, and their descendants are numerous: Miss Mary Ann Gardner, their only living child, resides in Summerville; Gen. Wm. Montgomery Gardner, who died recently left a daughter, Miss Marion Gardner; Mr. James Gardner, another son, left children;

and Mrs. White, Mrs. Stokes, Mrs. Ridgely, Mrs. Hale
Barrett, Mr. Colden Rihnd, and many others, are from
James and Eliza Gardner.

Another daughter of Mrs. Elizabeth McKinne married
Thomas Gardner, their descendants are Gardners, Gaird-
ners, Fosters, Weeds, Smiths, etc. Mrs. John Mackintosh, whose tomb is near that of her mother, Mary Mc-
Kinne. One of the daughters of Mr. and Mrs. Mackintosh married a Dent, and has descendants in Waynsboro:
Dr. John Dent, Dr. A. S. Whitehead and others. Another
daughter married Governor Crawford and left children.

Mrs. Elizabeth McKinne's name appears at the head
of the list, in the "Church Manual" when there were only
fourteen members of the Presbyterian Church in Augusta
and a large number of her descendants are of the same
faith; but many are Episcopalians, and one is the wife
of a Bishop.

———

Standing alone, and not far from those of the McKinne
family, is the tomb of *Alexander McLaws*. If there were
ever any dates on this tomb, time has effaced them. His
daughter has placed a stone over the body of Alexander
McLaws. His daughter was the wife of Governor Reid
of Florida. Their daughter, Flora Reid, married Colonel
Dancey, an officer of the Seminole war. James McLaws,
the son of Alexander McLaws, married and left descendants. The sons of James McLaws were Judge William
Raymond McLaws, General James La Fayette McLaws,
Mr. Abram H. McLaws. The grave of the "stranger" is
here: Robert Mitchell of Queens County, New York, died
March 22nd, 1808, in his 32nd year.

———

III.

Sarah Hull Campbell, daughter of Edward and Marie
Campbell, died July 6th, 1815.

Macartan Campbell, died July 31st, 1818, at Summerville. Another Macartan Campbell died in Savannah, May 13th, 1871, and was buried there.

———

"This tablet is erected by the Vestry in grateful memory of *Edward Fenwick Campbell,* one of the builders of this church, Senior Warden of the Parish. Died September 27th, 1861, at the age of 75 years."

———

Anderson Watkins, M. D., a native of Virginia, but for many years a resident of this city. He died near Lexington, Kentucky, September 16th, 1828, in the 56th year of his age.

———

Richard Tubman, born in Charles County, Md., May 17th, 1767, and departed this life July 11th, 1836. He was a member of the Vestry of this church for sixteen years.

———

Gerrard McLaughlin, born July 3, 1798, died April 22, 1857. For thirty years a faithful member of the vestry of St. Paul's Church, Augusta.

———

The graves of *Bishop Polk* and his *wife* are under the chancel. The beautiful chancel railing, which was placed as their memorial, is just above them. These tombs can be seen, by lifting a door and lowering a lighted lantern into the crypt-like space.

———

Leonidas Polk, first Bishop of Louisiana, born April 10th, 1806, died June 14th, 1864.

———

Frances Annie Devereux, wife of Leonidas Polk, born March 22nd, 1807, died April 17th, 1875.

———

The tablet in memory of *Bishop Polk,* near the altar, is very beautiful. Above a shield of black marble, lettered in gold, is a bishop's crown. Right Rev'd Leonidas Polk, D. D., missionary bishop of the South West, First Bishop of Louisiana and Lieut. Gen. in the army of the Confederate States. Born April 10th, 1806. Fell at Pine Mountain, Georgia, June 14, 1864.

The tombs of *Rev. William H. Clark* and his wife are also beneath the church, under the "Angel Stairway."

Rev. William H. Clark, born Jan. 22nd, 1820, died Aug. 10th, 1877.

Mrs. Sophia Green Clarke entered into rest 1870. There is also a tablet in memory of Rev. Clarke near the altar and opposite that of Bishop Polk.

Lewis De Saussure Ford, M. D. L. L. D., born December 31st, 1801. Entered into rest, August 22, 1883.

Frances Emily, born December 5th, 1807, died June 23rd, 1884.

The massive doors, leading from the vestry room into the church were the gift of the daughters of Dr. Flournoy Carter. Capt. John Carter, 1760-1820. An officer in the Continental Army, and First Senior Warden of St. Paul's Church.

Dr. John Carter, 1793-1854.

MEMORIAL WINDOWS.
In memory of *Theodosia,* wife of *Rev. Edward G. Ford,* Rector of St. Paul's. Died April 1st, 1873.

.. *Grace Sterling King,* wife of John B. Connally, died December 31st, 1875.

Louise Woodward King, Died December 7, 1878.

Katherine Gregg McCoy, wife of W. E. McCoy, passed from death unto life November 20th, 1882.

Charles Adolphus Platt, December 11th, 1814-July 21st, 1887. *Josephine Elliot Platt,* daughter of *Charles A. Platt,* May 11th, 1865-May 18th, 1882.

Mattie F. Alexander, died March 30th, 1883. Aged 23 years.

There are the *Reredos* windows in exquisite mosaic setting. The *Dunbar* memorial, known as the "Angel Stairway." Paintings of the Apostles, in memory of *Judge King.*

Rev. Edward G. Ford, who was Rector before Rev. William H. Clark, is buried beneath the church.

IV.

Sacred to the memory of *Mrs. Hannah Anderson,* widow of Mr. Robert Anderson, late merchant in Charleston, S. C. She was a native of Pennsylvania and for 30 years a resident of Charleston. She died September 30, 1814.

Alexander Hutcheson, son of Adam and Elizabeth Hutcheson, born Aug. 7, 1809, died April 2, 1810.

Adam Hutcheson, son of Adam and Elizabeth Hutcheson, born Feb. 2, 1811, died March 7, 1813.

John Hutcheson, son of Adam and Elizabeth Hutcheson, born Oct. 20, 1815, died June 28, 18—.

In memory of *Sarah Foulk McKinney,* who departed this life October 10, 1809, age 26.

In memory of William Wigfall McKinney, son of David and Sarah McKinney, died Nov. 10, 1809, age one month.

In memory of Caroline McKinney, daughter of David and Sarah McKinney.

In memory of David Bull, a native of Hartford, Conn., a merchant of Augusta, Ga., died October 23d, 1809, age 26 years.

Mrs. Elizabeth Isaacs, wife of Ralph Isaacs, about April 9, 1809, age 45.

Charlotte W. Isaacs, youngest daughter of Ralph and Elizabeth Isaacs. October 2, 1809. Age 15.

In memory of *John W. Buckle,* who departed this life July 20, 1809, age 31.

This tablet records the death of *John Weltheim Berrien,* only son of John McPherson Berrien and Eliza, his wife, who departed this life Aug. 22, 1810. Age 1 year 10 months.

Sacred to the memory of *John Bacon,* born September 28, 1769, died April 15, 1812. His son Edmund Bacon, was a friend of Judge Augustus Longstreet.

The Bacons, Barretts, Glascocks, Wares and others trace their family lines from Captain John Bacon.

Governor Matthews is buried in St. Paul's church-yard. This may be news to some of his descendants for he has many. His tomb is by that of Robert Forsythe and not far from the monument of John Bacon. The inscription of his tomb is characteristic of the man, brief and to the point:

"In memory of General George Matthews, Aug. 30, 1812. Age 73."

The old monument of "John Wilson, Esquire," is one of the best known. "In memory of *John Wilson, Esquire,* late of Augusta, Ga., who departed this life May 2, 1813. A native of Ireland and a resident of this country for 54 years."

In memory of *Mrs. Eliza Thompson,* wife of Rev. B. Thompson, who succeeded Rev. Washington McKnight and took charge of the Presbyterian Church in 1807, who departed this life on the 14th of July, 1814, age 21 years.

In memory of *Samuel William Miller,* who was a member of a family which still has a representative in Augusta. He was born in Newport, R. I., December 21, 1791, but resided in Georgia until a few years of his death, when he removed to Augusta, Ga. He died September 18, 1817. Age 25 years, 8 months and 28 days.

To the memory of *Mrs. Corally Jones,* consort of the Captain William Jones, of the U. S. army, who departed this life Nov. 6, 1812, age 22 years.

In memory of *Rebecca Fullerton,* the wife of Hugh Fullerton, who died May 9, 1810, age 29. Also Mary, daughter of Hugh and Rebecca Fullerton, died October 27, 1801. Age 6 months.

Sacred to the memory of *Bridget Cooper* who departed this life January 15, 1813. Age 70 years.

In memory of *Alexander Sturges,* second son of Dimas and Isabella Ponce, who was born August 6, 1809 and departed this life July 22, 1813.

———

Lewis Cooper, a native of Newark, N. J., who died September 28, 1817. Age 32 years.

———

Sacred to the memory of John Beale Barnes, Esq., who departed this life, Nov. 6, 1815. 36 years.

———

Sacred to the memory of *Bernard Bignon,* a native of France and a resident of the United States for 23 years, who departed this life on August 14, 1816. Age 75 years.

———

V.

The simple headstone of marble, which marks the grave of William Longstreet, is by the west walk. His remains were there interred, near the grave of his daughter, in 1814.

Sacred
to the
memory of
William Longstreet,
who departed this life
September 1st, 1814,
Aged 54 Years,
10 months and 26 days.

———

William Longstreet, born in 1759, discovered the secret of steam navigation sometime before the year 1788, and his name can be justly placed among Georgia's "Inventors." The ridicule he endured, is evident, from his letter to the Governor. Whether the "jeering" of the thought-

less crowd retarded the progress of this energetic genius
is unknown; but a certain license of "much liberty,"
which marked the early times of "Independence," made
the jokers impudent, and a song, about Longstreet's
boat, is remembered in the traditions of Augusta:

"Can you row the boat ashore,
      Billy boy, Billy boy?
Can you row the boat ashore,
      Gentle Billy?
Can you row the boat ashore,
Without a paddle or an oar,
      Billy boy?"

The letter, preserved in the archives of the state, is as
follows:

"Augusta, Sept. 26th, 1790.

Sir:—I make no doubt but you have often heard of my
steamboat, and as often heard it laughed at. But in this
I have only shared the fate of all other projectors, for it
has uniformly been the custom of every country to ridicule even the greatest inventions until use had proved
their utility. In not reducing my scheme to practice has
been a little unfortunate for me, I confess, and perhaps
the people in general; but until very lately I did not think
that either artists or material could be had in the place
sufficient. However, necessity, that grand science of in-
vention, has furnished me with an idea of perfecting my
plan almost entirely with wooden materials; and by such
workmen as may be got here, and from a thorough confidence of its success, I have presumed to ask your assistance and patronage.

"Should it succeed agreeable to my expectation, I hope
I shall discover that source of duty which such favors always merit; and should it not succeed, your reward must
lay with other unlucky adventures.

"For me to mention to you all the advantages arising
from such a machine, would be tedious and indeed quite

unnecessary, therefore I have taken the liberty to state in this plain and humble manner my wish and opinion, which I hope you will excuse, and I shall remain either with or without approbation.

Your Excellency's most obedient and very humble servant.

"Wm. Longstreet.

"To Governor Telfair."

———

William Longstreet was the father of Judge Augustus Longstreet.

———

Duncan Matheson, a native of Ross Shire, Scotland, who died September 30th, 1812. Aged 32 years.

———

Daniel Starnes who died February 4th, 1814, aged 50 years. His stone was placed by his brother Samuel Starnes.

———

The monument of marble, surmounted by a cross, near the church on the east side is the tomb of Seaborn Jones, born at Halifax, N. Carolina, June 15th, 1759, died at Augusta, Georgia, July 24th, 1815. Age 56.

———

VI.

Josiah Sturges, son of Seaborn and Elizah Jones, born 1810, died Jan. 30th, 1813.

———

Robert Walker, son of Seaborn and Elizah Jones, born 1810, died July 22, 1815. Aged 5 years, 4 months and 11 days.

———

The monument to the memory of *Mrs. Margaret Phinizy,* is like that which markes the grave of Mrs. Elizabeth McKinne—five marble balls rest on the body of the tomb and support the pedestal of the urn shaped figure on tops. It is near the west wall. Mrs. Margaret Phinizy, who having adorned the doctrine of God her Saviour, by a life of exemplary piety and usefulness. Died August 22nd, 1815, aged 55 years.

Eliza Mary Joyner, wife of Wm. H. Joyner and only daughter of Dr. James Hartly of South Carolina, who departed this life on the 10th day of October, 1815. Aged 19 years and 6 months. Also their infant son.

Rachel Danforth, wife of James R. Danforth, who departed this life January 19th, 1816, in the 22nd year of her age. Also Anderson W. Danforth, son of James R. and Rachel Danforth.

Daniel Dill, died August 15th, 1816, in the 88th year of his age.

Nathan Gasque, who died October 1st, 1816, in the 41st year of his age.

Roderick William, son of Alexander and Mary Mac-Kenzie, born April 19th, 1815, died October 1st, 1817.

Caroline Elizabeth, only child of Denis and Mary Small born 28th December, A. D. 1800, died 21st September A. D. 1817.

.. *Maria,* wife of Samuel G. Starr, died November 5, 1817. Age 28. She was daughter of Eben R. and Hannah White, Danbury, Conn.

Louisa, wife of Wm. Smith and daughter of Claiborne and Elizabeth Watkins, of Abington, Virginia, who departed this life November 26, 1817, in the 17th year of her age.

John Bab Frances, son of F. B. and Jane Coquillon, born December 1871, died January 16, 1818.

————

Thomas P. Moffett, died May 22nd, 1818, aged 22 years.

————

The section, where members of the Campbell family are buried, is near the graves of Seaborn Jones and his sons. A monument bears the inscription:

The Resting Place of
Edward Fenwick Campbell
and his wife,
Maria Campbell.

————

Sextons
of
St. Paul's Church.

————

Abel Wright,
Died December 25, 1887.

————

Benjamin Whitehead,
Died April 2, 1894.

————

I do not know whether it was one of these who rang the church bell when a freshet had overflowed the streets of the city, or another who was buried elsewhere. But it is a true story of faithfulness.

St. Paul's stands on a slight bluff—lifted above freshet water—and when the old Sexton hired a boat and was ferried over and rang the bell for services, it was quite a surprise to those who heard it. He declared, however, it was "nothing but his duty."

SECTION II.

Public records of Franklin County, Georgia, 1777-1867, consisting of abstracts of wills, marriages, deeds, administrations, declarations of service, jury lists, grants and court dockets.

Transcribed under auspices of Daughters of American Revolution of Georgia, 1924, by Carrie Price Wilson (Mrs. Walter S.), State Consulting Registrar, Ex-Regent Lachlan McIntosh Chapter, D. A. R. Member of the League of American Pen Women and Georgia Historical Society, and Grace Gillam Davidson (Mrs. John L.), State Chairman Historic Research and Preservation of Records, Regent of Hannah Clark Chapter, D. A. R.

FRANKLIN COUNTY, GEORGIA.

An Act

For laying out two more counties to the weftward, and pointing out the mode of granting the fame.

(1) Whereas it is neceffary in order to ftrengthen this State, and for the convenience of the inhabitants, that new counties fshold be laid out and properly fettled,

Therefore, be it enacted by the reprefentatives of the freemen of the State of Georgia in general affesmbly met, and by the authority of the fame, That the prefent temporary line circumscribing the Indian hunting ground, fhall be marked by a line drawn from that part of the north branch of Savannah river, known by the name of Keowee, which fhall be interfected by a line running north-eaft from the Okunna mountains, thence in the fame direction to Tugalo river, from thence on a direct line to the top of Currohee mountain, thence to the head or fource of the moft fouthern ftream of the waters of the fame, thence down the faid river to the old line, thence along the faid line.

(11) And be it further enacted by the authority afore-faid, that is to fay, beginning at Savannah river where the weft line of Wilkes county fttrikes the fame, thence along the faid line to the Cherokee corner, from thence on the fame direction to the fouth branch of the Oconee river, thence up the faid river to the head or fource of the moft fouthern ftream thereof, thence along the temporary line feparating the Indian hunting ground to the northern branch of Savannah river, known by the name of Keowee, and down the faid river to the beginning: and all that tract of land, included within the aforefaid lines fhall be a county, and known by the name of Franklin.

(Signed) James Habersham, Speaker.
Savannah, Feb. 25, 1784.
(Watkin's Digest of the Laws of Georgia, pp. 290-291.)

Declaration of Revolutionary Soldiers for Pensions under Act of Congress June 7th, 1832. From Minutes of Franklin County (Georgia) Court of Ordinary, Commencing May 4th, 1829, and ending November 4th, 1844. (Abstracts).

John Albritton.

Of Capt. Vaughn's District, aged about 85. Entered the service of United States about 1774 as a volunteer in militia of Virginia. Private in Capt. George's Company; Lt. Fr. Underwood, Col. Charles Scott. Marched to Williamsburg in search of Gov. Dunmore and remained in service 4 weeks. Removed to Union District, South Carolina, and volunteered in Capt. Joshua Pelmore's Co., and afterwards in Capt. Hughes' Co. and served in Col. Brannan's Regt. for three or more years. Was at Battle of Cowpens where Gen. Morgan commanded, and was marched to Augusta, Georgia, and Bacon's Bridge. Taken prisoner by British and retained by them 6 months or more. Peace was declared soon after deponent's release and he was never discharged. Was born in Newcastle, Hanover County, Virginia, December 6th, 1747, and later lived in Goochland Co., Va., from whence he removed to South Carolina until close of war. Afterwards moved to Elbert County, Georgia, and finally to Franklin County. Known to and testified by William Glover and Rev. Dozier Thornton.

———

Richard Bond.

Resident of Capt. Watson's District, aged 69. Entered service of United States from Amherst Co., Va., in 1777, in militia and was drafted as a minute man; marched to Albermarle Barracks and placed under Capt. David Shelton, Col. Richardson. Was again drafted in Amherst Co., in 1779, and appointed orderly sergeant—was marched under command of Capt. Higginbotham to mouth of Gillis's Creek below Richmond and discharged. In 1780 was again drafted in Amherst Co., and as orderly sergeant marched to New Glasgow in lower Amherst and again discharged. In 1781 entered as substitute for his father, Nathan Bond and was marched under Capt. Franklin to Guilford, Carolina, but did not serve until 3 days after the Battle. Col. Rose was in command of the regiment, and Maj. Gabriel Penn of the battalion. At Guilford there was a dispute as to who should command, and Gen. Greene permitted us to choose our own captain, and we changed from a volunteer captain instead of militia, and was placed under command of Capt. James Dillard, Col. Lynch's regiment.

Marched across Deep River towards Cross Creek, and learning that the British had taken to their ship, was marched and discharged by Capt. Dillard. Afterwards served several small tours as a scout, and guarding prisoners, serving 10 months—6 months as orderly sergeant. In the last tour was a part of the infantry rifleman attached to Washington's Light Horse. Testified to by Rev. John Bramblett, Edward Ware, and Gabriel Smith.

James Cash.

Resident of Capt. Vaughn's District, aged 67. Entered service in Granville Co., N. C., militia about 2 months previous to Gates' defeat near Camden, Aug., 1780; marched to Hillsboro and Cross Creek, now Fayetteville, from there to Camden, S. C., to join Gen. Gates. Was under Capt. Peter Bennett, Maj. Telmar Dixon and Col. Ramsay—was in Battle at Gates' defeat and escaped, but in a few days rejoined the army at Hillsboro. Marched again towards Camden and discharged by Capt. Harris for two 3 months' tours. About October, 1781, entered army again at Granville under Capt. Samuels, Major Crafton, and marched to Hillsboro to guard Legislature of North Carolina. Afterwards was marched into South Carolina near Georgetown after Fanning and Scotch tories; returned to Hillsboro with prisoners and remained there as guard until discharged by Capt. Lewis, October 12, 1782, for a 12 months tour.

Born October 25, 1764, in Fairfax County, Virginia, but was living in Granville when called to service, removing afterwards to Montgomery County, North Carolina, and thence to this county. The first 6 months service was as substitute for brother-in-law John Williams, and then drafted and served 18 months as private soldier under Generals Butler and Gates of Regular Army. Received discharge from Capt. Harris. Endorsed by Elisha Dyer and Rev. Samuel Hymer.

William Cheek.

Resident of Capt. Watson's District, aged about 80. Entered service of United States in 1777, in militia of South Carolina in Laurens District under Capt. William Berry, and marched to Ramburns Creek on Indian Frontier to guard against the Indians; was discharged and revolunteered after 3 months under same officer, and served again on same Indian Border for another 3 months. Col. John Hunter commanded in both tours. Was dis-

charged by Capt. Berry. In 1779 again volunteered at
Laurens under Capt. Lewis Duvall and Col. Benjamin
Kilgore and served another 3 months tour on said Indian
Border, discharged and remained at home for 3 months.
Served every alternate 3 months on that order for four
years. Was in no battle and was stationed at no other
place than Block House Station.

Was born in North Carolina, September 29, 1752. Entered service in Laurens District where lived until 1804,
from there to Pendleton District and from there moved in
1818 to Franklin County, Ga. Testified to by Rev. John
Bramlett and Joseph Attaway.

Thomas Clark.

Resident of Capt. Adams' District, aged 71. Entered
service of United States in Camden District, South Carolina, March 1779. Drafted under Capt. Joseph Finister,
Col. Joseph Brown. Marched to Columbia and to Orangeburg, and shortly afterward to Charleston, into which city
we were chased by the British; detached on a party to
James Island. Recollects Pulaski, a commander of horse
at Charleston. Discharged, and again drafted in 1780-
81 at Camden under Capt. John McCool, and joined Gen.
Sumter at Orangeburg—no fighting, except a little skirmish at Geisenters on Edisto River. Capt. McCool was
not with us but were commanded by Lt. Hezekia Lewis
(?). In summer of 1781 was marched to join Gen. Henderson at Orangeburg and to station on Edisto. After 4
months was again drafted, and after 2 months was discharged. Served 3 months as volunteer after tories; 13
months in all.

Was born in Granville County, July 22, 1761; lived
in Camden, now Chester, when entered service. Since
peace, lived 2 years in Rutherford County, N. C., moved
to Jefferson County, Georgia, and from there to Franklin
county.

Endorsed by Rev. Mathew W. Vandivere and George Garner.

Elisha Dyer.

Resident of Capt. Newell's District, age 69. Entered service in Granville County, N. C., March 1778, then 16 years of age, under Capt. Abram Potter, Col. Farrar and was marched to Brier Creek where he was engaged in a skirmish with the British at Stono, S. C., and was shortly afterwards discharged for a 3 months tour by Capt. Carrington of Orange County, N. C. Again entered North Carolina militia in Granville about 2 weeks before Gates' defeat near Camden, 1780, under Capt. Peter Bennett, Col. Ambrose Ramsay of Guilford, and Gen. Butler. Marched to Cross Creek, now Fayetteville, and placed under command of Gen. Carswell and kept scouting until marched to Camden and put under Gen. Gates, at which time his father sent Jesse Gaskins to serve out the tour as it was the sickly season. Was discharged by Col. Ramsay, but again entered the North Carolina militia at Granville previous to battle of Guilford, March 1781, under Capt. John Henderson, Col. Malbady (sic), a French officer, and Gen. Greene. Was in Battle of Guilford, marched near Fayetteville and discharged for a 3 months tour by Capt. Henderson. Entered again at Hillsboro under Capt. Frederick Dubois from Caswell County (month not recollected), 1782, stationed as guard to Legislature then sitting. Was under Col. Hugh Linnon and was discharged by Capt. Dubois for a 3 months tour. Served altogether 12 months, that is 4 three months tours as private soldier, 3 months in addition as an express under Col. Potts at Hillsboro and found his own horse as a volunteer. Was born in Virginia near Big Falls of Potomac in May, 1763. Was called into service when living in Granville County, from whence he removed after the war to Rockingham County, N. C., thence to Pendleton, S. C., and finally to Georgia, about 1800, has resided ever since in Franklin

County, except 7 years which he spent in Walton County, Georgia. Was never drafted—always volunteered and never served as a substitute. His discharges were in a chest which his sister took to the Western County, and does not know where she now lives, if living. His neighbor, James Cash, a Revolutionary soldier, knew him during service. Testified to by Rev. Samuel Hymer, and Jesse M. Million.

Ambrose Downs.

Declaration of Ambrose Downs, November 12, 1832. Aged about 71. Entered service in Richmond County, Georgia, in Fall of 1779, under Capt. Isaac Skinner, Col. Clark's Regiment, marched to Blackstock's Mill where engaged in small skirmish with enemy. Then to Ramsours Mill where joined Gen. Sumter and took British and Tory prisoners. From there to Long Cone when had a small engagement, and thence to Kings Mountain where Ferguson was, but not having sufficient ammunition did not attack him, but went over to Nullichucky until we were ordered back to Kings Mountain, but did not reach there until after the battle. From here we were marched to Mechlinburg County, N. C., from there to Auson old Court House on Pee Dee, where we had a brush with the tories. Being placed under General Greene were marched to Guilford Court House thence to Taylors Ferry on Roanoke River in state of Virginia, thence to Mechlinburg (Va.?) from there to Prince Edward and intended to go to little York but did not reach there in time for the engagement with Cornwallis. Returned to Mechlinburg and thence home. Served in all about three years. Knew Generals Sumter and Greene, and a Major Gaston. Born in Richmond County, Georgia, about the year 1761, removed to Laurens County, S. C., thence to Edgefield, back to Richmond County and finally to Franklin County, Ga., where he has since resided except six years he lived in Pendleton District, S. C.

Testified to by Rev. Mathew W. Vandiviere and Lewis D. Holsonbake.

Joseph Edwards.

Resident of Captain Newell's District, About 77 years old. Entered service in Surry County, N. C., 1776, as a volunteer under Capt. Shepherd, Col. Armstrong's Regiment. Marched to Cross Creek and remained there some time guarding the British and tories; from there to Hillsboro and thence home to recruit horse and clothing but was soon recalled and remained in service, with short intermissions for about three years. Was in no great battle but in many skirmishes, and also to the Indian border. Moved to Wilkes County, N. C., but was drafted to serve in Capt. Martin's company under Col. Cleveland, and marched into lower North Carolina, after Col. Fannin and the tories. Was discharged after about 45 days. Drafted again and served 33 days under Capt. Isbel in Col. Isaac's Regiment. Discharged and again drafted and served 15 days under Capt. Sloan and Col. Cleveland and marched near Virginia line after a Tory Captain, Cox, and his company, and took Capt. Cox, but could not find his company —was discharged and returned home. Served three years as Sergeant Horseman under Capt. Shepherd and found his own horse—served three or four months afterwards as foot private. Was born in Maryland—about 1756. Came to Surry County, N. C., and from thence, in 1784, to Franklin County where he has since lived. Was volunteer for three years but drafted for remainder of service.

Testified to by Rev. Dozier Thornton and John Stonecypher.

Thompson Epposon.

Resident of Capt. Mangrum's District. Aged 79. Entered service in Albermarle County, Virginia, 1777, under Capt. Robert Harris, marched to Williamsburg and put under Gen. Nelson—thence to little Hampton and back to Albermarle—discharged for a tour of duty by Capt. Harris. Re-entered service in Wilkes County, N. C., under Capt. Moses Guest in Horse County and served from June 1780 to January, 1781. Was at Battle of Kings Mountain and dismissed by Capt. Guest. Removed to Virginia July 1781, and entered service from Albermarle under Capt. John Martin, marched to Richmond, Va., and placed under Marquis De La Fayette, marched to Williamsburg and was discharged by Capt. Martin and Col. Richardson. Was born in Albermarle County about 1757 and lived there about 5 years and in 1790 and in 1790 to his present residence. Was drafted for both tours in Virginia, but was a volunteer in North Carolina.

Testified to by Rev. David Garrison, Capt. Moses Guest and John Stonecypher.

John Farrar.

Declaration of John Farrar, November 7, 1831, age about 71, to obtain provision under the Act of Congress, March 18, 1818, and May 1, 1820. Enlisted in service, year not recalled, for 5 years, in North Carolina, in company of Capt. White, Col. Ledbetter's Regiment. Also served in Capt. Clements company in Col. Marbury's Regiment in Continental Establishment. Served 5 years and was discharged from service in Lancaster District, S. C. Had not applied earlier for this pension because he had been able to support himself. Is now infirm. A blacksmith and farmer but unable to pursue either avocation. Has one child, a son, about 17 years old.

Capt. Moses Guest.

Resident of Capt. Mangrum's District, age 81. Was commissioned Capt. of North Carolina Militia by Governor of that state 1775—served 2 months tour against the Indians, under Col. Armstrong and Gen. Rutherford. As Capt. of Horse marched under Cleveland to Ramsours

Mills, but arrived too late for battle—was marched home to Wilkes County (N. C.) thence through Burke and Rutherford by the Cowpens after the tories, and met them at Kings Mountain, where we defeated them. Col. Cleveland was only Commander of Horse at that battle. Was sent as guard to about 700 prisoners to Moravian Town, N. C., thence back to Wilkes. Afterwards was put continually with Minute Men on scouting parties until nearly end of war. At Kings Mountain commanded a Horse Company of about 50 men and was in command of same immediately after the Indian Campaign, when he was put in command of a foot company. Was in service during entire war, and does not think he had one year's rest altogether. Was born in January, 1750, in Faquher County, Va. Was living in Wilkes County, N. C., when he entered service; removed from there to Pendleton, S. C., about 45 years since and about 32 since removed to present residence. Knew Cols. Shelby Lenoir, Sevier, Campbell, Williams and Cleveland.

Testified to by Rev. Dozier Thornton, Thompson Epposon, Henry Parks, John Stonecypher, and William Glover.

William Glover.

Declaration of William Glover, age 72. Entered service of United States at Wilkes County, N. C., in militia about 1778-9 as private under Capt. Shepherd and Col. Gordon. Was marched to Hamilton's Old Store, from there to Shallow Ford on the (Y) Adkin, crossed Dan River into Virginia with some prisoners at Dick's Ferry where we met a new guard and returned to Wilkes and received a discharge from Major Lewis for a 3 months tour. Immediately reentered the service under Col. Cleaveland and remained with him under Capt. Barton and Capt. Keys scouting for 6 months, when again entered regular service in 1780 in Wilkes County, N. C., under Capt. Noll, Col. Isaacs and Gen. Rutherford. Marched to Salsbury by way of Charlotte, thence to Camden where we were defeated under Gen. Gates. On the way was detached under Col. Davidson and was in a skirmish at the mouth of Rocky River, where Col. Davidson was wounded. Returned home for three days and entered army at Wilkes Court House under Col. Gordon. Marched to Shallow Ford where defeated the tories in battle. Had previously served 3 months under Col. Armstrong and Capt. Bushwick and Gen. Sumter and was in Battle of Hanging Rock near Camden. Returned to Wilkes and entered Capt. Keys and Col. Cleaveland and was ordered to guard prisoners taken at King's Mountain to Virginia line. Returning to Wilkes joined Col. Cleaveland and ordered under Capt. Key to scout duty to Flower Gap and lead mines on New River on Virginia line. Placed as guard over the mines. Returned to Wilkes and was under Capt. Gordon, Capt. Key, Capt. Bacton, Maj. Lewis and Col. Cleaveland until war was over. Was in fight at King's Creek. Served 3 years.

Born in Prince George County, Md., 1760, and was living in Wilkes County, N. C., when entered service. Came to Elbert County in 1786, thence to Franklin County, Ga., in 1800, where has since resided. Was once drafted but other times volunteered—was never a substitute. House burned 1801 with all papers.

Endorsed by Rev. Dozier Thornton and John Stonecypher.

Andrew Lee.

Resident of Capt. Adam's District, aged 72. Entered service from Wilkes County, Georgia, under Col. Elijah Clark as a volunteer in the militia September, 1780, after the first siege of Augusta. Was placed under Capt. George Walton and marched to Holston at head of Wautauga River in North Carolina, from there, having been joined by Gen. Sumter's command, was marched to Blackstock's on Tiger River where had a battle with British

and tories under Tarleton, November 20, 1780, where Gen.
Sumter was wounded. Was here discharged by Capt.
Walton, having served 3 months and returned to regular
residence in Abbeville District, S. C. In January, 1781,
volunteered here as minute man and was marched tow-
ards Augusta where engaged in a fight with Indians on
Oconee River. Joined Gen. Geene's army at siege of
Ninety-Six in June 1781, and was detached to go with
Gen. Pickens to 2nd siege of Augusta. Was returned to
Abbeville with Gen. Pickens and did scout duty to end
of war. Served about 2 years and 6 months as private
in Light Horse, furnishing own horse.

Born in Augusta, Georgia, 1761. Was living in Abbeville District, S. C., at time of entering service, and went
over to Georgia to join Gen. Clark. Removed from Abbeville in 1811 to Lincoln County, Ga., until 1827, when finally settled in Franklin County, Georgia.

Endorsed by Rev. Samuel Hymer and Thomas King.

Burdett Leech.

Resident of Capt. Grimes' District, age 70. Entered
Virginia Artillery as substitute for George Leech, October, 1780, year before the taking of Cornwallis—entered
at Little York under Capt. Edmunds, Col. Thomas Marshall. Marched to Williamsburg, and when the British
landed at Burrell's Ferry drove them up into Albermarle
County, where were joined by Gen. Lafayette and marched back to Williamsburg where we were joined by Gen.
Washington and marched down to the siege of Little
York, when my brother's time expired, my service for him
being 9 months. I was here discharged by Capt. Blackwell and entered as a volunteer in the Virginia militia at
York under Capt. John Banyan, Col. Churchill's regiment. Served there until Cornwallis surrendered October 19, 1781, and was discharged.

William Murdock.

Resident of Capt. Watson's District, age 73. Entered service in fall of 1776-7 at Ninety-Six District, now Newberry, as substitute for father, Hamilton Murdock, who was drafted for a 3 months tour. Placed under Capt. Robert Gillam, Col. James Williams' Regiment of Horse. Marched to Kellott's Station on Reedy River to keep off Indians, and was discharged by Lt. Samuel Saxon. Returned home, but was drafted in June, 1780, and marched to Stono to relieve men there, but met them returning, having been defeated. Returning home were discharged at Newberry by Capt. Gillam for a 3 months tour. Deponent, with father then moved to what is now Laurens District and volunteered there under Capt. Henderson in Col. Williams' Regiment of Horse. Marched to White Hall in Abbeville District and thence into Georgia against the Indians. Was kept marching about but no battle and was discharged by Lt. Christopher Hardy, Capt. Henderson. Served 9 months, the first 3 and last 3 as horseman, finding own horse.

Born in Ireland, March 15, 1759. Lived in Newberry and from there to Franklin County, Ga.

Endorsed by Rev. John Sandige and James Wilson.

William Mitchell.

Resident of Capt. Newell's District, age 71. Entered service in Union District, S. C., in militia, July 1780, under Captains Duff and Samuel Atterson. Marched through the country scouting and skirmishing until Duff was taken prisoner and Atterson had his arm broken. Served until February, 1781, and was then discharged, but immediately enrolled as volunteer horseman under Capt. George Avary to serve 15 months. Was kept riding through the country until June, 1781, when was marched to siege of Ninety-Six, and put under command if Maj. Ben Jolly and Gen. Greene on his way to Eutaw Springs and was in that battle. After this was kept on scouting parties when was sent under Capt. Avarey and Col. Kilgore after the Cherokee Indians and engaged in several skirmishes in which towns were burned. Returned to Union County and finished 5 months tour and was discharged by Capt. Avary. In June, 1782, entered service for one month as a substitute for Richard Barrett under Capt. Atterson, Col. Fair. When Barrett's term was finished deponent re-entered as substitute for John Ham for one month, after which he entered at once as substitute for James Hogan for 2 months in Capt. Avary's Company, served these 2 months at Bacon's Bridge on Ashley River, and was discharged at Union by our officers who had been discharged by Gen. Greene.

Born April 1, 1761, probably in Virginia. Was living in Union District when entered service. Was volunteer 22 months and substitute 4 months.

Endorsed by Rev. Samuel Hymer, Charles D. Jenkins and John L. Reid.

Samuel Moseley.

Resident of Capt. Briant's District, age 72. Entered the service in militia of North Carolina at Lewisburg, in Franklin County, N. C., May 1, 1780, as private under Capt. Harrison Macon, and marched to Cross Creek to join Gen. Caswell's regiment, and was placed under command of Col. Dixon, probably a continental officer. About August 1, was with Gen. Gates at Lindsay's Creek and at Battle of Camden, after which we were dispersed. Was wounded 3 times at this battle: first by a ball above right eye, second by bayonet in side, and third by ball in left thigh. Was thrown down and rode over by British Light Horse, and placed in wagon and carried to Hanging Rock about 30 miles—traveled about 5 or 6 days and came up with the army at Randolph and was there discharged by Gen. Caswell. Returned home and confined with wounds until about January 1, 1781, when volunteered at Franklin, C. H., under Capt. Bledsoe, and marched in scouting parties through counties of Wake, Edgecombe, Nash and Franklin, and was discharged by Lt. Swantrouter. Remained at home until after Cornwallis marched through North Carolina and in September, 1781, enlisted at Warren, C. H., Bute County in a company of horse of Regular Continental State Troops, for 12 months under Capt. Samuel J. Jones, and was marched by him to subdue the tories in the lower and southern parts of North Carolina. At end of enlistment was discharged by Capt. Jones. There were some French officers along. Afterwards volunteered under Col. Ben. Seawell and Capt. James Smith; served 5 or 6 months until peace was proclaimed.

Born in Bute County, N. C., September 23, 1759. Was living in Franklin County, N. C., when entered service. Since the war lived in Wake Co., and Edgefield and Abbeville Districts, S. C., and for the past 12 years in Franklin County, Georgia.

Endorsed by Rev. David Garrison and John H. Patrick.

Julius Nichols.

Resident of Capt. Fleming's District. Entered service as volunteer in militia of North Carolina, in Wake County, in September, 1776, under Capt. James Jones, and marched towards Charleston, but after crossing Coles Bridge were informed that Lee had left Charleston. We were ordered to Cross Creek and marched to Tarboro, thence to Halifax and Wilmington. Returned home and joined Capt. Jones at a moments notice. Ensign Armstrong and Lt. Medici were in command in our company which was a Light Horse Company. Served 6 months in this tour. In September, 1778, enlisted at Salsbury, N. C., militia for 9 months under Capt. John Lopp and marched under Col. Purvard to Purysburg, S. C., where we mustered under command of Gen. Lincoln. In the spring we were marched to Sister's Ferry and were stationed there when the Battle of Briar Creek was fought on Georgia soil. Remained in that vicinity until the term was out, and discharged by Capt. Lopp and returned home. Enlisted March, 1780, at Hillsborough, N. C., militia for 3 months under Capt. James Christmas and Col. Tinnan, marched to Charleston and taken prisoner by the British, May, 1780—was discharged by them on parole and returned home in June. In November, 1780, turned out with Capt. King and served 2 months collecting provisions for army at Cross Creek and placed under Capt. Fletcher, Commissioner of the county and was under command of Gen. Butler. Returned home but was immediately drafted for another 3 months. Was given furlough but returned at once to army at Cross Creek under Col. Armstrong and kept on foraging duty—discharged by Capt. Fletcher. Served 2 years and 2 months.

Born in Granville County, N. C., March, 1759. Entered service in Wake County, where was living until about 20 years since when settled in Franklin County, Georgia.

Endorsed by Rev. Mathew W. Vandivere and William Turk.

Henry Parks.

Resident of Capt. Guins (Givens?) District, age 74. Entered militia of North Carolina in Wilkes County 1774-5, under Capt. Guess as volunteer under command of Gen. Rutherford—marched to the Valley Towns in Cherokee Nation on scouting parties—served 2 months and was discharged by Col. Armstrong. Afterwards in militia for 6 months as minute man under Lt. Benjamin Cleaveland and Capt. Walton; was marched against the tories and Scotch to Cross Creek, and at the end of 6 months was discharged by Capt. Walton. Next entered the army under Capt. Gilreath and Gen. Rutherford and marched to Purysburg and staied there and at Sisters' Ferry where was discharged after 5 months. Entered again as volunteer at Wilkes County, N. C., under Capt. Lewis and Col. Benj. Cleveland. Marched to King's Mountain and was in that battle where was wounded by rifle ball through the arm and returned home until wound was healed, when volunteered under Capt. John Cleveland and Col. Lenoir, under command of Gen. Rutherford. Marched within 2 miles of Wilmington and placed as guard at a bridge. Was marched back to Wilkes and discharged by Capt. John Cleveland, after a service of about 6 weeks. Again volunteered under Capt. Lewis and went to join Gen. Green. Marched with his army to High Rock Ford on Haw River and was out about a month as a scout against the tories. Served about a month before Gates defeat, scouting after tories who were under command of Gen. Bryant. At that time he was a volunteer under Col. Lewis and was joined by Gen. Rutherford when the tories marched off and were defeated by Sumter at Hanging Rock. Served about 3 years as private soldier.

Born in Albermarle County, Virginia, May 1758; record in possession of Thomas or James Parks, in Burke County, N. C.

In 1784 removed from Wilkes County, N. C., to Wilkes County, Ga., and about 36 years since came to Franklin County, Ga., his present residence.

Testified by Rev. David Garrison, Moses Guest and John Stonecypher.

Abner Sheridan.

Resident of Capt. Catlett's District, age 72. Entered militia of North Carolina at Hillsboro under Capt. John Taylor and was there placed as a guard to the Legislature, Burke being Governor. Served 3 months and was discharged by Capt. John McConly, Capt. Taylor having been tried and broke for cowardice. Enlisted under Capt. John Elliott in state troops in Orange County, N. C., and was marched to Hillsboro in Capt. Jones' company. Maj. John Lewis. Marched to Lindley's Mill on Cain Creek in Orange County, N. C., and to Brewer's Mill on Haw River, Chatham County, where was stationed for some time. From there was marched to Redfield Ford on said river and from thence to near the head of Cape Fear River. Went back to Lindley's Mill and to Hillsboro where was discharged by Capt. Jones for 9 months tour.

Was born in Maryland—year not known. Lived in Orange County, N. C., then Greenville District, and from there to present residence in Franklin County, Ga.

Endorsed by Rev. David Garrison and Samuel Jackson.

John Stonecypher.

Resident of Capt. Bryant's District, age 75. Entered service in North Carolina May or June, 1779, at Wilkes C. H., under Col. Cleveland and placed as a guard over some prisoners at Salsbury. Served a 3 months tour and returned to Wilkes C. H. and was marched to Ramsaurs on Catawba River where engaged in battle. From there was marched to New River to try to stop the Roberts (sic), and a gang of tories came up at King's Creek where there was battle and drove the tories off. At the end of this 3 months tour again entered service at Wilkes C. H., about June 1780, in militia under Capt. Rutledge, and thinks the regiment was commanded by Cols. Locke and Isaacs. Was placed under Gen. Gates and served 3 months. Again entered the militia at Salsbury and marched to Charlotte and thence to near Camden and was in that battle at defeat of Gates. Escaped and returned home for a few days when again entered service at Wilkes C. H. under Col. Cleveland, with whom he remained until Battle of King's Mountain, October, 1780. Was in that battle and was afterwards put under command of Gen. (formerly Col.) Davidson and was engaged at battle at Beatty's Ford on Catawba River, where our forces were trying to prevent the British, under Cornwallis, from crossing. At this battle Col. Davidson was killed and we were defeated and retreated to widow Tarrances, where we were attacked next morning in her lane and again defeated. Returned to Wilkes C. H. and joined the militia under Col. Cleveland and served with him until he left the service to go to Legislature, when deponent was placed under command of Col. Hearne and was with him at the Battle of Guilford, March 1781, at which time was placed among the riflemen under Col. Campbell—was wounded in this battle and returned home until wound was healed and re-entered army in October, 1781, at Wilks C. H., under Capt. Key, Col. Hearne and Gen. McDowell. Marched to Pleasant Gardens on Catawba River, and from thence to Cherokee County against the Indians, and was present at the burning of Wataga Cowl(sic) Sugar and Burning Towns and several Indian villages. Served until December, when was discharged at Wilkes C. H. by Col. Cleveland. Served more than 3 years as a private soldier.

Born 1756 in Culpepper County, Va. Record in possession of Peter Stonecypher in Wilkes County, N. C. Lived in Wilkes County until 1784 when he removed to Franklin County, Ga., where he has since remained. Received discharge from Captain Keys, De Moss, Sloan, Jackson, Allen, Lenoir, Rutledge, Barton, Henderson (who afterwards became a tory), Shepherd and Robert Cleveland. Never received one cent of pay other than the Liberties of his Country.

Testified to by Rev. Dozier Thornton, Moses Guest and Wm. Glover.

Jesse Smith.

Resident of Capt. Edwards' District, age 67. Drafted in militia in Camden District, S. C., under Capt. John Steel, in May or June, 1780. Joined Gen. Sumter at Chester, S. C., and was in regiment commanded by Col. Bratlow—was in an engagement at Henderson's Ford on Catawba River, August 18th, 1780, where we were defeated. Received, after this 3 months tour a discharge from Capt. Steel. In May 1781 while in service was in defeat at Camden, and was marched to Rocky Mount and back to Camden where we joined the Regulars under Gen. Greene and

was marched to Ninety-Six and was ordered with Lacy's
command at Orangeburg during battle of Ninety-Six.
Again joined Gen. Greene and was marched to Eutaw
Springs in which battle Maj. O'Neal was killed. After
this tour of 3 months was discharged by Capt. Steel, and
in June, 1782, volunteered for 7 months at Camden under
Capt. Cook and Col.Taylor and was marched from Orangeburg to Four Holes, thence to Bacon's Bridge and
Monk's Corner where was discharged by Capt. Gordon.
Capt. Cook having become ill, and returned home. Had
no fighting in last tour except we took one Col. Moore and
60 or 70 tories; hung him and 4 of his men at Orangeburg.

Was born in Montgomery County, N. C., April 16th,
1765. Called into service in Chester District, S. C., where
was then living. Since the war have lived 3 years in Laurens District, S. C., from there back to neighborhood of
birth, thence to Franklin County, Ga., his present home.

Testified to by Rev. John Sandige, John Stonecypher,
and John Cleveland.

Warren Stow.

Resident of Capt. Catlett's District. Entered Connecti-
cut State Troops in the town of Sheffield under Capt.
Noah Phelps, about one year after commencement of war.
Marched to Hartford and put aboard ship to New York,
from there marched to White Plains, West Chester and
Fish Kilns, and from there crossed Hudson River and
joined Gen. Washington at Morristown, N. J. Wintered
there and was discharged after service of 12 months, by
Capt. Phelps. Returned to Suffolk and enlisted there under Capt. Remington; marched to Rhode Island and was
stationed in an old field besieging a seaport town. After
3 months service was discharged by Capt. Remington.
Returned to Suffolk and enlisted under Sergt. White,
marched to Albany, N. Y., and placed as guard—discharged after 3 months service. Returned to Suffolk and re-

moved to New Mulberry, possibly in New Hampshire, where volunteered and was placed as guard in a stockade block house near Bennington, against Indian attack. Was discharged after 3 months and returned to New Mulberry, from thence to Sheffield, over the line into Massachusetts, and enlisted under Capt. Flowers (thinks it was James Flowers), in the Regular Continental Army for the remainder of the war. Marched to Peekskill, N. Y., and was under command of Col. Sumter and Gen. Washington. Was detached from the army to join Gen. Greene in the South and was marched to near the High Hill of Santee in S. C., where lay sometime at Pond's Ford in tents. Marched to Eutaw Springs where we had battle. Returned to Pond Ponds (Pon Pon?) where received discharge at close of war. Was under command of Col. Dixon, and served about 6 years.

Born in Sheffield, Conn., year not known, but record possibly in possession of Mr. Hitchcock, Parish Register of Suffield(sic). After the war settled in Wake County, N. C., and from there to Elbert County, Ga., but for the last 20 years in Franklin County, Ga., his present home.

Endorsed by Rev. David Garrison and Samuel Garrison.

Gabriel Smith.

Resident of Capt. Edwards' District, age 67. Entered militia in Montgomery County, N. C., August 1780, under Capt. Thomas Childs and marched to join Gen. Gates at Camden, but did not reach there before the battle—retreated and was discharged for furlough. In 7 days returned and was marched to Mars' (?) Ferry where we had a skirmish in which Capt. Childs was wounded through the arm. We were then placed under Capt. Samuel Pond and marched to Drowning Creek, Bettises' Bridge, where we were defeated in a skirmish and returned home. After a few days being reinforced returned to the attack and was there taken prisoner by tories in fall of 1781, and kept about 3 weeks and made escape. During these campaigns was under command of Adjutant David Jameson and Col. Thomas Wade. After 3 weeks volunteered in Montgomery County under Capt. Joseph Paison, Maj. James Crump and Col. Thomas Childs (promoted). Marched after the tories into Randolph County but had no battles of note—took some prisoners. Continued to serve until Cornwallis was taken at York, October, 1781, and until peace was declared—altogether about 18 months. Served with Theophilus Taylor of Habersham County, Ga., a Revolutionary soldier.

Born in Montgomery County, N. C., December 12, 1764. Removed to Wilkes County, Ga., 1784, and to Franklin County, Ga., in 1802, where have since lived.

Endorsed by Rev. Mathew W. Vandivere, Tryon Patterson and Theophilus Taylor.

William Smith.

Resident of Capt. Edwards District, age 69. Entered service in South Carolina militia in Ninety-Six District November, 1780, as a substitute for William Flanigan, under Capt. Nathaniel Alston and marched into the Indian Lands and placed at Drury Lews Station where remained the 3 months and was discharged by Capt. Samuel Walker at Ninety-Six for 6 months tour and marched to the tories near Orangeburg under Maj. Dillard and Col. Benj. Kilgore and Col. O'Neal. From there to Bush River and to Savannah River above Augusta, pulling down tories' houses, etc., until the 6 months was out, when was discharged by Capt. Walker and returned home. Served 12 months. Has a sister in Jackson County by name of Polly Patterson, a widow, who knows of service.

Born in Moore County, N. C., February 26, 1763. After the war lived in Moore and Montgomery counties and from there to Elbert County, Ga., but has lived in Franklin County, Ga., for the past 42 years. Received a certifi-

cate of land bounty in South Carolina which was sold to
Capt. Raney for 20 lbs.

Certified by John Williams, who as a young boy saw
deponent go out to service; also endorsed by Rev. Mathew
W. Vandiver and Jesse Smith.

John Tate.

Resident of Capt. Andrew's District, age 74. Entered
United States Service in militia of Pennsylvania the 12th
or 13th of December, 1776, as a volunteer under Capt.
Robert Culberson, Maj. Davis, at Shippensburg, Cumberland County. Marched to Philadelphia and to Bordentown, N. J., where had a skirmish at Monmouth with
Tories and returned with Prisoners to Bordentown. From
there marched to Trenton and thence to Heights of Middleton where in March, 1777, was discharged at Philadelphia by Capt. Culberson. Was hired by Lt. Blythe to
serve 2 months to fill out a draft at Shippensburg under
command of Capt. Ersky and Col. Dunlap at Carlisle—
from there to Lancaster and joined Regiment in Regular
army. We reached Brandywine 2 nights before the battle
and was under command of Brig. Gen. Potter, Genls.
Wayne, Greene, Sullivan, Sterling and Armstrong. Gen.
Washington was there also and Brig. Erwin. Fought in
this battle and retreated to Chester, Philadelphia up the
Lancaster Road and had a skirmish near 28 mile store—
marched to Warren Hill Tavern—to Bull Tavern—to
Gordon's Ford on Schuylkill River. Was there taken
sick but had a skirmish and was marched to the line of
the regular army below Pottsgrow and placed on an out
guard without food for 3 days—recalled for rations but
was not sent with the army to the Battle of Germantown.
Afterwards marched to Chester, thence to a tavern called
Fox Chase where received discharge after 2 months tour.
Entered the Light Horse at Shippensburg, July or August, 1781, under Capt. Johnson, a militia major. Marched to Philadelphia thence to Newtown, Bucks County, and

was there discharged by Gen. Lacy(?), under whom this tour was made. Served 7 months.

Born in Ireland, 1758, and came to America 1763, and was living in Shippensburg when entered service. Since the war lived in Baltimore 9 months and drove wagon to Pittsburg. From there removed to Morgan's District, Burke County, N. C., and from there in 1796 to his present residence.

Endorsed by Rev. S. Hymer and James Morris. Stephen Grove of Madison, Ga., had known of part of above service, but was now so infirm that his memory has almost failed.

William Thomas.

Resident of Capt. Davis' District, age about 69 years. Entered service in the militia of North Carolina at Guilford C. H., as a volunteer under Capt. John Leek and Col. James Martin. Marched to Cross Creek where defeated the Scotch and returned to Guilford and was marched after the tories to Little River, but they had dispersed and we were discharged after a tour of 3 months. In August, 1778, volunteered under Capt. John Leek, Cols. Paisley and Martin. Marched to near head of Catawba, waited reinforcements and proceeded to Cherokee Nation, where helped burn towns, cutting down corn, etc. Served 3 months tour. Again entered at Guilford into the Continental Army for 9 months about, and was marched by Capt. Leek to Purysburg, and there put under Lt. Lewis, Capt. Ralph Chapman and Col. Lytle, Continental officers, wintered there and in the spring marched to near Augusta, Ga., where deponent was taken ill and sent to hospital. Again volunteered under Capt. Richard Varium at Guilford in February or March, 1781, and served about 10 weeks. In October, 1781, was ordered out after Col. Fannin and other tories to Deep River and served 3 months tour. About 21 mos. regular service besides considerable irregular service. Sometimes on horse back and other

times on foot. Has grant of land for Continental service.
His first 3 months service was substitute for his brother.

Born in Culpepper County, Va., January 20, 1763. From
Guilford County, N. C., removed to present residence in
Franklin County, Georgia.

Endorsed by Rev. Henry David, Gabriel Martin and
Jesse Thomas, brother of deponent.

James Wilson.

Resident of Capt. Watson's District, age about 73. Entered militia of South Carolina at York while on a visit
there about March, 1780, as a volunteer under Capt. Mc-
Kensie, to go after the Tories near Turkey Creek, but on
reaching there found that they had been defeated, so returned to York and was sent out as a spy under command
of Capt. McCool, under Gen. Sumter. Went down towards
Savannah to —— company of Tories under Turnbull, but
they had been dispersed so returned to Sumter's Army
and marched to Catawba River to guard fords and fer-
ries. Was stationed under Capt. McCool at the old Nation Ford and was then marched towards Hanging Rock
where we found the British and Tories too strong for us
so retreated to the Fords and ordered to guard Col. Hills
Iron Works in York County. After this served as scout,
was discharged and returned home to Orange County, N.
C. This service covered 6 or 7 months. Volunteered in
Orange County as a minute man in Capt. Wilson's Company of Horse in October or November, 1780, and did
scout service and pilot to Maj. Reed's Horse Co., to Buffington's Iron Works and also acted as pilot to other
Companies and Detachments until March, 1781, when he
had leave of absence to remove his mother. This tour was
3 or 6 months—more than one year as horseman, finding
his own horse. William Hall, of Alabama, could attest
his services.

Born in Pennsylvania July 12, 1758, and removed to
North Carolina at 6 years of age. Lived in Orange Coun-

ty, N. C., but was on a visit to York, S. C., when enlisted. After the war lived in York County, N. C., until about 20 years since when removed to his present home.
Attested by Rev. Nelson Osborn and Richard Bond.

Elisha Wilkinson.

Resident of Capt. Newell's District. Entered Militia in Virginia at Sussex C. H., under command of Capt. Green Hill, Lt. John Foreman, Ensign John Tyas, Maj. Jarrold, Col. Joseph Jones and Gen. Lawson in November 1780. Marched to Cabbin Point, drew arms and was marched to Bobbs Old Field, 7 miles from Hampton Road. From there to Petersburg where was discharged after 6 weeks and 3 days service—was made Corporal after 3 days service. Re-entered service January 4, 1881, as substitute for Simon Shell of Brunswick County, Va., and marched to Petersburg and to Coffins Point to Babbs Old Field under command of Col. Meriwether, Maj. Nathaniel Lucas, Capt. Edmun Wilkins, Lt. Joel Wilkinson, Ensign Thomas Cook, and served until April 15, 1781, as 2nd Sergeant and was discharged after service of 3 months and 11 days. Entered army again July 14, 1781, at Sussex C. H., under command of Col. Boyd Blount, Maj. William Boggs, Capt. Sterling Howell, Lt. Gardner Howell, Ensign William Mogit. Marched to Baker's Old Field and put in Light Horse Co., under Capt. James Vaughan. Marched to Hall's Mills thence to Portsmouth where remained until August 28, 1781, when was sent to Sussex by Col. Benj. Blount with an express to Col. David Mason. Rejoined the army at Jamestown and was here discharged. All service being about 6 months and 14 days.

Born in Sussex County, Virginia, in 1763, and lived there until 1789, when removed to Dinwiddie and lived there 5 years and removed to Mechlinburg County, Va., where remained until 1807, when came to Franklin County, Ga., present residence.

Endorsed by Rev. Mathew W. Vandivere, L. D. Holsonbake and Thomas Farmer.

The following Declarations of Revolutionary soldiers
were found in Will Book, 1814-1829.
Inferior Court, January 20, 1823.

Warren Stoe, age 68, appears to obtain the provision
made by acts of Congress, March 18, 1818, and May 1820.

Enlisted for 12 months in the first 12 Months Men that
were raised after the first 8 months in the state of Con-
necticut in the Company commanded by Capt. Phillips,
1st Regiment, in the line of the state of Connecticutt, in
the old Continental Establishment; served the entire enlistment, was duly discharged. In 1776 or 1777, enlisted
in Conn., Capt. Flowers Co., Col. — — Regt., who left it,
and it was then commanded by Maj. Sumner, in which he
continued to serve until the close of the war—in all about
5 years, was discharged in New York state, not far from
New York City. Was in the battles of White Plains,
and Eutaw Springs; that he has no other proof of service,
other than his oath; that he has not disposed of any property, with the intent to diminish it so as to take advant-
age of the Acts of Congress aforesaid; that all his property consists of

14 head of hogs	$14.00
1 axe, 3 hoes, 1 mattock	3.00
1 shovel plow, 1 gofer	1.00
	$18.00
Indebted to William Wiley......	$45.00
Indebted to Harris Toney	97.00
Indebted to Thomas Davis	18.00
Indebted to William Bush	4.00
	$164.00

That he is a farmer, unable to do much work; has seven
in family, his wife, age 50, unhealthy and unable to la-

bor, son Hudson 18 years, healthy; daughter Martha 14 years has a phthisic affection which renders her unhealthy; son William, 12 years, healthy; daughter Nancy 8 years old, son Presley, 6 years old, both healthy.

Sworn to and subscribed on the 20th Jan. 1823.

Warren Stoe.

Test, Frederick Beall, C. C. O.

———

Inferior Court, January 20th, 1824. (Original claim.)

Personally appeared Edy Holbrooks, a resident of Franklin County, age 62 years, makes the following oath in order to obtain provision made by act of Congress March 18, 1818, May 1, 1820:

Enlisted October 10, 1780, in Virginia, in the company commanded by Kirkpatrick in the old Continental Establishment; continued to serve till the end of the war when was discharged at the Ponty Lock in the state of Virginia; was in the battle of Camden, but has no proof of his service except his own oath and the oath of Jesse Holbrooks. In pursuance of the Act of May 1, 1820, he swears that he was a resident citizen of the United States on the 18th of March, 1818, and that he has not since, by gift or sale disposed of his property thereby to diminish it so as to come within the provision of the Act of Congress to provide for certain persons engaged in the land and naval forces of the U. S. in the Revolutionary War, passed on March 18, 1818, nor has any person in trust for me any property, etc., than that contained hereunto annexed by me.

Edy Holbrooks.

To-wit:

120 acres of land	$120.00
1 colt	10.00
8 head of cattle	64.00
1 sow and 12 shoats..........	17.00
3 sheep	6.00
2 pots, 1 oven, 2 skillets	7.00
2 plows and 3 hoes	8.00
2 axes, 2 augurs, drawknife, etc.	4.50
1 rifle gun	12.00

$248.50

By occupation a farmer, unable to work because of age. Family consists of wife upwards of 50 years, unable to work; two daughters, one 20, the other 12, both able to work.

Sworn to January 20th, 1824, before:

Asa Allen, J. I. C.

Garrett L. Sandridge, J. I. C.

James Ramsey, J. I. C.

James Mitchell.

Georgia, Franklin Co.:

Personally appeared in open court Jesse Holbrooks, and being sworn, saith that the Revolutionary Service and claim are correctly stated thereon, and were performed by him. Sworn to and subscribed this 20th, day of Jan. 1824.

Jesse Holbrooks.

Peter Grover.

On the 5th day of March, 1827, personally appeared before the judges of the Inferior Court, Peter Grover, a resident of said county of Franklin, aged about 60 years, who being duly sworn, made the following declaration to obtain provision made by the acts of Congress of the 18th of March, 1818, and of May 1820:

That he enlisted for 12 months, the day and year not remembered, in the state of North Carolina, Continental Establishment and served the full enlistment of 12 months, when he was discharged in Orange County, N. C. That he hereby relinquishes every claim to a pension except the present, and that his name is not on the roll of any other state except North Carolina. That the following reasons are why he has not applied for pension earlier; he has heretofore been able to work and support himself, but lately he has become very infirm and weak, and is unable to support himself; therefore wishes to avail himself of the Act of Congress, May, 1820. He solemnly swears he was a resident citizen of the United States on March 18th, 1818, and that he has not since by gift or sale or in any manner disposed of property so as to diminish it to bring himself within the provision of said act to provide for certain persons engaged in the Land and Naval service of the U. S. in the Revolutionary War, passed 18th of March, 1818, and that he has not, nor has any person in trust for him any property or securities, contracts or debts due him, nor has he any income other than that is contained in the skedule here annexed and by him subscribed, and that since March 18th, 1818, has there been any changes whatever in his property.

Sworn to and declared on 5th day of March, 1827, in open Court.

Skedule of Property:

50 acres of land, very poor......$20.00
1 spider and frying pan........ 2.00
1-2 doz. plates, in use 13 years.. 2.00
An old axe .... .50

$24.50

The declarant is a farmer, and is unable from bodily infirmity to pursue that business. Has but one child, a

female who resides with him, about 22 years old, who is
able to work and does support this deponent.

his
Peter x Grover.
mark

Witness, Thomas King, Clerk.
Pension Records, found in box of loose papers.

William Ray.

Pensioned by the War Office January 29, 1825—pension
No. 19,360. Transfer is made to William Allen, in letter
signed by I. L. Edwards from War Dept., Pension Office.

J. C. Calhoun, Secretary of War.

William York.

Pension No. 19,185. Appoints F. W. Heinemann his
attorney to receive pay in Savannah, Ga.

Edy Holbrook.

Pensioned May 2, 1828. Appoints James M. Wayne his
attorney. Was a private in Capt. Kirkpatrick's Co., Col.
Hawes' Regt. Had lived in Franklin Co. 32 years, and
previously to that resided in Spartanburg District, S. C.,
and Wilkes County, North Carolina, and Goochland
County, Va.

Signed by   James Barbour, Secretary of War.

Harry Terrell.

(Found in a book of Deeds and Administration—not
numbered.)

Our father, Harry Terrell, formerly of Bedford County,
Va., but lately of Pendleton District, S. C., died in the
late Revolutionary War under military service in Virginia Continental Line both in the grade of Captain and Major, for which services it appears the said Harry was entitled to lands according to his grades, in conformity to
the provisions made by the state of Virginia for her offi-

cers and soldiers, in lands for that purpose reserved.
Now know you that we, George W. Terrell, lately of
Pendleton District, in State of South Carolina, David Mo-
seley, who intermarried with Elizabeth A. Terrell of the
said District, and Wm. H. Terrell, of Chuttuckmuck, be-
ing the only legal heirs and representatives of the said
Harry, do by these presents appoint John D. Terrell, of
Franklin County, who is the fourth legal heir and repre-
sentative, our lawful attorney and solicitor in fact, to
secure land, etc. Witnessed by:
Charles Ward, Benjamin Cleveland, James Blair.
March 3, 1813.

BOUNTY GRANTS FOR REVOLUTIONARY
SERVICES.
ORIGINALS FOUND IN BOX OF LOOSE PAPERS.

Unless otherwise stated the grants are for 187 1-2 acres.
1784, May 26—To David Stone—renewed in the name
of Walker Richardson. (John Habersham.)
1784, May 26—To James Flynn—renewed in the name
of Walker Richardson.
1784, May 26—To Joseph Trap—transferred to Bedford Beaver.
William Entrecan—transferred to John Colten. Gr. in
Washington Co.
Jesse Garden or Gordon, grant in Washington Co.
Alexander Anderson—transferred to George Barber.
Bounties of Jonathan Jamison and Robert Flowers;
warrant to Jas. Matterson.
1786—800 acres to Thos. Wooten, renewed to Wilie
Pope, Jan. 3rd.
1784—Sept. 14—John Yarbroth—signed by J. Houston.
1784—Jan. 17—Peter Inlow. Israel Smith.
1785—Jan. 18—Moses Collins—Signed by S. Elbert.
Certificate of Col. Elijah Clark that Thomas Rennals
"never refused going on duty from the Reduction of Au-

gusta to total expulsion of the British from this State,''
etc:, and is entitled to bounty, etc.

Ditto—for Richard Rennals.

1796, Oct. 26—William Hay transferred his bounty to
George McFall.

William Daniel transferred his bounty to Walker Richardson.

Arnold Atkins transferred his bounty to Absalom Jackson and Jos. Ryan.

1784—Apr. 20—William Daniel transferred his bounty
to John Farler Thompson, 250 acres.

1784—Sept. 27—Benjamin Chisholm transferred his
bounty to 460 acres.

1784—Feb. 20—Richard Berry—certificate of duty—
signed by Elijah Clark.

Ditto to Wilden Owsley, Lymon Keeth, Isam (or Isaac)
Justice and William Gente.

1785—Feb. 14—Bounty to Abraham Wood and Edward
Barber—signed S. Elbert.

1785—Feb. 23, bounty to Daniel Bankston, trans. to
Zach Cox, signed S. Elbert.

1784—May 14, Isham Young 575 acres transferred to
Walker Richardson.

John Crittenden, renewed in Basil Lamars name.

Levi Marshall, renewed in Thomas Connells name.

William Terrells bounty from David Thurman bounty, endorsed; Thomas Shannon and David Thurman—
500 acres in name of Richard Hartfield; the rest in name
of Thomas Wooten.

Israel Smith to James McCutchen(?).

William Wallice trans. to William Moses.

1784—May 14—Henry Hellenberger 230 acres for de-
serting from the enemy. J. Habersham.

1784—May 17—Bounties to: Edward Williams, Lemuel Keith, Jr., Darby Ragans, Jesse Hunter, Thomas Sullivan, Edward Gortney Haile, signed John Habersham.

1784—July 16—John Boyd.

1785—June 5,—1150 Bounty Reserve to Francis Woodward on certificate of Stephen Williamson, Robert Walker, John Walker, Elias Davis and James Adams.

1785—Dec. 15—Thomas Wooten, old warrant of Thomas Washington, Peter Allen, Richard Call, and "8 others" to Micajah Williamson.

To Grant Taylor, old warrants of William Philips, George Clough, Michael Hawse, John Crawford, Joseph Cook. Confirmed July 2, 1787.

1785—Oct. 3—2300 acres on bounty certificate of Abraham Munford and "9 others."

1784—May 17—Daniel Butler 275 acres.

1785—May 15—Old warrant of John Cox to James Freeman.

1785—Oct. 3—Reserve 3450 acres to Richard Call on bounties of John Cobb, H. Marbury, Abraham Mixon, William Moore and William Nicholson.

1786—Aug. 7—Edward Stephens 460 acres in Green Co., in lieu of old warrant.

Jan. 6, 1791—John P. Waggoner 1000 acres. An old warrant made out to John Gorham.

**—no date. Renewed in name of Richard Hartfield 500 acres; Thomas Wooten 500 a. and 650 a. old warrant of Andrew Frazer and David Shannon Bounty Reserve in Thomas Wooten's name. Thomas Shannon's name Interlined.

1785—Oct. 3—Bounty certificate of Daby (sic) Henderson and "8 others" and Peter Major and "9 others," to H. Marbury.

. 1790—Aug. 2.—Grant Taylor 920 acres to John Smith —renewed for A. Powell.

1785—April 6.—John Talbot 230 acres Washington County, assine of Litt. Mosby, who was asine of Jas. Stephens, and of Thomas Deal and William Harrass.

1791—Nov. 28—Thomas Lamar 1000 acres signed by Rene Fitzpatrick, which warrant with like number of acres of William Morgan and Hezekiah Johnson were renewed by Capt. S. Weatherby, Green Co.

1785—May 5—Bounties of Joseph Braswell, Henry Beall, Penman Floyd and Henry Davis, Minute Men, trans. to Peter Carnes, Esqr.

1785—Feb. 14.—Certificates to Alex. McQueen, Jesse Howard, Peter Lockhart, Miles Platen, Adam Rozer, Peter Turner, John Bradshaw, Balie Grimes, Abraham Grimes, John Grimes, Abraham Canady, William Brakens, John Brewer, Silas Beard. By E. Clark as having served in Minute Batt.

1785—June 2—Certificate of Capt. E. Clark to John Smith for service in Capt. Richard's Co.

Minute Men's Bounty, certified by S. Elbert and Col. E. Clark, Act of March 3, 1777.

1785—March 22.—Certificates of John Chissor, Daniel Jackson, John Wickham, "citizens and refugees," trans. to John Tolson Lowe.

1785—March 22—The following certificates were transferred to Edward Telfair, Esqr.: Hugh McDonald, Amos Rozer, James Simmons, William Evins, Allen Braswell, James Braswell, William Gay, Thomas Hawkins.

1785—March 22.—The following certificates were transferred to James Jones: Bailey Gains (Grimes?), Elijah Dumass, William Brake.

1785—Feb. 22.—Henry Howard trans. to Alethia Anderson Jones, who petitions land court for warrants on bounties of William Moore and Benjamin Nicholson.

James Jones petitions for warrants on bounties of Andrew McGreen, Baily Gains, John Thegott and William Brakes, each 575 acres and Elijah Dumass 287 1-2.

1785—March 10—To the heirs of Devereaux Jarratt, deceased.

575 acres to the following: Thomas Williams, Henry Anderson, John Butler, Richard Leavens, William Young, and Peter Roquemore.

287 1-2 acres to: John Philips, Henry Howard, James Dunman (500), Robert Higgins, David Rowling, James Carter, George Cloudas, James Carters Heirs (to Thomas C.), Henry Nail, John Marshall, John Scott, Sr., Jacob Curry, John Rowling, Peter Bradshaw, Richard Cowlsey, Conrod Ellrod, Richard Tate, James Clark, Henry Green, Reubin Jackson, Moses Bruer, Darby Rozer, Harris Roberts, Jeremiah Polhill, Peter Hill, Jesse Cooper, John Green, John Beall, George Beall, Joshua Gillison, Peter Gillison, Sampson Porter (?), David Langston, Hugh Paskins, Demcy Pollard, Ralph Vann, Robert Cary, Peter Anderson.

1785—July 16—Certificate of Col. John Stewart, to following as Minute Men: John Butler, Hugh Anderson, John Studstill, Jonathan Reese, Reubin Baine, John Ryly, David Cooper, Peter Newel (or Nevil), Peter Price, Cooper Welborn, Richard Simmons, Samuel (?) Simmons, Jesse Gordon, Joshua Powell, John Scott, Edward Wardman, Isaac Wardman, George Milder, Hugh Wardman, Benjamin Pinkins, David Robinson, Noel Jones, Peter P. Ward.

Col. E. Clark certificate to Minute Men: Samuel Miller, Thomas Holland, John Denthan, Nicholas Gunnels, Lawrence Fulsome, Philip Whitton, Thomas Stockwell.

1785—Feb.—S. Elberts minute bounty to heirs of James Jones, and Dancy Summers. March, 1785.

1785—Feb. 4.—Elijah Clarks certificate for service in Minute Batt.: Isaac Johnston, Levy Johnston, David Adams, Hugh Adams. "For duty performed" to Lymon Keeth.

1785—Jan. 3—Same to Cezer Hawkins.

No date. The following Minute Bounties were transferred to Horatio Marbury: James Brown, Hugh Ward, May 6, 1785.

James Russells bounty was transferred to David Young, June 7, 1785.

Leonard Marbury asks warrants on enclosed certificates: John Rowley, Thomas Stockwell, John Dentham, Richard Cawley, Thomas Holland, Arch. Nicholson, Peter Bradshaw, Conrod Ellrod, Nich. Gunnels, Philip Whitton, Lawrence Fulsom.

April, 1785—Certificate of service signed by Elijah Clark, to men of Minute Battalion: Peter Bradshaw, Arch. Mickson, Nich. Gunnels, John Wooten, Zach. Henderson, George Runnalds, Andrew McGruen, John Thegott, William Russell, James Hill, Amos Razon, James Anderson, Richard Cawley, John Soulter, William Cucksey, Wm. Odior (Osier), Jacob Wardman, George Miller, Benjamin Perkins, John Bratcher, Hugh Woods, John Woods, Edward Williams, Bailey Gains, Sabry Dinkins, David Burks, Catlatt Cawley, Anthony Cooper, William Rogers, Philip Steed, Philip Rasberry, John Cawley.

Feb. 14, 1785—Certificate of same to: John Whitten, Peter Pittiman, or Tilliman, John Davis, Alex. Davis, John Hawkins, Peter Lucas, Thomas Williams, John Holland, Peter Holland, Peter Stockwell, John Love, Ambrose Gaines, Peter Hath(?), Jesse Taylor, Abraham Turner, Joshua Edmunds, Elisha Peters.

May 17, 1785—Certificates issued by John Habersham: Lewis Powell, Stephen Pennington, David Rice, Elisha Burress, John Young, Sr., and Jr., Philip Sommerhill, John Ferguson, Augustin Harris, John Summers, Edward Simol, James French, James Loyd, Christopher Woods, John Smith, Isaac Averit (2), David Thurman, John Thurman, John Beard, Cuthbert Hudson.

Feb. 14, 1785—To Robert Simol—Signed S. Elbert.

July 21, 1784—To Martin Shirley—signed J. Houston.

July 19, 1784—To John Duffy—Signed J. Houston.

May 17, 1784—To Sherwood Beckham—Signed J. Houston.

June 19, 1784—To Thomas McKenny—Signed J. Houston.

Sep. 27, 1784—To Edmund Whatley—Signed J. Houston.

July 16, 1784—To Robert Owsley—Signed J. Houston.

May 17, 1784—To John Collins—Signed J. Houston.

Oct. 1, 1784—To Felix Ragan—Signed J. Houston.

Oct. 11, 1784—To Ayers Gorley—Signed J. Houston.

Oct. 26, 1784—To Jacob Fortene—Signed J. Habersham.

June 18, 1784—To Brantley Moseley—Signed J. Habersham.

Dec. 8, 1784—To Joshua Woods, John Stedome, Joseph Wells, Nathaniel Williams, Robert Butler, Henry Hartley, James Morris, William Kemble, John Jackson, Benj. Kemple, John Ramsay, Jr., Jacob Watson (By J. Houston.)

Feb. 14, 1785—To Jonathan Webster, John Webster, Samuel Braswell, William Yarbrough, James Cunningham. (S. Elbert).

Aug. 13, 1785—John Mobley—certificate of Walker Richardson.

Sep. 13, 1785—James Bryant—certificate of J. Houston.

Nov. 7, 1785—Warrant of 6,305 acres to Robert Middleton on bounties of James Allen and 21 others as per cert. of Elijah Clark to Richard Call.

Ditto of 7.187 1-2 acres bounties of John Jones and 25 others. Renewed by Ambrose Gordon; also 5.750 acres bounties of John Young, cert. of Col. John Stewart, to Richard Call.

March 16, 1785—Bounty and cert. of service from E. Clark to Isaac Patterson, John Gaster, Arch. Grigsberry.

9,000 acres in grants of 1,000 acres each, purporting to be in lieu of a part of John Marcus' Reserve Bounty, are laid out to Sampson Dugger, by the following signers: Edward Hunter, Samuel Beckham, B. Tennille. November 7, 1791.

Aug. 1, 1791—To Samuel Jack, 1,000 acres, renewed to Solomon Slatter.

Aug. 1, 1791—To Evan Harvey, 1,000 acres, renewed to Septimus Weatherby.

Nov. 7, 1791—To Robert Middleton 1,000 in lieu of old Warrants in part for James Ellis on Reserve, renewed in name of William Dozier, who by cert. of Geo. Weatherby, "bears the character of an honest man and good citizen."

Nov. 17, 1791—Reserve renewed by Harris Bryan of 1,000 acres. Ditto by John Myrick, Jr., William Dozier, Harriss Bryan.

Tracts laid off to Sampson Dugger, Nov. 7, 1791, were renewed by Daniel McCowen, George Terry, Solomon Slatters, George Weatherby, Hezekiah Johnstone, Alexander Flewellen, Septimus Weatherby, John Myrick, Sr.

At same time and place to Sampson Dugger in tracts of 1,000 acres each, purporting to be in lieu of part of bounty reserve to Andrew Frazer—7 warrants; renewed in the name of Dr. Septimus Weatherby, Harris Ryan, Capt. George Weatherby, James and Thomas Lamar. Reference is made to an "old warrant" of 3,000 acres in name of Andrew Frazer, dated Nov. 7, 1796, Bounty for Reserve, which same is disposed to Capt. George Weatherby.

Nov. 21, 1791—To Wm. Green, Surveyor for Green County, to lay off 1,000 acres on Reserve to Daniel Smith. Signed Rene Fitzpatrick.

The same to John Adkinson.

Nov. 1792—The same to Henry Kass, old bounty for Cont. soldier and seaman, March 9, 1786.

Aug. 7, 1786—The same to John Farmer, 460 acres (Thomas Harris, Adj.)

Dec. 4, 1786—The same to Wm. Phillips, 862 1-2 acres and to Benajah Smith 1150 acres in lieu of 3 reserve bounties in name of Robert Flournoy, and 1 in name of Thomas Booker.

Jan. 1, 1787. Signed Wm. Cochran, Adj. Test. by Henry Graybill, clerk Green Co.

May 5, 1785—To grants to Samuel Ward, 230 acres in Franklin County, signed by Walker Richardson; and 287 1-2 in Washington County, May 17, 1784, signed by J. Habersham.

June 7, 1785—To John Freeman 287 1-2 acres, and 690 acres on bounties of Wm. Anderson, Wm. Maxwell, Robert Martin.

Jan. 18, 1785—Wm. Giddens(?), 287 1-2, signed S. Elbert.

Wm. Gibbons, Jr., warrant for Cezer Hawkins' bounty as minute man, and of Darby Roser, John Butler, and Morris Bruer, "citizens."

June 18, 1785—Bounty warrants of Yarbrough and Brazel belong to Thomas Payne.

July 5, 1790—5360 acres reserve lands to Capt. Thomas Porter, sign. John Smith, C. F. C.

May 17, 1784—J. Habersham's certif. to John Nelson, Isaac Vansant, Thomas Smith, Jacob Gossett. The last named trans. to Peter Stubblefield.

July 20, 1784—J. Houston's certif. to Wm. Bryant, and John Appling, July 23.

Dec. 20, 1784—Joseph Anderson, "Refugee to N. C." entitled to Bounty. E. Clark, certif.

The above sold to Frederick Sims, who also has bounty.

———

Certificates of Litt. Mosby, Capt. and P. M. 2nd Ga. Batt.

Feb. 9, 1784—John Stephens and William Davison, 3 years service in 2nd Ga. Batt.

May 4, 1785—Joseph McLain, 3 years service in 2nd Ga. Batt.

May 8, 1785—Thomas Davison, 3 years service in 2nd Ga. Batt.

May 14, 1785—Edmund Anderson, 3 years service in 2nd Ga. Batt.

Jan. 9, 1785—William Allen, 230 acres trans. to Danl. Young. "Served his time faithfully."

Third Regiment Continental Troops. Captains Fred. Tennille and Raleigh Dourman.

Dec. 17, 1784—William Thompson, Jr., "good and faithful soldier, entitled to every emolument," etc. Trans. the above to William Thompson, Sr. Marked Virginia at the top. Wit: by Hartwell Hobbs, Samuel Wainwright.

3rd. Georgia Battalion—Samuel Scott, Captain.

Dec. 10, 1784—William Anderson—served 3 years enlistment.

Dec. 10, 1784—Stephen Johnson and Simon Jackson—Ditto.

4th Regiment of Horse, Leonard Marbury Lt. Col. Com. of the Cont. Regt. of Light Horse for State of Georgia.

Jeremiah Cloud, Menoah Cloud, and John Cloud—soldiers' discharge. Nov. 19, 1777. On back is written Ezekiel Cloud's warrant to be cancelled Down to Meeting at Coleman. 1806.

April 30, 1785—Cont. Light Dragoons; William Paxton, sergeant—on his certificate is written: Mary Hooper, who was the widow of Wm. Paxton, deceased. Prays that the warrant may be issued to her orphan son Thomas Paxton.

Service and discharge to John Troy, James Johns, William Jenkins, Isaac Jackson, William Baldwin, William Jeans, Aaron Owens, John Sanders, John Dobey, William Dobey, Abel Jones.

The following grants were for Minute Men, and were attested by Horatio Marbury, and transferred to Leonard Marbury.

John Jackson, John Butler, John Wilkinson, Daniel Marcus, Francis Heath, John Harvey, William Sinquefield, John Turner, Reuben Jackson, Elias Spikes, James Ratliff, William Arraday(?), Solomon Turner.

Minute bounty of Edward Williams and John Studstall to Horatio Marbury. To John Butler, 2nd Cont. Batt.—certif. of Col. Bush and Isaac Jackson.

May 1, 1785—"Absalom Roberts in Regt. under my command," etc. (Leonard Marbury.) The following served 3 years in Cont. Line under L. Marbury: John Guy, William Gay, John Watts, Dennis Gay, John Dennison, John Hartford, Walter Harrison, John Horner, Moses Ware, James Ware, James Parker, John Parker, Peter Wise, Joseph Spikes, William Wallace, Thomas Walker, Joseph Walker, John Hearn. All received discharges. David Butler in same regiment.

Aug. 31, 1785. Certificates of L. Marbury that Stephen Moore was a sergeant in his regiment, and lost his life in service of his country. His widow, Mary Moore, asks for his bounty, which is transferred to Capt. H. Marbury.

Continental Bounties.

To Joseph Martin, 1897 1-2 acres on bounties of: John Turley, Richard Gray, Henry Dean, William Bennett, John Bennett, John Bennett and James Clark, 230 acres each and William Cousins of 287 1-2 acres.

Joseph Martin bounty certif. of John Bullman, Wm. Lyles, James Arey, Jonathan Turner—also in his own right 2000 acres and in John Gorham's name 1000 acres.

May 6, 1785—Certif. of service given by Leonard Marbury to John Bullman, Wm. Lyle, James Ayre, Jonathan Turner, continental soldiers, serving 3 years and more were discharged, petition that their bounties be granted to Col. Joseph Martin.

Also same service to: Joseph Way, John Way, John Arnold, Wm. Terrell, John Henby, James Harley, Robert Harrod, Eph'm Hardy, Robert Hardy, Wm. Finley, James Fenton, Robert Farling, Peter Eaton, Jno. Doer

(?), Wm. Fleming, Jno. Arrenton, Jno. Bartley, Owen Basil(?), Henry Barclay, Wm. Booth—bounties trans. to H. Marbury.

May 6, 1785—Service and discharge to Wm. McCarter, trans. to Moses Clark.

July 15, 1785—Certif. from L. Marbury for cont. service and discharge to: Henry Johns, Wm. Bentley, Wm. Stokes, Wm. Johns, John Keble, trans. to Henry Evans.

Bounties of Wm. Hearn, John Oliver, Robert Watson, Thomas Watson, Wm. Owens, Robert Dennis, James Henson, Peter Turley, to Col. Micajah Williamson.

May 10, 1785—Same to John Adamson, Wm. Robertson, Thomas James, Joseph Anderson, trans. to Bryan Ward.

April 26, 1785—Wm. Hertford, Cont. sol. trans. to John Clark, Jr.

Service, and discharge, to Henry Daniel, Peter Downey, Wm. Moore, James Moore, John McRae, Arthur Allen, 3 years service—trans. to Stephen Potts, July 17.

Discharge to John Freeman as reg. soldier, cert. by John Cloud.

April 18, 1785—Discharge from Lt. Col. Leo'd Marbury to James Edwards, John Edwards, Thos. Bolling, Robert Jenkinson, Wm. Hancock.

April 20, 1785—Ditto to Thomas Williams, Eli Williams, James Anderson, Frederick Michael, John Adams, soldiers in Cont. Regt.

April 23, 1785—Ditto to Russell Jones and Alexander Scott; Cont. Lt. Dragoons.

Feb. 10, 1785—Ditto to Thomas Jones, Wm. Alenxander, Robert Jackson, Wm. Nelson, soldiers in Cont. Regt., faithfully served term of enlistment.

April 30, 1785—The same to Archibald Roans, Wm. Evans, Reuben Bryan, James Bryan, John Elvin(?)

Land Reserve of Continental Line and Navy.

April 6, 1785—To Hezekiah Robertson 230 acres also

same to James McDonald, trans. to John Talbot; cert. by Thomas Napier, Adj.

Jan. 21, 1785—Bounties of Josiah Sanders, Henry George, Ralph Edwards, Ezekiel Highland, John Sulter, aggregating 2,300 acres, trans. to Harriss Ryan, and from him to John Myrick, Sr. To Benjamin Porter 1,000 acres.

Jan. 21, 1786—To Richard Claiborn Napier 1,000 acres (Th. Napier), to B. Porter 540 and 410 acres.

Jan. 2, 1786—To Benjamin Porter 940 acres.

Jan. 31, 1785—To Capt. Thos. Threadgill, 690 acres (S. Elbert). Renewed in names of Ebenezer and Benjamin Smith, and Isaac Alexander, November 11, 1790.

July 27, 1778—Liberty Co., Ga.—Certificate and discharge to James Hays, soldier in my Battalion, asks for a grant of 287 1-2 acres in name of Francis Hardgrave. Signed, Sam'l Jack, Coln.

Dec. 2, 1786—In Glynn and Camden Co. Bounty to Robert Montford, Esqr., for 10,000 acres in lieu of old warrants on Bounty. H. Osborn, Adj.

South Carolina Militia.

March 27, 1786—Union County, S. C. Certificate that Joseph Michel has lived in this settlement eighteen months in this place and have deserved a certificate of me, given under my hand and seal. Thos. Brandon, Col.

Nov. 3, 1783—The same to Joseph Kelley, "having applied for his caractor as he is aimed to take land in state of Georgy, this is to certy has suported the caractor of an honis man ever since he has lived in those parts. Given under my hand this 3 day of Nov., 1783.

Jan. 10, 1785—Simon Salter of S. C. capt. Henry Dukes Co. of Minute Men, Col. John Stewarts Batt.—Certificate of bounty to Thomas Mash of S. C., Bailey Gaines, of S. C., and William Ammons, of S. C., by E. Clark. Abraham Gaines of S. C. (Capt. Duke).

March 24, 1784—Brantley and Thomas Moseley bind themselves to David Greer of state of S. C., to transfer the bounty of Brantley Moseley. Wilkes Co., Ga.

Georgia, Wilkes Co. To all concerned: The bearer hereof, Moses Spencer, Bears the character of an honest Industrious Man. He distinguished himself as a soldier in the Defence of his country during the contest between Great Britain and the United States of America. It is hoped he will be permitted to pass unmolested. Given under our hands this 3rd September, 1785. Thomas Carter (?), J. P.

April 26, 1785—Richardson Hunt an Inhabitant of the State aforesaid (S. C.)

April 15, 1784—David Little, sol. in Militia, service and bounty. (E .Clark); also "warrants of George Bowers and Palashiah Stalings with this certificate and his own bounty, to be made out in the name of John Pope.

Dec. 20, 1784—William Walker, soldier in Militia, certificate for Bounty. (E. Clark.)

Feb. 8, 1785—Certificate of service attested by Elijah Clark to Shadrach Kimbrough and Joshua Glass and Zach. Henderson, whose bounties are made out to John Pope.

May 17, 1784—To Nath. Offutt—J. Habersham granted to Wm. Walton.

To Thomas Green, Jr., and Horatio Marbury, "captain applens warrt." (J. Habersham).

May 26, 1784—To Henry Britton—sold to Jesse Walton.

May 5, 1785—To Wm. Russell and James Hill—bounties to Elijah Clark. Also to Jno. Appling.

June 6, 1785—To Wm. Davis, Wm. Anderson, Wm. Lewis and Benj. Allen, laid out to Joseph Cook.

June 5, 1790—To Thomas Porter, Bounty Reserve 1,000 acres in part of old warrant.

May 17, 1792—To William Allen Bounty Reserve 287 1-2 acres.

May 17, 1784—To Sterling Jinkins—(J. Habersham.)

Oct. 1, 1784—To Dempcy Philips and Andrew Frazer. (J. Houston).

Dec. 4, 1786—To Robert Flournoy 920 acres in Green County in Reserve. Certificate by Wm. Patrick, Clerk.

March 6, 1786—To Abraham Hill, 460 acres in Green County in Reserve. Certificate by Wm. Patrick, Clerk.

June 6, 1785—To Dennis Henley prays for bounty.

—— 1785—Isaac Smith and Wm. Hudson, partially destroyed but signed by J. Habersham.

August 5, 1785—Certificate of Leonard Marbury to service and discharge as Continental soldiers in Georgia line to: Thomas Rogers, Edward Rogers, Walter Dodson, Thomas Jolly, William Dodson, Wm. Jackson, John Peterson, Wm. Peterson, Robert Davidson, John Davidson, Wm. Hadding, James Hadding, John Hardy, James Hardy, John Eldridge, Thomas Eldridge, James Beckman, Robert Beckman, James Peterson, Peter Beach, whose bounties are granted to Dr. William Baker.

July 20, 1785—To William Rider, Thomas Rudd, James Reeden, William Reeden, Henry Reed, Willis Redman, all petition Land court that their bounties be granted to Col. William Deakins.

April 30, 1785—Certificate of L. Marbury that Capt. Drury Cade was a captain in Regiment of Light Dragoons under his command. Received grant of 575 acres.

Same that Mark Philips was a soldier in Cont. Regt. of Light Dragoons, 230 acres.

May 4, 1785—As above to Bryan Ward, Samuel Ward and John Ward.

June 1, 1786—As above to James Anderson, transferred to Bryan Ward.

April 25, 1785—As above that John Pope, Esqr., was a Lieut. in Cont. Regt. of Light Dragoons, 450 acres.

Jan. 1, 1786—To James Wood, bounty for Cont. Line & Navy (T. Napier) 5690 acres in Washington County.

Surveyors of Revolutionary Grants.

John Gorham, Joseph Pannill, D. Rees, Dep. Sur., John Walton, Francis Tennille, Samuel Criswell, Larkin Cleveland, William Greer, John Martin, Jesse Walton.

The following forty-nine (49) marriages were found among some papers in the vault of the Ordinary's Office, and, compared to the Index of First Book of Marriages, but not found recorded.

The first date following refers to date of issue of license; the second to the date of marriage, with name of Minister or J. P.

William Glover-Elizabeth Pullum; Nov. 27,—28, 1812. Benjamin King, J. P.

James Hodge-Jinny Bond; Dec. 30, 1813—July 6, 1814.

Randle Brewer-Leanna Cox; July 26,—30, 1815. John M. Gray, M. G.

William Williams-Jinsey Holbrooks; Aug. 21,—24, 1815. Richard Shockley, J. P.

Benjamin Baker-Polly Williamson; Dec. 10, 1815—,same date. W. L. Bagwell, J. P.

Thomas Mays-Luvice Brinlee; April 25,—27, 1815. Thomas Newton.

Allen B. Holland-Patsey B. Cobb: March 17, 1815. George Stovall, J. P.

Jonathan Carpenter-Peggy Cash; June 1, 1815.

Griffin Watters-Matilda Tolbert; July 13,-14, 1815. Francis Calloway.

Burwell Heggons-Charity Heggons; March 29,-30, 1814. Francis Calloway.

Vincent Wadkins-Elizabeth Henderson; Sept. 7, 1815. William Hulsey, J. P.

Aaron Sanders-Morning Thomason; Feb. 14, 1817. John Duncan, J. P.

Miles Bauzewell (Boswell?)-Eleanor Holbrooks; Sept. 14, 1814. Wm. Hulsey, J. P.

Thomas Smith-Ruth Beall; Sept. 15, 1814. William Jones, J. P.

Daniel Gober-Elizabeth Arendal; Dec. 22, 1814. James H. Little, J. P.

William Chatham-Ruth Payne; Dec. 23,-25, 1814. Francis Calloway.

Thomas Munn-Fanny Woodale (Woodall?); Aug. 17,-19, 1813. James Allen, J. P.

Robert Harrison-Sarah Miller; June 15, 1815. W. Hulsey, J. P.

James Brasdle-Eleanor Covington; Jan. 4,-5, 1812. W. T. Bagwell, J. P.

James Ashworth-Jamimy Braisher; Jan. 26, 1815. Wm. Hulsey, J. P.

Jeremiah Chandler-Sarah Macky; Oct. 18,-19, 1815. James H. Little, J. P.

Martin Russell-Polly Hanes; March 1,-2, 1815. Francis Calloway.

Harris Toney-Rebecca Roberson; Aug. 21,-24, 1815. Henry David, M. G.

James McCarter-Jinsa Brown; Sept. 1, 1812. James H. Little, J. P.

William Gulley-Elizabeth Thompson or Thomason (top of her name gone); April 10,-18, 1815. John Warmack, J. P.

*Thomas Goraham-Mary A. Avery; license issued October 10, 1815. Married October 18, by Edmund Hulsey, J. P.

James Robertson-Margaret Lowery; Feb. 19,-20, 1815. Absalom Holcomb, J. P.

Isom Cardle-Elizabeth Cardle; Aug. 7,-13, 1815. A. Holcomb, J. P.

Thomas Gazzaway-Patsey Walker, May 1,-2, 1815. Moses Guest, J. P.

*There were two licenses found on these names—one of which was signed.

John Gruver-Elizabeth Wilson; Sept. 6,-7, 1815. Wm. Brown, J. P.

Thomas Watters-Ann Brown, Sept. 12,-17, 1815. John M. Seay, M. G.

James Isom-Elizabeth Everett; March 30, 1815. Wm. Hulsey, J. P.

James Dobs-Ann Armstrong; July 12, 1815. Clemond Quillian, J. P.

James Quillian-Sarah Prickett; May 16,-18, 1815. Clemond Quillian, J. P.

Henry Wade-Tempy Jordan; Aug. 15,17, 1815. Absalom Holcomb, J. P.

James Brown-Peggy Figgens; July 12,-14, 1815. Absalom Holcomb, J. P.

Pleasant Hulsey-Elizabeth Byrd; Jan. 24, 1815. Wm. Hulsey, J. P.

James Conch-Abagal Watson; Jan. 30, 1815. Richard Shockley, J. P.

Nicholas Bellamy-Rhody Jones; Oct. 27,-Nov. 9, 1815. James H. Little, J. P.

Francis Calloway-Elizabeth Taylor; Aug. 18,-Sept. 11, 1814. Francis Calloway, M. G.

Benjamin Lowery-Charity Bond; April 28,-May 2, 1815. Asa Allen, J. P.

James Langston-Elizabeth Davis; June 21,-22, 1813. Littleton Meeks, M. G.

Peter Epperson-Rhody Wadkins; Oct. 28,-29, 1812. Wm. Jones, J. P.

Barnet Wadkins-Hannah Epperson; Nov. 9,-12, 1811. Wm. Jones, J. P.

Cornelius Reburn (Rayburn?)-Becca Baxter; June 17,-22, 1815. James H. Little, J. P.

Russel Daniel-Elizabeth Gilbert; Apr. 3,-6, 1815. Gabriel Martin, J. P.

John Whitaker-Susan Sutley; Aug. 7,-10, 1826. Frederick Freeman, J. P.

Henry Hampton-Eliza Thornton; Nov. 26,-28, 1825. Littleton Meeks, M. G.

Abram Echols-Mary Hays; Aug. 23, 1821. Littleton Meeks, M. G.

FIRST BOOK OF MARRIAGES

Franklin County, Georgia, from 1805-1825.

Transcribed by order of Inferior Court of 1857.

1805.

Dec. 19—John Sissom and Sarah Dodd.

1806.

Feb. 5—Jacob Carlton and Sally Chitham.

April 14—James Wilkins and Ann Sowells.

April 14—William Smith and Tempy Beall.

April 14—Starling Harris and Elizabeth Gober.

May 1—James Ramsey and Jane Misser or Messer.

May 18—Absalom Adams and Mary Prickett.

May 22—John Stowers and Margaret Forester.

June 26—Thomas Jinkins and Frances Barton.

June 29—David Buckner and Neilly or Milly Holbrooks.

July 16—David Warren and Dera Kindrix.

July 31—Nathaniel Sims and Winnefred Bulloch.

July 26—James Lyner and Elizabeth Merrell.

Sept. 18.—James Daniel and Charity Pairpoint.

Oct. 4—James Bohannan and Rachel Patterson.

Oct. 26—Jesse Parker and Polly Herron.

Oct. 30—John Baker and Amelia Brown.

Nov. 20—James Allen and Polly Halley.

Dec. 25—William Bush and Joicy King.

1807.

Dec. 19—Allen Chandler and Mary McDonald.

Feb. 9—Charles Baker and Polly Stowe.

Feb. 19—George Stovall and Nancy Christian.

April 9—William Wallace and Janet Black.

April 11—William C. Millican and Rebecca Coyle.

April 28—William Robins and Mary Hollingsworth.

May 4—Mordeca Stringer Hamilton and Debery (Deborah?) Cooper. No return.

June 23—Michael Walden and Lucy McNeil.

Oct. 12—Richard Ross and Catherine Denman (No return).

Oct. 12—William Smith and Delilah Kees (no return).

Nov. 23—William Forsyth and Rhoda Morgan.

Dec. 24—Isaac Alexander and Susannah Thomas.

Dec. 26—Thomas Smith and Martha Jackson.

Dec. 29—Greenberry Sewell and Ann Brasdell.

Dec. 31—Levi Banks and Elizabeth Alexander.

Dec. 27—Richard Roberson and Elizabeth Kelly.

1808.

Feb. 5—Enoch Anders and Malissa Crump.

Jan. —James Smith and Elizabeth Poe.

March 20—William Swain and Rebecca Williamson.

March 3—John Hargroves and Rebecca Brown.

March 17—John Brown and Mary Crawford.

May 15—Hendrick Vaughan and Polly Bagby.

June 23—William Grady and Elizabeth Collins.

July 25—Joel Pricket and Elizabeth Dobbs.

Aug. 16—Charles Lowery and Elizabeth Toney.

Aug. 25—Flemen F. Adrine and Mary McDonald.

Sept. 8—Thomas Carter and Jinny Davis.

Nov. 29—William Scott and Ann Coil.

Oct. 11—Burrell Cook and Ann Lowery.

Oct. 13—James Lowery and Katy Dorsey.

Oct. 11—Caleb Garrison and Rachel Box.

Dec. 1—Thomas McCalla and Margaret Ramsey.
Dec. 8—Reuben Harrison and Bathana Dixon.
Dec. 27—Moses Trimble and Peggy Baker.
Dec. 29—Daniel Dixon and Priscilla Dorsey.
Dec. 25—John Brown and Mary Stovall.
Dec. 13—Thomas Harber and Elizabeth McKee.
Dec. 29—William Dean and Peggy Tolbert.
Dec. 3—Thomas Collyer and Mary Collins.
Nov. 17—William Glenn and Rosa Aron.
Oct. 3—Henry Holland and Priscilla Brown.
Oct. 14—William Smith and Drucilla Wade.

1809.

Jan. 1—William Denman and Mary Hicks.
Jan. 7—Robert R. Cox and Elizabeth Moulder.
Jan. 19—Thomas Milligan and Elizabeth Cleghorn.
Jan. 25—Mathew McCarter and Peggy McIntire.
Feb. 13—William Bullin and Amey Bolling.
March 31—Peter McKinsey and Cloe Ray.
March 19—Absalom Cornelius and Margaret Ward.
March 23—Wilson Strickland and Polly Conley.
March 25—John Carpenter and Esther Canady.
Jan. 6—James Smith and Patsey Allen.
March 18—Thomas Harris and Joannah Talley.
April 6—Reuben Hagin and Susannah Hooper.
May 25—William McCeiver(?) and Sarah Shield.
May 7—Davy Connally and Nancy Moore.
May 2—Joseph Cleveland and Patsey Weeks.
June 3—Robert McDowell and Rebecca Covington.
Sept. 3—William Nix and Susannah Stonecypher.
Sept. 3—Benjamin Hollingsworth and Joicy Jones.
Sept. 28—Robert Harrison and Pheroby Smith.
Sept. 7—Samuel Mangrum and Elizabeth Brawner.
July 20—Nathan Lowery and Rebecca Pool.
Aug. 10—Thomas Rose and Ann Bronner (Brawner?).
Dec. 23—Ezekiel Neal and Elizabeth Sparks.
Oct. 15—James Boswell and Lena Mullin.

Oct. 22—Thomas Payne and Sarah Carlton.
Oct. 29—Reuben Warren and Elizabeth Davis.
Oct. 12—John Mills and Ellender Forester.
June 20—Drury Roland and Ann Johnston.

1810.

Jan. 3—Stephen Dye and Elizabeth Woodson.
Jan. 14—Edmund Henley and Hepsibeth Denman.
Jan. 18—Charles Harris and Elizabeth Thompson.
Jan. 18—Obed M. Christian and Anna Barnes.
Feb. 2—George Bates and Edith Bryan.
Feb. 4—George Babs and Edith Bryan.
Feb. 6—Peterson Dodd and Abba Mullin.
March 21—John Hewell and Ellender Becker.
March 1—Edward Ryley and Polly Westbrook.
March 18—William Deale and Nelly Hailing.
·April 5—William Baker and Catherine Boaron.
April 26—Jesse Blackwell and Sarah Wilkins.
May 12—John Black and Polly Cannon.
July 8—John Towers and Elizabeth Spears.
July 30—Thomas Lewis and Rachel Day.
Aug. 30—Isaac A. McQueen and Cinthia Carruth.
Sept. 11—Isaac Brown and Nancy Lovelady.
Sept. 25— — Dodd and Polly Sheffield.
Sept. 27—John Holbrooks and Polly Dorsey.
Oct. 25—James Johnston and Sally Mize.
Nov. 15—William Dobbs and Catherine Covington.
Dec. 8—Elijah Thornton and Jane Fleming.
Dec. 19—George King and Elizabeth Lawrence.
Dec. 20—Jenidran Hendrick and Polly Williams.

1811.

Jan. 22—William Hall and Mary Bennett.
Jan. 3—Jonah Stovall and Lucy Farmer.
Feb. 3—John Denman and Patsey Hooper.
March 7—James Baker and Mary Sewell.
March 7—William Thompson and Elizabeth Davis.

March 20—Lewdeary Haley and Winnafred Arendall.
March 26—John W. Carrell and Elizabeth Redwine.
April 8—David Payne and Polly Chatham.
April 2—Garrell L. Sandridge and Frances Smith (original license "Garrett.....)
July 23—John Meeks and Elizabeth Henderson.
July 25—John Sewel and Elizabeth Christian.
Aug. 13—William Tatum and Parthenia Thurmond.
Oct. 31—David Dodd and Sallie Sanders.
Dec. 12—John William Yow and Sarah Bradlet.
Dec. 17—Thomas Brown and Barshelia Williams (original license "Barsheba").
Dec. 21—Absalom Denman and Clarissa Wilcox.
Dec. 24—Joseph Morris and Ann Moore.
Dec. 28—John Sanders and Abby Robins.
Dec. 29—George Tailor and Lathy Mullins.
Nov. 25—John Cane and Lidy Hall.
May 12—David Ballenger and Rebecca Stephenson.
June 27—Mat. W. Beall and Rebecca Stephens. Prob. intended for 1814.
Oct. 28—Cade D. Strickland and Jincy Burton.
Nov. 11—Aquilla Shockley and Melia King.
Dec. 18—Benjamin Stonecypher and Elizabeth Collins.

1812.

Jan. 2—Sandlin Hardin and Polly Stephenson.
Jan. 14—Jesse Prickett and Elizabeth Elliott.
Jan. 19—Roland Gatewood and Sina Lane.
Feb. 25—Hull Sims and Polly Allen.
Feb. 27—Job Brooks and Priscilla Woods.
March 5—Samuel Holbrooks and Hannah Wilson.
March 31—William Aron and Deonnoa Brasker.
April 22—Thomas Gazaway and Lucy Wheeler.
July 16—Hezekiah Smith and Polly Thomas.
Aug. 6—John Hodge and Dolly Gober.
Aug. 7—John Connor and Polly Chappelear.
Sept. 4—Absalom Carter and Nancy Wilkerson.

Sept. 6—Thomas Payne and Elizabeth Dobbs.
Sept. 10—David Ellison and Charlotte Mays.
Oct. 7—William Davis and Nancy Mahoe (Mayhew?)
Oct. 8—Richard Crump and Elizabeth Wheeler.
Oct. 26—Mark Philips and Mary Cann.
Dec. 19—Asa Ayres and Olive Vesils(?).
Dec. 24—Josiah Hancock and Nancy Goodwin.

1813.

Jan. 9—Thomas Beall and Elizabeth Cleghorn.
Jan. 29—Frederick Gowdy and — — Adarine(?).
Feb. 10—William Sandridge and Jerusha Pulliam.
Feb. 18—William H. Hall and Lucy Merida (Meredith?).
March 4—James Bagley and Elizabeth Allen.
March 18—John Ash and Margaret Newton.
March 25—Berry King and Rebecca Bray.
April 6—William Mays and Elizabeth Thomas.
April 8—William Bohannon and Polly White.
May 16—James Hollingsworth and Mary Jones.
July 27—Alexander Murphy and Susannah Coleman.
July 29—Chaffin Chatham and Polly Payne.
Aug. 5—William Penn and Abigail Wilson.
Aug. 26—Morgan Denman and Elizabeth Gray.
Sept. 9—James Phillips and Sarah McIntire.
Sept. 30—George Lowery and Elizabeth Cox.
Oct. 22—James J. Holmes and Elizabeth B. Newton.
Oct. 27—Benjamin Whitaker and Winnifred Brasdle.
Nov. 2—Francis Callaway and Sallie Russell.
Nov. 19—David Nichols and Minna Gibbs.
Nov. 21—Allen Elstur(?) and Mrs. Anna Terrell.
Dec. 2—Joseph Jones and Hepsy Bowen.

1814.

Jan. 2—Ralph Smith and Sally Arthur.
March 3—Moses Manley and Lina Attaway.
March 27—George Carpenter and Nancy Hendrick.

May 27—William Smith and Sabra Nail,

July 8—William Gilbert and Priscilla Gilbert.

July 23—Adam Witt and Rachel Johnson.

Sept. 11—Matilla Smith and Susannah Garrison.

Sept. 29—Solomon Rackley and Charity Lotty Bright. (In license it is "Charlotte).

Sept. 29—Robert Burton and Sarah Conally.

Oct. 27—James Ash and Nancy Martin.

Nov. 10—Wyatt Chandler and Polly Liner.

Nov. 21—William Reid and Polly Sims.

Dec. 11—Asa Hogwood and Elizabeth Higgins.

Dec. 20—Frankey Holbrook and Jiris Mulligan.

Dec. 22—William Irons and Elizabeth Brassons. (Beasons, in license).

Dec. 25—Norman Dobbs and Sarah Cape. (Moseman Dobbs in license.)

1815.

Jan. 4—Thomas H. McIna and Ann Blackwell.

Feb. 19—John Gibson and Ruhoma Gibson.

March 26—Asa Payne and Linna Gess(?).

July 28—Francis Gideon and Susan Hendrick.

Aug. 10—James L. Fleming and Jane Ash.

Nov. 16— — Reddin and Rachel Ing——.

1816.

Feb. 6—John Nix and Elizabeth Holmes.

Feb. 10—Andrew Watson and Elizabeth Isaac.

Feb. 5—David Theyrs(?) and Deicy Ragan.

March 20—Mathew Davis and Darkes (Dorcas) Holbrook.

March 21—John Williamson and Elizabeth Thompson.

March 26—John Miller and Anny Hulsey.

March 27—James Nix and Lucy Holmes.

April 14—Jonathan Bush and Dinoelondy Crump.

April 18—Seborn Thompson and Fanny Loughridge.

April 29—Richard Gober and Polly Ayres.

April 28—Moses Shannon and Jemime Cleveland.

April 18—William Turk and Jane Mays.

May 23—Eber M. Bolls and Elizabeth B. Taylor.

May 30—Armistead Dowdy and Elizabeth Cross.

June 20—Jesse Aron and Patsey Flood.

July 18—Warren Stoe and Elizabeth Medlock.

July 18—Jesse Rose and Permelia Fleming.

July 24—Moses Ellison and Nancy Dixon.

July 26—Moses Rice and Cinthia Holcomb.

July 3—William Garrison and Elizabeth Craft.

July 18—John Knox and Elizabeth Denman.

Aug. 15—Freeman Hardy and Kizziah Linnear (Lanier?).

Aug. 6—John Allred and Nancy Warren.

Aug. 1—Allen Wood and Ann Ramsey.

Aug. 1—William Thrasher and Elizabeth Smith.

Aug. 1—Elijah Crawford and Clarissa Beasley.

Sept. 30—James Mays and Lucinda Brindley.

Sept. 28—Jonathan Terrell and Elizabeth Ramsey.

Oct. 3—Thomas Westbrook and Elizabeth Allen.

Oct. 20—Nathaniel Harris and Argent Wellborn.

Oct. 30—Joseph Clarkson and Nancy Gober.

Oct. 27—Joseph Henderson and Nancy Reid.

Oct. 15—James L. Thomas and Rebecca Everett.

Oct. 18—Enoch Heggins and Polly Heggins.

Nov. 6—Thomas Thrasher and Mihelia Elliott.

Nov. 23—Joseph A. Brantly and Martha Meeks.

Nov. 24—John Hollingsworth and Matilda White.

Dec. 10—John T. Smith and Elizabeth Shotwell.

Dec. 26—Josiah Rickols and Polly Tucker.

Dec. 19—Enoch Brady and Nancy Davis.

Dec. 23—Anderson Worthy and Susannah Andrews.

Dec. 22—William Andrews and Rebecca Poe.

Dec. 23—William Boswell and Louisa Whitworth.

Dec. 29—David Anthony and Elizabeth Chandler.

Dec. 8—Hope Sims and Hannah Varner.

Dec. 8—William Put (Peet in license) and Nancy Sanders.

Dec. 9—David Lowery and Sarah Cook.

Dec. 19—Gray Jordan and Peggy Chandler.

Dec. 24—John Isham and Sinah(?) Henderson.

1817.

Jan. 22—Thomas Mays and Martha Chandler.

Jan. 29—John Ivie and Nancy Glass.

Jan. 23—John Hulsey and Elender Garrison.

Jan. 28—John W. Lowery and Elizabeth Trimble.

Jan. 30—William Wilson and Elizabeth Sisson.

Jan. 28—John Ivins (Evans?) and Nancy Baugh.

Jan. 6—John Shotwell and Sally Henly.

Jan. 2—Michael Mullin and Sarah Jones.

Jan. 25—Martin Ingram and Nancy Peek.

Feb. 18—James Lowery and Nancy Toney.

Feb. 20—Jediah Blackwell and Nancy Henderson.

Feb. 20—Robert Miller and Elizabeth Wallraven.

Feb. 4—Aaron Anderson and Morainy Thompson.

Feb. 2—Jesse Redwine and Elizabeth Hunt.

Feb. 13—John Ayres and Edy Payne.

March 6—Asariel Miller and Dicey Holley.

April 17—Dyall Mills and Judah Gibson.

April 13—Jesse Thompson and Charity Smith.

April 3—James Russell and Ann Acols.

April 8—William Arthur and Mary Miller.

May 15—Joseph McIntire and Nancy Little.

May 29—William Martin and Nancy Rucker.

May 29—James Dunahoo and Elizabeth Wilson.

June 15—Samuel Headen and Mary Norwood.

June 1—John Tilman Carter and Katy Starns.

June 12—William Brown and Nancy Reese.

July 24—Jacob Molder and Martha Westbrook.

July 15—Lewis Ballard and Meeky Dobbs.

July 3—John Lowery and Elizabeth Ayres.

194 GEORGIA D. A. R.

July 29—William Brooks and Hannah Hollingsworth (William Brock in license.)
July 31—Thomas West and Eleanor Hervey.
Aug. 26—George Thrasher and Alender White.
Aug. 21—Hugh McDonald and Ann Loggins.
Aug. 21—Gaines Chandler and Polly Howington (Green Chandler in license).
Aug. 28—John Payne and Ruth York.
Aug. 31—Martin Anthony and Elizabeth Chandler.
Sept. 23—James Poole and Martha Burton.
Oct. 3—Daniel Chitwood and Polly McCracken.
Oct. 18—John Fannin and Zaland McIntire.
Oct. 30—James Shalleen and Elizabeth Yearlow.
Nov. 13—John Ramsey and Elizabeth Tate.
Nov. 13—David S. Henslee and Rhoda Payne.
Nov. 5—David Vaughan and Sarah Sewell.
Nov. 19—Josiah Prickett and Polly Baker.
Nov. 25—David Candell and Rebecca Sims.
Nov. 27—Elijah Walters and Nancy Bolin.
Nov. 13—Peter Combs and Elizabeth Collum.
Nov. 18—John Ballenger and Elizabeth Stephenson.
Nov. 20—Robert Lane and Annie Cleveland.
Dec. 5—John Carroll and Priscilla Bolen.
Dec. 7—(man's name not on license)-Ann Micholds..
Dec. 7—Job Thompson and Judah Hall.
Dec. 27—James A. Thompson and Martha Linch.

1818.

Jan. 28—David Robertson and Sally Thomas.
Jan. 12—Leonard Bond and Sally Cash.
Jan. 11—Daniel Osburn and Dicey Stout.
Jan. 15—Asa Griffin and Nancy Little.
Feb. 1—Robert Ray and Mary Bramlett.
Feb. 17—Daniel B. Manley and Winney Hopper.
Feb. 19—Wright Bond and Polly Wilkinson.
Feb. 26—Abcol Carter and Maledda (pos. Matilda) Chandler.

Feb. 19—Martin Jones and Mrs. Juda E. Garrison.

March 3—John Westbrooks and Nancy Jones.

March 15—Seaborn Hall and Nancy Smith.

March 19—John McMillen and Dicey Clark.

March 22—Thomas Aron and Susannah Smith.

March 29—Drewry Jones and Dolly Barton.

March 3—James Pedan and Polly Baker.

April 30—Membrum Keith and Nancy McCoy.

April 5—William Jones and Annie Howell.

April 25—Nathaniel Wilson and Susannah Birt.

April 16—James Denman and Sarah Lecat, or Secat.

May 1—Daniel Ingland and Susannah Field.

May 17—John Dooly and Zeberia Gartney.

May 27—Claburn Cawthan and Jerusha Pulliam.

June 18—Col. Asa Allen and Mrs. Ann Wood.

June 25—William Dean and Elizabeth Pearce.

July 30—John Poe and Winny Davis.

July 2—Thomas Heggins and Elizabeth Smith.

July 16—John Dudley and Ann Jones.

July 16—John Moss and Nancy Boatright.

Aug. 13—Russell G. Beall and Cole S. Dent.

Aug. 20—William Woodson and Caty Swan.

Aug. 24—William Dean and Louisa Hobbs.

Sept. 22—Stephen Bramblett and Martha Andrews.

Sept. 14—John Crawford and Polly Vessels.

Oct. 1—William Herrin and Sally Molder.

Oct. 8—Asa Brendlee and Polly Bowen.

Oct. 8—Thomas Pulliam and Matilda Burrice.

Oct. 29—Micajah Jones and Elizabeth Ashworth.

Oct. 29—John H. Patrick and Nancy Mitchell.

Oct. 29—William Akins and Rhoda Chatham.

Nov. 22—Elisha Limme(?) and Ann Trentham (Treutlen?).

Dec. 9—Samuel Sewel and Lucy Trimble.

Dec. 24—Haleman F. Simmons and Sarah E. H. Burns.

1819.

Jan. 17—Hillary Stone and Matilda Bagwell.
Jan. 31—William Hill and Harriet Nance.
Feb. 14—Henry Smith and Margaret Herring.
Feb. 21—Henry H. Davis and Mrs. Polly Watters.
March 11—Isham Morel and Phebe Watters.
March 15—Jeremiah Garreld(?) and Jene Barnett.
May 2—Barney Athu (Askew?) and Sophia Jones.
July 6—Asa Turner and Martha Jones.
July 11—Tignal Meredith and Mary Ann Stovall.
Aug. 19—William Harris and Dicey Miller.
Sept. 23—William Baxter and Thursy Conally.
Sept. 23—John M. Brown and Elizabeth Cheek.
Sept. 30—Felix G. Denman and Ann Hutchinson.
Sept. 30—Isaac Tabor and Abba Wheeler.
Oct. 3—Brasel Addison and Jane Crump.
Oct. 10—Hiram Taylor and Sally Blair.
Oct. 29—Berryman Shoemake and Pussy Farrow.
Nov. 1— — —McLure and Charity Feno—?
Nov. 9—Roland Spears and Comfort Sewell.
Nov. 18—James Smith and Sarah Burt.
Dec. 21—Nelson Osborn and Lucy Watson.
Dec. 28—Wesley Martin and Betsy Rogers.
May 13—William McMullin and Amelia Bell.

1820.

Jan. 4—James H. Davis and Sally McFarland.
Jan. 13—John Birt and Polly Smith.
Feb. 3—William Burns and Jane Cheek.
Feb. 13—William Pierce and Betsy Holbrook.
Feb. 15—Joseph Dunnessin(?) and Lucy Beall.
Feb. 17—Nathaniel Brumlett and Jinny Gober.
Feb. 24—Hezekiah Hopgood and Patsey Edwards.
Feb. 29—Eli Ramsey and Elizabeth Strange.
March 9—Peter Vaughan and Deborah Sewell.
March 9—John C. McNeal and Polly Beard.

March 26—Sampson Barber and Polly Bush.
April 10—Mark Smith and Ally Smith.
May 31—William Attaway and Lucy Dunlet(?).
July 23—Henry Freeman and Abisha Hutcherson.

1821.

March 20—Darling B. House and Jinny Bryant.
Aug. 30—Pleasant Holley and Matilda Allen.
Oct. 15—John Lnading(?) and Amelia Jones.
Dec. 13—William Holley and Elizabeth Ramsey.
Dec. 20—John Sartin and Nelly Bond.

1822.

Jan. 24—Hudson H. Allen and Miss A. ———
Feb. 14—William J. Sparks and Naomi Prickett.
July 11—Tyre Swift and Rhoda Chandler.
Aug. 21—William Brown and Morning Smith.
Oct. 15—Josiah Beall and Ann Dent.
Oct. 31—Lewis Tucker and Maria Gober.
Oct. 10—John W. Payne and Julia Hall.
Dec. 3—Amos Lowery and Eliza Allbritton.
Dec. 12—Daniel Shannon and Mary Hunt.
Dec. 29—Cornelius R. Donahoo and Nancy Parks.
Feb. 16—James Brown and Sarah Smith.

1823.

Jan. 26—Russell Holcomb and Susan Meeks.
Jan. 2—Joshua Westbrook and Leroycy Bellamy.
Jan. 14—Levi Hamby and Elizabeth Clark.
Jan. 2—William R. Wellborn and Melissa Bush.
Feb. 6—Wilkey Shelton(?) and Sarah Huln(?).
March 11—Thomas Austin and Mary Woolbright.
March 16—Peter Wilson and Jinny Baker.
March 20—Michael Sutley and Polly Wilson.
April 24—Richmond Shelton and Nancy Garrison.
April 24—Wright Williams and Rhoda Robertson.
July 11—Solomon Tate and Mary Chandler.

Aug. 28—Willis Tapp and Nancy Wade.

Aug. 31—George Hall and Lucy Thomison.

Nov. 18—Francis Hickumbotham and **Martha** Jones.

Oct. 30—Daniel Gibson and Mary Conch.

Oct. 16—John Williamson and Eliza Carlton, or Carttin.

Dec. 11—Joel Henson and Eisu (?) Chatham.

Nov. 20—James Donahoo and Jane Jordan.

Dec. 19—Martin Payne and Kesiah Payne.

Dec. 21—Berry King and Lucy Cook.

1824.

Jan. 16—Charles M. Conley and Disa Conley.

Jan. 25—Zachariah Walls and Sally Moseley.

April 1—John A. Willis and Elizabeth Davis.

April 1—George Humphries and Zilla McIntire.

April 17—John Tony (or Long), Jr., and Eliza Brumly.

June 3—Christopher Holbrooks and Sarah Christian.

July 26—Tandy H. Green and Obedience White.

Aug. 19—Reuben Conch and Jinny Sewel.

Aug. 19—Jesse Brown and Sarah Smith.

Aug. 5—Lewis Sanders and Prudence Miller.

Aug. 24—Hiram Gober and Belvy Gober.

Aug. 31—Frederick Cockrum and Dorcas Baxter.

Oct. 7—Alexander F. Ash and Elizabeth McCracken.

Oct. 7—Stephen Chandler and Anna Adderhold.

Nov. 18—Christopher Baker and Centhia Spears.

Nov. 25—James Stovall and Nancy Garner.

Sept. 2—George Kitchen and Anna Johnstone.

Dec. 23—Calvin Sanders and Sarah Miller.

1825.

Jan. 6—Samuel Johnston and Cinthia Rucker.

Jan. 13—Arnsted Hardy and Lucy Norwood.

Jan. 13—James S. Bathen and Mary Pulliam.

Feb. 12—Daniel Chandler and Anna Geargin(?).

March 21—Robert H. Hall and Louisa Lowing.

March 22—James Humphreys and Buyna Jordan.

April 21—Henry Freeman and Martha Mayfield.

June 16—Christopher Connally and Elizabeth McIntire.

June 18—Francis T. Cook and Eda S. Hood.

1825.

June 20—Austin Carter and Polly Finch.

June 21—Samuel W. Connally and Prude Christian.

July 5—Young Standin and Jane McIntire.

July 26—William Conley and Cinnis(?) Christian.

Aug. 15—Samuel F. Garrell(?) and Nancy Blankenship.

Aug. 18—Thomas Wells and Martha Ramsey.

Aug. 31—William Hony(?) and Jirsay(?) Parr.

Aug. 21—David Sutly and Martha Whetycar (Whitaker?).

Sept. 6—Little Harris and Anny Hanley.

Nov. 20—Adam Bell and Eleanor McFarland.

Nov. 26—John Strange and Ann Johnson.

Nov. 28—Joshua Carpenter and Azzie Sims.

Nov. 29—Jeremiah Watters and Eliza C. Tate.

Dec. 4—Absalom J. Baird and Sallie Bryan.

1826.

James Hollingsworth and Mary Jones.

Jan. 31—Lewis Chandler-Polly Prewett.

May 4—Dozier Thornton-Jane Pulliam.

Nov. 9—John Camp-Fanny Cawthon.

——

FRANKLIN COUNTY MARRIAGES

1827-1834.

1827.

Feb. 4—James Haley-Elizabeth Keisler. Asa Payne, J. P.

March 7—Ingram Pair-Airy Vaughan. Royal Bryan, J. P.

Feb. 1—William Keel-Ann Echolls. Robert Williams, J. P.

March 29—Joshua Maybry-Drusilla Defoor. C. D. Jenkins, J. P.

May 3—Ambrose Chandler-Jerusha White. C. D. Jenkins, J. P.

March 4—Sterling Pinson-Polly Burton. George Vandiver, M. G.

Jan. 23—Zedediah Meadows-Margaret Gober. W. J. Parks, M. G.

April 8—Thos. J. White-Mary Connally. William Gilmore, J. P.

March 8—Daniel Bush-Elizabeth Neal. W. J. Parks, M. G.

Feb. 22—Alvin E. Whitten-Cath. W. Jones. Thomas King, C. C. O.

April 14—Wm. Jones-Rachel Higginbotham. Robert Williams, J. P.

April 26—David Candle-Elizabeth Bridges. Samuel Jackson, J. P.

March 29—Burrell White-Frances Pulliam. Royal Bryan, J. P.

July 26—James H. McCarty-Nancy Stoe. Samuel Mosely, J. P.

July 29—Larkin Harrison-Frances Harrison. Dozier Thornton, M. G.

July 3—Warren Mize-Elizabeth Clarkson. William Turk, J. I. C.

June 9—Andrew Wilson-Lincy Stegall. Maxfield H. Payne, J. I. C.

July 5—George M. Christian-Sarah J. Jones. William J. Parks, M. G.

Oct. 16—Wm. W. Baird-Rebecca McCall. **Royal Bryan,** J. P.

Oct. 24—Richard Minyard-Rebecca Chandler. Frederick Freeman, J. P.

Oct. 14—Saml. C. Lovil-Ella Blalock. **John Crocker,** J. P.

Nov. 1—Thomas M. King-Mary Sutly.

Nov. 8—Solomon D. Thompson-Harriet Word.

Nov. 13—Edmund D. Puckett-Nancy **Pulliam.**

Nov. 13—Robert Brown-Hannah Caudle. Samuel Jackson, J. P.

Nov. 15—Lewis D. Jones-Mariah L. Bush. William J. Parks, M. G.

Dec. 13—Isaac D. Manley-Tabitha Attaway. J. Hammond, J. P.

Dec. 13—Robert Hemphill-Mary Brannan.

Nov. 8—Christopher Denman-Sary Cagle. F. Calloway, M. G.

Dec. 18—Randolph Crow-Elizabeth Sewell. Frederick Freeman, J. P.

Oct. 25—Joel W. Townsend-Mary D. Acker. David Garrison, C. M. C.

Nov. 15—James H. Garrison-Nancy B. Davidson.

Oct. 11—Moses Roberts-Milly Tabor.

Dec. 2—John K. Houston-Harriet J. Watson. John B. McMillan, J. P.

Dec. 20—Lodowick Dobbs-Delilah Dobbs. **Asa Payne,** J. P.

Dec. 25—James Chatham-Nancy Yarbrough. Frederick Freeman, J. P.

Aug. 9—John McKelvy-Christian Attaway.

Oct. 11—John T. C. Attaway-Mary Avery.

Aug. 7—John Wade-Lucy Peak.

Nov. 22—John C. Sandridge-Elizabeth Murdock. Elijah Stephens, J. P.

Nov. 19—John Sims-Rhoda Rogers. Robert Williams, J. P.

Nov. 22—Darling B. House-Margaret Rogers.

Dec. 19—Simeon Turman-Nancy Avery. John Bramblett, M. G.

March 7—Tapley Sartain-Rachel Williams.

July 29—Chaltm(?) Coker-Matilda Chandler.

April 4—James Avery-Sarah Pulliam. John Bramblett, M. G.

Nov. 11—Johnson T. Smith-Margarett English.

July 16—Elijah Hillhouse-Nancy Maulding.

Nov. 8—Joel H. Dyar-Rachel Sanders.

June 14—Henry McJenkins-Narcissa Vaughan.

1828.

Jan. 1—Garrett Gray-Jinny Jinkins.

Nov. 6—John Thomas-Elizabeth Mitchell.

Jan. 1—Wm. Bryan-Alis Bryan. John Sandridge, M. G.

Jan. 1—Wm. Heaton-Mary Aderhold. John Crocker, J. P.

Jan. 24—Stephen B. Westbrook-Elizabeth Hunt.

Jan. 17—James Attaway-Matilda Avery.

Jan. 17—Wm. Angling-Elizabeth Sewall.

Jan. 17—Drury V. Motes-Frances Brannum.

Jan. 3—John Deverall-Elizabeth Hudson.

Jan. 8—Wm. Allman-Nancy Fowler. Zachariah Chandler, J. P.

Jan. 16—Elisha Williams-Cyntha Toney. Howell Mangum, J. P.

Jan. 10—Saml. T. Payne-Margaret McCracken.

Jan. 20—Thomas Mize-Lavina Cape. Thomas Garrison, J. P.

Feb. 21—Zachariah Clark-Polly Ann Davis. Samuel Jackson, J. P.

Feb. 28—Jonathan Graham-Irene Payne. William Beall, J. P.

Feb. 28—John P. Alexander-Elizabeth Tate. Charles D. Jenkins, J. P.

Feb. 12—Jackson M. Watters-Polly Cawthon.

Jan. 24—Samuel Sandres-Anne Skelton.

March 6—Andrew Bowen-Milly Grover.

March 23—John Jeffers-Frances Nixon.

March 27—Jeremiah Cockburn-Joanna Henson.

April 17—Ely Woods-Mary Abbott.

May 10—Wm. Bryant-Sally Hyde. William Gilmore, J. P.

June 1—Moses Fagans-Phebe Smith.

June 15—Wilkinson T. Cawthon-Sarah Camp.

July 10—Christophers Meaders-Candace Garrison.

May 15—Joseph E. Philips-Harriet Paschal.

May 13—Henry Carver-Barbara Whisonant. Samuel Mosely, J. P.

Aug. 3—John J. Hendricks-Sarah Grose.

Aug. 12—John Clark-Ann C. Baird.

Sept. 7—Samuel Noles-Sarah Robertson. Elijah Stephens, J. P.

Sept. 9—James S. Teasley-Susan W. Reed. Joel W. Townsend, E. M. C.

Oct. 9—John F. Wilson-Polly P. Stubbs.

Oct. 9—Wm. Mitchell-Rebecca Baird.

Oct. 12—Barnet Roberts-Phebe Candle.

Oct. 23—Ferdinand Stovall-Cynthia Reed.

Oct. 25—James Freeman-Martha Chandler. Job Hammond, J. P.

Oct. 30—Thomas M. Shannon-Avis Gunnels.

Nov. 4—Wm. Ford-Cerren Smith.

Nov. 6—Levi Blair-Nancy Smith.

Nov. 18—Johnson M. Hooper-Bernicy Chattham.

Nov. 20—Daniel Chandler-Catherine Harbour.

Aug. 17—James Hammet-Sarah Tate.

Aug. 7—Franklin Glenn-Susan T. Carson(?).

May 8—Reuben Thornton-Elizabeth Waters(?).

May 9—Wiley Clark-Frances Whitehead.

Nov. 9—Joshua Sewell-Nancy Johnson.

Oct. 28—Adam Andrews-Adaline Sanford.

Sept. 7—Lemuel Dodd-Diannah F. Smith.

April 17—Ezekiel Thomas-Sally Cockrum.

Oct. 4—Parnal Attaway-Annah Cox.

Dec. 23—Josiah Murray-Sarah Catlett.

Dec. 24—Hardy Rose-Polly Freeman.

Dec. 25—James Gillespie-Elizabeth Yarbrough.

Dec. 30—Eli L. Nance-Tabitha Lualling. Richard Smith, J. P.

Dec. 4—Reuben W. Westbrook-Tabitha Hill.

Dec. 28—Richard Ramsay-Elizabeth Gentry.

1829.

Jan. 1—Jesse Johnson-Alsey Henson.

Jan. 8—James Philips-Elizabeth Dearing.

Jan. 25—Wm. Hathcock-Arminda Trimble. Nathan Gunnels, J. P.

Jan. 14—Micajah Jones-Mary Ashworth. Maxfield H. Payne, J. I. C.

Jan. 15—Charles Jones-Sarah Christian.

Jan. 13—Mathew Allen-Lucinda Vaughters.

Jan. 22—Madison Ramsey-Ratha Crump.

Jan. 14—Cooper B. Tate-Nancy White. Job Hammond, J. P.

Jan. 27—Chesley Payne-Matilda Burgess. B. T. Merrell, J. P.

Jan. 29—Berry G. Tilman-Armanda Martin.

Jan. 25—John Johnson-Mary Gober.

Jan. 13—Robert W. Prewitt-Isabella Little. Littleton Meeks, M. G.

Feb. 19—Hugh Brown-Mary Caudle.

Feb. 10—Wm. Morrow-Mary Mitchell. John Maples, J. P.

Feb. 4—John Langston-Sophia Shannon.

Feb. 10—Samuel Knox-Mary M. Reed.

March 12—Wm. N. Staple-Martha G. Thornton.

March 24—Bartley Barry-Mary Bruce.

March 29—Henry W. Hardy-Sarah Isbell. James R. Smith, M. G.

March 22—Isaac E. Cobb-Frances C. Chandler.

March 30—John Bellamy-Rebecca Jones.

March 26—Jesse Thomas-Rhoda Jackson. Chesley Cawthon, J. P.

March 24—Wm. Neal-Elizabeth Gober.

Feb. 4—Alex. Langston-Elizabeth Shannon.

March 10—Freeland T. Willis-Caty Oliver.

April 6—Jesse Roberts-Martha Bryant. Howell Mangrum, J. P.

April 9—Wm. Wilson-Elizabeth Watters.

April 16—James Martin-Katherine Wheeler. Dudley Ayers, J. P.

April 19—Martin Dobbs-Partheny Fulbright.

May 26—Wm. Sloan-Eliza Hackett. A. W. Ross.

July 4—James V. Ledbetter-Martha R. Lisk. John B. Chappel, M. G.

July 18—Benjamin H. White-Margaret Smith.

Aug. 5—Jedediah Garrison-Elizabeth Bradley.

Aug. 26—Elijah Sartain-Sarah Williams.

Sept. 3—Henry Wideman-Milley Sewell.

Sept. 13—James S. Alexander-Elizabeth Humphries.

Sept. 20—John Harper-Mary Sanders. Reuben Thornton, M. G.

Sept. 10—Wm. Chandler-Nancy Harbour.

Sept. 24—Wm. S. Crow-Malinda West.

Sept. 7—James Ramsey-Fanny Christian. G. L. Sandridge, J. I. C.

Sept. 22—Aaron Wetherby-Mary Robertson.

June 14—Hiram B. Perkins-Susan Ray.

July 23—Wm. S. Denman-Darkis Paire.

Aug. 27—Asa Chandler-Jane Clark.

May 26—Geo. A. Bolch-Letty McClay.

May 26—William York-Tabitha Martin.

Oct. 27—Wm. S. Acker-Elizabeth White.

Oct. 26—Green B. Sewell-Susannah Vaughan.

Sept. 6—Wm. York-Nancy Cosby. Samuel T. Payne, J. P.

Nov. 3—Wm. Aaron-Rebecca Rudd.

Nov. 18—Wm. A. Perry-Sarah Williams.

Nov. 2—Ely T. Wilmot-Jane Wyley.

Nov. 8—Thomas Payne-Olive Ayers.

Nov. 10—Saulbury Garrison-Sarah Brawner. David Garrison, M. G.

Oct. 8—Asa Sewell-Nancy M. Mitchell.

Dec. 22—Caleb Hill-Margaret Russell. John Catlett, J. P.

Dec. 24—James Vaughan-Nancy Sewell.

Dec. 19—Peyton Tiller-Sally Baker.

Dec. 6—Obadiah White-Jemima Sparks.

Nov. 26—Thomas Chandler-Mary Jackson. Asa Chandler, M. G.

Dec. 10—Joseph C. Lowery-Permelia Wright. John Burton, J. P.

1830.

Feb. 23—Austin W. Crosby-Margaret A. Reed. Robert Pulliam, J. I. C.

Feb. 16—Hedrick Toney-Anny Rose.

Feb. 15—Squire Mason-Louisa Mills.

Feb. 14—John W. Thomason.

Feb. 9—John G. York-Anny B. Thomason.

Feb. 2—Benajah Freeman-Susan McCarter.

Feb. 4—William Robertson-Matilda Mays.

Jan. 17—Wm. A. Barber-Nancy Hudgins.

March 25—Nicholas Sewell-Elizabeth Towns.

May 30—Linsey Chandler-Matilda Sewell.

April 25—David White-Mary H. Jones.

April 22—Joseph Slack- Mary J. Tatom. Hiram Russell, J. P.

March 31—David Stovall-Margaret McCalla.

April 1—Samuel Watson-Harriet Jones.

March 3—Alford Smith-Caroline Neal.

March 11—John C. King-Mary Borum.

March 25—Solomon Dobbs-Fanny Carson. Lewis Bullard, M. G.

March 4—James Wade-Elizabeth Ryley.

March 24—Sion B. Pritchard-Elizabeth Headen.

March 23—Absalom H. Shelton-Milly Patterson. Berry Laughridge, J. P.

April 6—Pickens Gillespie-Nancy Morrow.

Dec. 27—Johnson Gray-Liley Jinkins.

Oct. 10—Wm. Stokes-Barbary Iley.

Sept. 14—Martin Defoor-Susan Tabor. Oliver C. Miller, M. G.

May 12—Wm. Dunson-Sarah Cook.

June 22—Benajah Williams-Malinda Sparks.

Aug. 12—Robert T. Banks-Frances S. Jones. S. Hymer, M. G.

March 18—Larkin C. Ayers-Elizabeth Ayers. Asa Payne, J. P.

July 29—Samuel Nuckols-Eliza C. Sandridge.

Aug. 11—Henry Parks-Sarah Pulliam.

Sept. 23—John H. McFarren-Elizabeth Maulden. Asa W. Allen, J. P.

Feb. 11—Orville Cauthon-Elizabeth Harrison.

Oct. 3—Robert Rodgers-Nancy Rudd.

Feb. 24—Agrippa Scott-Jane Gray.

Sept. 23—Thomas G. Edwards-Sophia Wilkinson.

Sept. 23—John Gober-Sarah Jones.

Sept. 29—Jacob Smith-Eliza Ann Williams. Samuel McCollum, J. P.

Aug. 22—Alex. McCarter-Lucy McDow.

Oct. 16—Ichabod Sayer-Mary Thomason.

Jan. 13—Cloud Barton-Martha H. Bird.

Nov. 17—James Anderson-Martha Arrowood.

Nov. 18—Levi Crow-Mary Carson.

Nov. 11—Riley Mitchell-Harriet M. Combs.

Nov. 28—Philip L. Allbritton-Mary F. Merrell.

Dec. 9—John Green-Elizabeth Hughes.

Dec. 10—Thomas J. Crow-Jane Sewell. Woodson Blankinship, J. P.

Dec. 30—John Ledbetter-Susan Williams. John B. Chappel, M. G.

Dec. 23—John B. Wiley-Nancy Jones.

Dec. 23—James Stovall-Sarah Edwards.

Sept. 25—James Davis-Mary Anthony.

Jan. 2—Wiley Watkins-Permelia N. Reed.

Nov. 30—Wm. Simmons-Arcada Mitchell.

Sept. 7—Wm. Sheerdon-Tryphena Garrison.

Nov. 4—Wm. Anderson-Elizabeth Morgan.

Aug. 10—Capel Garrison-Elizabeth Baker.

Dec. 20—Wm. F. Neal-Mary D. Key.

Aug. 21—Jacob Clark-Lucy Ausburn.

Oct. 17—Hugh Harrison-Caroline W. Harris.

Nov. 4—Asa Scott-Lucinda McFarland.

Oct. 20—Osborn Garner-Mary Baldwin.

Oct. 10—Jacob Noggle-Martha Bing.

Nov. 12—Abner Sosebee-Malinda Payne.

June 14—Wm. B. Smith-Sarah Age (Agee?).

Nov. 16—Drury Fry-Margaret Freeman.

April 22—John Berry-Martha Ellis.

Oct. 14—William Parks-Nancy Haynes.

Nov. 4—Stephen Haynes-Mary Parks.

Nov. 3—Marshall Parks-Mary Macbourn.

1831.

Jan. 13—Spencer Holcomb-Peggy Lawrence.

March 8—Chas. R. Glazier-Sarah McCarter.

March 15—Waddy Stokes-Malinda Starrett. Nelson Osborn, M. G.

Jan. 20—Dudley J. Chandler-Nancy Jolly. Nath'l R. Hood, J. P.

Jan. 13—Green B. Sewell-Winney Seegar.

Feb. 24—Henry J. Morris-Aseth Allen. William Alexander, J. P.

March 22—Samuel Field-Martha W. Bagwell.

Feb. 15—Benjamin Starrett-Cynthia Iley.

March 10—Greenberry Dobbs-Patsy Goodsom. Absalom Holcomb, J. I. C.

March 3—Wm. R. Howing-Susannah Seegar. Jacob Strickland, J. P.

Oct. 30—Martin Williams-Mary Kesler.

Oct. 13—Martin Meeks-Susan Morris. Littleton Meeks, M. G.

Sept. 22—Wm. Stoe-Susannah Catlett.

Aug. 21—Benjamin Chappleer-Elizabeth Milum(?).

May 27—Hezekiah Buckner-Rutha Ayers. Robert Wilbanks, Esqr.

Aug. 9—Frederick Beall-Margery McMillion.

May 22—Nathan L. Reed-Sarahann Downs. Wm. Burroughs, J. P.

May 31—Horatio Beall-Polly Starrett.

June 28—Chafen Chatham-Sylvania Lacy.

June 30—Thomas C. McIntire-Louisa H. Allen.

May 19—Francis McCall-Nancy McNeal.

April 25—Wm. Harris-Mandy Melviry Woods. Richard Smith, J. P.

May 24—Mathew B. H. Cockeram-Martha Hooper.

Aug. 25—Edmund F. Bush-Adaline Borders.

July 3—Martin Rouz-Drecy Jackson. Bartlett Jones, J. P.

Aug. 4—Ottoway W. Vaughan-Elizabeth Dodson.

Sept. 25—Seabern Whitaker-Denersa Compton.

Oct. 6—James H. Wilson-Sarah T. Stubbs.

Sept. 6—John M. Payne-Elizabeth Bellamy. Hiram Bennett, J. P.

Oct. 20—John W. Crow-Aves Porter. George W. Humphries, J. P.

Oct. 6—Theodore Turk-Elizabeth M. Little.

Nov. 3—John W. Stubbs-Martha P. Wilson.

Feb. 3—Amos Osborn-Rachel Davis.

Dec. 22—Hampton Ramsey-Sarah Henson.

Aug. 4—Nacy Meeks-Eliza Chalmers. Samuel Morgan, J. P.

Dec. 7—John Boswell-Louisa Johnson.

Dec. 23—Benj. S. Pulliam-Elender Turman.

March 17—Archibald Jordan-Lucinda Tate.

Oct. 30—Thomas Payne-Sillender Varner.

Dec. 27—Joel Blackwell-Judah Ann Edwards.

Nov. 3—Jeremiah Hendricks-Sarah Crawford.

Sept. 29—Benjamin Tucker, Jr.-Sarah Legrande.

Dec. 15—Johnson Rogers-Aggy Johnson.

Sept. 27—Wm. Manley-Nancy Tucker.

Dec. 16—Thomas Payne, Jr.-Mary Ann Adcock.

Dec. 5—Brinson Martin-Sally Meadows.

Dec. 8—James Mills-Elizabeth Bennett.

Nov. 13—Thomas Jackson-Mary Catlett. Joseph Byers, M. G.

Dec. 20—Elihu Langston-Martha H. Neal.

Aug. 11—Isom Lowery-Mary Baskin.

Dec. 23—James A. Sewell-Mary Vaughan.

Oct. 18—John Williams-Elizabeth Neal.

June 26—Ambrose Payne-Loradee L. Briant.

July 14—Micajah Garvin-Ann Kelly.

Sept. 27—Middleton Finn-Syntha Skelton.

Dec. 22—John Burton-Nancy Harrison.

Nov. 18—Curtis Tapp-Nancy Cary.

Dec. 11—John F. Carroll-Nancy Kirk. Carter White, J. P.

Sept. 25—Wm. Mills-Rutha Jones.

Nov. 27—Jesse Warmack-Malinda Scott.

1832.

Jan. 12—Samuel F. Alexander-Matilda Neal. John S. Wilson, M. G.

Jan. 12—Benjamin H. Bobo-Mary Faire.

Jan. 26—Jackson Hays-Nancy Green. Benjamin Stonecypher, J. P.

Jan. 1—Hezekiah Davis-Sarah Brewer.

Jan. 1—Cooper Bennett-Nancy Mills. Hiram Bennett, J. P.

Jan. 1—James Saxon-Nancy Harrison.

Jan. 4—George W. Wesley-Jane Jones.

Jan. 8—Elza Chandler-Elizabeth Johnson.

Feb. 16—Cooper B. Feller (Fuller?)-Amy Stonecypher.

Feb. 12—Johnson Weems-Pamelia Leach.

June 28—Wiley Smith-Prudence Murdock.

June 10—John Ray-Sarah Howell.

March 1—Daniel Goode-Artemissa Horton. John Catlett, J. P.

Jan. 1—John P. Jolley-Mary Cook.

April 5—Pleasant Bellamy-Sarah Chatham.

April 3—Samuel Knox-Mary Ann Swift. Asa Chandler, J. P.

Jan. 26—George Kesler-Mary Miller.

Jan. 13—Micajah Walters-Mary Cickeram.

March 1—William Riley-Lucinda Chandler.

Feb. 23—Hiram Vaughters-Elizabeth Glenn.

April 6—John Vaughan-Sarah Black.

June 17—John M. Burgess-Martha S. Mitchell.

Jan. 31—Esley Hunt-Susan Dailey.

March 11—William Flood-Rebecca Smith.

April 30—James Morgan-Mary Burgess.

Jan. 29—John Sartain, Sr.-Mary Ann Coker. John Bramblett, M. G.

Jan. 24—John Ballenger-Liney Williams.

Dec. 20—William Vaughan-Mary Wilkinson.

Dec. 31—Levi Hosey-Harriet Dilport. Robert Mitchell, J. P.

Dec. 13—Elisha Lowery-Polly Hand.

Aug. 20—Gilford E. Hendricks-Susan Crider.

July 19—Peter Bennett-Ann Cobb.

Jan. 5—William Anders-Mary McCarter.

June 7—William Duell-Elizabeth Felgham (Fulghum?)

March 8—John Bramblett-Dicey Clark.

March 8—James Mabry-Sarah Colyer.

April 19—Baker Ayers-Elizabeth Shelnut.

May 22—James H. Hood-Emily Cook. Joseph McEntyre, J. P.

Feb. 9—Calvin W. Patterson-Elizabeth Attaway.

Aug. 16—James King-Virginia N. Neal.

Oct. 11—Joel Dickerson-Elizabeth Slaton.

Oct. 11—H. K. Philips-Nancy Patterson. James Attaway, J. P.

Sept. 20—Allen Warwick-Louisa H. Holley.

Sept. 20—Michael Cox-Mary Thornton. R. Thornton, M. G.

Oct. 23—John M. Allen-Marta Mackie.

Dec. 27—Asa Bellamy-Katherine Yarbrough.

Oct. 11—Wesley Royster-Polly Murdock.

Nov. 8—Wm. R. Graham-Malisa Payne.

April 8—Alison Bell-Matilda Freeman.

Oct. 25—James M. Black-Mary M. Conch.

March 11—Thomas Childers-Milly Vickry.

Aug. 24—Marcus W. Pair-Hannah Keesler.

June 28—Littleberry Underwood-Louisa Key.

Nov. 18—Wm. Hughes-Nicey James.

Nov. 25—Joseph Coker-Cloe Bridges. Wm. King, J. P.

Oct. 18—Barnabas Garrison-Jane Candle.

Dec. 27—Joel M. Westbrook-Lucy Riley.

Nov. 20—John R. Pack-Leah Waters.

Oct. 25—Thomas J. Langston-Elizabeth Neal.

Sept. 4—John A. Fowler-Katherine Keesler.

Oct. 15—McKenny Lilt-Patsy Robinston. Chesley Cawthon, J. P.

Dec. 22—James A. Read-Mrs. Margarett Chiles. W. Blankenship, J. P.

Feb. 15—John Peterson-Parmelia Hobgood.

Dec. 27—Allen Scott-Polly McFarland.

Oct. 21—Martin Caloway-Lucinda Scott.

March 8—Allen Holmes-Hester Ann Ramsey.

1833.

Jan. 25—Allen Isbell-Sarah Burton.

Dec. 13—Wm. R. Pool-Susannah Stovall.

Sept. 10—Micajah Martin-Lucy Williams. C. Addison, J. P.

Nov. 7—James Williams-Esther Medders. George W. Key, M. G.

Dec. 5—Richard Wheeler-Caroline Mills.

Jan. 20—Wm. Chatham-Mary Tate.

Jan. 31—Francis Sewell-Lucy Blackwell.

Oct. 13—Gillum Word (Wood?)-Lydia Roper.

Dec. 12—Jarret Purcel-Mary Mabry.

Nov. 21—Daniel Bush-Emily Jones.

Dec. 19—Pleasant Holbrook-Mary Harbour. A. E. Whitney, J. I. C.

March 3—John B. McMillon-Elizabeth Hall. Job Bowen, J. P.

April 26—Wm. Henson-Nancy Ramsey.

July 11—Wilson F. Hunnicut-Elizabeth Hyatt.

May 10—Benjamin Howard-Lucinda Bryan.

Feb. 10—John Isbell-Elizabeth Cockeram.

Dec. 26—Wm. Teasley-Elmiry Reed.

Nov. 1—Moses Collyer-Susan Barnett.

Feb. 12—Perry M. Vaughan-Virginia Mauldin.

March 5—Henry Keesler-Nancy Haley.

April 4—John Cheek-Anna Duncan.

Nov. 21—James Boswell-Elizabeth Graddy James Stovall, J. P.

Feb. 14—James Carpenter-Eliza H. Barrett.

March 15—John Curry-Susan Purcell.

Nov. 7—Dr. Terrell H. Jones-Judith A. Bush.

Dec. 5—John Mulkey-Elizabeth Leach.

Dec. 19—Andrew Norwood-Elizabeth Mitchell. Robert Mitchell, J. P.

Oct. 17—Wm. Shearly-Adaline Eavans.

Aug. 27—Alexander Pickens-Elizabeth Pickens.

Nov. 28—Albert G. Bagwell-Rebecca Walker.

April 30—R. W. Whitten-Mary Phips. Wm. R. Wellborn, M. G.

June 3—Martin Pierce-Nancy Burgess.

April 8—Joseph H. Vickrey-Patience Sanders.

Jan. 17—Wilkins Stovall-Mahaley Garrett.

March 12—John G. Baker-Frankey Mullinix.

Feb. 18—Alfred Smith-Cassandra Chapplear.

Aug. 18—Thomas Wilkerson-Clarkey Isbell.

Dec. 20—Andrew K. Harper-Anna Little.

Oct. 15—Eda Bowers-Jane Glover.

June 9—Daniel McIntire-Sarah Kerk.

March 31—Jesse Bryan-Sarah Horton.

Aug. 25—Hampton Patterson-Mary Bowers.

1834.

Jan. 18—Wm. L. Martin-Lance E. Miller.

Jan. 26—Gillam Wilbanks-Rebecca Callahan.

Oct. 30—Oliver Harrison-Susan Stone. Thomas Farmer, J. I. C.

Nov. 15—Eli L. Maberry-Martha Scroggins. S. G. Thomason, J. P.

Feb. 12—John R. Dickerson-Elizabeth Adge (Edge?).

Feb. 10—Benjamin B. Parker-Sarah Wilson. J. Crandal, J. I. C.

Dec. 25—Talbot Key-Mrs. Effa Burgess.

Aug. 3—Alex. Powers-Nancy Howell. R. A. R. Neal, J. P.

Dec. 14—Michael Betenbee-Caroline Hemphill.

Nov. 6—Daniel Anders-Lucinda Vessels.

Nov. 5—Garland Hooper-Atena Payne.

June 10—Benjamin R. Hill-Sally Maulens. Harvey M. Mayes, J. P.

Nov. 30—James Murphy-Anna Garner.

Nov. 7—James R. McCalla-Pelonia A. E. Yancey. R. McAlpin, M. G.

Dec. 17—Joel Purcell-Martha Guest.

Dec. 28—Eppa Morris-Eliza Turman. Abram Dean, J. I. C.

Nov. 4—N. E. Hilburn-Martha E. Bird. Wm. Shackelford, J. P.

March 30—Wm. L. Westbrook-Mariah Vaufgan.

March 19—Wm. Ray-Matilda Holcomb. John A. Davis, M. G.

March 13—Stephen B. Westbrook-Mary Shannon.

Aug. 17—Richard L. Aycock-Rachel Leach.

Dec. 18—James Bell-Welthy Ann Wood.

Feb. 20—John Hardy-Elizabeth Freeman.

Oct. 12—Chuff Martin-Annes Jolly.

April 23—Richard Hooper-Adene Miller.

Jan. 1—Richard Jenkins-Alpha Pulliam.

Dec. 29—Moses B. Crawford-Nancy Smith.

Aug. 20—Joel Scott-Vesta Smith.

Nov. 8—David Guest-Matilda Hicks.

1835.

Jan. 5—Harvy Hix-Sarah Mixon. Robert Crump, J. P.

Jan. 14—Fleming Winyard-Mary Guest. Asa York, J. P.

Jan. 1—Eli F. Haines-Martha Harbour. D. L. Ballens, Elder in M. E. Church.

Jan. 29—James Mitchell-Lucy Bond. Mathew M. Vandiver, M. G.

Feb. 12—Wm. P. Watters-Mary B. Black.

Feb. 6—John Crider-Sophia Crider. Thomas H. Murdock, J. P.

Feb. 5—David Barton-Winney Mitchell.

April 2—Jacob P. Reed-Teressa C. Hammond. W. Magee, M. G.

Feb. 21—Pendleton Garrett-Frances Hutchens.

March 17—Wm. C. Wright-Delilah Bridges. John B. Wade, M. G.

From Deed Books in Clerk's Office, Carnesville, Franklin County, Georgia, and rearranged in regard to dates. All deeds are for lands or slaves.

1785

James Cobb to Nicholas Long, Sr., of Halifax County, N. C.

Joseph Jeter and wife Mary make various deeds.

Richard Hill and wife Elizabeth make various deeds.

1786

John Hutchings Johnson and wife Sarah.

1787

Amon Ayers to George Cockburn.

Sevastin Inlow of Wilkes County.

Stephen Carsey and wife Nancy.

John Partin and wife Sary.

John Golson and wife Ann of Wilkes County.

John Hubbard and wife Elizabeth.

Thomas Gilbert and wife Hannah.

John Cobbs and wife Mildred.

Malachi Jones to Henry Chappelear.

John Rose's heirs: Thomas Rose sen. and jun., and Henry Rose of Wilkes County.

1788

Reuben Ballard and wife Absilla A.

John Palmer and wife Susannah.

Manoah, alias Noah, Cloud and wife Ennoler of Wilkes County.

Robert Poague and wife Margaret.

Jesse Webb of Green Co., N. C.

John Carter and wife Ann.

Temus Spratlin and wife Winifred of Wilkes County.

1789

Ralph Banks and wife Rachel.

Daniel Ayers and wife Agnes.

Henry Wilson of Abbeville, S. C., Witness by John Wilson.

Ambrose Downs and wife Sabra.

James Hill and wife Mary.

Berryman Shumate of S. C.

1789

Thomas Cotham and wife Elizabeth.

William Lucas and wife Barbara.

Pendleton Isbell and wife Sarah of S. C.

Nathan Barnett and wife Lucy.

William Wheeler and wife Mary of Wilkes County.

Benjamin Echols and wife Sabra.

Michael Wilkerson and wife Elizabeth of state of N. C. and Abbeville Co.

John Bryan and wife Nancy.

John Morgan and wife Betsy.

Daniel Morgan and wife Deborah.

Benjamin Ashworth and wife Sarah.

Charles Bedinfield and wife Sarah.

John Clark and wife Rosanna.

George Ogg of Tarboro N. C., but formerly of Richmond Co., Ga.

William Reynolds and wife Martha.

Benjamin Porter and wife Patsy Claborn of Wilkes Co.

1790

Reuben Allen and wife Elizabeth of Wilkes Co.

Christopher Lyner and wife Jane of Wilkes Co.

Hannah Bell, widow of George Bell, of Franklin Co., late of Rockbridge Co., Va., appoints Joseph Strickland, of Rockbridge, as her atty. to recover from Samuel Wilson.

John Stonecypher and wife Ann.

William and Joseph Gibbons, brothers, of Chatham Co., Ga. Witness: Francis Courvoisie and Baruch Gibbons.

Thomas Carter and wife Mary.

Richard Runnels and wife Margaret.

Robert Cogbil Burton of Abbeville, S. C.

David Hillhouse and wife Sarah.

Silas Mercer and wife Dorcas.

1790

William Seay and wife Phoebe.

Nathan Coffey and wife Mary.

John Carter and wife Nancy.

Thomas Scott and wife Elizabeth.

Joseph Humphreys and wife Rebeckah.

Thomas Patton and wife Arcada.

Benjamin Hubbard and wife Catherine.

John Depriest and wife Jane of Wilkes Co.

William George and wife Dolly.

Thomas Bush and wife Elizabeth.

1791

Robert Thrasher and wife Elizabeth.

Joseph Martin Russell and wife Ailsey.

William Brown and wife Sarah.

Micajah Williamson and wife Sally.

Mordecai and Nathan Benton.

Richard Call and wife Alethia Anderson Call.

John Barnett and wife Caroline.

John Brown and wife Dolly.

Josiah Woods and wife Sarah of Wilkes Co.

William Hightower and wife Amelia.

William Tindall and wife Betty Ann of Columbia Co.

Wilkins Richardson and wife Prudence.

John Tweedle and wife Sarah.

Mark Phillips and wife Nancy.

Thomas Payne sen., Ex. and heir of Thomas Payne decd. Other heirs: William, John, Nancy, Nathaniel, Moses, Champneys, Shorsbury and Ruth Payne.

Obadiah Hooper of Pendleton, S. C.

Aquilla Burns to Philemon Martin of Spartanburg, S. C.

Leonard McGruder of Prince George Co., Md., to James Williams of Annapolis, merchants.

1791

Henry Osborne to George Naylor. Both of Augusta, Ga.

Robert Means and wife Margaret.

John Peter Wagnon and wife Rebeckah of Augusta, Ga.

James Lamar, Jr., and wife Alasannah, of Columbia Co., Ga.

Jeremiah Cleveland and wife Mary.

Walton Harris senior and wife Rebeckah.

Samuel Gardner and wife —— of Wilkes Co.

John Walters and wife Mary.

John Colman and wife Polly.

William Lewis and wife Catherine.

1792

John Lindsay and wife Mary.

William Arnold and wife Susannah.

John Goodwin gift to son John Goodwin Jr.

Benjamin Fry and wife Mary.

Gideon Davis and wife Milly of Elbert Co.

John Neale and wife Joanna (sometimes spelt Nail).

Samuel Sherrill and wife Mary.

John Payne and wife Nancy.

Joshua Sledd and wife Winifred.

Henry Langford of Greenville and Eli Langford of Pendleton (S. C.)

Jesse Stallings and wife Sary of Wilkes Co.

Jonathan Palmer and wife Ruth of Wilkes Co.
Jeremiah Cleveland and wife Nancy Sutton Cleveland.
John Clark and wife Rosannah.
John Cloud and wife Elizabeth.

1793

Thomas Harrington and wife Sarah.
David Terrell and wife Mary.
John Freeman and wife Catherine.
Moses Payne and wife Jenny.
Thomas Harrington and wife Caty to son Drury. (See above.)
Robert Thrasher and wife Elizabeth.
Julian Neal and wife Mary.
William Reilly and wife Barbara.
Patrick Vance and wife Sarah.
Thomas Carter and wife Elizabeth.
Joseph Cloud Thrasher of Rockingham Co., N. C.
Absalom Smith and wife Winny of Hancock Co., to William Person, son of Enoch Person and wife Diana. Deed is signed as ''Abraham Smith.''
William Stone and wife Mary.
Nathaniel Allen and wife Permelia of Elbert Co.

1794

John Doolen and wife Nancy.
Abraham Shelly, deed of gift to son John Shelly.
John Diamond and wife Elizabeth of Oglethorpe Co.
Stephen Heard and wife Betsy.
Philemon Martin and Tax Collector.
John Cunningham and wife Ann of Elbert Co.
Absalom Thurman and wife Elizabeth of Wilkes Co.
Thomas Smyth and wife Ann of Augusta, Ga.
Nice Cleveland and wife Jane.
Robert McGowan and wife Mary.

Major George Naylor, formerly of Augusta, now of Philadelphia, to Nathaniel Fields and Joshua Harlan, merchants of Philadelphia.

Basil Lamar and wife Mary of Wilkes Co.

John King and wife Nancy of Greene Co.

Susanna, wife of James Clayland of Augusta, Ga., relinquishes her dower.

Julian Neal, Jr., and wife Mary of Elbert Co.

Asa Estes and wife Anna.

Hugh Hay to Gilbert Hay, Physician.

1794

Peter Thompson and wife Lamentation of Abbeville, S. C.

Patrick Cruikshanks of Chatham Co., Ga., to Thomas Fitzsimmons of Philadelphia.

Joseph Wilson and wife Margaret.

George D. Moore of Maryland to William Bagley.

William Baker, Surveyor, was of Maryland.

1795

John Harrington and wife Agatha (sometimes spelt Agnes.)

James R. Whitney, Tax Coll. to Angus Martin of Augusta.

Thomas Gragg to Robert Williamson.

Edward Rice and wife Sarah to William Nicks.

George Kenny, Sheriff, to Nimrod House—executed as property of Lewis Bobo, decd.

William Moss and wife Drusilla of Elbert Co.

George Pettigrew and wife Jene.

John Lane and wife Betsy.

Abraham Pierce of Edgefield, S. C., and George Ogg, of Augusta.

Division of estate of Charles Finch, Dec'd. In Re: William Finch, Susanna, Betsy and Burdett Finch, Thomas Willingham and Judah his wife of Oglethorpe Co.; Starke

Saunders and Nancy his wife, James Comer and Fanny his wife of Hancock Co. and Charles Finch; William Anderson and Sarah his wife of Wilkes Co., being heirs of said estate. Joyce Finch and Richard Copeland Exrs. of one part, and Josiah Goldsby of Oglethorpe Co. Ex. of the other part.

Thomas Murray and wife Janey of Wilkes Co.

Samuel Gardner of Wilkes Co. to Jesse Pie.

Robert Pulliam and wife Mary.

William Bailey of Amherst Co., Va.

Joseph Pulliam and wife Jean.

Mathew Arthur and wife Caty to John Gilbert of Guilford Co., N. C.

Lewis McLain and wife Rhoda of Wilkes Co.

William Sloan sr. and jr. of Pendleton, S. C., and David Sloan.

James Coile and wife Jean.

1795

Thomas Martin of Augusta Co., Va.

Aaron Campbell and wife Lydia.

James Brady and wife Mary of Elbert Co.

Warren Philpot and wife Martha.

Hugh McDonald and wife Helen of Elbert Co.

Charles Gilbert and wife Sarah.

Richard Aycock and wife Judith Crawford Aycock of Wilkes Co.

Joseph Humphreys and wife Hannah.

Henry Lyner and wife Margaret.

Thomas Gilbert and wife Hannah.

Leonard McGruder of Md. and Gen. James Smith of Baltimore.

1796

Henry Holcom to son Henry, deed of gift. Wit. by Ann Holcom, Smithy Dooler, Jeptha White, Edward McGarey and wife Margaret of Elbert Co.

William Strong senior and junior.

Daniel Saffold and wife Elizabeth.

George Furman and wife Elizabeth.

Thomas Cox and wife Mary.

Bethuel Riggs and wife Nancy.

1797

George Stovall and wife Ann of Elbert Co., to William Wilkinson.

Benjamin Echols deed to Nancy Purcel.

James McClain and wife Minney to James Cotton.

James Freeman of Elbert Co. to Talmon Harbour of Franklin Co.

James Tait and wife Rebeckah.

Cuthbert Hudson and wife Elizabeth to the heirs of David Hudson.

George Shenald and wife Elizabeth, formerly widow of John Morgan, and mother of William Morgan.

Daniel Morgan sen. and wife Deborah.

Larkin Prestidge appoints his father John Prestridge his atty. for property in Pittsylvania Co., Va.

Thomas Garden and wife Lette, formerly Prestridge, appoints John Prestridge atty. for her property from her grandfather, John Prestridge of Pittsylvania Co., Va.

William Payne to Thomas Cotton sen.

Philamon Martin deed of gift to son Aaron and daughter Elizabeth.

John Cook and wife Alsey.

John Wilson and wife Mary.

Edward Bryant and wife Susannah.

William Bridges and wife Elizabeth.

Barnabas Pace and wife Agnes.

George Naylor and wife Henrietta.

Daniel Easley of Jackson Co., to Samuel Gardner.

1798

Reuben Allen of Elbert Co., to John Holland.
Henry Head and wife Elizabeth of Orange Co., Va.
James H. Little and wife Anna.

1799

Malachi Jones to Sherrod Holcomb.

1800

Elizabeth, Jane and Margaret Gillespie and James S. Baskins of Abbeville Dist., S. C., and John Allison of Wilkes Co., N. C., and Alexander Patterson of Elbert Co., to Lowry Gillespie. Land formerly of James Gillespie. Wit: John Cowan, Mathew Gillespie, James Vernon.

1801

Jonathan Beeson and wife Elizabeth.

1802

Christopher Williams, Gent., of Charleston, S. C., and wife Mary to Charles Ingram.

John Holland to Jesse Holland.

William Arnold and wife Polly.

Charles Young of Philadelphia to James Patton of Alexandria, Va., for 5 shillings of Pennsylvania money for 24940 acres of land in Franklin Co., Ga., patented to Isaac Randolph, who by his attorney Gideon Dennison transfers to David Allison.

Henry Holcomb and wife Priscilla, to Samuel Baker, land in Botetourt Co., Va. (Bedford Co.) Wit. by Sherwood and Richard Holcomb, and Jane Dooley. (Recorded 1804).

George Sibbalds of Augusta to Lewis Sewall of Columbia Co.

Barbara Moss to Thomas West Brook. Deed.

Lewis Small of Columbia Co., to Andrew Millican.

Vincent Garner and wife Elizabeth.
William Bowman and wife Sarah.
James Wyly and wife Barbara.
John Odell of Newberry S. C. from James Odell.
Robert Middleton and wife Elizabeth.
Philip Vineyard to John Williams of Buncombe Co.,
N. C.
Isaac Strickland and wife Priscilla (deed of date
1800).
John Owen and wife Rhoda.
Rial Price to John Haggard.
William Black and wife Elizabeth.
Elizabeth Bush to son in law Samuel Headen and wife
Lydia.
George Prickett and wife Sarah.
William Lowery and wife Mary land granted to Eliza-
beth Nunnelee.

1803

Lewis Dickerson to James Stogaler. Wit: John J.
Dickerson.
Littleberry Shields and wife Susannah.
John Caen and wife Anne Whitworth Caen.
Daniel Morgan and wife Patience.
Zebulon Garrison and wife Rebeckah.
William Hall and wife Jean.
Jonathan Jackson Hays and wife Jenett who had a
bequest from Samuel Heartson of Va.
William King and wife Polly.
Maj. John Holland to Daniel Bush, minor.
Thomas Payne and wife Milly.
James McClain and wife Jemimah.
William Henley and wife Mary.
James Garner and wife Sarah.
David Dodd and wife Abigail.
John Daricott Esq. and wife Rebeckah.
Edmund Henley and wife Sara.

Charles and William H. Tait, exrs. of James Tait of Elbert Co., dec'd.

Levin Dixon J. P. attests to deed of John Parker to Lewis Dickson.

Augustine Webb and wife Alice. Wit: Christopher Tyner and Joseph Black.

Christopher Clark and wife Rebeckah. Wit: Sterling Strange and D. Hudson.

Joseph Gunnalds of Jackson Co., Tenn., appoints William Black his atty.

Joseph Pane Kennedy of New Haven, Conn., now temporarily in Co. of Franklin, appoints trusty friend Obadiah Hooper as his atty.

James Hunt of Sumner Co., Tenn., appoints Nathaniel Hunt his atty.

1804

William Varnall and wife Elizabeth.

Gilbert duBois Berranger of Wilkes Co., Ga., to Lewis Picquet for his son Antonne Picquet, land in Franklin Co. "For natural love and affection."

William Varnall and wife Elizabeth.

James Sparks and wife Nancy.

Attestation of Sterling Tucker that he had married Mary Ann Ingram, the widow of Thomas Ingram. That John Ingram, brother of Mary Ann had departed this life and Sterling Tucker relinquishes any rights he may have, to Charles Ingram. Wit: Robert Lanier, Jon. Lanier, William Ingram, John H. Harper.

Mathew Jordan of Oglethorpe Co.

Stephen White of Jackson Co. to adms. of Ishmael Vineyard.

Stephen Beaver and wife Nancy.

John Harris to Elijah Martin, both of Franklin Co.

William Henley and wife Mary.

John Gilbert and wife Mary.

Dixon Naylor and wife Mary.

George Pettigrew and wife Jean.

George Potts and wife Judy.

Poyndexter Payne and wife Anney.

Samuel Morgan sen. and wife Nancy.

Samuel Ward deed of gift to niece Lucy, wife of Joel Yowell.

Solomon Potter and wife Patsey.

Joel Doss and wife Mary.

Pleasant Webb and wife Nancy.

Elijah Christian and wife Elizabeth.

John Philip Aduner(?) and wife Jane.

Joseph Payne and wife Mary.

Michael Borden and wife Mary.

Thomas Holcomb and wife Penelopy.

Samuel Philips to nephew John Philips Hays.

John Elkins of Franklin Co. to John Baker.

William Dean and wife Susannah.

John Turman and wife Polly to George Turman.

William Jackson and wife Nancy.

George Sibbald and wife Rachel of Augusta.

Charity Jones appoints her son Tignal Jones her atty. to recover property from William Parker, Ex. of James Parker—land on Roan Oak River, N. C. Charity was sister of James.

Joel Prickett and wife Mary.

Thomas Roberds and wife Anna.

John Cross and wife Nancy.

William Little and wife Elizabeth.

William David and wife Lucy.

Swift Mullins and wife Anna.

Edmund Henley and wife Jane.

William Samson and wife Elizabeth, of Wilkes Co.

John Morris and wife Sarah.

Julius Howard and wife Susannah.

Rowland Horsley and wife Sarah.

William Gober, jr., and wife Margaret.

Moses Sanders' gift to his son Moses.

William Craine gift to son Abijah.

1805

John Easley and wife Sarah.

Warren Stoe and wife Sally.

Richard Hooper and wife Jemima.

John Mullin, jr., to Lucy, Patty, and Dorothy Farmer (sale).

Peter Carrell and wife Mary.

Joseph Pulliam and wife Jane.

Philip Mulkey, sr., to gr. son Mark Mulkey, minor. Wit: Nancy Mulkey, Peter Shepherd, A. B. Harris.

Henry Rose, by his atty. Drury Rose, to John Tatum.

Josiah N. Kennedy of Warren Co. adm. on estate of Joseph Kennedy.

Elijah Renshaw and wife Margaret.

John Baker and wife Sarah to Benjamin Baker (sale).

Jeremiah Taylor and wife Leah.

Robert Todd of Elbert Co. to John Nesbit. Wit: John Barber.

Randolph Walker and wife Sarah.

Israel Pritchett and wife Sarah.

Martin and John W. Kidd of Elbert Co.

John Hubbard and wife Salley of Elbert Co., to John Holcombe.

Richard Dodd and wife Mary.

Joachin Hudson and wife Nancy.

William Fleming and wife Mary.

Robert Bean and wife Martha of Rutherford Co., Tenn.

William Eatherington and wife Eunice of Jackson Co.

Nancy Newberry, widow, to Moses Walters. Deed.

William Swift and wife Lucy.

Swift Mullins and wife Anna.

Thomas Payne and wife Yanaka.

Charles Ingram, bro. of Benjamin dec'd, and **wife** Elizabeth.

John A. Baker and wife Jane.

Reuben White and wife Elizabeth.

John Westbrook and wife Ellender.

John Dorsey and wife Rebeckah to Basil Dorsey.

Farley Thompson and wife Elizabeth.

John McGowan and wife Hannah.

Burrell Whitehead and wife Frances.

John Forsyth and wife Clara.

John Owens and wife Rhoda.

John Warren, Reuben and Thomas Warren at this time.

Jesse Holland and wife Mary.

William Pulliam and wife Sally.

Hannah Wright (widow of Obadiah Wright, and formerly Hannah Roberts) gift to son John Wright of a legacy from her father, Alexander Roberts, of 100 lbs. of Virginia currency, in his will of date Feb. 15, 1779. Her deed is of date of Aug. 11, 1805, and on the 18th of this month she entered in marriage agreement with Dan'l Beall, which was witnessed by an Obadiah Wright, presumably her son.

John Sapp and wife Elizabeth.

Robert Shewmake and wife Dicey.

David Greer and wife Hannah, of Pendleton, S. C.

1806

Obadiah Jones, gift to daughters Mary and Margaret Jones.

Gyllum Hudson to Stephen Garrett, tract originally granted to Cuthbert Hudson; Witnessed by Joachim Hudson.

John Newman and wife Mary to John Martin.

Tryon Patterson and Joseph Kiser, witnesses.

Stephen Garrett of S. C. to Thomas Thornton. Wit: Andrew Mauldin, Gabriel Martin.

1806

Frederick Stevilie of Burke Co., N. C., atty. of John Henry Stevilie, to Charles Warren, tract formerly granted to Thomas Carter, Dec. 6, 1785, on Shoal Creek.

Sterling Williamson and wife Leah.

John Brown deed of gift to son Peter.

George Cockburn and wife Elizabeth.

Edward Moore and wife Lucy.

Benjamin Pruitt and wife Mary.

John Williams and wife Rachel.

Randolph Walker and wife Sarah.

William, John and Lewis Gober, appoint George Gober their atty. in re estate of George Gober, dec'd of Granville Co., N. C.

Charles Angle deed of gift to minor son Thomas, daughters Sally and Lucy, step son John Banister Collins, step daughter Mary Collins. Wit: Philip and Mary Mulkey.

John Mullins in behalf of Martha Mullins, late Martha Farmer, with Lucy, Dorothy and Thomas Farmer, heirs of Josiah Farmer, late of Granville Co., N. C.

John Mayfield of Warren Co., N. C.

James McBee and wife Sarah.

Joshua Prestridge and wife Elizabeth.

James Gardner and wife Elizabeth.

Jesse Thomas and wife Nancy.

Thomas Smith and wife Sarah.

Samson Lane and wife Polly.

Julian Neal and wife Mary.

William T. Cook and wife Frances.

Larkin Prestridge and wife Elcy.

John Herrington, now of Ky., appoints Thomas Herrington his atty.

Thomas Davis and wife Kesiah.

Thomas Thomas and wife Christian.
Lewis Small and wife Elizabeth.
Christopher Baker and wife Mary.
Thomas Farrar gift to grand son Francis Howard Farrar. Wit: Richard Arrington.

1807

John Sandige and wife Susannah.
Ruth Barton to David Bryant. Wit: Presley Barton and Flower Swift.
John Loden and wife Susannah of Pendleton, S. C.
William W. Walton and wife Elizabeth.
John Erranton (Herrington?) to Daniel Johnson.
Nimrod House to Vineyard Crafford.
Francis Cook and wife Betty.
Frederick Beall and wife Martha Peyton Beall.
Nimrod House and wife Ruth.
Thomas Barton to Richard Hutcheson of Va.
Edmund King and wife Elizabeth, to Jacob Purcell, land on Tugaloo River where he now lives.
Benjamin Baker, son of Absalom Baker to Benjamin Baker, jr.
Moses Deman and wife Elizabeth.
Isaac Barrett of Elbert Co., to Ninian Barrett, sen.
Abner Franklin and wife Rhoda.
James Blair to Evin Todhunter.
John Barnett of Clark Co., to Esaias Harbour.
Joseph Nail (also Neal) to William Smith. Both of Wilkes Co.
James Shepherd of Elbert Co., to John Connally.
Nathaniel Williams and wife Hannah. Wit: Robert Williams.
Thomas Jordan and wife Sarah.
Benjamin Barton and wife Rachel.
Henry Black and wife Susannah.
John Shankle, sen. and wife Betsy, to Eli Shankle. Wit: Abraham Shankle.

John Tabor and wife Elizabeth, of Elbert Co.

William Scott and wife Polly.

Benjamin Martin and wife Elinor.

Christopher Baber and wife Nancy.

1808

John Neal and wife Joanna, land formerly granted to Julian Neal.

Joseph Walker to John and Derrell Martin. (These were brothers of Philemon and Elizabeth Martin, heirs of Philemon Martin, sen. Elizabeth died a minor.)

Henry Strickland and wife Ruth to William and Felix Gilbert of Wilkes Co. Wit: O. H. Prince.

Gabriel Long of Abbeville, Dist. S. C. To Stephen Dixon.

Jasper Smith of Bedford Co., Tenn., to Charles Ingram, land of James Easther, whose daughters were Teary, wife of Jasper Smith, and Sophea, wife of Joseph Howard. 287 1-2 of this tract was granted to James Easther (on Tom's Creek) and 287 1-2 acres had been the grant of William Bailey, and bought of him by James Easther, April 1788.

Barnard Franklin and wife Patsey.

John Bowman and wife Winnifred.

Reuben Pettijohn of Jackson Co. to James Kirkpatrick.

Jesse Holbrook to John Adam Miller of S. C.

Zachariah White and wife Jincy.

Wyly Rogers and wife Lurany.

Charles Kennon of Wake Co., N. C., to John Kennon, of Hancock Co., Ga. Wit: Lewis Kennon.

John Payne, dec'd, late of Pittsylvania Co., Va. Thomas and Jonathan Payne appoint Reuben Payne their atty. Wit: Swann Hardin, Jerusha Hardin.

Benjamin Barton and wife Rachel.

John Bannett, sen., and jun., of Elbert Co.

Thomas Ward of Pendleton Dist., S. C., to Thomas Baldwin.

Daniel Thornton to Edmund King, quit claim and title to 500 acres for 25 cents.

Moses Randle and wife Rebeckah.

Thomas Covington to "true and affectionate child, Nutty Silman."

Lucy Wilkerson, late Lucy Abernathy, heir and legatee of Tignal Abbernathy, Dec'd. late of the county of Mechlinburg, Virginia, appoints her husband Elisha Wilkerson her atty.; to receive of Burrell Abbernathy, the adm. of Signal Abbernathy, her legacy.

William Calloway and wife Patsey, lottery on Wilkerson Co., to Hannah Hail.

Thomas Carter and wife Elizabeth of Elbert Co.

John Hutchins, formerly of Franklin Co., now of Jackson Co.

Edward Lloyd Thomas to Elizabeth Covington Thomas, deed of sale.

Rowland Cornelius and wife Ellen.

Jesse Hill and wife Margaret.

Samuel Headen to William Bush. Wit: Joshua and Elizabeth Hudson.

William Calloway and wife Linah (or Sinah).

Absalom Carter and wife Rachel.

Elias Sanders and wife Mary.

Joseph Chandler and wife Salley.

Robert Walton and wife Mary.

Thomas Wilburn and wife Mary of Putnam Co.

Thomas Cox and wife Mary.

Barzellia Harrison and wife Ann.

1809

Elijah Martin of Franklin Co., appoints Isaiah Bagley his atty., concerning legacy from Zachariah Martin,

dec'd, late of Chatham Co., N. C., left to son Josiah to pay
to Elijah or his order. At same time Moses Terrell of
Franklin Co., appoints his son Hyram Terrell his atty.
to secure legacy left to Nancy, wife of Moses, by her father Zachariah Martin. Wit: James Martin.

Zedekiah Payne and wife Elizabeth .

Zachariah Thomas and wife Susannah.

William Hall and wife Jane.

Benjamin Jones and wife Susannah.

Croatia and Martha Hartgroves, appoint John Martin
their atty. for legacy from their father, Henry Hartgroves, whose estate is adm. by Royal Barnett of Spartanburg, S. C.

Solomon Hix and wife Tabitha.

John E. Carson and wife Margaret.

William England to Merick Martin.

Elijah Martin appoints James Martin his atty. in re
a tract of land in Wilkinson Co., now Pulaski, part of a
tract obtained from Creek Nation of Indians by a treaty.

Gabriel Martin and wife Delilah.

Isaac Love and wife Nancy.

Philip Maberry and wife Fanny.

Thomas Covington deed of gift to wife Susannah, and
to children: Rebeckah McDowell, Polly and Catherine
Covington, and grand son Isaac Whitaker.

John Easley and wife Sally of Tenn.

Seth Strange and wife Mary.

Gilbert Hay appoints R. Walton his atty.

James Garner and wife Sarah.

Benson Henry and wife Kesiah.

Enoch Brady and wife Lydia.

William Denman and wife Sarah.

Ferdinand Phinizy and wife Margaret of Richmond
Co.

Sampson Lane and wife Polly.

Thomas Whitehead and wife Nancy.

Polydone Naylor, heir of George Naylor.

John Duke and wife Delilah.

Nancy Tucker, relict of John Tucker. Wit.: Samuel, Joseph and John Tucker.

James Quillin and wife Susannah.

1810

Samuel Waters and wife Molly.

Charles Williamson and wife Patsy.

Philip Prewitt and wife Anna to Samuel Prewitt, Jun.

David Terrell and wife Mary of Wilkes Co.

Deed of gift for "natural love and affection," from John James Sweatman to William, Augustine, John, James, jun., and Polly Sweatman.

Obadiah Hooper and wife Sally.

William White and wife Nancy.

William O. Whitney and wife Ruth.

Thomas Gilbert to daughters Polly and Elizabeth.

Zachariah Bryan and wife Sina.

Philip Payne and wife Milly.

Susannah Covington, wife of Thomas, and William Dobbs, divide tract of land given to them by Thomas Covington, sen.

Robert McDowell and wife Rebeckah.

Eli Bryan took oath as Major in 57th. Battalion of Georgia Militia. Sept. 3.

Joseph Martin to James Denman.

Thomas Brooks and wife Elizabeth.

Aaron Campbell and wife Lydia.

Peter Carrol and wife Mary.

Moses Collyer and wife Darcus.

Elizabeth Martin, adm. of estate of late John Martin, appoints Simon Terrell, atty.

William Mitchell and wife Catherine.

William Flanagan and wife Mary.

William Wyly and wife Mary.

Thomas Sparks and wife Elizabeth.

Joseph Penn to Isaiah Bayley or Baxley.

John Able of Lincoln Co., Tenn.

1811

Elizabeth Bush, ex. of Daniel Bush, dec'd. Legatees: Sally Easly, Judah Holland and Susannah Norris of Tennessee, Lydia Haden, John, William and Thomas Bush, of Georgia.

William Bush gives to his sister Susannah Norris of Dickson Co., Tenn., some slaves in trust for her minor daughters, Elizabeth, Orrey and Lidiath Norris.

Thomas, John, Reuben and Charles Warren, are of record.

Henry Sanders and wife Jane.

Christopher Gardner and wife Clary.

Obadiah Hooper and wife Betsy.

Tignal Jones and wife Rhoda.

Gabriel Martin and wife Delilah.

William Shields and wife Mary.

William Young and wife Susannah.

William Smith of Lenoir Co., Tenn.

William Holbrook and wife Priscilla.

Absalom Pregnalls and wife Nancy.

William W. Walton of Giles Co., Tenn.

Samuel Woods and wife Susannah.

Daniel Morgan, sen., and wife Patience.

Daniel Morgan, Jr., and wife Deborah.

Joseph Chandler and wife Nancy.

1812

John Burgess and wife Polly.

John McNeal and wife Hannah.

Zedekiah Payne of Bedford Co., Tenn.

Jesse Hill and wife Margaret.

Seth Hodges of Lincoln Co., Tenn., appoints Thomas Delanoy to represent him in suit for his share of Robert Thrasher's estate, in right of his wife, Elizabeth, now dec'd. John Bryan and Joell Yowell, admns. (Elizabeth wife of Seth Hodges, had previously to her death, deeded her part of this land away. The rest of the heirs are Sary, Represented by James Blair Gorden or Garden, Joseph and Thomas Thrasher.

Burrell Whitehead and wife Frances.

Sarah Bryan, Boley Cannon and Bethel Bryan, admns. of estate of Eli Bryan.

John Cox and wife Nancy.

Margaret, Catey, Eavy Lyner, Thomas Stowers and wife Mary (Lyner) heirs of Henry Lyner. (This name may be Tyner.)

Jephtha Harrington and wife Fanny.

Andrew Williamson and wife Ruth.

Lewis Molder and wife Catherine.

Mark Hardin and wife Nancy.

John Morris and wife Sarah.

Julius Sims and wife Maria.

Thomas Connolly, of Halifax Co., Va., the guardian of Polly, Charles, Archibald, George, Milly and Angelica Connally, heirs of John Connally of Franklin Co., dec'd.

Hutchins Burton and John Ragsdale of Franklin Co., appoint Drury Ragsdale of Mechlinburg Co., Va., atty. in re estate of John Ragsdale, dec'd.

Caleb Garrison and wife Sally.

Levi Garrison and wife Patsey.

Joseph Dudley and wife Mary, who was child and heir of John Lancaster of Charlotte Co., Va., who was a son of Richard Lancaster, and heir of William and Joseph Lancaster, Va. Mary Dudley and her brother William

Lancaster are the only heirs of John Lancaster, and are coheirs with Elizabeth Lancaster, only heir of William Lancaster. In May, 1813, Elizabeth was the wife of Leonard Starke.

Henry Higgins and wife Mary.

Charles Reagan and wife Mary.

Gilbert Hay, exr. and heir of William Hay of Wilkes Co.

John Hubbard and wife Salley.

Sampson Lane and wife Polly.

Aaron Martin of Amit Co., Miss., sells negro to George Martin of same county. Wit: by William Martin. Aaron also releases part of estate of Philemon Martin. Wit: Archibald Martin.

1813

Drury Hutchins and wife Sarah.

Mary, widow of John Cole, to recover from estate of Richard Cole of Louisa Co., Va., property in hands of Samuel Cole.

Jesse Goodwin of Franklin Co., Tenn.

John Pettigrew of Christian Co., Kentucky.

John Burgess and wife Polly.

Solomon Hix and wife Tabitha.

Lemuel Herston and wife Nancy.

Robert Walters and wife Nancy.

Moses Ayers gift to sons David and Daniel.

Jeremiah Yarborough of Oglethorpe Co.

Christopher Kelley and wife Elizabeth.

Julius Sims and wife Halinda.

Thomas Payne and wife Sarah.

James Adams and wife Dorcas.

James Rylee and wife Anna.

John Hooper to William Heckett, land granted by Gov. Mitchell to John Hooper.

John Robins and wife Lucy M.

Moses Collyer and wife Dorcas.

Signatures to Deeds in Franklin Co.

1798—Philip Prewit and wife Anne.

1799—John Crawford and wife Mary.

1805—Peter B. Terrell and wife Penelopy.

1809—Zachariah Thomas and wife Susannah.

1807—Russel Jones and wife Anna.

1808—Wm. Jackson and wife Nancy.

1798—Eli Langford and wife Sarah (of Pendleton District, S. C.)

1807—Wm. Bulloch and wife Spicey.

1809—Samuel Morgan and wife Nancy.

1809—John Sandridge and wife Susannah.

1809—Moses Trimble and wife Catherine.

1808—Jesse Hill and wife Margarette.

1809—Marriage contract of Russel Jones and Polly Nees. Signed by Dudley Jones, Poyndexter Payne, and Thomas Nees.

1807—Daniel Brown and wife Rhoda.

1807—James W. Cook and wife Susanna.

1809—Abraham Whitaker and wife Martha.

1797—John Mullin Sr. and wife Elizabeth.

1795—Robert Williamson and wife Elizabeth.

1794—John Depriest and wife Jane.

1794—Nathaniel Durkee and wife Catherine of Wilkes Co.

1793—Daniel Ayers and wife Nancy.

1795—Leroy Pope and wife Judith of Elbert Co.

1795—John Cunningham and wife Ann.

1805—Sampson Lane and wife Polly.

1808—William Cleveland and wife Rhoda.

1797—Richard Call and wife Alethia A.

1808—John Black and wife Margarette.

1808—William Asna(?) and wife Mary.

1809—Thomas P. Carnes and wife Susan.

1809—Thomas Farmer and wife Doratha.

1804—Jacob Pusley and wife Mary.

1808—William Graham and wife Dicey.

1808—Nathan Bond to Susannah Bond, dau. of Joseph (deed).

1808—James Burgess and wife Mary.

1808—Moses Walters and wife Elizabeth.

1808—James Garner and wife Sarah.

1807—Samuel Banks and wife Elizabeth.

1809—Robert Barnwell and wife Egness (Agnes?)

1809—Philip Mulkey and wife Fanny.

1809—William Gober and wife Margaret.

1809—George Rucker and wife Catherine.

1810—Starling Harris and wife Betsy.

1810—Allen Harris and wife Patsy.

1811—Russell Jones Sr. and wife Sarah (had a son Dudley).

1786—John Castleberry and wife Mary of Washington Co.

1786—Daniel Mathews of Edgefield Co., S. C., sold his orig. gr. to John Hancock.

1793—Garnett Turman and wife Mary.

1793—James Stringer and wife Aggy. of Wilkes Co.

1793—James Tait and wife Rebecca, of Elbert Co.

1793—Thomas Howell deed to Wiley Rogers; both of Elbert Co.

1791—Thomas Carson and wife Jenny, of Greene Co.

1791—Robert Brown and wife Catharine of Elbert Co.

1791—Moses Spencer and wife Betsy, of Pendleton Co., S. C., to Nath. Williamson.

1790—John Coleman and wife Polly of Wilkes Co.

1792—Jesse Hooper and wife Elizabeth of Elbert Co.

1792—Stephen Westbrook and wife Arphilladay.

1794—Robert Walters power of atty. to son Robert to sell land in Pittsylvania Co., Va.

1794—Nathaniel Allen and wife Pamelia, of Elbert Co.

1794—Abigail Grizzle and son Samuel, to Edward Prince, land, original gr. to Elam Grizzle.

1794—Samuel Gardner deed to Mary Gibson, both of S. C., grant to Samuel Sliker, 1785.

1793—Leonard Marbury of Richmond Co. power of atty. to Wm. Baker of Pr. Geo. Co. Md.

1793—Samuel Hemphill of Green Co., Ga., from John Berry of Lancaster Co., S. C.

1792—Basil Lamar and wife Mary of Wilkes Co.

1794—Nicholas Koger and wife Darkis (Dorcas).

1794—John Harrington of Lincoln Co., Ky., to Benj. Roberts of Franklin Co., Ga.

1794—Mary Bobo, adm. of Lewis Bobo of Elbert Co., to John G. Rainer of Franklin Co.

1794—John Clark and wife Sarah.

1791—Josiah Woods and wife Sarah.

1791—Araminta Stewart, widow of Elbert Co.

1791—Hugh McDonald and wife Helen.

1792—Robert Bean and wife Martha.

1805—George Longmire and wife Mary.

1806—James Reed and wife Susannah to Eli Bryan.

1806—James Armstrong and wife Darkes.

1807—James Anderson and wife Sarah.

1807—James R. Wyly and wife Sarah.

1809—Lewis Davis and wife Peggy.

1809—John Tate and wife Ann. Signed "Nancy."

1809—Isaac David and wife Susannah.

1810—Claiborn Cawthon and wife Hannah.

1810—Thomas Davis, Sr., and wife Kesiah.

1811—Thomas Payne, Jr., and wife Milly.

1811—Andrew Carothers and lawful atty. Zachariah Thomas, both of Hickman Co., Tenn.

1811—Archer Scott and wife Sarah.

1811—Thomas Brooks and wife Elizabeth.

1811—William Berry and wife Elizabeth, of Smith Co., Tenn.

1811—William Polk and son John of Franklin Co.

1811—Lewis Sowell of Clark Co., Ga.

1811—Emanuel McConnel and wife Martha.

1811—William Vaughan Sr. says: that some time in the year 1789, April, his property being in possession of his son George Vaughan, there was taken from him a certain negro woman, Nann, by Samuel T. Mett (or Fillett). The said woman has just been found in possession of John McDonald living near the Federal Road in the Cherokee Nation of Indians. Wm. Vaughan Sr. app. James Blair atty. to recover said negro.

May 1809—Deed of gift, Marbit Sloan to his children; John, Rene, Walter, Joshua, Slone, and Frances Jackson Pitman.

Nov. 23, 1807—John Holland of Dickson Co., Tenn., app Jesse Holland Jr, and Richard Wilkins of Franklin Co. his attys.

1797—Malachi Jones, sheriff of Franklin Co. and Russel Jones of Charleston, S. C.

1806—Thomas Thornton to Mark Hardin.

1809—Oct. 7.—Drury Rowland apps. friends James McMullins and Esther Johnson to recover property from Silas Pearce of Albermarle Co., S. C. (? and signed Rachel Burton, "formerly Rachel Rowland."

Index of Will Book "B" 1848-1867.

Will of Thomas Payne, Jr.

Found in an old book of loose records, the rest transcribed to other books. This will entirely to itself, the edges worn away, probably part of the first book of wills which could not be found. Full copy.

In the name of God, amen. I, Thomas Payne, Junr. of Franklin Co. and the State of Georgia, being in perfect health of body and perfect mind and memory, thanks be given unto God. Calling in to mind the mortality of my body, and knowing that it is appointed for all men once to die, do make this my last will and testament, that is to say principally and first of all, I recommend my soul into the hand of Almighty God who gave it, and as touching such worldly estates as wherewith it hath pleased God to bless me with in this life, I give, desire and dispose of in the following manner and form. First I give and bequeathe to my beloved brother Nathanial Payne one tract of land lying in said county and lying on Dosses Creek being the first creek that mouths in on the south side of the south fork of Broad river above the mulberry grove. Containing one hundred and fifty acres, the original grant in the name of William Payne. Secondly, I give and bequeathe to my beloved brother Moses Payne one tract of land in said county and lying in the south fork of Broad river being my first tract I hold on said south fork below Nathanial Payne's own survey containing two hundred acres. Thirdly I give and bequeathe to my beloved brothers, Champness, Shreesberry (Shrewsberry), Zedediah, Poyndexter and Cleveland Payne and my sister Ruth Payne one tract of land, a piece, of some of my land to be as near the valley of the other tracts I have given my aforesaid brothers Nathanial and Moses Payne, and neither of my aforesaid brothers or sister to be vested with authority of making sail or of conveying the aforesaid lands and without the approbation of a majority of my executors hereafter mentioned and then the rest of my estate both "rail" and personal after my Lawful debts are paid to be disposed of as follows, that is to say the negro that Col. Benjamin Cleveland is owing me in case my beloved father should die before the death of my beloved mother, I give and bequeather unto my beloved mother, Yamaky Payne said negro dueing her life and after her deceast to be equally divided together with the rest of my estate between all my beloved brothers, step brothers and sisters—and in case all of my brothers and sisters or either of their death without having an heir of his, her, or their body, that their part—said estate shall be equally divided between the rest of my brothers and sisters and I do also hereby constitute and ordain my beloved father, and my friend John Gardram, Wm. Cawthon and Richards White my soul executors of this my last will and testament in witness whereof I have hereunto set my hand and seal this Fifteenth day of May, in the year of our Lord one thousand seven hundred and eighty six and in the tenth year of American independency signed sealed and acknowledged in presence of us who in his presence and in presence of each other have hereunto subscribed our names.

Thos. Payne, Jr. (L. S.)
Proved the 1st day of June 1787 by the oaths of John Walters and Clabon Cawthon before me.
Nathanial Payne, R. of P.

John Walters.
Mathew McBee
    his
Clabon X Cawthon
    mark.

Administration and Wills. (Franklin Co.)

Book unmarked and not indexed.
Estate of Bazzel Dorsey, adm. by John Dorsey and Charles Baker, exrs. Wit: John Tabor, Zachariah Tabor,

and Joseph Penn. Oct. 13, 1807.

Inventory of Owen Forester, Aug. 3, 1804.

John Evans appointed adm. of estate of William Isam, dec'd, Oct. 1804.

James Sartain appointed adm. of estate of Arthur Jones, dec'd Oct. 1804.

Will of Jacob Strickland—dearly beloved wife Faithee and her 2 daughters Priscilla and Elizabeth Meyers. Tamer my 2nd child, Isaac the next, Jacob, Mary, Hardie, Selah, Elizabeth, Henry, Wilson, Nancy, Sarah. John Gilbert and Hardie Strickland Exrs. Apr. 4, 1804. Codicil: to gr. son Isaac Gilbert. Wit: James Goodlett, John Hodge. Probated Oct. 1804.

Will of John Gilbert—Wife Mary—sons William, James and John. Daughters Elizabeth and Nancy ("loving mother"). Exrs: wife Mary, Abner Franklin and Isaac Strickland.
April 6, 1803.

Will of Mary Gilbert—Son John and his son William. Dau. Elizabeth Kinnings and her children, Edward and Mary, and her other children. Gr. son Edward Gilbert and gr. dau. Mary Gilbert chil. of son William. Exrs: John Gilbert and Abner Franklin. Wit: William Black and M. Wilcox, J. P. Apr. 6, 1803—Apr. 11, 1803.

Will of Obadiah Hooper—Daughters Mary White, Nancy Goodlett, Milla Munro, and Susannah Perry. Sons: James, Thomas, John, Obadiah, Mathew, William, Richard. Wit: David Humphreys, William King and —?— Humphreys. July 16, 1800. April 6, 1803.

In Re of above:

Tushaloosa county court, September Term, 1818.

Ordered by the county court of Alabama Territory that Obadiah Hooper be and he is hereby appointed guardian for his children who became heirs to the estate of Moses Saunders, dec'd in the state of Georgia, Franklin Co., viz: for William S., Obadiah Jun., Elizabeth, Amelia and James Hooper—he having entered into bond in the sum of $2,000, with John Hooper and Elisha Colbert as securities on 22nd Sept. 1818.

I, M. B. Clark of the county court of Tuskaloosa county Alabama Territory, do hereby certify that the above is a true copy of the order of the county court of Tuskaloosa county and Territory aforesaid held on the 22nd. of Sept. 1818.

Given under my hand having no real office I have hereunto affixed my privet seal this 30th day of Sept. 1818.

M. B. Clark, Clerk.

1804—Charles Payne asks for titles from estate of John Payne dec'd. 1805, Feb. court. Est. of Joseph Pruett, adm. by Samuel Pruett.

1805, Feb. court. Est. of John Christian, adm. by Abda Christian. Bondsmen: Sam'l Lisucers(?), Charles and Thomas Conally, John Ubanks, John Burns, Cornelius McCarter, Benjamin Vaughan, Hezekiah Wheeler.

1805, Feb. court.—Estate of Jonathan Werkman, adm. by Charity Werkman.

1805, Feb. court.—Estate of Isaac Whitman, adm. by William Williamson.

1805, Feb. court.—Estate of Samuel Whitaker, adm. by Wm., Andrew and John Wmson.

1805, Feb. court.—Estate of Samuel Whitman, adm. by Polly Whitman and Wm. Graves.

1805, Feb. court.—Rufus Christian chose Ruben Christian his guardian.

1805, Feb. court.—Nancy Christian chose Robert Christian her guardian.

1805, Feb. Court.—Richard Allin appointed guardian for Sally, minor dau. of Peter Williamson.

1805, Feb. court.—Estate of Isaac Whitehead adm. by Thos. Covington, and Epps Chatham.

1805—March court.—Estate of Japheth Pruett, adm. by Joakim Hudson, William Ash, Henry Parks and A. Franklin. Among his effects were a sword and pair of pistols.

Oct. 30th, 1817—Martin Anthony receipts as legatee for his part of the estate of James Chandler, to David Anthony Adm. in rite of his wife.

In Re will of Robert Thrasher; Sales to—Thomas, E., and J. Thrasher, James Wyley, John Mullins, sr., J. Hawkins, J. Taylor, Thomas Jinkins, J. Grimmett, C. Gilbert, P. Hawkins, Wm. Hackett, A. Fitzjerrell, Obadiah Hooper, T. White, J. Summerell, J. Brown, J. Hill, G. Taylor, J. Hancock, Swift Mullins, B. Baker, Jesse Legrand, Wm. Davis, J. Harrison,—returned Jan. 5, 1798.

Accounts rendered by Warren Philpot, Dec. 26, 1799. To schooling Betsy Thrasher, "his dau."

Inventory of Isaiah Haly, dec'd. Jul. 5, 1800.

List of debts due estate of John Gorham, dec'd.

Date	Name.	Residence
August 2, 1785	Thomas Payne, dec'd	Franklin Co.
May 7, 1792	Robert Singleton	Franklin Co.
April 19, 1794	Daniel Beall	Franklin Co.
November 1, 1795	George Naylor	Columbia Co.
April 15, 1796	George Weatherby	Warren Co.
February 21, 1794	Aquilla Scott	Warren Co.
September 17, 1790	H. Saxon	Jackson Co.
January 1, 1790	Henry Strickland	Franklin Co.
May, 1789	Robert Dixon	Richmond Co.
February, 1796	William Cox	Wilkes Co.
May, 1796	John Greenwood	Elbert Co.
January, 1794	J. Watkins, James Leak	Green Co.
August, 1791	J. Embree	Wilkes Co.
January, 1792	H. Graves, dec'd	Richmond Co.
March 1794	Duncan Carmical	Green Co.

Inventory of Samuel Eperson, dec'd, "To 549 days spy wages." Appraisers, George Christian, William Black, John Gilbert. Feb. 22, 1796.

Will of Robert Watters, planter—Sons: William, John, Robert, Elijah, Peter, Samuel, and Moses. My four daughters, Betty, Susannah, Hannah and Mary.

Wit: John Smith, Joseph Humphreys. Nov. 2, 1793—Oct. 9, 1794.

Admrs. Bond for 2.000 lbs. signed by all the sons and Fred'k Stevellie, Oct. 9, 1794.

Appraised Nov. 14, 1794, by Thomas Carter, Aaron Camel, John Payne.

Will of Robert Thrasher—wife Elizabeth and all my children. Exrs. John Bryan and Warren Filpote. Wit: John Bryan, Martha Jennings, John Goodwin. Jan. 5, 1797—Feb. 4, 1797.

Willoby Hammack and Jacob Loughridge bond as Exrs. of will of John Moore, dec'd. July 9, 1795. Adms. Elijah Gentry, James Scott, Mathew Willey, James Wyatt, and Peter Having, sr.

Bond on estate of Elijah Strong, signed by Rebecca Strong, Louis Pope and Burwell Pope of Oglethorpe Co. Nov. 20, 1795. Wit: John Barnett, J. P. Appraisers, Robert Thomas, Thomas Johnson, John Cunningham.

Sales to Lewis Pope, William Dukes, Burrell Brewer, Joseph Pitman, John Barnett, William Strong, James Pitman, Alex. Patrick, John Linsey, Hugh Reed, Samuel Bridgewater, Absalom Rainey, David Criswell, Presley Thornton, William Pace, Miles Barnett, Benjamin Eperson.

Inventory of James Hayes, dec'd. Appraised by Jacob and Samuel Hollingsworth and Elijah Martin. Recorded Sept. 14, 1796.

Inventory of property of John Bullard, dec'd. One mare, one rifle gun, one saddle, clothing. An amount against Joseph Box.

Some wages, value unknown.

98 days in Capt. Bowen's Co.

55 days in Capt. Norris Co.

54 days in Capt. Bowen's Co.

Appraised by Joseph Box, John Gatten, and John Dunsey (Dancey?). Recorded June 10, 1796, Joseph Chandler, R. P.

Inventory of goods, etc., of Jonathan Bowers, by Malaki Jones, Adm. Appraised by James Terrell, Dan'l

Beale, Jonathan Hilton, Aug. 9, 1796. Jos. Chandler, R. P.

Will of Peter Williamson—wife Elizabeth,—Daughters: Elizabeth, wife of Richard Allen; Patsey, wife of Josiah Pritchett; Jennett Hanby, Mary wife of William Henby (Hanby?), Fanny, Nancy, Sally. Sons: Robert, Richard, John, and Peter Griffin Williamson. To Thomas Gorham. Wife Elizabeth sole Exr. June 4,-17, 1798. Wit: James Terrell, Joseph Dobbs, Joseph Chandler.

Appraised Oct. 18, 1798, by James Terrell, James Chandler, James Hooper, Zachariah Bryan. Notes due from James Hooper, Benj. Beason, Samuel Garner.

Will of John Shipley—wife Martha—Sons: William and George. Daughters: Nancy, Naomi, Elizabeth and Polly. Exrs. Robert Shipley, sen., Nathaniel Shipley. Wit: H. McCracken, Moses McCrea. Nov. 23,—Dec. 3, 1799.

Inventory Jan. 10, 1800. Notes against Martha Shipley, Horatio Bealls, James Little, Henry Sewell, Robert Shipley, jr., Robert Todd, Samuel Glenn, Moses McCheves, Wm. Thornton, Philip Brown, John Arnolds, George Cogburn, Peter Hutson, James McDowell, Joseph Terrell, Joseph Shipley, Abner Farrar, Wm. Caldwell, John Mitchell, Peter Jaitell(?), Obadiah Hooper, James Elliott.

Inventory of estate of James Wofford, dec'd. Appraised by Moses Terrell, Jacob Hollingsworth, George Vaughan, Sept. 13, 1796.

Payments made by Benj. Wofford to the creditors; John C. Walton, Wm. Wofford, Wm. Hewett, Augustus Brown, from Aug. 24, 1796, to Nov. 7, 1797.

Proven Accounts, Jan. 8, 1798—Andrew Hemphill, Benjamin Robertson, George Vaughan, H. Johnson, James Scott, Sutten Green, Clement Wilkins, Eli Silman, Samuel Philips, Wm. Christian, James Gates, James Coil, Aquilla Burroughs, Thomas Eperson, Wm. Patton, John Reynolds, Jonathan Lane, John Fanning.

Court of Ord'y., Feb. 4, 1801—Present: Larkin Cleveland, Russel Jones, Daniel Beall, James H. Little, Esqrs. On motion council for Robert Walton, son of Mary Walton, late of the county, dec'd temporary letters of administration be granted said Robert on the estate of said Mary, etc.

Court of Ord'y., Oct. 3, 1801. Abner Vaughan dismissed as adm. of estate of John Murphy, dec'd.

Will of Thomas Woodward—Son Thomas when he comes of age 21, my children names not given. Exrs.; Wife Mary and her brother John Howard. Wit: Henry Chappelear, William Leach. Made March 16, 1800. No date of probate.

Will of John Conn,—Wife Elizabeth. Sons Simon and Samuel, and daughters Caty Martin and Peggy Murphy have received their share. Sons John, Thomas, and Isaac, and daus. Jane, Mary and Agnes Conn. Wit: Wm. Hamilton, Samuel Jackson, Frederick Beall. July 3, 1800—Feb. 4, 1801.

Letters of adm. granted James Brown on est. of Hugh Brown, dec'd.

Letters of temporary adm. granted Killy Walton on est. of Edward Rice.

John Easly appointed guardian of John, William and Thomas Bush.

(July Term, 1801.)

At same term James Freeman qualified as an exrc. of will of Daniel Bush, and Joakim Hudson, Elizabeth Bush and James Freeman have temporary letters of adm. on est. of Daniel Bush.

Martha Shipley appointed guardian of George and Polly Shipley. Mary Trimble given final letters of adm. on est. of Conmack Haggins, dec'd.

Petition of James Young that Lewis Bobo gave his bond in his lifetime to make titles to a tract of land and died without executing it. All concerned notified at the end of three months titles will be made.

Will of Daniel Bush—wife Elizabeth—Daus: Easly, Judith Holland, Susannah Norris, Lydia. Sons: William, John, Thomas. Wit: Mam. Jones, Isham Clayton, Joel Mabry. Sept. 6, 1800—July 9, 1801.

Will of Edward Rice—wife Sarah—sons, Claborn, Leonard, William and Killis; daus: Polly and Elizabeth. Land not to be divided till William is 20 years old. Beloved son Killis to be supported by all the others. Exrs: wife Sarah and Killis Walton. Wit: Henry Holcom, Priscilla Holcom, Rachel England. Made Jan. 23, 1801—probated July 9, 1801.

Feb. 4, 1801—Estate of Robert Thrasher, to Warren Philpot, to keeping Elizabeth Thrasher, dau. of dec'd, to schooling. Robt. and Gilbert Thrasher,

Joseph Glenn.

Jan. 17, 1810—May term 1810.

Wife Nancy—sons William and John, minors, wife Nancy their step mother. Sons Thornton T., Mathew Hopson, Simondon Goslander, sons of Nancy, also minors. Dau. Lucy Brown, dau. Sally Barnett, note on Hugh McDonald, son Joseph, son Edward and dau. Polly Emory already received their portions. Exrs: wife Nancy and brother Simon Glenn, brother in law William Goolsby. Wit: William Cook, Hugh McDonald, Mary Cook.

William Harden.

Oct. 17, 1803—no date of probate.

"Beloved wife," sons Martin, Mark, Swan, Henry, Richard. Daus: Cynthia, Sarah and Sucka (Sookey). Exrs: Beloved wife, dutiful sons Mark, Swan, and Martin. Wit: Mary Whitney, Gadwell Ayers, Obadiah Tremmer. May Term 1810.

Edmund Chandler declares that James Chandler, dec'd had sold unto him 310 acres in waters of Unamattee, orig. grant of Daniel Brown. Joseph and Elizabeth Chandler,

Admrs. of James Chandler dec'd, ordered to execute deed to Edmund Chandler.

Sept. Term, 1810.

Robert Burns app. admr. of estate of William Huxham, dec'd.

March 23, 1810.

Thomas Storey and John Chalmers, appraisers of est. of James Brock, dec'd. Notes payable to this estate; Charles Warren, Clemmonds Quillian, Thomas Mills, John York, Benjamin Cooper, James Mills, Washington Sowells, Hezekiah Chandler, Thomas Sisson, John Collins, Nimrod Hendricks.

Sept. 7, 1810.

Boley Conner, Thomas Hamblen, Zebediah Payne, app. adms. of Joseph Glenn. Notes due on this estate; Charles Gorden, Joel Sutton, Abner Sutton, Israel Sneed, William Mobb, Thomas Harris, Capt. Joshua Clark, Nathaniel Statom.

Jan. 7, 1811.

Joseph Terrell, Security for Sarah Williamson, admrx. of Wm. Williamson. At same time letters of adm. granted on est. of Henry Terrell ——?

May 6, 1811.

Rebecca and Polly Stephenson, orphans of William Stephenson, ask that Woodson Roberts be app. their guardian.

Smith Cammel bound to Alex. Williamson till he is 21.

Sept. 18, 1810.

Est. of Col. Wm. Harden, appraised by Sampson Bobo, John West, and Boley Conner.

July 1, 1811.

Elizabeth Martin widow, app. adm. of est. of John Martin.

Sept. 2, 1811.

Sally Thrasher, orphan of Robert Thrasher, late of Franklin, chooses Capt. James Blair her guardian.

Same time John James bound to Hugh. B. Greenwood.

July 17, and Aug. 31, 1811.

Jacob Hollingsworth, Jr., Thomas Hollingsworth, James Martin, Esqr. appraisers of est. of John Martin. Nov. 1, 1811.

Simon Terrell app. guard. of the orphans and heirs of John Martin, viz: Van Allen Martin, Philip Martin, Charlotte Martin, James Van Martin, John Washington Martin, and William Terrell Martin. Elizabeth, the widow took her "thirds."

Reuben Thornton petitions that a bond for title given by Jack Hendrix, late of Franklin Co., dec'd, to half of the tract of land or bounty he lived on, Jan. 5, 1805, adjoining Thomas Thornton, to John Hosey. John Hosey assigned his right to Reuben Thornton.

James Sewell applies for execution of a deed given by Eli Bryan in his lifetime.

Ordered that John Bryan, exr. of Robert Thrasher advertise for sale 210 acres, orig. grant to Thrasher, for the benefit of the heirs. Signed by the following heirs: Lincoln Co., Tenn., Sept. 11, 1811, Robert, Joseph and Thomas Thrasher, Thomas Deloney, Seth Hodges, and James Blair for Sally Thrasher.

John Neal, adm. of est. of Joseph Neal, applies for permission to sell 287 1-2 acres of original grant to Stephen Casey, on N. Fork of Broad River, adj. widow Wheeler, Akins and others, in Franklin Co.

Abigail Wilson chooses William Wilson as guardian.

Moore Stephenson chooses Woodson Roberts as guardian.

Hannah Hollingsworth chooses Jacob Hollingsworth as guardian.

Woodson Roberts app. guardian of Elizabeth Stephenson.

Will of Christopher Garrison:

Wife Benor; my three children: first Levi, second David, third Barnabas, all under age. Exr. brother Levi Garrison. Wit: Jeddediah Garrison, David Garrison, Tre-

phenah Garrison. Dec. 5, 1811—Jan. 6, 1812.
March 2, 1812.

James Blair app. adm. of est. of Joseph Terrell.

Polly, Charles, Archibald, George, Milly and Angelica
Connally, orphans of John Connally, choose Thomas Connally as guardian, all being 14 years old or upward.

Zebadiah Payne, adm. of Cleveland Payne, authorized
to sell 80 acres, orig. grant to Thomas Payne, on middle
fork of Broad river, adj. Cockburns and said Thos. Payne.

Sally Bryan, Wm. B. Bryan and Boley Conner, app.
admrs. of Eli Bryan.

Henry Bresdle(?) bound to Washington Allen.

Jan. 1812.

Elizabeth Bush, Exr. of Daniel Bush, dismissed, having finished.

May 4, 1812.

Granted petition of Thomas Wright to be relieved as
security for John Wright and Daniel Beall, in right of his
wife, Hannah Beall, formerly Hannah Wright, admrs. of
Obadiah Wright, dec'd.

James Long app. admr. to William Dunn, dec'd.

Winkfield Bagwell and Martha McDowell app. admrs.
on James McDowell.

Application of William Wilson to be relieved as sec. of
Daniel Manley, admr. of est. of Isaac D. Manley.

Joseph Willis.

Apr. 9, 1812—May 4, 1812.

Wife Peggy, daus: Elizabeth, Lucinda, Charity and
Partheny Willis. Son William not of age and child in
esse. Exrs: Wife Peggy, and Thomas Payne, Sr. Wit:
George Taylor, Andrew Dorsey, John R. Brown, J. P.

July 6, 1812.

John Payne, Thomas Akins, William Reynolds, appraisers.

John G. Williamson chooses Samuel H. Everett, guard.

Rhoda and William Cawthorn, app. admrs. of William Cawthorn, dec'd.

Kenith McKensie app. guar. of Rutha Payne, orphan of Cleveland Payne.

Henry Hollingsworth chooses Benjamin Hollingsworth as guard.

Capt. James Blair relieved as sec. for Ann Sparks, adm. of James Sparks, dec'd.

Will of Shadrick Chandler.

April 5, 1812—July 1812.

Wife Martha, son James and dau. Elizabeth Millican. Four sons; Gedediah, Samuel, Daniel, William, when of age. Daus: Mary Westbrook, Tabitha Gorden, Susanna and Peggy. Two youngest daus. Sally and Martha. Exrs. wife Martha and friend Charles Jordan. Wit: Jonathan Gibbs, Jesse Thrasher.

Will of Anday Williamson.

July 13, 1812—Sep. Term 1812.

Wife Ruth. Children: Mary, John, Elizabeth, James, Nancy and Anday Williamson, Jr. All chil. are under 14. Exrs: wife Ruth, Frederick Beall, John R. Brown. Wit: Sampson Lane, Zachariah Chandler, T. Terrell.

Will of William Wheeler.

June 27, 1812—Sept. Term 1812.

Two youngest brothers Freeman and Richard Wheeler. Exr. John Echols. Wit: Thomas Gorham, Ignatius Percel, Jeremiah Dobbs.

April 6, 1812—Nacey Meeks, Killis Walton, Chas. England, apprs. of Joseph Terrell's est.

May 20, 1812—John and Alex. Williamson, Wm. Terrel, apprs. of Jas. McDowell's est.

July 18, 1812—Rich. D. Gray, Kenneth Finley, Martin Harden, Robt. Walters, on Wm. Cawthon's est.

Sept. 18, 1812—Washington Allen, Jas. Hooper, W. F. Bagwell, apprs. of Andy Williamson's est.

Feb. 11, 1812—Inv. of est. of Eli Bryan. Sally Bryan, Joseph Chandler, Boley Conner, adms. Notes due est.: John D. Terrell, Richard Shockley, Steedley and James Blair, Isaac D. Manly, William Baker and Andrew Elliott.

July 31, 1812—J. Gibbs, Geo. Thrasher, Stephen Westbrook, Esaias Harbour, apprs. of est. of Shardick Chandler. Debtors: Stephen, Hughes, Right Berry.

Nov. Term 1812—Gilbert Hay, surviving Exr. of Wm. Hay, applies to sell land.

Jan. 4, 1813—Robt. Laughbridge bound to Darby Henly. Frederick Beall, Clk. of Court.

July 16, 1812—Apprs. of est. of Isaac D. Manly; Woodson Roberts, Joseph Attaway, John Watson. Notes due by Henry Smith, Henry Burroughs, John Moody, Wm. England, Thomas Carter, dec.

March 1, 1813—Est. of Eli Bryan insufficient for support of children, so Royal Bryan was bound to Boley Conner and Catherine Bryan was bound to John Neal.

Elizabeth Robertson mother of infant son Terrell Robertson, asks that her father Frederick Brasdlee be app. guardian.

John R. Brown app. guardian of Senica and Ebolina Dedman.

Matilda Chandler, minor dau. of Robert Chandler bound to George King.

Boley Conner, adm. authorized to sell land of Eli Bryan, dec'd for benefit of heirs, land in 5th Dist. of Wilkinson Co., granted to Elizabeth Watters.

Thomas Payne, adm. in right of wife, formerly Sarah Carlton.

Epps and Stephen Chatham to be relieved from sec. for Robert Carlton and Sarah Carlton now Sarah Payne, on est. of Jacob Carlton, dec'd.

Royal Bryan asks to be released from sec. for William Bryan, one of admrs. of Eli Bryan, as he, William, has removed from the Co.

May 3, 1813—Elijah Coleman bound to John Clark.

Toliver Hooper bound to Isaac Brown.

Will of David Clark.

March 13, 1813—May 3, 1813.

Wife Martha—"My children." Exrs: Thomas Mays, Samuel McKee. Wit: James Allen, William Ash, Ellender Huey.

Will of Robert Mercer.

Oct. 1, 1809—May 1813.

Wife Elizabeth. Two sons: John and James. Six daus: Elizabeth Berry, Isabella Hemphill, Margaret Hemphill, Mary Hall, Agnes McFerin, Rachel Foster. Wit: Joseph Morrison, John Blackwell, James H. Little.

May 3, 1813—Aquilla and Robert Shockley granted letters of adm. on est. of James Shockley.

Alexander Williamson app. adm. of Thomas Williamson.

Robert Chandler informs the court that Samuel and Sarah Lard, minors bound to Joseph Yates are inhumanly treated. James Carroll. John Stubbs, Lucinda Dunn, witnesses. Yates was put in jail, and the children were bound to John Dorsey.

April 7, 1812—James Sewell, George Stovall, Jr., James Hooper Sr. apprs. of est. of Eli Bryan.

July 5, 1813—Latha Bryan bound to Elias Burgess.

John Ayers app. guard. of Jincy Ayers.

Will of Charles Taylor.

Sept. 6, 1810—July 5, 1813.

Wife Anna, and son George Exrs. Daus. Betsy Taylor and Patsy Prickett. Wit: Frederick Beall, W. F. Bagwell, J. P., James McDowell.

(George Prickett, in right of wife Patsy, enters caveat, July 8, 1813. Atty. James Smith.)

Sep. 6, 1813—Mary Wheeler app. adm. of est. of Wm. Wheeler, Jr., dec'd.

Signal Meredith, 14 years old, chooses Wm. H. Hall as guardian.

John Tabor, Richard Allen and Abel White, app. apprs. est. of William Wheeler Jr.

Jan. 3, 1813—David Payne and Groves Yarborough app. admrs. of est. of James Yarborough.

Russel and Julia Bryan, orphans of Eli Bryan, bound to Joseph Chandler.

Asa Allen returns as guardian of Mary D. and Virginia Hudson, orphans of David Hudson of Elbert Co.

March Term 1811—Edward Carrell made guardian —

May 8, 1816—Elizabeth Burk ordered to bring two orphans in her possession into court.

Jesse Holbrook asks release as sec. for Daniel Manley.

Wm. Thomas, James Ramsey, Wm. Ash. app. apprs. on est. of Daniel Clark, dec'd. May 8, 1813.

Sept. 10, 1813—Frederick Beall, Epps Chatham, Francis Calloway, app. apprs. of est. of Charles Taylor.

July 19, 1810—Sale of est. of James Brock.

Voucher: David Wright received his share of est. of Obadiah Wright. John Wright, adm.

Persons holding claims against the est. of Joakim Hudson dec'd 1808; John Weems, Elisha Valler, John Clarkson, Beal Baker, Jesse Patterson, Richard Say, Frederick Beall, George Christian, George Silman, John Dixon, James Lowery, Jr., Joshua Hudson, Eli Bryan, William Jones, William Christian.

Sale of effects of John Martin, dec'd. Elizabeth Martin adm. Thomas Hollingsworth, and Edmund Strange, Clerks.

Henry Parks, adm. of est. of John McKee, rendered statement of expense, six days traveling to Rabun's Creek, S. C., to get Wm. Thomason sworn as witness in case of Samuel McKee vs. Henry Parks, Jan. 1812.

Feb. 10, 1812—Samuel Poe gives receipt in full to William Wilson as guardian to Mary Wilson, now wife of Samuel.

Receipt from James Smith atty. from William Wilson, guardian of Mary Wilson, for prosecuting a case against Barnabas Pace in Elbert Co.

In 1809 the following promissory notes were given Mary Wheeler, as exr. of est. of William Wheeler:—Lucy Wheeler, Elizabeth Wheeler, Mary Wheeler, Wm. Wheeler, Lizbeth Wheeler and Robert Williams. Wit: John Simmons.

From George Cogburn, Coroner for inquest on Wm. Wheeler.

Notes from Daniel Coleman, Abner Echols, James R. Wyly, Nacy Meeks.

1811—1814—Returns of John Tabor, guard. of Thomas Gorham.

1812—Receipts from legatees of John Lowery, dec'd: Nathan, Charles, Elizabeth, Shadrick, or Frederick, Lowery. Frederick Beall.

1812—Receipts of debtors of est. of James Brock; John Goodwin, James Williams, James Little, Adam Sheffield, Nimrod Hendrix, Ben. Cooper, Fleming F. Adrian, Wm. Brock, John Collins, Adam Andrews, Caleb Garrison, Wm. Chalmers.

Promissory notes due est. of Joseph Terrell: James Blair, adm. Larkin Holt, N. Dotson, Andrew Barwood, Joseph Whitehead, Tillman Powell, Aaron Terrell, Sr., and Jr., James R. Wyly, Walter Adair, Jeremiah Taler (Taylor or Tabor?), Fanch Cleveland, Almond Powell, John Harrison, Anny Terrell, David Poor, Robert Kyle, Edward Adair, Starrett Osborn, Burrell Whitehead. 1812.

July 23, 1812—Receipt of Samuel Holbrook to William Wilson, agent for Hannah Wilson, now the wife of the said Samuel Holbrook.

Jan. 1, 1798—Daniel Brockington, vs. John Fergus and Malachi Jones. M. Williamson, atty. for plff. Wit: Thomas Jones, Robert Shepty. James Hooper, foreman of jury.

1791—''Sometime in the year,'' Christian Rhinehart vs. John Hooper, the value of service of a negro man name Bustol. Plffs. attys: Peter Early and Archibald Martin. Moses Payne Dep. Sheriff. Fred'k Beall, C. I. C.

May 1, 1797—William Allen vs. John Conner, Sr., Moses Payne, Dep. Sher. Wit: Robert Allen, Charles Tait, atty. Sworn to in Elbert Co., March 7, 1799.

Sept. 5, 1792—Nathaniel Durkee vs. Daniel Beall. P. Alen, plff. atty. F. C. Terrell, sheriff. Attested in Richmond Co., Gad Young, J. P.—Peter Early, plff. atty.

Sept. 26, 1796—N. Durkee empowers Miss Sarah F. Willis to give Daniel Beall an ample discharge from all transactions. Washington Wilkes Co.

April 20, 1790—Charles McDowell and James Greenlee, for the use of William Quillen, vs. Daniel Beall 30 lbs. of N. C. currency, rent of plantation on Hunters Creek, known by the name of Killions or Hillions Place. Samuel Hillingsworth, foreman of jury. Wit: Thomas White. Note was transferred to Wm. Darnall, wit: Thomas Juaron(?).

May 1, 1798—Elizabeth Williamson exr. of Peter Williamson, vs. John Williamson for 6 cows and calves. M. Williamson, plff. atty.

May 1, 1799—John Milton vs. George Henning. Thomas P. Carnes testifies that Henning had paid 95 dol. on said note Oct. 19, 1797, to Elisha Brewer. On Nov. 24, 1799, Richard T. Cosby was authorized by Thomas B. Scott to liquidate above note by payment of $85.

Nov. 6, 1798—Charles Kennedy vs. Samuel Whitaker, to recover value of horse.

Nov. 24, 1797—John Greenlee vs. Robert and Hamilton Montgomery and Samuel Hollingsworth debt due to James Greenlee of the Co. of Burke, state of N. C. Judgment obtained in Superior Court of Morgan Dist., at instance of Hezekiah Hyat in N. C.

Jan. 10, 1798—Nathan Stedman vs. Nimrod House; note given Hugh Crumliff, who endorsed to John Martin.

June 10, 1796—Malachi Jones vs. John Dempsey, "who is about to remove from the state," ("as is supposed"). Moses Terrell, J. P.

July 2, 1798—Daniel Beall vs. Edmund Henley and Janet Hendley, sheweth that said Janet Gorham (now wife of Hendley) was in her widowhood indebted, etc.

June 20, 1795—Seaborn Jones vs. George Henning, note payable to Philip Clayton for fees on plats of Richard Dawson. The following jury found for Plff: Elias Baker, Frederick Steville, Benjamin Echols, Bassile Harriss, Thomas Smith, Francis Guttery, Samuel Conn, William Hendley, Abraham Casey, William Patrick, Christopher Hudson. Talman Harbour.

Nov. 9, 1798—James Terrell, Sheriff, levied on property of Daniel Beall to satisfy a debt due to Ananias Cooper. Fred'k Beall, C. I. C.

May 6, 1796—Sidney Redding vs. Tryon Patterson for horse which she recovers.

Nov. 1, 1799—Stephen Young vs. Henry Strickland for slander, on the plantation of Daniel Robertson in Elbert Co., D. C. Cleveland, C. I. C. Young Gresham and J. M. Dooley, attys.

Dec. 8, 1798—Hugh Pierce vs. Abraham Odum.

March 9, 1800—Henry Sewell vs. Absalom Baker.

July 9, 1797—James Crow vs. Joseph Dunegan, for note to John Depriest, who endorsed it to Isaac Ford. Wm. H. Crawford pro querente. Attest: Philamon Martin. John Shackelford, Deft. Atty.

Jan. 1, 1800—John Clarkson vs. Jas. Freeman, to recover horse used in service of U. S. army.

Dec. 25, 1799—Francis Smith and Jesse Holbrook vs. Alex. Colewell and John Rabourn.

Jan. 1, 1799—William Wimbish vs. William Jones.

Dec. 5, 1799—Elbridge Hargroves vs. Malachi Jones. Wit: Harris J. L. Wyly. Stephen Beaver was added to jury in place of Samuel Conn.

March 18, 1800—Jacob Dyer vs. John C. Linch.

Aug. 1, 1799—Daniel Jones vs. Charles Bond.

Nov. 15, 1800—Jeptha Rush vs. Andrew Reid.

April 14, 1798—John Milican vs. Stephen White.

Nov. 15, 1799—Robert Barnhill vs. John Cain and Robert McFarland.

April 8, 1800—Peter Hudson vs. Malach Jones, Jr., Jere Sparks, J. P.

July 28, 1800—Edward Payne vs. Edmund Hendley.

Aug. 15, 1800—George Thrasher and wife Casia vs. Francis Barden, at house of John Thrasher.

April 11, 1799—James H. Little vs. Abner Farrar; Obadiah Hooper security for Farrar.

Dec. 11, 1799—John Ralston, of Augusta (merchant), and Hugh Nesbit, vs. Chas. Bond. Wit: David B. Butler, J. P. of Richmond Co. Chas. Walker, sec., in place of Robert Skelton.

Jury—Wm. Little, Obadiah Hooper, Wm. Hall, Wm. Jones, Wm. Burt, Thos. Meadows, Elijah Bankshaw, Joseph Chandler, Champneys Payne, Joseph Pulliam, James Reed, John Lowry.

Dec. 15, 1796—William Glover vs. Arthur Jones.

May 30, 1800—Samuel Isaacs vs. Evan Todhunter; B. Franklin, Plffs. Atty.

July 26, 1800—Joel Youell vs. John Cleveland.

Feb. 5, 1800—William Mood vs. William Wilson.

Oct. 8, 1794—John Milton vs. John Garrett and Thomas P. Carnes. Obadiah Jones, Atty.

May 5, 1799—Nathaniel Shipley vs. Abner Farrar.

Aug. 22, 1799—Arthur Jones vs. James Sartain.

Sept. 29, 1800—Howel Adamson vs. Joel and John Rabourn.

Oct. 4, 1800—Edmund King vs. Benjamin Echols.

Sept. 25, 1800—Rowley Howel and John Tate to Peter Hudson. James Martain, J. P. and Elijah Martain Wit. Peter Hudson has removed from the county.

March 29, 1800—John Cleveland and Thomas N. Gibson vs. Thomas Kelley.

Sept. 23, 1800—Mathew Alexander vs. Peter Jailet, Zellet, (spelt variously). Wit: William Spradling, David McCracken.

April 4, 1798—John Milican vs. Stephen White. Hon. Larkin Cleveland, Judge. D. Cleveland, C. I. C. Jurors: David Northington, Robert Armstrong, Robert Walton, Beall Baker, Solomon Potter, Wm. Ash, Wm. Haley, Sr., Absalom Treutham, Jas. Chandler, Obadiah Hooper, Mark Haley, Moses Trimble.

Oct. 10, 1800—Russel Jones vs. Moses McClure. Robert and Nath. Shipley Secs. for McClure.

Dec. 13, 1709—John McIntosh vs. Thomas P. Carnes—promissory note to John Bostwick at Louisville. Wm. Robertson J. P. Henry Chappelier sec. for Carnes. Wit: Henry Burroughs and James Cash. Jury: Wm. Cleveland, Wm. Blackwell, Solomon Hicks, And. Williamson, James Jackson, Wm. Harden, Ezekiel Thomas, John Collins, Simon Terrell, Jas. Chandler, Wm. Young.

Oct. 7, 1800—Hugh McDonald vs. Edmund Henley.

Dec. 19, 1801—James Manning vs. William Hooper.

April 8, 1800—John Keys vs. Thomas Gorden or Garden and John Cleveland. B. Franklin, atty.

April 7, 1801—James McKey vs. Chas. Bond. Attest Frances McKey apparently wife of James McKey. Order on Wm. O. Whitney.

Feb. 5, 1801—Hugh McDonald vs. John Temples. Moses Haynes, J. P.

April 6, 1802—Thomas Westbrook and James Terrell bond to Beverly and Whitfield Broaddus.

April 13, 1802—Land on Indian Creek, granted to William Way, joins D. Jones's land, and Zachariah Harris is summoned as garnishee.

Feb. 15, 1803—Jurors: William Cleveland, William Blackwell, Joel Hicks, Andrew McManus, James Jackson, William Harden (foreman), E. Thomas, John Collins, William Young, Simon Terrell, James Chandler, John Lain.

Aug. 10, 1801—Henry Gragg vs. Royal Bryant.

June, 1802—Jurors: William Ramsay, Tyrus Swift, Nathaniel Payne, Benjamin Baker, James Pulham, William Hooper, Little B. Bottes, Benjamin Cleveland, George Cogburn, Josiah Burgess, Asa Allen, James Mitchell.

Oct. 1, 1799 Francis McCall and John Neal vs. Charles Bond, "late of Franklin Co."

Sept. 15, 1800—James Blair vs. William Welbourne, Joel Crain, and Evan Todhunter.

March 16, 1802—Dudley Jones and Daniel Beall vs. Benjamin Cornelius.

April 15, 1802—William Wood vs. Chas. Bond, at which time Maj. Thomas Crews and Samuel Leathers were summoned.

March 25, 1803—Moses Terrell vs. James McConkey. Samuel Everett, sec.

Dec. 23, 1800—Rusel and Dudley Jones vs. Andrew Glenn. Wit: David Glenn and Frederick Beall.

Feb. Term, 1804—Jurors: Gabriel Jones, Zebulon Savage, John Williams, Gabriel Martin, James Malonie, Philip Brown, Joseph Sewall, Zachariah White, Andrew Corathen, John Arnold, John Payne, Sr., John Martin, foreman.

March 10, 1803—Richard Ward and Jordan Lacey bond to James Odell, Henry Garrett. Wit: Peter Walters, J. P. Nathan Camp, Constable.

April 14, 1802—Felix Gilbert vs. William Walker Walton. Hon. Abner Franklin, Judge. William Malone, sheriff.

July Term, 1804—Jurors: Christopher Lyner, Abel Coleman, Joseph Terrell, Larkin Prestridge, Henry Black, Edmund Chandler, Samuel Morgan, John Morris, John Bartow, John Hill, Thompson Epperson, Samuel Bean.

May 28, 1803—Samuel Watkins and Co. vs. Silas Twedell.

Feb. Term, 1805—Jurors: Joseph Dobbins, James Cook, John Tait, James Garner, Joseph Holcomb, Samuel Howell, John Goodwin, Peter Jones, John Martin, Wm. England, Thompson Moore, Thomas Newton.

Feb. 28, 1803—Edward Payne vs. Samuel and Benjamin Whitaker and John Williamson. The Whitakers were served in Richmond Co., J. (or H.) McTyre, sheriff.

Feb. Term, 1805—Jury No. 2: Joshua Hudson, Henry Wall, Nathaniel Williams, Stephen Poe, Henry Burroughs, David Clark, Benjamin Cherry, John Michum, Thomas Jordan, Isaac Strickland, John Forester, James Denman.

Sept. 11, 1800—James Alston vs. Frederick Thompson. Arthur Markham sec. for Thompson. Wit: John Sapp.

April 28, 1804—Elias Earle and Baly Elkins vs. James and Peter Rentfro.

Oct. 6, 1798—Part of jury list: John Stowers, Absalom Cleveland, Wm. Blackwell, Wm. Leach, Amon Airs, John Silmon, John Wright, Benjamin Jackson, John Casey, James Neal, Peter Jones, Richard Thomas, Jesse Thomas, Samuel Howel, Nicholas Swet, Thomas Clark, James Casey, John Graves, Wm. Tackett, John Hewett, James Gates, Hugh Bean, Thomas Parish, Christopher — —.

Dec. Court, 1798—Jurors present: Moses Colier, Robert McFarlin, Benjamin Pulliam, Edmund Hendley, Amon Avis, John Silmon, Peter Jones, Nixholas Suel, Thomas Clark, David Ellison, William Harden.

Jurors 1801—William Little, Daniel Manly, Obadiah Hooper, Henry Strickland, Jesse Shumate, George Pierce,

William Hall, Robert Morris, William Jones, William Birt, Harriss Wyly, Thomas Meadows, Ely Rentshaw, Peter Hudson, Joseph Chandler, Champneys Payne, Joseph Pullim, James Reid, John Lowery, Moses Bradwell, Benjamin Thrasher, Charles Walker, Thomas Cathamge(?), Moses Trimble, Moses Saunders, George Garner, Daniel Bush, Nathan Reed, Francis Saunders, Jacob Burton.

1797—Francis Tennille and wife Winnyfred, Robert Morris and wife Mary, Francis Fitzsimmons and wife Catherine, sold lands in Franklin, Washington and Effingham counties, through Robert Morris, Jr., of Philadelphia, to Robert Morris, and John Nicholson.

1794—George Naylor and wife Henrietta of Augusta to Robert Morris of Phil. and James Greenleaf of New York city.

1792—John Hinson of Greenville Co., S. C., to James Barr of Albermarle Co., E. S.(?).

1796—Solomon Thornton, exr. of William Thornton of Wilkes Co., Ga., to Robert Hill of Stokes Co., N. C.

1807—Mary Whitaker widow of Samuel, of Wilkinson Co., Territory of Miss., app. Francis Graves of same place as her atty.

1809—James Sartain of Franklin Co., Tenn., to Charles Warren of Franklin Co., Ga.

Oct. 1809—Jeremiah James and Nancy Sparks give power of atty. to John Gittens to collect their part of the est. of Edward Sparks, dec'd of Goochland Co., Va.

March 14, 1809—Joseph Pulaski Kennedy of Washington Co., Miss., app. James Smith, Esqr., of Franklin Co. his atty. Made in Jackson Co., Ga. Wit: Joseph Barr.

1809—Thomas Crews of Smythe Co., Tenn., app. James Smith his atty.

1811—Edy Holbrook to Edwin Barham of Stokes Co., N. C., 100 acres in Franklin Co.

1811—John Robins app. Richard L. (or S.) Arrington atty. to sell land in Halifax Co., Va., of est. of late Richard Arrington, dec'd.

1811—Oliver C. Cleveland and Polly Payne, wid. of Champneys Payne, to Dudley Jones.

1807—Richard Echols of Baldwin Co., to George Kelleay (Kelly) of Franklin Co.

1803—Moses Sanders to son David, of Franklin Co., Tenn.

1788—Thomas Stanton, Simon Thomason an old man, and Jacob White, Sr., were living in South Carolina.

1811—Poindexter Payne to Kenneth McKensie of Pendleton Dist., S. C.

1811—John Robins and wife Elizabeth.

1809—William Hemphill and wife Margaret.

1811—John McCurdy and Samuel Graves admrs. of est. of Ishmael Vineyard.

1807—Obadiah Hooper and wife Sarah.

1808—Johnson Randall of Wilkerson Co., Miss.

1806—William Turner and wife Sarah.

1805—Heirs of James Wofford, dec'd; Ann Clark, now Ann Bright, wife of William; sister of James Wofford, dec'd, coheir with Benjamin and Nathaniel Wofford, Mary Witherspoon, Charlotte Baker and Sarah Gillespie. Benjamin Wofford, adm.

1807—Benjamin Pulliam app. Abner Tatom of Lincoln Co., atty. to demand from the Exrs. of Absalom Tatom, dec'd late of the town of Hillsboro, N .C., "My part of the legacy out of said estate, in consequence of my marriage with Jemima Fullilove, dau. of Henrietta Fullilove."

1807—James Haley (signed Hailley), wife Elizabeth.

1806—W. O. Whitney, wife Ruthy.

1806—Jesse Blackwell, wife Mary.

1806—Philip Prewitt, and wife Anna.

1806—Benjamin Jackson and wife Nancy.

1807—William Hooper and wife Joicy.

1807—Huson Moss to receive lot of land, if any, drawn by Nancy Reddin's ticket, as she is moving away.

Nov. 2, 1807—Nancy Martin app. John Martin of Union Co., S. C., atty. to recover certain property given by her mother, Sarah Martin (relict of James Martin), who afterwards married Richmond Terrell, who sold the property to Moses Guiton of Union Co., S. C., before the said Sarah became of full age.

1789—William Mathews of S. C. his orig. grant to Jefferson Co.

Ephraim Peebles of Burke Co., who in 1805 is "of Jefferson Co., and transfers it to Roderick Easly of Clarke Co.

1805—H. McClacker of Barren Co., Ky., to Thomas Covington.

1808—Micajah Johnson and wife Elizabeth.

Nov. 1807—Obadiah Wright app. Daniel Beall to obtain a grant drawn in the late land lottery, 202 1-2 acres, lot 241 8th Dist. Wilkerson Co.

Nov. 3, 1807—Samuel Boling app. Wingfield Bagwell to receive lot 173—6th Dist. Wilkinson Co.

Oct. 11, 1807—Sarah Nix app. John Stonecypher to receive her grant in late lottery.

1806—John Harrington of Lexington Co., Ky., to Benjamin King of Franklin Co., Georgia.

1806—Daniel McDougald app. John Bennett, Jr., to act with respect to a tract of land, part of which was granted to Alex. McDougald.

1806—Joel Crain to Daniel McDougald part of above tract. Wit: Swann and Jerusha Hardin.

1806—Joseph Prine app. James Martin to receive his lottery.

1806—Lewis Davis to Henry Davis, part of tract of Thomas Payne, Sr.'s survey.

1807—John Hamner and Henning Jordan to John Moore of Oglethorpe Co.

1807—Thomas Covington app. William Malone to receive his lottery. Lot No. 135—29th Dist. of Wilkinson Co.

1807—James Tait to Mark Hardin.

1807—George King of Columbia Co., Ga., app. Sampson Lane atty. in impending lottery.

1807—David Morgan and James Garner to Thomas Hollingsworth.

1807—James Haggard of Jackson Co., to Wm. Howinton.

1807—George Hinkle to John Holland, both of Dickson Co., Tenn., orig. grant to Reuben Allen.

1807—Jacob Womack to Wm. Polk. Wit: Hartwell Freeman, Evan Polk, Dolly Mitchell.

1807—William W. Walton to John Hooper, orig. grant to Larkin Cleveland.

1807—Moses Randall, wife Rebecca, and Thos. Randell, wife Margaret, to John Morris.

1808—Zachariah White, in right of his wife Ginsey, formerly Cockeram, and Richard Cockeram, heirs and legatees of Edy Cockeram, late of state of Va., dec'd, app. Peter Cockeram to demand of the admrs. of Richard Stone, late of Va., dec'd, a sum of money bequeathed to Edy Cockeram by Richard Stone.

1808—David Crews and wife Judy to James Hooper.

1808—Baker Ayers and wife Betsy to John Payne.

1808—John H. Jones of Clark Co., to Reuben Payne and Robert Walters, exrs. of Benj. Thrasher.

1808—John Henderson and wife Betsy to John Mayfield of Warren Co., N. C., original grant to George Pettigrew.

1802—Thomas Jenkins to John Duke.

1805—James Tate to Joseph Williamson.

1805—Uriah Barnett to Charles Williamson.

1805—Elijah Martin to Samuel Moss.

1806—Thomas Harrington of Claiborn Co., Miss., app. Thomas Harrington his atty.

1806—James Flood sells to Boley Conner his draw in lottery.

1806—John Robins to James Sartain.

1806—John Byford to William McMillian.

1800—John Easly, agent of William Norris of Tenn., to Joseph Hunnicutt.

1804—Tignal Jones, adm. of Arthur Jones dec'd, to James Sartain.

1790—Zachariah Cox of Wilkes Co., to Wm. McRee and James McCammon.

1796—Henry Rose of Ky., to John Tatom.

1799—Josiah N. Kenner of Warren Co., to John Tatom.

1806—Fermin H. Byford to Jacob Womack.

1806—Joel Crain to Evan Todhunter, orig. grant to Thomas Kelly, Sept. 17, 1798.

1806—David McCracking to John Cox.

1806—Paulser Ingle to Shadrack Holt.

1806—Gilbert Hay app. Robert Walton atty. concerning tracts granted to his bro. Wm. Hay.

1807—Samuel Moss of York Dist., S. C., to Joseph Walker, Hollingsworth Dist., Franklin Co.

1807—Presley Barton and Benjamin Cherry to John Swift.

1807—John Armstrong of Wilson Co., Tenn., to William Gober.

1807—Moses Denman to Elisha Wilkinson orig. gr. to Benj. Harrison and Wm. Bridges.

1807—Elizabeth was the wife of Moses Denman.

1807—Abner Cleveland and wife Elizabeth to William Cleveland and William Calloway.

1808—John Purcell to Polydore Naylor.

1808—Elizabeth Taylor, widow of Richard Taylor, app. Polydore Naylor her atty. in lottery.

1808—William Wood of Jackson Co., to John R. Brown.

1808—James Freeman of Elbert Co. to Ignatius Purcell.

1808—Joshua Kennedy of Washington Co., Miss., to William Malone.

1808—Stafford Selman to James Nettles.

1800—Alexander Caldwell to George Thrasher, orig.

gr. to Wm. Hay—the plantation on which he, the said Caldwell now lives.

1802—John P. Adinger to Robert Barnwell (or Bamwell) and wife Patsy.

1803—James Riley of Elbert Co. to Henry Avery.

1804—Bailey Brooks and wife Charity to James Riley.

1805—Robert Brown to John Brown.

1799—Thomas Raburn to Alex. Caldwell.

1799—John Newman to William Thomas.

1800—James Coil and wife Jane to John Connally. Wit: Andrew Holland.

1800—George Sibbald of Augusta to Lewis Sewall of Columbia Co. orig. gr. to Wm. Call.

1807—Mary Patrick of Oglethorpe Co. to George Williamson. Wit: David Patrick.

1807—John Connally and wife Sisley to Kesia Connally and the heirs of Chas. Connally. Wit: James Rylee, Robert Eubanks, Charles Connally.

1804—Tirey Guntry and wife Delilah to William Rook, part of grant to Wm. Willburn.

1805—John Yarborough of Oglethorpe Co., to George Williamson, "being my part of legacy from James Yarborough, dec'd."

1805—William Baldwin and wife Polly (signed Mary), to Benjamin Whitehead, part of bounty grant to Joseph Pullum.

Nov. 26, 1806—Sarah Terrell sells slave to James Martin. Wit: Jepha and Fanny Harrington.

1803—Lewis Dickerson to James Stogaler. Wit: John Parker and John Stogaler.

1803—Richard Downs to Alex. Smith.

1801—Wm. Hewitt, Sr., to Richard Dobbs.

1798—Colbarn Barrell and Henry Cervantes of Ingram Court, London, agents for Joseph Barrell of Charleston, in the commonwealth of Mass., and Daniel Neal Lister of New York, gentleman. Whereas by letters patent, Jared Irwin, Gov. of Ga. on Sept. 26, 1796, granted to John Col-

lier of Columbia Co., Ga., 1000 acres in Franklin Co., Ga.
John Collier made Thomas Smythe, late of Richmond Co.,
Ga., then residing in London, his atty. who sold to Joseph
Barrell of Charlestown, Mass., from whom it was bought
by Daniel Lister for his son Daniel Neal Lister. Wit: Par-
don T. Taber, of Ship "Independence," of New York,
Sandeman Barrell, Clerk to Barrell and Cervantes, Thom-
as Callaway, Steward Guy's Hospital. Certified by Chas.
Price, Lord Mayor of London, 1803. Robert Robson of
London, Notary Public, certifies to the signature of Chas.
Price, Lord Mayor. W. Shockley, N. P. and T.; Atkin-
son, N. P. certify that Robert Robson is a notary public
duly authorized.

1803—Peter Watters to John Cross.

1803—James Sparks to Samuel House.

1803—John D. Terrell to John Cleveland.

1803—Thomas and William Williamson to Andrew
Williamson.

1807—David Worthington to Bassil Dorsey.

1807—John Duncan to John Henderson.

1807—John Banks of Elbert Co., to John Duncan.

1807—Abner Farrar and William Malone to Robert
Malone.

1807—Hezekiah Terrell, Sheriff, to John Griffin of
Wilkes Co., land orig. granted to John Gorham, dec'd.
Thomas Carter one of the admrs.

1802—James Wyly to Randolph Holbrooks, lot where
Holbrooks now lives, and where Harris K. Wyly, lived.
Wit: Berry Cleveland, Jr. In 1807 this land was trans-
ferred to Winkfield Bagwell. Commissioners: John R.
Brown, James Hooper, Samuel Shannon, Asa Allen.

1806—Henry Tyler and wife Annis, of Oglethorpe Co.
to Benjamin Brooks.

1806—Richard Woods and wife Susannah to John Sewell.

1804—100 acres granted to John Hubbard by George Handley, sold by Samuel Dailey and wife Mary, legatees to Thomas Jones.

1804—John Williams and Abner Dunigan to Nasel (Nacey) Meeks.

1804—Wilkes Co. Henry Strickland authorized to sue for 500 acres on Broad River, granted to Wm. Hay, dec'd, Gilbert Hay, Exor.

1806—John Harrington of Lexington Co., Ky., and Thomas Harrington, agent for John, to Geo. Stovall, land on Bear Creek, granted to John for services in the war.

1806—Thomas Harrington and wife Catey.

1806—Thomas Covington to John Covington.

1806—James R. Wyly to Nasel Meeks.

1806—William Pulliam, John Laine, Sr., and John Smith to Peter Odum.

1806—Valentine Warren to Charles Warren.

1801—Hugh McCracken to Thomas Covington, late of Rutherford Co., N. C.

1805—James Nettles, and wife Polly, to Thomas Covington, Sr.

1805—Andrew Walker to Richard Taylor.

1805—Clement Wilkins and wife Clarice, to Samuel Daly.

1807—Charles Dean of Elbert Co., John Dean of Franklin Co., to George Stoval, part of grant to Thomas Arrington 1787 on Bear Creek. (The name Arrington appears to be the same as Harrington).

1807—James Quillian and wife Susannah, formerly wife of Wm. Dean, relinquishes dower.

1807—Thomas Westbrook and wife Mary of Jackson Co., to Samuel Shannon, on Little's Creek granted to William Guy, surveyed to Christopher Hudson, from him to Westbrook.

1807—Thomas Willingham to Absalom Trentham.

1807—John Merrell, Jr., to John Brewer. Wit: John Merrell, Sr., and Benjamin Brewer.

1801—Richard Allen and wife Elizabeth to George Kelly, land bought from Eli Langford.

1803—Thomas Connally pays William Pritchford and wife Judy for land. Wit: Hermon Bagley, Nathan Pitchford, Craddock Gober.

1803—Joseph Terrell and wife Ann to Epps Chatham of Wilkes Co.

1803—Thomas McDowell and wife Martha to Absalom Trentham, orig. grant of Ralph Banks. Wit: S. Glenn, J. P., and Elizabeth Glenn.

1802—Johnson Randell to Samuel Headen.

1805—Enoch Smith to Joseph Kiser.

1805—William Rook to Moses Ayres, Jr.

1806—Alex. Saxon and wife Mary to Wm. Goodson. Orig. grant to Wyatt Langford.

1806—James Reed and wife Jane to William Wilson.

1806—Chapley Ross Welborn of Wilkinson Co., to George Watkins, part of est. of John Cleveland, late of Franklin, father of Nancy, wife of Welborn.

1804—Amos Bratcher, one of the admrs. of est. of Amos Bratcher dec'd, being about to leave the state, turns over everything to Daniel Beall, the other admr.

1811—Benjamin Whitehead and wife Mary to Edward E. Swards.

1811—John Brown and wife Martha to John, son of Meredith Brown and Rigdon, son of Meridith.

1808—John Dugless to Japheth Yarborough.

1801—James Brazzell to William Wilson.

1809—George Carpenter and wife Polly to Joseph Nix.

1809—Catherine Dye to Jesse Blackwell.

1807—Benjamin Cleveland to George Watkins, part of est. of John Cleveland, dec'd. Argin, wife of Benjamin, relinquishes her dower.

1810—Clement Wilkins, and wife Clarissa, to John Mayfield, Sr., of Warren Co.

1810—Robert R. Cox to James Tate.

1812—Sheriffs deed to Dr. Anderson Watkins of Richmond Co., sold as property of Robert Watkins, dec'd for the use of Robert Walton.   Part of orig. gr. of Benj. Cleveland.

1812—George Gober and wife Nancy to Thompson Epperson.

1812—James Brooks app. James Martin his atty. to recover from William Stanton of Pendleton Co., S. C., four slaves, given by Simon Thomason, dec'd to his daughter, Margaret, now the wife of James Brooks.

1812—Mary Cole, widow, app. Charles Sisson atty. to demand of Samuel Cole of Louisa Co., Va., a slave left in his hands by Richard Cole, son of the said Mary Cole.

Later she app. Seth Strane to represent her.

1812—Thomas Bush app. Seth Strange to recover money from the estate of his father Henry Bush of Caroline Co., Va., dec'd.

1808—Esaias Harbour to James Tate.

1810—Josiah Burgess and wife Verlinder to Thomas Cox.

1810—Gabriel Smith to Tryon Patterson.

1810—Richard Downs to Tryon Patterson.

1809—Redfern Weems and wife Elizabeth to William F. Garrett.

1809—James Haggard of Zane Co., Tenn., to Jonnakan Haggard.

1808—Absalom Trantham to Peter C. Ballinger.

1800—Alexander Beard of Jackson Co., to David Shelton.

1811—Elizabeth Thrasher, widow of Robert, sells to Thomas, Robert, Joseph and Sarah Thrasher, and Thomas Delmy and Seth Hodge her life estate.

1811—William O. Whitney and wife Ruthy to Lewis Moulder.

1811—Joseph Woodall mortgage to Garrett L. Sandidge.

1811—John Swift of Morgan Co., to Tryon Patterson.

1811—John Anderson of Elbert Co., to Joseph Morris.

1811—Robert Neal and wife Tabitha to Edward Riley.

1811—Capt. Samuel Tate wife Nancy of Pendleton Dist., S. C., to Allzemedon Thompson.

1811—Benjamin Cleveland and wife Arglin to John Elston of Pendleton Dist., S. C., land on Tugalo River, orig. granted to Thomas Payne and Benjamin Cleveland.

1811—Presley Barton and wife Elizabeth of Morgan Co., to Hugh Crawford.

1811—Barnabas Pace and wife Mary of Elbert Co., to Lowry Gillespie.

1811—Levi Thomas Davis to son William, gift of his home. Test: Thomas Davis, Jr.

1810—Asa Ayers gives a list of his property May 1810, when his wife Elizabeth eloped.

1810—William Hemphill and wife Margret to Thomas Gober.

1810—Mathew and Martin Sims to James Starrett of S. C.

1810—Robert Walton to Kenneth Findley.

1910—Richard Hooper to John A. Miller, Sr.

1810—Isaac Love to Wiley Dyar, lot No. 165, 5th Dist., Wilkinson Co. Granted to Love.

1809—Jesse Goodwin wife Elizabeth to James Starrett of S. C., Pendleton Dist.

1809—Mary White to John Morris, land where she now lives. Orig. grant to Chas. Butt.

1812—William Morgan of Franklin Co., Tenn., to John Morris.

1812—Richard White to Dudley Jones.

1812—John Hooper and wife Mary to Wm. Hackett.

1806—George Cockburn and wife Elizabeth to John Aaron.

1806—John Brown deed of gift to son Peter Brown.

1806—William Hemphill to James Armstrong.

1806—Stephen Hughes to William Ramsay.

1806—Barbara Moss and Amos Bratcher to John Westbrook.

1805—William Haley to James Mills.

1805—James McClain to Moses Ayers.

1801—Jacob Strickland and wife Priscilla to son Hardy Strickland. (Priscilla is pos. 2nd wife).

1802—Philip Vineyard to John Williams of Buncum Co., N. C.

1804—James Haggard to Hardy Strickland.

1805—Nancy Newberry, widow, sells lot No. 18, 3rd Dist. to Moses Watters.

1805—William Swift and wife Lucy to James Gibson.

1805—Thomas Payne, Sr., and wife Yanaky, to Moses Ayers. Wit: Zebediah and Cleveland Payne.

1805—Joshua Kennedy to Joseph Canterbury; both of Washington Co.

1805—William Wood to John Nesbit, of N. C.

1805—Benjamin Prewit and wife Mary to Reuben Shotwell.

1805—William Moore of Abbeville Co., S. C., to Chas. Ingram.

1805—John Blackwell to Chas. England of Pendleton, S. C.

1805—Randolph Walker and wife Sarah to Redfearn Weems.

1804—Thomas McDowell to John Walraven, grant to McDowell Feb. 3, 1785.

1806—Swift Mullins and wife Anna to Robert Hackett.

1806—Larkin Cleveland deed of gift to son David, orig. grant to Ezekiel Offutt.

1806—Chas. Ingram and wife Elizabeth to Sterling Tucker of Brunswick Co., Va.

1806—Thomas Harrington, atty. for John Harrington, to Thomas Stovall.

1806—John Robins to Gabriel Jones.

1806—Chas. Toney to Thomas Bush. Wit: John and William Bush .

1806—William, John and Lewis Gober, interested in the est. of George Gober of Granville Co., N. C., app. George Gober as atty. of Franklin Co.

1806—Chas. Angle deed of gift to son Thomas Angles, minor, to two daus. Sally and Lucy. Stepson John Banister Collins, stepdaus: Betsy and Mary Collins. Wit: Philip Mulkey, Jr., Mary Mulkey.

1802—John McKie, and wife Elizabeth to John Easly.

1800—Edward Moore, Esqr., and wife Lucy of Wilkes Co., to Thomas Grant.

1806—Lucy Farmer, John Mullins in behalf of Martha Mullins, late Martha Farmer, Dorothy Farmer and Thomas Farmer, heirs of the late Sarah Farmer of Granville Co., N. C. appoints Joseph Chandler, Esqr., one of the legatees, atty. to demand from John Graves of Granville Co., N. C., their several legacies.

1804—George Pricket and wife Sarah to James Read.

1804—Edward Megarcy of Elbert Co., to Robert Brown.

1804—John Harris to Elijah Martin.

1804—Thomas Moore of Augusta to Walter Mackall.

1804—William Henly and wife Mary to Edmund King.

1804—Dixon Nalor and wife Mary to Samuel Sewall.

1804—George Petigrew and wife, Jane, to Samuel Sewall, signed "Jean," Wit: James Petigrew.

1803—George Mathews of Oglethorpe Co., to Adam Cloud of Savannah, gr. to John and Manoah Cloud.

1803—John P. Adams app. Christian Adaner atty.

1803—Stephen Beaver and wife Nancy to Francis Hemley.

1803—William Few of Columbia Co., to William Turner.

1803—David Dodd and wife Abigail to Benjamin Slaton.

1803—James Neal to George Pettigrew. Wit: James and John Pettigrew.

1803—John Gilbert and wife Mary to William Howington.

1800—Charles Dean to John Burt, Sr.

1802—Aaron Arnold, Jr., to Elias Welman. Wit: James Welman.

1802—Thomas Hansy of Pendleton Dist., S. C., to Solomon Potter.

1802—William Henning to Hezekiah Stephens.

1802—William Eddins to Joel Garrell. Wit: Allen Garrell.

1802—Littleberry Shields to John Kelly.

1802—William Thomas to Aaron Arnold.

1801—John Watters, Sr., to John Henry Stevile of Burke Co., N. C. Wit: Nathan Camp and Frederick Stevile.

1801—Henry Chappelear to Edmund Henley.

1801—Elijah Christian and wife Elizabeth to Russell Jones.

1804—Henry Gordon to William Welman.

1804—Josiah Box to Anderson Ivy.

1804—Poyndexter Payne and wife Ann to Lewis Davis.

1804—Samuel Morgan Sr, and wife Nancy to Japheth Pruitt. Wit: Samuel Morgan.

1804—Samuel Ward deed of gift to his niece Lucy Yowell and her husband Joel Yowell. Wit: Joshua Yowell and William Eddins.

1804—Joel Doss and wife Mary of Elbert Co., to Thomas Jordan.

1804—Benjamin Allen and wife Elizabeth to Samuel Sewall.

1804—Nathaniel Hunt to Wiatt Langford.

1804—John Banks and wife Rebecca, to John Evins.

1804—William Quillin, Jr., to Jacob Carlton. Wit: John Tweedell.

1804—Michael Borders and wife Mary of Jackson Co., to George Stovall.

1804—Moses Payne atty. for Robert Shoemaker to William Cawthon.

1803—James Young to Richard Mauldin.

1803—David Glenn to William Glenn. Wit: Samuel Glenn.

1803—Thomas Carter and wife Elizabeth of Elbert Co., to Henry Walls.

1803—John Roberts, Jr., to John Roberts, Sr.

1803—Pleasant Webb and wife Nancy of Oglethorpe Co., to Robert Mercer, surveyed for William Webb, in 1785.

1803—Joseph Payne and wife Mary to John Meadows.

1803—Thomas Holcomb and wife Penellipey, to James McDowell. Where said Thomas now lives and where Sherwood Holcomb had resided.

1803—George Potts and wife Judy of Pendleton Dist., S. C., to Ephraim Dixon. Wit: Mary Dixon.

1802—Solomon Potter and wife Patsy to Henry Gordon.

1802—Richard Goolsby of Oglethorpe Co. to John Roberts, Sr. and Jr.

1802—John and Fanny Forsyth of Augusta, to James Miller.

1802—John McGowan and wife—to Robert Brown.

1802—Henry Millirons to John Walter Key, both of Columbia Co.

1802—Alexander McDougald to John Bennett. Wit: James Bennett and John Bennett, Jr.

1802—Jesse Dodd to Thomas Dobbins.

1798—Josiah N. Kennedy of Abbeville Co., S. C., to Anna Goodwin of Greenville Co., S. C.

1798—John Elkins to John Baker.

1796—Thomas Gregg of Elbert Co., to Stephen Poe.

1803—Receipt from Mary Gilbert to John Gilbert.

1803—John Roberts Sr. and Jr., to Philip Mulkey.

1803—William Dean and wife Susannah to George Turman.

1803—John Harrington and wife Agatha to Jeremiah Birks.

1803—Mark Haley to Barzillia Harrison.

1803—William Jackson and wife Nancy to John Boswell. Wit: William Boswell and Thos. Nunn(?)

1803—Andrew Innes(?), merchant of Augusta, to Thomas Talbot of Wilkes Co.

1804—William Henly and wife Mary to Samuel Philips.

1804—Samuel Philips deed of gift to nephew John Philips Hays.

1804—Moses Alread(?) to Mary Price.

1804—William Croslin to William Doss.

1804—Jeffery Cobb app. John Easly his atty.

1804—Stephen Beaver and wife Nancy to Castleton Lyon of Elbert Co.

1804—James Terrell app. John D. Terrell of Franklin Co., Ga., and James Terrell of Rutherford Co., N. C., to collect judgment against Edwin Lunsford of Rutherford, late of Greenville Co., S. C.

1804—John Burke of Pendleton Dist., S. C., app. Simon Terrell atty. against Thomas Davis, and revokes his appointment of Moses Terrell.

1804—William Gunter to Joshua Word(?).

1800—John Turman and wife Polly to George Turman of Elbert Co.

1800—George Sibbald and wife Rachel of Augusta, to James Hulsey.

1804—Charity Jones and Tignal Jones to collect from Wm. Parker of N. C. Exr. of Jas. Parker.

1804—Robert Brown of Broad River to Morgan Gunter.

1804—Warren Philpot of Pendleton Dist., S. C., to John Swift.

1804—Daniel Morgan, Sr., to Benjamin Morgan of Pendleton Dist., S. C.

1804—Isaac David and wife Susannah of Elbert Co., to Henry David.

1800—John Jack, gentleman of Philadelphia and wife Lettis, to William Eaton of N. Y. City.

1800—Andrew Burns of Columbia Co., to John Collins.

1800—Nimrod House and wife Ruth to William, Thomas, and Alex. Williamson of Lincoln Co.

1800—John Marcus of Washington Co., to Wm. Bullock. Wit: John and Mary Smith.

1798—James R. Whitney, T. C., to Andrew Burns of Jefferson Co. Wit: Bridget Whitney.

1798—Malachi Jones to Howell Adams.

1798—William Wilkerson and wife Priscilla of Wilkes Co., to Gilbert du Bois Berranger.

1798—George Garner and wife Betsy to John Smith.

1799—William Aldread to Patrick Taylor.

1799—John Hardin of Oglethorpe Co., to John Haggard.

1801—Fitz M. Hunt and wife Sarah to John Collins.

1801—Thomas Cawthon to Hugh McCracken.

1807—Howell Adams of Tenn., to Thomas Hailey.

1795—William Slatter to John Acworth, both of Warren Co.

1795—John Acworth sells the above to David Hale of Vermont; sale made in New York City.

1799—Jacob Goare and wife Rachel of Hancock Co., to Wm. Booker of Wilkes. Sam'l Dent, J. P.

1799—Malachi Jones to Caleb Jones. Wit: Malachi Jones, Jr., and Patrick Taylor.

1799—John Hubbard and wife Sally to Samuel Daily of Elbert Co., granted to said John By George Handley, Gov. Wit: Thomas Cook, J. P., and Susannah Hubbard.

1800—Thomas Gregg of Elbert Co., to Moses Trimble.

1800—Lewis Sewall of Columbia Co., to Patrick Scott, of Elbert Co.

1800—James Hay, exr. of William Hay of Oglethorpe Co., to Jeptha White.

1800—Grant Taylor of Jackson Co., to James Crow.

1800—Edward Prickett to Benjamin Love.

1800—William Morris and wife Jenny, to William Pool, orig. grant to Jeremiah Nicholson.

1800—James McBee and wife Sarah to John Temples.

1800—Mathew Talbot of Wilkes Co., to Richard Eubanks.

1800—James Airwicks(?) of Pendleton, S. C., to John Smith, Sr.

1798—James Denman and wife Clary, to Christopher Denman of Wilkes Co.

1798—Malichi Jones to Frederick Keel.

1798—Stephen Casey and wife Nancy to Robert Bond, all of S. C. orig. gr. to Casey from Gov. Elbert.

1799—Isaac Thomas to Jacob Hollingsworth. Wit: Thomas Hollingsworth.

1801—John Swift to Flower Swift, Sr.

1801—Thomas Westbrook and wife Mary to Beverly Broadus of Albermarle Co., Va.

1801—Samuel Bean to Maj. John Holland.

1801—William Huitt, Sr., and Robert Black (of Elbert Co.) to Joseph Terrell.

1801—John Trimble and wife Charity to David Clark.

1801—Thomas Gregg and wife Anna, to Jesse Branner.

1801—William Holley deed of gift to his children John and Elizabeth Holley.

1797—Robert Boyd and wife Agnes of Abbeville, S. C., to David McCracken; S. Casey's grant.

1797—Elijah Fleming of York Co., S. C., to Wm. Fleming. Orig. grant from Gov. Telfair.

1795—William Wilburn and wife Mary to William Dilham.

1795—Harris K. Wyly to Malachi Jones.

1786—Thomas Washington of Savannah to Robert Middleton of Green Co., orig. gr. of 1786.

1799—Wyatt Cleveland of Elbert Co., to Lott Ivy.

1801—Dower to Martha Shipley, widow of John Shipley, dec'd.

1801—John Flanigan to William Bates of Pendleton, S. C.

1801—Clement Watters to Caleb Jones, John Williams and Sherrold Holcom.

1801—John Parker to Henry Parks. Wit: Benjamin Cooper and Daniel Parker.

1801—Enoch Norton of Pendleton, S. C., to Samuel Earle of Greenville, S. C.

1801—Obadiah Hooper to Joseph Starkey.

1801—Edmund Snow to John Nix.

1801—David Clark of Elbert Co., to Arthur Jones.

1800—Elias Welman to Samuel Jackson.

1800—Absalom Franklin and wife Margaret to Thomas Roberts.

1800—John Mullins, Sr., to Swift Mullins.

1800—Malachi Jones and wife Susannah to Dudley Jones.

1803—William Ramsey and wife Rhoda to William Payne.

1803—Joseph Pulliam and wife Jane to Thos. Barton. Wit: Cornelius and Benj. Cooper.

1803—Millington Ledbetter and wife Mary to Robert Williamson.

1803—Benjamin Vermillion of Jackson Co., to Joseph Rogers.

1802—Adam Southerland to Shrewsberry Payne.

1802—Hezekiah Ledbetter, Sheriff, to James Lawson; property of Daniel Beall, levied on by Ananias Cooper.

1802—John Smith to Isaiah David. Wit: George and Elizabeth Garner.

1802—Richard Downs to Gabriel Smith.

1802—Ralph Banks to James Brock.

1793—Alex. McDougald and wife Elizabeth to Alex. Moss of Wilkes Co.

1795—James R. Whitney, Sheriff, to Elizabeth Whitney of Elbert Co., a survey of Fr. Mitchell.

1802—Wm. Pulliam and wife Sally of Elbert Co., to Sampson Lane.

1802—Travis Reas of Greenville, S. C., to John Nix.

1802—Thomas McCall of Camden Co., Ga., to Chas. Kennon, of N. C.

1802—Mathew Jordan of Elbert Co., to Fleming Jordan of Oglethorpe Co.

1802—James Brock of Elbert Co., to Benjamin Cooper.

1802—Amon Ayers to Stephen Huse.

1802—Lewis Sewall of Columbia Co., to David Montgomery.

1802—William Baldwin app. his son William Baldwin, Jr., atty. to collect share of his father William Baldwin's estate in Berkley Co., Va.

1802—Edmund King to William King.

1802—Killis, Robert, George Walton and Joseph and Mary Martin, app. our brother William Walker Martin atty. to collect their legacies from est. of Henry and John Mullins dec'd, their said uncle and cousin; property in Goochland Co., Va., in the hands of Thomas and Conley Mullins, Admrs.

1802—Jeremiah Sparks and wife Nancy, app. William Walker Walton atty. to collect their share of father's estate, Edward Sparks, dec'd of Goochland Co., Va.

1802—Charles Warren app. Peter Watters, "Capt. in the County" to confirm titles to land whereon John Cross now lives.

1802—James Blair to John Blackwell.

1802—Robert Crockett of York Dist., S. C., adm. of est. of Samuel Crockett dec'd, to Moses Trimble, orig. grant to said Samuel Crockett, Mar. 17, 1786.

1802—Ebenezer Fain of Buncombe Co., N. C., to James McCracken, orig. grant to Joseph Martin Russell, Aug. 19, 1790, conveyed by him to Rachel Hamilton, and by her to E. Fain. (This property was resold to Robert Crockett in same year.)

1802—Mary Parks, adm. of Lewis Bobo, dec'd, resident of Elbert Co., to Thomas Westbrooks, of Franklin Co. Wit: John Parks.

1802—James Dial and wife Mary, to John Gilbert.

1802—Edward Bryant and wife Susannah to William Cawthon, Jr.

1802—James Young to John Tate.

1802—James Jones app. Joseph Jones of Franklin Co., atty. to sell land in Frederick Co., Va.

1802—Thomas Standridge, Sr., to son Thomas, Jr., deed of gift. Wit: Jas. Collins, Susannah Standridge.

1801—John Tweedle of Elbert Co., to Dunmark Rayburn.

1801—Buckner Harris of Jackson Co., to John Jenkins.

1801—Edmund Taylor of Jackson Co., Rolen Weedon.

1801—Jacob White and wife Mary to Samuel Payne.

1801—William Ross of Pendleton, S. C., to William Crain.

1801—David Worthington and wife Elizabeth to John Grimes.

1801—John Hardin of Oglethorpe Co., to James Haggard.

1801—Littleberry Shields to Henry Hardy.

1800—James Freeman to George Rucker.

1800—Jacob Walker to Volintin Warren.

1800—William Lowery to John Graham.

1800—Andrew Cornelius and wife Patty to John Martin.

1800—Christopher Williman, Gentleman, of Charleston, S. C., to David Worthington, bounty of Landerdale for his services in the late Revolutionary War. (Mary, wife of Christopher.) Wit: Jocob Williman.

1784—James Yarborough to Adam R. Lister.

1798—Jonathan Hilton and wife, Elizabeth, to Russell Jones.

1799—Thomas Kelly to James Blair.

1799—John Cobbs of Jefferson Co., and Eldridge Hargrove of Jackson Co., to James Young.

1799—Eliza Carnes, sole Exr. of Peter Carnes of Richmond Co., to Mal. Jones and Clement Watters.

1799—William Quillian to Abner Farrar of Greenville Co., S. C.

1797—Elijah Williamson of Buncomb Co., N. C., to Thomas Cox.

1797—Daniel Beall and wife Martha to George Naylor of Columbia Co.

1797—George Naylor to Joseph R. Tatom, merchant of Philadelphia.

1797—Baker Ayers to Amon Ayers. Wit: Moses and Jane Payne.

1802—Thomas Hanay of Pendleton, S. C., to Benjamin Jones.

1802—John Moreland and wife Ann, of Jefferson Co., to Beall Baker.

1802—Randolph Holbrooks to George Estes of Oglethorpe Co.

1802—James Blair and wife Elizabeth.

1802—Joseph Terrell and wife Anna, to Peter Kinsey.

1802—Thomas Stripling of Wilkes Co., to William Ramsey.

1802—David Denman and wife Mary, to Christopher Denman.

1802—William Williford of Elbert Co., app. John Payne atty. to collect all the property of Sarah Williford, formerly Sarah Thomason, given to her by the will of her grandfather Macksfield Henslee, formerly of Caswell Co., N. C.

1802—Absalom Baker and wife Mary to Martin Sims.

1802—Dr. Charles Syndenham Morton to John Neal.

1802—Philip Vineyard and wife Catherine to Thompson Moore of Edgefield Co., S. C.

1802—Charles Quillian to William Quillian, Sr., who transfers to James Quillian.

1802—Polly Howell to George Knox.

1802—Francis Vitteloe deed of gift to minor dau. Fanny Allen, in care of Michael Box.

1802—Mark Haley and wife Sarah to Thomas Payne.

1803—William Quillian, Jr., to David Bullock.

1803—Thomas Rutledge of Jackson Co., and Hezekiah Chandler of Franklin Co., legal heirs of Mark Smith of Fayette Co., Ky., being married to sisters of dec'd Mark Smith; app. Daniel Glenn their atty.

1801—Christopher Hudson and wife Patsy to Thomas Westbrook.

1801—George Humble and wife Sarah to Benjamin Cleveland.

1790—Zachariah Cox to George Whitsall, both of Wilkes Co.

1798—Moses Watters and wife Elizabeth to Robert Watters.

1795—William Gough and wife Judith to Milly Sparks.

1795—Absalom Cleveland to John Roberts.

1795—Joseph Briars to Benjamin Parr.

1795—Sarah and Isaac Morris of Elberton Co., admrs. of James Morris to John Armstrong.

1795—Garrett Tureman of Elbert Co., to John Armstrong. Wit: Agnes Pace.

1795—Peyton Wyatt and wife Hannah, of Wilkes Co., to William Ratliff of same.

1795—Daniel Ayers and wife Anna to Mark Hardin.

1795—William Crain and wife Mary to William Harden.

1794—Samuel Isaacs of Pendleton, S. C., to John Kelly.

1794—Joseph Sinclair and wife Sarah to Jesse Carter of Greenville Co., S. C.

1794—Zachariah Cox of Montgomery Co., to Thatcher Vivion of Washington Co.

1794—Joseph B. Spencer and Charity M. Spencer to William T. Booker, all of Columbia Co., land in Franklin Co., which was granted to Charity M. Spencer, before her marriage. Land grant dated Nov. 1786, on Oconee River.

1794—John Tatom to Daniel Molder of Elbert Co.

1794—John Starr to Samuel Gardner of S. C.

1794—Joseph Wilson of Oglethorpe Co., to John Williamson of Wilkes Co.

1794—John Cobbs and wife Polly of Hancock Co., to David Ross of Richmond, Va.

1794—Basil Jones of Columbia Co., to John F. Hardy of Prince George Co., Md.

1793—John Henderson of Elbert Co., to Samuel Gardner of S. C.

1793—Julius Howard and wife Susannah of Elbert Co., to Joseph Pulliam.

1793—Joseph McCutcheon of Green Co., to John King.

1796—Philip Shelly to Stephen Smith.

1796—Isaac Stewart and wife Susannah of Green Co., to Geo. Naylor of Columbia (Spelt Stuart also).

1796—George Ogg, to Thomas Bray, both of Augusta.

1796—Deed of gift from Benjamin Cleveland of Pendleton, S. C., to Nancy Hardin; and to William Hardin his grant of 1786.

1786—George Naylor of Columbia Co., to Lewis Yancy(?) of Georgetown, Md.

1793—Henry Hayes to John Abelle.

1796(?)—Nathaniel Pearre and wife Annis of Columbia Co., to James Pearce of Richmond Co.

1796—Jesse Carter and wife Lydia of Greenville, S. C., to Robt. Langridge of same place.

1796—Malachi Jones, Daniel Beall, Asa Estes, bond to Joseph Chandler, Adm. of Jonathan Bowen, dec'd.

1796—James Gates, Thompson Epperson and Henry Hardy, bond to Joseph Chandler as Adm. of Samuel Epperson, dec'd.

1796—Malachi Jones, Frederick Beall and John Hewitt, bond to Joseph Chandler for Malachi Jones, adm. of James Hays, dec'd.

1796—John Gatlin, William Varnall, security for Asa Estes as adm. of John Bullard.

1796—Samuel Hollingsworth and Samuel Philips, sec. for Benjamin Wofford, adm. of James Wofford, dec'd.

1796—Joseph Pulliam and wife Jean to John Stonecypher.

1796—John and Abram Shelly to John Ward.

1796—Love Stathem of Wilkes Co., to Larkin Davis of Elbert Co.

1790—Absalom Cleveland to Humphrey Gibson, Jr., of Pendleton, S. C.

1795—Edward Rice and wife Sarah to Leonard Rice, of Elbert Co.

1795—Duncan Camron of Greene Co., to Thomas Coaker.

1795—Thompson McGuire of Elbert Co., to Hugh McDonald.

1795—Thomas Coker of Pendleton, S. C., to William Varnall, of Franklin Co.

1795—Simon Terrell and wife Sarah to Jacob Pennington.

1795—William Hughett and wife Mary to Joseph Terrell.

1797—Warren Philpot, Zachariah Bryan and Jonathan Hilton, Securities for John Bryan and Warren Philpot as admrs. of est. of Robert Thrasher.

1797—William Caldwell and Malachi Jones, sec. for Alex. Caldwell, adm. of John Caldwell.

1792—Peter Wyly to Joseph McCutcheon, both of Wilkes Co.

1793—William Waggoner and his wife to David Terrell, land in Franklin Co., originally granted to Willlam Waggoner. All of Wilkes Co.

1794—Joseph McCutcheon of Oglethorpe Co., to Richard Lockhart of Hancock Co. Wit: Priscilla Pope and Burwell Pope.

1806—Isaac Hancock app. Laughridge his atty. to convey all lands he may draw in the Lottery, as he has sold his rights to John Nail.

1794—Jesse Rowell declares before William Hardin, one of the justices of Franklin Co., that he was a soldier in 1st N. C. Regt., gives John Conner power of atty. to sell, assign or transfer a certificate issued in his name from the War office of the U. S. for personal services.

July 4, 1794—John Tweedle, late a soldier in the 1st Batt. of state of Ga., com. by Lt. Col. Harris, app. John Conner atty. to receive any land bounties to which he is entitled to by virtue of levies in the late Continental service. Sworn to before Wm. Hardin, J. P.

In another declaration he says he was Sgt. in 1st. Batt. and app. John Conner to sell or transfer a certificate issued in his name.

— — Peter Shepherd app. Nicholas Tuttle of Jackson Co., his legal atty. to ask and receive from the proper officer, a certificate concerning certain service in the U. S. in Gen. George Rogers Clark, or other officers commanding the troops, commencing in 1780 and continuing three years, at the following places; at the falls of the Ohio River and below the mouth of that river on the Mississippi, also at the last river at the Illinois settlements, and also at St. Vincent at the Wabash, and lastly at the Falls of the Ohio, where I was discharged by my Capt. John Bailey, Major Wails and Gen. Clark. Said atty. to collect any bounties, etc., pay, emoluments, etc.

(Signed)

Peter Shepherd.

Before us—

S. Lane, J. P.

James Pulliam.

FRANKLIN COUNTY WILLS AND TESTAMENTS
1827-1850

Robert Walters (or Watters), Sr., Planter.

April 1827—July 1827.

Wife Mary. Son Joseph, land conveyed to me by Moses Walters and Elizabeth his wife, on Shoal Creek. Dau. Rhoda Cawthon. Dau. Martha Looney land bought from Chas. Warren. Dau. Phoebe Marett. Two daus. Elizabeth and Leah, and Leah's two little daus. Mary and Martha, in case Leah does not remarry. Children of dec'd son John. To John Cannon and my dau. Mary Prewett. Exrs: son Joseph, Wm. Cawthon, and Isham Merrett. Wit: James H. Belise(?), Wm. Ray, Eli Woods.

John Mays

Oct. 11, 1827—Nov. 1827.

Wife Margarette. Son Newton, land bought of Chas. Lowery. Sons Edward, Robert and daus. Malinda and Synthia, not of age. Sons Thomas and William. Dau. Jane Turk. Exrs.: son Edward and son in law William Turk. Wit: James Anderson, Sr., Hall Sims, Thomas Bush.

James Miller

March 15, 1824—Sept. 1827.

Wife Adeania to choose her co-executor. All children to share alike when they come of age. Wit: James Martin, Jr., James M. Miller, Robert Williams.

Henry Avery.

Oct. 26, 1827—Jan. 1, 1828.

Wife Nancy, son James. Dau. Mary M. Attaway land in Appling Co.; dau. Jane Baird lot in Irvin Co., daus. Sarah Donahoo (land in Early Co.), Nancy A. Avery, Matilda Avery. Exrs: James Avery, John Deavours. Test: Joseph Reed, John Devours, Henry I. Mitchell.

Russell Jones.

Dec. 21, 1827—March 3, 1828.

Wife Sarah. Son Russell: son in law Allen Daniel; children of my dau. Polly Daniel, except William, deduction from Olive Powell's proportion. Grand chil. the chil. of Dudley Jones dec'd. Grand dau. Nancy Hooper; son in law Benjamin Cleveland; chil. of dec'd dau. Amelia Allen; son in law Charles Sorrels; son Lewis Jones, sons Thomas, William and James. Exrs: wife Sarah and son Russell. Wit: Gray Allen, Hugh A. Thompson, Russell T. Jones.

John W. Key.

Dec. 2, 1827—March 3, 1828.

Wife Jenny, son Pierce and Gabriel Martin Exrs. Daus: Lucinda Steel, Aggy. Harrison, Elizabeth Embry, Patty Thomas, Winny Embry, Sally Bailey. Grand chil. Louisa and George W. Bailey. Sons: Talbird and George W. Wit: Nathan Gunnels, John Sewell, Mary Sewell.

Robert Hemphill.

March 12, 1828—July 7, 1828.

Wife Riddy and Chas. D. Jenkins, Exrs. my five children until they come of age. Wit: Jesse Jenkins, Garrett Gray, Jonathan Humphrey.

William Pulliam.

June 30, 1828—March 29, 1829.

Wife Sarah. Sister in law Elizabeth Lee. To John Pulliam. Thomas King Exr. Wit: John Morrow, George Goody, Frances Goody.

Jairus Vaughan.

March 4, 1829—May 4, 1829.

Wife Hannah P. Exr. Son Ottoway W. Daus. Mariah, Harriette Mullinax, Elizabeth Ann Baker, Arra Pare, Narsipa Jenkins. Wit: John Sandige.

David Sloan, Sr.
(of Pendleton, S. C.)

Oct. 29, 1821—Oct. 16, 1826.

Wife Susannah and son David Exrs. 10 children. To Jesse Stribling. Dau. Susannah, wife of Robert Bruce. Sons: Thomas M., William, and youngest son James Madison. To Joseph Taylor and wife Nancy; to Joseph B. Earle and wife Rebecca; to John P. Benson and wife Catherine, my youngest dau. Grand child. David S. and Susannah Taylor, and grand son Charles Bruce.

Wit: Joseph Grisham, James Harrison, John Mathews.

Zacheus Herring.
(of DeKalb Co.)

Nov. 15, 1829—Jan. 4, 1830.

Wife Polly. Brother Isaiah, and orphans of brother Elbert Herrin. Wit: William I. Rusk, William Cheek, Micajah Carter.

William Wilkerson, Sr.

Nov. 21, 1829—Jan. 4, 1830.

Wife Fanny. Sons James and William H. Exrs. Daus: Fanny Nelms and Orpah Tate. Wit: Benj. Pulliam, James Wilkerson, John B. McMillion.

Samuel Philips.

Feb. 25, 1830—March 1830.

Nephews: Jackson Hays and Dennis Philips, exrs. To Louisa, Jane Amanda, and Thomas Gorham. Wit: John A. Green, Dennis Philips, Nancy Green.

John Bellamy.

May 26, 1829—May 3, 1830.

Wife Lucy Exr. Sons: William, Nicholas, John, Richard, Asa, Pleasant, Gilbert. Dau. Lucy Moats, entailed to her children: likewise to dau. Patsy Brawner, dau. Nisy Westbrook, dau. Elizabeth Bellamy. Speaks of the following property: Original grant to Richard Bellamy on Nails Creek; tract of land No. 166, 13th Dist. Houston Co., drawn by himself and No. 134 11th Dist., Muscogee Co., drawn by his mother, be divided among the children of son Gilbert. Wit: Joshua Wood, Chafin and William Chandler. Co-exrs: Wm. Bellamy and John Brawner.

William York.

June 24, 1830—July 5, 1830.

Wife Nancy and "all my children." Exrs. Dudley Ayers and John M. Payne. Wit: Abram Drain, Thomas Payne.

James McCarter.

May 20, 1830—Sept. 6, 1830.

Wife. Children who are living with me, namely: son John, daus. Polly, Sally, Betsy. Sons James and Mathew. Exrs. son John and friend Samuel Shannon. Wit: James Ramsey, Ely Ramsey, Chas. Tony.

Jane Robertson, widow.

March 12, 1829—Nov. 1, 1830.

Daus: Elizabeth Brixy, Sarah Ragsdale, Rebecca Tony, Margaret Robertson. Grand dau. Jane Lucinda Robertson, dau. of my beloved dau. Rhoda Williams. Sons William and Samuel Roberson. Exr.: son William. Wit: A. Freeman, Robert R. Ash, Malinda Mayes.

John Stubbs.

Dec. 13, 1830—Jan. 3, 1831.

Wife Nancy. Dau. Polly P. Wilson, and "Other children, when they come of age." Son John and son in law John F. Wilson, Exrs. Wit: Thomas King, R. Weems, George Garner.

John George Goody.

Sept. 8, 1829—March 7, 1831.

Wife Frances, sole heir and exr. Wit: Noah and Joseph Looney.

John Morris.

Apr. 18, 1830—May 2, 1831.

Wife Sally, and sons James and John, exrs. Other children: Epps, Thomas, Franklin, Susannah, Patsy Stonecypher, Lucy Jackson, Milly Meeks, Polly Coffee, Betsy Parks. Mentions lease to James and Leander Smith for 10 years on 2 tracts of land "as far as the mineral goes."

Wit: William A. McMillion, Alvin E. Whitten, Martha W. Bagwell.

John F. Pulliam.

Nov. 10, 1830—May 2, 1831.

"My mother." Kesiah Pulliam next youngest sister; Jemima Pulliam youngest sister. Wit: Robert Baskin, Reuben Payne, Benedict Payne.

Isaac Gray.

April 25, 1831—probated—

"My wife." Son Garrett, sole exr. Eldest dau. Susannah, next Letty, Mary, Elizabeth. Eldest sons John B. Gray, Johnston Gray. Daus. Nelly and Sally, and grand dau. Sarah Scott. Wit: Lewis Barton, Jonathan Humphries, James Tate.

John Strange, Sr.

Jan. 10, 1827—Nov. 7, 1831.

Wife Martha, two sons Seth and Sterling. Two lots, one in Troup Co., and one in Dooley, "drawn in my own name." Wit: Wm. Gilmer, Chas. Baker, Saml. Payne.

John Tabor.

Nov. 11, 1825—Jan. 2, 1832.

Wife Elizabeth. Sons: John H., William, Isaac, James, Francis W., and dau. Susannah. Land in the ensuing lottery. Three of his sons Exrs. Wit: Josiah Hix, Abraham Trail.

John Payne, Sr.

Dec. 7, 1831—Jan. 2, 1832.

"Being old" etc. Wife Ann. Eldest son Maxfield H., and third son David, exrs. Second son Thomas. Eldest dau. Elizabeth, 2nd dau. Nancy, widow of John Mills, son in law Chaffin Chatham, husband of dec'd dau. Polly, son in law William Chatham, husband of dec'd dau. Ruth. Wit: Thomas Payne, Sr., Samuel Payne, Baker Ayers.

John Allen.

Dec. 8, 1831—Jan. 2, 1832.

Wife Mary. Sons Richard and James, and son in law Pleasant Holley, Exrs. Other sons: Asa, John, Washington; daus. Elizabeth Kelly, Mary Lane, Nancy Carrell, Matilda Holley. Three grand chil. heirs of my dec'd dau. Sarah Christian. Gr. daus: Pilly Mayfield and Virginia Neal. Gr. son John, son of Washington Allen. Wit: Allen Weems, William Chandler, Woodson Blankenship, J. P.

John Clarkson.

Jan. 28, 1832—March 5, 1832.

"Being old and infirm" etc. Wife. Daus. Polly Boswell, Kesiah Pool, Milly Hill, Elizabeth Mize, Sally Shockley, Nancy Slaton, Jane Clarkson. Sons Joseph and David. Wit: Gabrief Martin, James Hargrove, Samuel Prewitt, John M. Prewitt, Jod Thomas.

William Jolly, Sr.
of Pickens Dist., S. C.

July 6, 1829—May 7, 1832.

Son James and his son and son in law; son Joseph's widow; dau. Patsy Hunnicutt's son and dau. To sons William and Jesse deducting what I gave to Eleanor Land. Sons: Maxey, John, and John's son. Son William Exr. with Charles J. Varner. Wit: John Varner, Richard Dean, Andrew Jenkins.

Lewis Chandler.

April 25, 1832—July 2, 1832.

Children of my first wife, Susannah. (Not named). Present wife Polly. All property to be divided between her and all my children. Excrs: Martin Anthony, Trench Hagard. Wit: Joseph Prewett, Warren Mize, John W. Prewett.

David Cawdle (Candell).

Dec. 30, 1829—Nov. 12, 1832.

Wife Elizabeth sole exr. Child in esse. Dau. Zillena. Wit: Samuel Jackson, David Candell, John Candell.

George Stovall, Sr.

Feb. 8, 1833—May 6, 1833.

Wife Rebecca. Sons: John, Sr., George W., William and David C. Sons in law: Tignal Meredith, James Rice, John M. Stovall. Son Joseph; dau. Susannah. Exrs: two oldest sons. Wit: John C. Watters, John Burgess, William Burroughs.

John Payne, Sr.

April 13, 1833—May 6, 1833.

Wife Polly, all estate for life, to be divided among all my chil. except Charles S. M. Payne. Exrs: Asa Payne, and Chestry(?) Payne. Wit: Thomas Payne, John M. Payne, John G. York.

Nathan Williams, Sr.

Feb. 28, 1833—May 6, 1833.

Wife Susan. Exrs: Thomas Horton and John D. Parker. Daus. Polly Hendricks, and children of dec'd dau. Sally Brown and Middleton Brown. Children of William Williams. Daus. Susannah Cheek, Rachel Sartain, Jemima Williams, Levicy Ballenger. Sons John E. Williams and Robert Williams. Wit: David Nelams (Nelms), Elizabeth Hall, John B. McMillion. A previous will, 1824, mentions gr. chil. Susannah, Polly, Middleton and Sally Brown, dau. Liney Ballenger and Nathan Williams, Jr.

Esaias Harbour.

May 29, 1832—Sep. 1833.

Beloved wife. Sons: John and Talmon. Daus: Rebecca Shelton, Catherine Molder, S lly Aderhold; grand chil. Talmon, Eli Jasper, Sally, Catherine and Polly Harbour. Wit: James H. Little, Robert G. Little, John H. Little.

Wit. to codicil of same date: Seaborn J. Harbour, Martha Harbour, James H. Little.

Elisha Wilkinson.

Aug. 31, 1833—Nov. 1833.

Wife Lucy and son Elisha Exrs. Other children: Tignal, Thomas, Polly Bond, Patsey Mitchell, Sophia Edwards, Fanny Wilkerson. Wit: Johnson Wiley, Westley Wiley, Linny Wiley, James Stovall, J. P.

Rowland Mitchell.

May 27, 1833—Nov. 1833.

All his estate to his sisters: Ann, Nancy, and Mary Mitchell. Wit: John C. Watters (Walters), Henry Pair, James Isbell.

Richard Malden.

July 22, 1833—Nov. 4, 1833.

Wife Elizabeth. Son Egis and John Henderson, Exrs. All my children. Son Egis is only one married. Wit: Nathaniel Harbin, George Y. Bond, Reuben Thornton, Harris Sanders.

Moses Ayers.

Oct. 6, 1827—Nov. 1833.

Wife Abigail sole heir and exr. Wit: John C. Aderhold, William King, Sr., Daniel Ayers.

Ann Payne, Sr.

Feb. 15, 1833—March 3, 1834.

"Being old and infirm." If she is fortunate to draw

gold or land in present lottery, it is to be divided among her seven children: Maxfield H., Elizabeth, Thomas, David, Nancy, Bennett (latter only life estate—to be given "her own born children." Children of my daus. Polly and Ruth Chatham. Exrs: three oldest sons. Wit: George Thomason, Willis Thomason, Solomon D. Thomason.

Joel Sartain.

June 7, 1834—Sept. 1834.
Wife Lilly, life estate. "Heirs," but not named. Exrs.: Wife, William Neal, Seth Strange. Wit: Samuel T. Payne, Richard Bellamy.

George Cockburn.

.. ... Probated Nov. 3, 1834.
Being 88 years old. Sons: Archibald, George, John, Josiah, Russel, Jeremiah, and Clark Cockburn. Daus: Jerushia Blackwell, Rachel and Sarah Cockburn. Son James and dau. Malissa all money, real estate, etc. Also 2 slaves to Malissa, "that unfortunate girl," and wants her to live with her mother and sister Sarah. Exr. James H. Little. Wit: Samuel Glenn, Thomas Howell, Charles Allen. Mentions Cherokee Lottery.

John R. Brown.
Citizen of Ammitt Co., Miss.

March 20, 1829—Sept. 26, 1829.
Daus: Martha McDowell, Arminda Weatherby, and Chlorinda, the latter having sustained an injury to her arm which incapacitates her, she is left all the slaves. To my much esteemed friend and son, Dr. Solomon Weatherby, all my surgical instruments, medicine, professional books and shop furniture. Copy of will to be forwarded to brother Abner Browne, Lexington, Henderson Co., Tenn., or to Samuel M. Caruthers, Hickman Co., Tenn., and that his death be published in the Nashville Whig, for the information of his friends in Tenn. Exrs: Solo-

mon Weatherby (also spelt Weathersly), Gabriel Felder, William Stewart. Wit: Minor M. Whitney, John Hall, Thomas Bachelor, Clk., R. M. Neilson, C. P. C.

William Neal.
(Nuncupative will.)

May 4, 1835.

Wife Lavinia. Daus: Arminda Ann Elizabeth, Lucinda Clementine, Eliza Kesiah, Harriett Tabitha. Son Thomas Anderson to have a liberal education. "As they come of age." Thomas Bush, Exr.

(William Neal died Saturday, April 4, 1835. The witnesses Elizabeth Bush, Tabitha Neal, William R. Wilburn giving the substance of what he said.)

William Glover.

Feb. 9, 1835—May 4, 1835.

Present wife Elizabeth Exr. Dau. Elizabeth Scales; other children under age and unmarried. Wit: David Carr, Joseph H. Jones, Job Bowen.

Thomas Covington.

Feb. 5, 1835—May 4, 1835.

All property to Thomas Farmer of Franklin Co., who is to give his childen Thomas J. Farmer, Jr., John N., Nancy and Susannah Farmer $25 each as they come of age. Wit: Josiah Stovall, James Stone, Oliver Harrison.

Burdet Leach.

April 22, 1835—July 6, 1835.

Wife Judith, son George only one of six children named. Wife Exr. Wit: Wm. Casey, Randolph C. Crow, Henrietta Hemphill.

Benjamin Slaton.

Oct. 14, 1835—Nov. 2, 1835.

Wife Ann. Sons: William (under age), Daniel, Samuel H. Daus; Patsy, Lucy, Cassey, Carryann, Nancy Baker, Elizabeth B. Dickerson. Grandchildren Olive and

Mary English. Exrs: Benjamin Evans, John and Thomas Bush. Wit: Daniel Bush, Wm. Mize, Thomas Mackie.

William Thomas.

July 1, 1835—Jan. 1836.
Wife Nancy and son Madison H. Thomas, Exrs. Daus: Sarah, Mary and Anny. Wit: Gabriel Martin, M. H. Thomas, Sarah Thomas.

Rachel Ramsay, widow.

March 31, 1835—March 7, 1836.
Son James Exr. All my children. Wit: Wm. R. Collon(?) Pierce Key, Caswell Ramsey.

Ely Ramsey.

Nov. 28, 1835—May, 1836.
Wife Elizabeth. Sons: Elonzo William H. Crawford Ramsay, Seth Strange Ramsey, Ely Harrison Ramsay. Dau. Rachel Colane Ramsay. Exrs: Robert Prewett and Seth Strange, Jr. Wit: Joseph McEntier, Crawford H. Little, Wm. Boswell.

Jesse Brawner, Sr.

Jan. 18, 1836—May, 1836.
Wife Sarah and son John Exrs. Dau. Susannah Westbrook. Other chil. names not given. Wit: Seth Strange, Jr., Richard Bellamy, Harrison Strange.

Sarah Parks.

July 4, 1834—July 25, 1836.
Robert Pulliam Exr. tract on which I now live, known as the Royston tract sold to Richard Royston by Thomas King. To Thomas William Walton Pulliam, son of Robert Pulliam. To Sarah Mackie, dau. of the late Isaac Herbert of Richmond Co., Ga. To Thomas, son of the late James Pulliam. Wit: Harner V. Pulliam, Henry W. Davis, John R. Stanford.

Thomas Mays.

May 2, 1837—July 1837.

Wife Martha. Children: Jeane, Nancy, Betsy, Polly, Peggy, Permelia and Harriett's children. Exrs: Joel Thomas and Newton Mays. Wit: A. F. Ashe, Clarkston Mize, Warren Mize.

Lucy Wilkerson.

Oct. 17, 1835—Sept. 4, 1837.

"Advanced in years." To daus. Polly Bond, Patsy Mitchell, Sophia Edwards, Sally Cawthon, heirs of dau. Silva Baker, dec'd. Sons: Elisha, Tignal, Thomas, and dau. Fanny Baldwin. Son Tignal, Exr. Wit: Josiah Stovall, Benjamin P. Hughes, Thomas Farmer, J. I. C., Jordan Farmer.

Julius Nichols.

March 28, 1838—July 1838.

"Old and infirm." Wife Sarah life estate to go to Ransom Nichols my nephew of Clarke Co., for the benefit of my dau. Agnes Anderson and her child; Sarah, Jane, and Candace Sabellah. Ransom Nichols, Exr. Wit: James Hargrove, Wm. Gober, Jidithan Porter.

Joseph McEntier.

May 28, 1834—Sept. 3, 1838.

Wife Nancy, James H. Little, James L. McEntier, Exrs. Eight chil: Minerva C., James L., John H., Robert H., Elizabeth A., Joseph W., and Nancy J. McIntier. Wit: Asa W. Allen, Samuel F. Wilkins, Hartwell Freeman.

John Burgess, Sr.

Nov. 16, 1838—May 6, 1839.

Wife Mary. Sons: Pleasant F. and Reuben C.—dau. Sarah. Son Pleasant Exr. Wit: not named.

James Stone.

Oct. 11, 1838—May 6, 1839.

Wife Elizabeth. Daus: Emily Griffin, Susannah Harrison, Julia Blair, Elijah G., William H., John F., James W. and Mary—calls the last five "My 5 youngest chil." Exrs: Oliver Harrison and son Elijah G. Wit: John Garner, Wm. H. Farmer, Josiah Stovall.

Thomas Akins.

Feb. 2, 1830—July 1, 1839.

Wife Polly. Sons: George, Thomas, William. Daus: Avarilla, Elizabeth White, Nancy Russell, Polly Watters. Mentions security for Willeford Watters to James Sullivan. Willeford appears to be husband of Polly. Exrs: Sons George and Thomas. Wit: Nathan Gunnels, Nancy Gunnels, Thomas M. Shannon.

Thomas Holmes.

Jan. 30, 1838—Sept. 2, 1839.

Alvin E. Whitten sole legatee and exr. Wit: Pleasant Holley, Mathew R. Rodgers.

William Bush.

May 1, 1839—Nov. 4, 1839.

Wife Joicy, son William F. and William R. Wilburn, Exrs. Dau. Louisa A. Jones. "Three children." One is not named. Wit: J. W. Bush, Menyard Sandres, J. P., Enoch Anderson.

Stephens Philips.

Dec. 28, 1840—Sept. 8, 1841.

Wife Mary Exr. "All my children." Wit: Joseph Parker, Nepolin Caveness, Job Bowers.

William Jones.

Sept. 9, 1841—Oct. 5, 1841.

"Old on the decline of life." Wife Sarah. Sons: Jasper N., James D., Russell T., and Walton H. Jones. Daus:

Harriet A. Watson and Nancy, wife of John Wiley. Exrs: Sons Russell T. and James D. Jones. Wit: Samuel Fields, James W. Payne, Temple F. Cooper.

Elizabeth Orr.

Nov. 3, 1840—Nov. 4, 1841.

Brother Durham Orr's sons Lewis and Samuel Exrs. His daus. Mary and Elizabeth. Wit: C. Meaders, A. N. Mays, G. W. Poole.

Jacob Strickland.

Nov. 5, 1841—Jan. 3, 1842.

Wife Clarisa and her 2 children, and such other of my chil. as shall remain with her. Sons: Isaac, Mathew, Tolbot, Jacob Sanders, Jesse White. Daus. Mary Mahulda, Eliza Caroline, Sarah Jane (Jacob Sanders Strickland is not of age). Exr: brother Hardy Strickland. Wit: Charles Strickland, Hardy Strickland, Jr., William C. Jolly.

Edward Carroll.

Sept. 18, 1841—Jan. 3, 1842.

Wife Ann, John M. Neal, Edward W. Mayfield, Exrs. Eight slaves conveyed to grand chil. Holis M., Mary F., Wesley M., and A. H. Neal. Wit: A. N. Mays, Nathan Gunnels, Alexander Langston, J. P.

Richard Freeman, Sr.

Jan. 18, 1841—Jan. 3, 1842.

Wife Elizabeth, "all my children." John, William, James, Francis, and Nathaniel H. and Richard Freeman. Sarah Chandler, Sidney Minnish, Elizabeth Hardyman. Son John Exr. Wit: G. L. Howell, Jacob Strickland, Dudley Chandler, John Megnis(?).

James Mitchell.

Feb. 27, 1842—May 2, 1842.

Wife Mary, son Reubin, Wm. Morrow, Exrs. Other sons: Daniel R., Jas. S., Beverly C., and Robert. Daus:

Arcadia Simmons and Mary Morrow. Land in Stewart Co. Wit: Simon Massey, Nathaniel H. White, James M. Edwards.

Charles Toney, Sr.

May 27, 1842—July 4, 1842.

Wife Nancy. Six children; Susannah H. Scott, Mary Anderson, Robert N., Charles, Jr., Nancy J. Norwood, Lourany E. Norwood. Wit: Clackston Mize, A. F. Ash, Floyd Parks.

John Martin, Sr.

Probated July 4, 1842.

Wife Rachel, sons: Micajah (land granted to Jacob Pendleton), William, Andrew, James, Aaron, John H., Josiah. Daus: Mary Martin, Sarah, wife of Wm. Belomel; Nancy, wife of John Ramsay. Wit: Math. B. and Garland Hooper, Alfred W. Davis.

John Burton.

Probated July 4, 1842.

Wife Mary and son Peter Exrs. Sons: Abraham, John H., Peter E. Grand son Benjamin H. Burton his father's share. To heirs of dau. Rhoda Ayers; to heirs of dau. Mary W. Pinson; to dau. Susan S. Aderhold; to heirs of dau. Sarah Isbell; to Evelina E. Harrison, dau. of John H. Burton, her father's share. Wit: Barthsheba Burton, Robinson Adams, H. F. Chandler.

Benjamin Harrison.

July 28, 1842—Sept. 5, 1842.

Wife Elizabeth. Son. Terrel L., and John B. Harrison. Granddau. Avaline Burton, dau. of John H. Burton. Dau. Frances Harrison, son in law Larkin Harrison and their dau. Nancy Harrison. Sons in law Talmon Harbour and John Morris. Grandson Benjamin H. Burton. Children of Terrel L. Harrison, names not given. Dau. Polly Morris. Two sons and infant of my dec'd dau. Elvira Caldwell, and niece Harriet Harrison. "The following children": John B. Harrison, Elvira Burton, David Dumass, and Elizabeth Cawthon. Son John B., son in law John Morris and David Dumass, Exrs.

Wit: Thomas King, D. A. R. Neal, J. J. M. Bagwell.

Elizabeth Payne.

April 30, 1839—Nov. 7, 1842.

Brothers David and Maxfield H. Payne. Three nieces Rutha Ann Chatham, Mary Amanda Chatham and Nancy Mills, daus. of my two dec'd sisters Rutha and Polly Chatham; my sister Nancy Bennett. All negroes to be sold and proceeds divided among brothers and sisters and their heirs. Brother Maxfield H. Payne, chil. of my dec'd sisters Rutha and Polly Chatham; Chil. of my brother Thomas Payne as follows: John H., William, Caroline Wheeler, Harriett Segers, Sary Ann Ayers, Oliver T., and Zebadiah C. Payne. Sister Nancy Bennett if she is living, if not to her children, her husband Cooper Bennett not to share. Exrs: Brothers David and Maxfield H. Payne. Wit.: Thomas King, D. A. R. Neal, Samuel Freeman.

Mary White.

Aug. 25, 1831—Jan. 2, 1843.

Married children; Jinny Smith, Sion White, Jerusha Chandler, Benjamin H. White. Other children: Vinda White, Martin, Pleasant and Samuel White, Mary Ann H. Jordan, dau. of Archibald and Elizabeth his wife. "My own daughter's child," less than 12 years old. Exrs. Martin White and Henry Smith. Wit: Graham Williams, Jeremiah Walls, David Hays.

Lucy Clements.

July 27, 1840—Aug. 3, 1840.

To son Mace and dau. Mary S. all the property I possess in Va., and half the slaves I own in Ga. The remaining half to son Meriwether and children of John S. Clements. Land in Ky. and Franklin Co. Exr. son Mace. Wit: Alice Smith, William A. Brackenbrough, Mary C. Brackenbrough. Probated in Richmond Co., Va. Bond given by Mace Clements in Richmond Co., Va., $40,000. Test: John T. B. Jeffries, Clk. A copy wit. by S. L. Jeffries, D. C.

Elias Burgess, Sr.

April 14, 1843—Sept. 4, 1843.
Sons James, Samuel, Evan, Benjamin. Grand dau. Peggy. Wit: Elias M. Burgess, Hezekiah Smith, John R. Smith.

David Anthony.

Probated March 13, 1843.
Wife Elizabeth and son Martin, exrs. Property at wife's death to go to her chil. except Elizabeth Anthony and Anna Chandler, wife of Stephen Chandler, dec'd. Notes against Stephen and Wyatt Chandler, and James W. Shankle. Wit: Gabriel Martin, Joshua Hudson, Madison W. Thomas.

Dozier Thornton.

July 27, 1837—Nov. 6, 1843.
Wife Jane, place on which I live, it being the place which she owned when I married her; a note on Benj. S. Pulliam for the sale of lot she drew as a widow. Balance to my own children, amounts advanced are recorded in my "Alphan Book," in the hands of my exrs., Joseph Chandler and Reuben Thornton.
Wit: S. Hymer, David Carr, Job Brown, J. P.
April 17, 1840—As son Reuben has moved to Ala. I appoint Henry F. Chandler in his place.
Wit: S. Hymer, James Attaway, Frances Pulliam.
March 14, 1842—Codicil: I give more to wife Jane, she having lived longer than expected.
Wit: James M. Glover, Benj. R. Pulliam, S. Hymer.

William Mitchell, Sr.

May 22, 1840—Nov. 6, 184

Wife Eleander and son William Exrs. Two lots drawn in the last gold and land lottery; lot No. 22, 9th Dist., 2nd Sec. and lot No. 218, 11th Dist., 2nd Sec. After wife's death all to be divided among my 5 chil: William, Jr., Eleander, sons in law Thomas Whitlow, David Barton and John Savage. Son Henry J. Wit: Wiley Clark, E. M. Knox, Samuel Knox.

Joshua Carpenter.

July 29, 1841—Nov. 6, 1843.

Wife Agnes, friends John B. Wade and Thomas Asku Exrs. Wit: Alex. Graham, John McDoogle, Wm. C. Wright. Son Martin and dau. Hester under age. Dau. Susannah Hannah, and her heirs; dau. Behemiah Nelams, sons James, Absalom, Joshua S., daus., Elizabeth Boatright, Fhoda Hammond and Leah Bond.

Archibald Cook.

June 25, 1843—Nov. 6, 1843.

Dr. Henry Freeman, Exr. All property to Cleverly Hughes, James L. Hughes, and Vincent Boswell. Mrs. Rachel Brown and Miss Anna Brown to continue to live in the house they now occupy. Wit: Henry Freeman, John H. Aderhold, Isaac M. Aderhold.

Josiah Hix.

Nov. 5, 1843—Jan. 8, 1844.

All property to remain in control of wife Elizabeth until youngest child is 21. Robert A. R. Neal, Exr. Wit: Henry Freeman, Johnson Weems, A. S. Jones.

Jesse Holbrooks.

May 6, 1844—July 1, 1844.

Wife. Dau. Elizabeth; sons John D. and Pleasant. Sons in law William Howell, John Arnold, John Hendricks,

George Gober.   Wit: Wm. R. Welborn, J. E. McCarter, Eli J. Harbour.

Hezekiah Prewett (Pruett).

June 9, 1844—Oct. 1844.

Sons: Robert, Joseph, William A., Samuel, Eli, Jeremiah, Hezekiah.   Daus: Eliza Patterson, Polly Freeman, Elizabeth Pruitt, and Lavinia Freeman; the latter's property to be in trust of John W. Pruett, and for her own heirs.   Some of the chil. are under age.   Wit: Nimrod Andrews, James McDonald, Wingard Sanders.

William Ford, Sr.

Oct. 29, 1839—Nov. 11, 1844.

Wife Sarah and sons Joel and William S. Ford Exrs. "My children."   Wit: James R. Haley, Joel Haley.

Lewis Ralston.

Oct. 21, 1844—Nov. 15, 1844.

"Of advanced age."   Wife Sally and grandson Edward H. Edwards, Exrs.   Dau. Elizabeth Edwards and her children, naming only one beside Exr., Francis T. Wit: R. G. Isbell, Franklin G. Morris.

Thomas Davis.

March 28, 1855—May 5, 1855.

Wife.   Daus: Elizabeth, Jane, Atermisia, H., Mary A. wife of Zechariah Clark, Nancy wife of Aaron Clark, Mary, wife of Hiram Forester, Hannah, wife of Albert Moss, Sarah Ann, wife of C. S. Wild, son William T. Davis. Daughters property left in trust of Seth Strange.   Exrs: Calvin S. Wild and Albert Moss.   Wit: Enoch Brady, Mathew B. Hooper, B. F. Willis.

Henry Parks, Sr.

April 11, 1844—Sept. 1, 1845.

Wife. Two shares of stock in Ga. R. R. Bank to dau. Elizabeth Hargroves, and same to son William J. Parks,

and son Francis A. Parks. If this stock is not disposed of
at the death of William J. Parks, to go to Annual Conference of M. E. Church, South. William J. Parks, exr. Wit:
Osborn B. Parks, Harwell H. Parks.

James Jackson.

Aug. 11, 1838—Sept. 1, 1845.

Wife Hannah. Sons William and Joseph Exrs. Daus:
Sarah Dobbs, Rebecca McFarland, Mary Chandler, and
Rhoda Thomas. Wit: William Burroughs, John T. Harri-
son, William Baldwin.

Sarah Gober.

June 4, 1834—Nov. 3, 1845.

"Old and infirm." All to beloved husband John Gober to carry out their marriage contract. No children
mentioned. Wit: Jas. Hampton, Jas. Hargrove.

John Semler.

Aug. 15, 1845—Nov. 3, 1845.

Wife. To Polly Richards, and the rest to John M. Neal,
who is also Exr. Wit: Nathan Gunnels, James L. Gillis-
pie, Thomas A. Smith.

Mathew B. Hooper, Sr.

Nov. 19, 1842—Jan. 12, 1846.

Wife Elizabeth. Children: John W. Justanse Beall,
Johnson M., Charles J., Richard, Elizabeth Butler and
the heirs of Martha H. Edwards, to-wit: William Russell
Edwards and Richard Mathew Edwards. Other children
not named have been provided for. Exrs. John W., Chas.
J., Richard and Benj. F. Hooper. Wit: Joshua and John
F. Wood.

Jonathan J. Hayes.

Aug. 13, 1845—March 2, 1846.

"Feeble and weak." Wife. Sons: John P., and Jackson J. To Sary Scales. Exrs: Jackson Hays and George
Shell. Wit: Jas. L. Smith, Willis Scales, Nelson Osbern.

Samuel McKee.

April 29, 1845—Jan. 12, 1846.
Wife Mary. Sons: Andrew H. William C., Thomas,
John, Samuel. Daus: Rosannah, Jane, Mary, Rachel,
Martha, Grand dau. Mary R. M. Allen, dau. of my dau.
Martha Allen. Exrs: Thomas and Andrew McKee. Wit:
Wm. Turk, John Langston, Leonard Shannon. (Mentions
lot in Carroll Co., 11th Dist. No. 210, and No. 1041, 4th
Dist., 1st Sec., formerly Cherokee Co.)

Samuel Prewett.

May 15, 1839—Jan. 5, 1846.
Wife Kesiah. Daus. Polly Chandler, Lucy Riley and
Polly Chandler's three sons, Wilkins, Daniel and Johnson
Prewett; grand sons Samuel W. Prewett & Samuel Riley
Sons Hezekiah and John W. Pruett. Orphans of Samuel
Robert W. and Joseph Prewett. Son John W. and George
F. Bond, Exrs. Wit: E. E. Sanders, Minyard Sanders,
William A. Young.

Moses Sanders, Sr.

Feb. 6, 1844—Dec. 8, 1846.
Sons: Harris, Minyard, Stephen; heirs and widow of
son John. Heirs of daus. Polly and Martha. Daus. Nancy, Sarah and Elizabeth. Exrs. Richard Wilbanks and
Minyard Sanders. Wit: William Perry, Donald McDonald, Jr.

Asa Bradley.

Dec. 22, 1846—May 3, 1847.
Wife Sarah house adjoining Martha B. Cooper. Daus.
Elizabeth Garrison, Martha Whitfield, Sarah Candle, Ma-
ry Segers, Margarette Candle, Priscilla Bradley, Harriet
Bradley and son George Bradley. Wit: Richard L. Hoop-
er, Mathew B. Hooper, Alfred W. Davis.

John L. Reed.

May 15, 1843—July 5, 1847.

Wife Eliza exr. son William A. P. Reed not of age. Mentions 202 1-2 acres in Upson Co., on Turkey Creek near Flint River. Wit: Joseph Chandler, Ann Willis, Lena Willis, William Burroughs, J. P.

Juda Walters (or Watters.)

July 26, 1846—recorded 1847.

Deed of gift to dau. Anna. Wit: N. Lindsay, J. M. Waters.

William Ramsay.

July 11, 1843—March 6, 1848.

Wife Rhoda and Thomas Morris Exrs. Son Wade H. Ramsay; dau. Nancy wife of David Scroggins; sons William, Jr., James, Drury M., Thomas J., and John. Wife and children of son George W. Ramsey; sons in law Andrew Martin, David Scroggins, and Asa York. Wit: John W. Verner, John E. Payne, John R. McMillion.

John McNeil.

Jan. 1, 1848—May 1, 1848.

"Of advanced age." Wife Frances with whom I have lived in social quietude 62 years; son Benjamin, daus.: Jerutha McNeil, and Francis Looney, property of both to be in trust of son Benjamin McNeil, who with "wife Frances" Exrs. Witnesses: John McFarland, Elijah Griffin.

Lewis Dortch.

March 17, 1848—May 1, 1848.

"Of advanced age." Wife Mary, with whom I have lived 53 years. Four children: Newnan R., James H., Spence D. Dortch, and Martha, wife of Carter White. Exrs: sons Newman R. and James H. Wit: Daniel Moseley, Bednego F. Wright, R. A. J. Wright, Sam'l S. McJenkins.

Gabriel Martin.

March 28, 1848—July 3, 1848.

"Old and infirm." Daus. Cynthia Neal, Sarah Tilman, wife of Berry G. Tilman; dau. Nancy Ash, son James D. Martin, heirs of son John Martin dec'd, namely, James B., Melvina E., John T., and Sarah A. Cahers or Cohers; sons Gabriel S. and James D., and James Hargroves, Exrs. Wit: Wm. H. Gober, Wesley A. Gober, G. N. B. Whitehead.

Royal Bryan.

Jan. 10, 1845—July 3, 1848.

Wife Harriett, S. C., and Joseph Jackson, Exrs. Sons: Robert R., Pleasant H., Thomas A., George N., and Benjamin K. Daus: Lucinda Howard, Elizabeth Bryan, tract of land on which Joel Bryan lives. To dau. Nancy Allbritton lot No. 803, Lumpkin Co., drawn by Tilman Bryan; also lot where James L. Allbritton now lives (Franklin Co.). Daus: Alice and Harriet C. Bryan. Wit: Robert G. and W. F. Isbell, Samuel Knox.

Thomas King.

Oct. 13, 1847—Jan. 8, 1849.

Wife Hannah all real and personal property in fee simple. Children; Nancy E. Neal, Jane C. Burton, Augustine W. King, Mary and Martha King, Benj. F., William P., Joseph B., and Milisa King. Wit: Thomas Morris, J. H. Mitchell, Isaac M. Aderhold.

Thomas Edwards.

Oct. 14, 1848—March 5, 1849.

"Of advanced age." Wife Sophia, married 18 years. All my children. Exrs. Thomas Baldwin to sell lot No. 9, 10th Dist., Carroll Co., Lot No. 51, Dist. 17, Early Co., lot 66, .. Dist. Fayette Co., for benefit of family. Wife Sophia and son Chas. G. Edwards Exrs. Wit: Micajah Estes, James T. Chaples, Joseph Garner, Martha Mitchell.

John Westbrook.

March 12, 1849—May 7, 1849.

Wife. Sons: Gillim H., Carroll, Basil and Glenn. Sons Stephen B. and Gillam H. Exrs. Wit: John H. Shannon, Russell J. Smith, Alex. Hampton.

John W. Stubbs.

June 6, 1849—July 2, 1849.

Wife Martha P. Children: Eliza Ann, Sarah Jane, William W., Leroy N., John S., and Thomas P., and Thomas the youngest son. Wit: Burgess Smith, W. M. Mitchell, Green B. Holbrook.

Caleb Barton.

Oct. 9, 1834—Jan. 2, 1849.

Wife Sarah. Sons: James H., Washington, Absalom, Henry M., William and Thompson Barton. Daus.: Polly, Matilda, Nancy Jackson, Sarah Messer, Susan King, Grand. dau. Rebecca Matilda Williams, not 18 years old. Son Absalom to take charge of his mother Sarah, and children, Polly, Matilda, William and Thompson, and educate them as well as the older children. Wit: John Crawford, Golom S. Rees, or Kees, Robert S. Hancock.

FRANKLIN COUNTY WILLS.

1814-1829.

John Anthony.

Aug. 21, 1814—March 6, 1815.

Wife Mary. Children: Lucretia, Willis, Willy, Waid, and Thomas. Exrs: Gabriel Martin and Thomas Perry. Wit: Martin Anthony, Pierce Key, Isaac Wimbish.

John Ayers.

Aug. 15, 1825—Jan. 2, 1826.

Children: Moses, John, Susannah Farmer, Leah McCarter, Polly Gober, Grand daus: Jenny Ayers, Susannah

McCarter, grand son William Jackson Gober, certain property for the support of son Joseph A. Ayers his lifetime. Exrs.: James H. Little, E. W. Mayfield. Wit: James Dailey, Samuel Dailey, Justma Sewell.

Asa Ayers.

Oct. 9, 1826—Nov. 6, 1826.

Wife Olivia-until youngest child comes of age. Note due from William T. Thompson. Exrs: Thomas Payne, Joseph Dunlop, James Little, Esqrs. If Little refuses to serve, appoint Maxfield H. Payne to take his place. Wit: Thomas Payne, John Payne, George Thompson.

Henry Avery.

Jan. 5, 1828—

Wife Nancy. Legatees: John T. C. Avery, James Attaway, Robert M. Baird, John H. Dunnahoo, Simeon Turman. Exr.: James Avery.

Richard Bellamy.

Aug. 20, 1813—Jan. 2, 1815.

Wife Nancy, dau. Susannah Webb, dau. Elizabeth Webb, dau. Polly Martin, dau. Elizabeth. Son John, grand dau. Ella Martin. Tract of 218 acres in Oglethorpe Co., to dau. Elizabeth where she now lives. Exrs.: son John and Stephen Westbrooks. Wit: Samuel Shannon, James Jones, Howell Mangum, John Westbrook.

Isaac J. Barrette.

May 5, 1828—

Heirs: James H. Barrette, John C. Mangum and wife, Micajah Carter by right of his wife Nancy, and he is also guardian for Judge H. Barrett, William and Eliza H. Barrett. Wit: Green B. Smith.

Henry Burroughs.

Feb. 16, 1828.

Legatees: William, Thomas, George N., Burroughs,

Royal Bryan, Thomas Pulliam. Wit: John M. Stovall,
Ferdinand Stovall.

Drewery Christian.
Friend Geo. Stovall.

Feb. 21, 1825—March 7, 1825.

Wife Frances. Friend Geo. Stovall, Thos. Jones, Exrs.
Four daus: Pyrean, Cainces(?), Sarah and Mary. Three
sons, Drewery B., Thomas C. and John A. Wit: James H.
Little. C. Christian, Margaret Jones.

James Lowery, Sr.

Dec. 9, 1820—Sept. 1824.

Wife Anna. Sons: Benjamin and John Wesley Low-
ery, Henry and Christopher. Daus. Mary Holbrook, Sally
Lowery, Aby Trimble. Wit: Clement Dallas, Burdett
Leach, Samuel F. Gerald.

Elizabeth Neal.

March 31, 1824—March 5, 1827.

Two sons Richard and Stephen Neal. Grand dau. Lil-
la Sartin, Nancy Neal (relationship not given), Son Richard and John M. Neal Exrs. Wit: Bryon H. Smithson,
Samuel Shannon, Bartlett Jones.

George Prickett.

Oct. 11, 1825—Nov. 1825.

Wife Patsy home and half the lot where Mrs. Reed now
lives; 1 lot in Early Co., known by No. 86, 12th Dist., and
granted to me. To cousin Bright W. Hargroves. Lot No.
25, 11th Dist. drawn by me in Irwin Co., One third of lot
in Appling Co., No. 110, 9th Dist. drawn by Daniel Gibson, now in the hands of James I. Millen. Exrs: Wife
Patsey, Readfern Weems, James H. Little. Wit: Maxfield H. Payne, Nathan Holley, Henry Freeman.

William Reynolds.

March 22, 1815—May 1815.

Wife Nancy. Daus. Lucy Turman and Elizabeth Reynolds. Exrs. Wife Nancy and Jesse Dobbs. Wit: Redfearn Weems, Peter Hobbs, William F. Gerald.

Ann Tate, widow.

Feb. 15, 1819—Aug. 12, 1827.

Exrc. Son Samuel. Children: William, Nancy Benton, Margaret Speaks (Sparks), Elizabeth Thompson, grand children: Samuel C. Tate, Anna Victory Tate, William B. T. Tate, James Tate, Catherine K. Tate, Thomas S. Tate, Frances C. Tate, not 18, Eliza C. Tate, Ann C. Tate. Wit: Thomas P. Carnes, William W. Carnes.

Alexander Williamson.

May 26, 1811—Nov. 1814.

Wife Clarica and her bodily heirs. If she dies without heirs to be divided between my brothers. Exrs: Frederick Beall, Macks F. M. Payne. Witt: H. Terrell, William Terrell, W. F. Bagwell.

Joseph Waters.

No date.

Heirs: William Carothers, Adam Looney, Robert Prewett, Isham Merritt, Larkin Cleveland, guardian for J. G. and R. Walters. Samuel Prewett by his agent, Joseph Prewett. Eliza, Lear, Larkin, and Polly Walters, and Berryman Prewett.

Samuel Sewell.

Feb. 15, 1815—May 1, 1815.

Wife Christian and sons John and James Exrs. Lands in Elbert Co. Dau. Mary. Sons Nicholas and Isaac. Wit: James Gailey, Wm. Redwine, William Pair.

James Little.

June 12, 1815—Sept. 4, 1815.

Wife Ann and John Chalmers Exrs. Five children: Sarah, Elizabeth, Polly, William Washington and James Monroe. Three daus. to be taught to read and write, two

sons to be taught reading, writing and arithmetic as far
as the Rule of Three. Wit: Isome Medlock, William Bale.

George Rucker.

Sept. 6, 1810—Nov. 6, 1815.
Wife Catherine and son George Jr. and Robt. Barnwell,
Exrs. Children: Indey, Nancy, Simeon, under age, four
eldest daus: Susannah, Elizabeth, Mary and Frances. Wit:
Joseph Payne, John Ross, Michael Hearndon.

Robert Stewart.

Nov. 12, 1814—May 1816.
About to take a journey from this state to North Carolina to dau. Sarah Ellison the land whereon he now lives,
during her life, at her death to her eldest son Stuart Ellison. To dau. Sarah Ellison lot No. 28, in 18th Dist. Wilkinson Co., and at her death to her son Robert Ellison.
To dau. Margaret Ellison lot No. 64, in 18th Dist. Wilkinson Co., at her death to her son Joseph Stewart Ellison. Personal property to grand children. Property in
North Carolina and Georgia. If any thing remains after
funeral and debts, I wish shoulder scofts (scarfs) bought
for Rev. Mr. Newton, Rev. Mr. Lair and one for each Excr.
The two ministers requested to preach funeral sermon
from the words: "I know that my Redeemer liveth."
Exrs: James H. Little, Thompson Moore, Samuel Shannon. Wit: Major Neal, Sally and Sarah Shannon.

William Hooper.

Aug. 20, 1815—May 1816.
Wife Joicy and son Joshua Exrs. Other sons William,
Obadiah, Richard. Wit: William Edwards, John Cleve-
land.

Epps Chatham.

March 19, 1813—May 1816.
Wife Sarah. Younger children: Chaffin, William, Rhoda, Elizabeth, Easter, and James, to be given property as

has been done for the older children: Joshua, Stephen, Sally and Polly. To Joel Glass $1. Exrs.: Stephen Chatham, Chaffin Chatham, David Payne. Wit: Francis Calloway, Peter C. Ballinger. William Chatham.

Richard Woods.

May 1, 1816—July 1816.

Wife Nancy all real and personal estate. At her death half of it to go to brother William Woods. All negroes to be freed at death of wife. Exrs: Wife Nancy, James H. Little, Samuel Shannon, and Samuel Strong of Oglethorpe Co. Wit: Nathaniel Hicks, Elizabeth Hicks, Pierce Key.

John Chalmers.

Dec. 17, 1815—Sept. 1816.

Wife Elizabeth and daus. Isabella and Ann. "All my children." John Chalmers Jr., sole exr. Wit: William Chalmers and William Boles.

Bryant Ward.

Aug. 18, 1815—Jan. 1817.

Wife Ann. Niece and nephew Susannah and Bryant Ward. Son John Ward. Sole exr. Joseph Martin of this Co., on Tugaloo River.

Moses Sanders, Sr.

Feb. 28, 1817—May 1817.

Wife. Sons John, Moses, Aaron, to Jones and Joel Sanders part of 400 acre tract granted to self, adjoining Aldred's old cabin. To Aron's Sanders Children: namely, Nancy, Joel, Jones, Moses, Nathaniel, Daniel, Polly, Sally. To grand chil. the children of David Sanders dec'd, namely, Marter, Hambleton, Sally, Nancy and David. Dau. Sally Hooper, and her child; William Sanders, Obadiah, Betsy, Carter, Milly and James Hooper. To Richard Maulden $2. Exrs. sons Moses and John. Wit: John Bush, William Legg, John Baugh, J. P. Codicil—that the portion of David Sanders' chil. be in trust of son John.

George Vaughan.

May 12, in 41st year of American Independence—July 7, 1817.

Wife Darchus. Sons: Henrich, Benjamin, John and George. Daus: Barbary Stephens, Rachel Martin, Nancy Cox, Polly Cox, Nelly McNeal, Priscilla Warren and Rebecca Williams. Exrs: John and Benjamin Vaughan. Wit: James Smith, Enoch Brady.

Robert Laughridge.

June 6, 1818—

Wife Susannah. Daus: Fanny, Susannah, Polly Hancock. Sons: Samuel, Jacob, James, Robert (where Allen Jones formerly lived), John, Benjamin (where William Scott formerly lived), and William. Exrs: Richard Gray, William Hackett. Wit: Van Davis, Sr. and Jr. and Cunningham Ellison.

William White.

Feb. 12, 1817—Nov. 1818.

Wife Mary. Daus: Pheeby Carter Smithson, Nancy Dixon, Polly Williams, Betsy G. Hunt. Sons: Zachariah, Thomas, William, Richard. Exrs: Sons Thomas and William. Wit: Henry Hardin, John Hollingsworth, Rice Green.

Benjamin Baker.

Dec. 10, 1815—Jan. 5, 1819.

Wife Cumfort. Sons: Benjamin and John. Daus. Jane and Onon, unmarried. Have given portions to other children. Land in Elbert Co. Exrs: son Christopher and Frederick Beall. Wit: Guilroy Sewell, H. Terrell.

Robert Neal.

March 9, 1818—Jan. 5, 1819.

Wife Tabitha. Sons: William, Joel, Stephen, Robert. Daus. Elizabeth, Mary, Tabitha, Caroline, Virginia, Su-

san. Exrs: son William, Gabriel Martin, James Allen.
Wit: Robert Malone, Lenny Randall, Patrick Mabry.

Thomas Davis, Sr.

Sept. 25, 1819—
Wife Kesiah. Sons: Lewis, Henry, Thomas, William.
Daus: Mary Terrell, Nancy Davis (now intermarried with
Enoch Brady), Elizabeth Davis, now intermarried with
Wolloam Ko(?). Exrs: Henry and Thomas Davis. Wit:
William Martin, George W. Lecroy, Thomas Hollings-
worth.

Stephen Westbrook.

Nov. 4, 1819—May 1820.
Wife Polly. Four youngest children: Reuben, Wiley F.,
Milton and Thompson. Daus: Bethesheba, Rhoda, Eliza-
beth Mayberry, Patsy Moulder. Sons: John, William,
Thomas, Joshua, Hudson, and Stephen B. Exrs: son
Joshua and friend Joseph Morris. Wit: Samuel Thur-
mond, Barret Jones, John Barber.

John Baugh, Sr.

Feb. 1, 1820—May 1, 1820.
Wife Darkus and her two little sons and dau: Joshua,
David and Patsy Baugh. Sons John, Mitchell, and William—the latter is sole Exr. Wit: John Duncan, Thomas R. D. Hicks.

Nathaniel Hix.

June 4, 1819—July 2, 1821.
Wife. Sons John and Absalom—the latter to take care
of his mother as long as she lives. Daus: Anna Haggard,
Elizabeth Turner, Polly Denman, Sally Key, Susannah
Shankle(?). Exrs: son Absalom, James H. Little, Sam-
uel Shannon. Wit: Joseph McEntire, James McCarter,
William Brown.

Thomas Hayney
of Pendleton Dist., S. C.

Jan. 31, 1821—Sept. 3, 1821(?).

Wife Elizabeth land in Franklin Co., Ga. Slaves to be freed at her death. Land in S. C. sold, and half to go to brother Hugh Haney, and to Elizabeth Blair and her heirs: both of whom if living are now in County Antrim, Ireland, near Clough Mills. If not called for in 7 years to be used for the poor of the district. Slaves not to be hired out or removed from Ga. or S. C. Exrs: James McDill, Hugh Wilson, William Turner. Wit: Robert McKenney, Margaret and Elizabeth McDill.

Magor Neal.

April 8, 1822—May 6, 1822.

Wife Nancy. John M. Neal, Edward W. Mayfield Exrs. Children: John M., Mary S., Elizabeth B., Hudson and Harriett—property to be kept together until Harriett is 21. Wit: Joseph Menness, Dickey Neal, Samuel Shannon.

Jacob Hollingsworth.

May 15, 1815—

"Advanced in years." Wife Mary. Four sons: Jacob, Thomas, James, and Benjamin. Dec'd dau. Sally Garner, her son Jacob Garner. Daus: Hannah Brown, Mary Wofford, Grand child: Sally Haynes, Mary Dolbens, John Hollingsworth, Henry Hollingsworth, Hannah Hollingsworth, children of my dec'd son Samuel Hollingsworth.

Nathan Arendall.

Oct. 28, 1822—May 5, 1823.

Wife Susannah. Sons John and Loughlin—"all my children." Sums equal to what I have already given to my daughters. Wife and son Loughlin, Exrs. Wit: John Silman, Samuel Dailey, James H. Little.

Dudley Jones.

Aug. 27, 1822—May 5, 1823.

Wife Clarisa and son Payton, Exrs. Oldest son Alswell

Beall, now known by the name of Oswell Beall Jones. Dau. Patsy. Wife of Asa A. Turner. To James A. Hooper $200. My children: Peyton, Sidney, Terrell, Kitty, Louisa, Francis, Jane, Emily and Harriett $2,000, each. Wit: William Beall, Thomas Payne, Garret L. Sandridge, Maxfield H. Payne.

William Payne.

May 8, 1823—July 7, 1823.

Youngest boys William and Harrison. All my children not named. Exr: Obadiah Ayers. Wit: Samuel Payne and Samuel F. Payne.

Martin Sims.

April 7, 1822—July 7, 1823.

Wife Anner Jane. Ten children, only son Julius named. Wife and Hull Sims Exrs. Wit: Samuel Yeargin, William Holbrooks, Samuel Holbrooks.

Legatees of John and Mary Christian.

Jan. 6, 1821—Wit: John Edwards.

Reuben, Drewry, Gabriel, Rufus, R. B., Christian, and William Oglesby and George Stovall.

Legatees of James Brock.

John Chalmers returns, Apr. 27, 1818.

William Chalmers, William Brock, James Brock, Elijah England.

Sale of Robert Roland's estate, Feb. 22, 1817. Aaron Tilman bought a shoe knife.

James Ramsey.

April 27, 1821—Nov. 3, 1823.

Wife Rachael and son James Exrs. Other children: Eli, Leonard, Jonathan, Martha Ramsey and Margaret McColley. Grand children: Harriet L., Thomas J., and Andrew H. Harper. Wit: James H. Little, William Ash, Sr., Samuel McKie.

John McEntire.

Aug. 26, 1823—

Wife. Daus: Margaret McCarter, Sarah Philips, Zelinda Fannin; three unmarried daus., Jane, Elizabeth and Zilla. Sons: Joseph and Thomas. Son in law James Philips. Tract in Monroe Co. Exrs: James H. Little, Samuel Shannon, Joseph McEntire. Wit: John Alexander. E. W. Mayfield, Mary D. Mayfield.

Flower Swift.

April 4, 1820—Jan. 1821.

Wife Sally. Children: William, John, and Tyre Swift, Vena Lagrand, Patty Duncan and Peter Barton. Wit: Robert Hackett, William Hackett, J. P.

Isaac D. Manley.

Sept. 9, 1811—March 1826.

Wife. Rodney and Elizabeth Hall, son and dau. of Ann Hall; Cineca and Evalina Deadman, son and dau. of Polly Deadman. Lot No. 13 in Dist. 24 of Wilkerson Co. Note against Richard M. Manly. Wit: Esaias Harbour, John Harbour, John Hamilton Blackwell.

Heirs of Martin Sims.

July 20, 1824—Agreement between heirs of body of Martin Sims, viz: Anna J., Hope. Hull, Sims of Franklin Co., and Richard Sims of Greene Co., Ala., and James Defour, Wm. Reed, Elisha and Agnes Sims, heirs of the body or constituted heirs by marrying daus. of dec'd Anna Jane Sims, widow of Martin Sims.

Stephen Chatham.

April 8, 1800—July 1826.

Wife. Daus: Hephizaba, Bevicy Green Chatham, Sarah Johnston Chatham, all unmarried. Sons: Elijah Jackson Japheth and Elisha Monroe Chatham, and Levi Chatham. Some of the sons are under age. Exrs: brothers:

Chaffin, William, and James Chatham. Wit: Maxfield Payne, Thomas Payne, Graves Yarbrough, Esaias Harbour.

William Pullam.

June 30, 1828—March 1829.

Wife Sarah. Sister in law Elizabeth Lee; John Pullam, Thomas King, Exr. Thomas King. Wit: John Morrow, George Goody, Frances Goody.

May 2, 1814—Wm. B. Wofford app. adm. in right of his wife on est. of James Thurmond, dec'd.

May 2, 1814—Sarah Scott adm. on est. of Archibald Scott.

May 2, 1814—James King chooses Adkinson Tabor his guardian.

July 12, 1814—James H. Little app. guardian of Fountain M. Thurman.

July 12, 1814—Maxfield H. Payne adm. in right of his wife, formerly Sarah Williamson.

July 12, 1814—Admr. of Wm. Williamson, dec'd.

July 12, 1814—Nelson Osborn, orphan, is bound to Jacob Redwine.

Sept. 5, 1814—William Rich app. adm. on est. of John Turk.

Sept. 5, 1814—Mary Long app. adm. on est. of James Long.

Sept. 5, 1814—Joseph Chandler app. adm. on est. of Sarah Bryan.

Sept. 7, 1814—John Williamson app. adm. of Thomas Williamson.

Sept. 7, 1814—Frances Allen and James Smith app. admrs. on est. of William Allen.

Sept. 7, 1814—Gabriel Martin app. admr. of est. of Drury Hutchins.

Sept. 7, 1814—Wm. Rich app. guar. of orphans of John Turk; Fondon Aderine, Salvador, Wm. and John.

Jan. 2, 1815—Thomas Wood app. guar. of Polly Wood.

Jan. 2, 1815—Henry Parks app. guar. of Isaac, orphan of Basil Dorsey, dec'd.

Jan. 2, 1815—Thomas Lenire app. adm. of est. of Polly Lenire.

March 6, 1815—Mary D. Hudson asks that Edward Carrell be her guard. instead of Asa Allen.

March 6, 1815—Thomas Connally makes returns as guard. of orphans of John Connally.

March 6, 1815—Francis Calloway makes returns as guard. of Alimpe(?) Martin.

March 6, 1815—Thomas Moore makes returns as exr. of David Clark.

March 6, 1815—Maxfield H. Payne app. guar. to John, Wm., and Sarah, orphans of Wm. Williamson.

March 6, 1815—Waitman Dishman app. guard. for Talliaferro Hooper in place of Isaac Brown.

July 3, 1815—John Hollingsworth app. guar. to James Hollingsworth.

July 3, 1815—Allen Daniel app. guar. to Russell J. Daniel.

July 3, 1815—Isaac Strickland app. guar. to John and Nancy, heirs of John Gilbert.

Sept. 4, 1815—Robert Burton app. guar. to Dempsey Connally.

Sept. 4, 1815—Samuel Prewett app. guar. to Levina Connally.

Sept. 4, 1815—Ignacius Purcell app. guar. to James Persel.

Sept. 4, 1815—Mary Wheeler, adm. of est. of Wm. Wheeler ordered to give bond.

May 14, 1815—Hannah Hollingsworth, heir to est. of Samuel Hollingsworth, debtor to Jacob Hollingsworth, Jr., Adm. of said est. for tuition vouchers. Wm. Robens, John Haynes.

May 1, 1815—Arthur Alexander app. guar. for Isaac Rush.

Jan. 1st, 1817—Inventory of est. of Joseph Shin, by Edmund King, Jr., adm.:

Cash received for his services in army, $21.06 1-4.

Sale of napsack and clothing, $3.43 1-4.

Milton and Boling's note, rent comm(?) $26.27 1-2.

Note on Lodowick and John Dobbs, $15.00.

March 4, 1816—Elias Baker app. guar. of John minor son of Basil Dorsey, dec'd.

March 4, 1816—James Sewell app. guar. of Samuel, minor son of Samuel Sewell, dec'd.

March 4, 1816—James Sewell app. guar. of Isaac, minor son of Samuel Sewell, dec'd.

March 4, 1816—Eli Ramsey app. guar of Harriet Lucinda, Thos. Jefferson and Andrew N. Harper.

March 4, 1816—John Stonecypher app. adm. of William Dun.

March 4, 1816—James McCarter app. guar. of Aly Martin.

May 16, 1816—Richard Brown and Darius Echols app. admrs. of Augustin Brown.

Aug. 5, 1816—William Hall app. adm. of David Meredith.

Aug. 5, 1816—James H. Little and Samuel Shannon app. admrs. on est. of William McCracken.

Sept. 1, 1816—John McDowell, Wm. Terrell app. admrs. of James McDowell.

Sept. 1, 1816—Sampson Lane and Matilda Bagwell app. admrs. of Winkfield Bagwell.

Sept. 1, 1816—Sampson Lane app. guard. of Henry Bagwell, minor.

Nov. 4, 1816—Thomas Towns app. admr. on William Ray

Nov. 4, 1816—Washington Weems app. adm. on Henry Brasele.

Nov. 4, 1816—Distribution of negroes of the est. of Charles Connally to legatees: Samuel Prewett, Robert Burton, Dempsey Connally, and Levina Connally.

Oct. 12, 1815—Ditto for the est of John Gilbert: James Allen, Russell J. Damel(?), Nancy, John and James Gilbert.

Jan. 13, 1817—Bedford Roland app. admr. on est. of Robert Roland.

Jan. 13, 1817—Nathaniel Wofford and John Beasley app. admrs. est. of Reuben Warren.

March 5, 1817—Isom J. Barrett authorized to sell land of Joseph Glenn, dec'd.

July 7, 1817—Edmund King and Wm. Bush app. admrs. of est. of Edmund King, Sr.

July 7, 1817—James Hooper Esqr., app. guar. of Wm. Sanders Hooper, Obadiah Hooper, Polly Carter, Milly and James Hooper, chil. of Sally Hooper, mentioned in will of Moses Sanders, dec'd. Aron Sanders app. guar. for Moses, Nathaniel, David, Polly and Sally Sanders, chil. of Aron Sanders, as mentioned in will of Moses Sanders, dec'd.

Sept. 1, 1817—James C. Watson, app. adm. of Thomas Woodward.

May 4, 1818—John Duncan and Mary Rice app. admrs. of Charles Rice, dec'd.

May 4, 1818—Moses Manley app. admr. on Daniel (or David) Manley.

May 4, 1818—Isaac Dorsey app. guar. for Berksley Dorsey.

May 4, 1818—Cornelius Murphy and Mary Tomlinson, exrs. of John Tomlinson late of Baldwin Co., ask that John Waters execute titles to land in Wilkinson Co., given before (by bond), Dec. 25, 1811.

July 6, 1818—William Blackwell app. adm. of William Blackwell, dec'd.

July 6, 1818—Andrew Thompson app adm. of Jesse Thompson.

July 6, 1818—Richard Manley app. adm. of Isaac D. Manley.

July 6, 1818—William Bole app. adm. of Daniel Kever.

Nov. 6, 1815—William Rich app guar. of Levy and Lettice, heirs of Richard Taylor.

July 6, 1818—John Chambers adm. of William Bole—publish citation.

Nov. 2, 1818—Martha Clark app. guar. for John Houston(?), Nancy Porter, William Henry, and Polly David Clark.

Nov. 2, 1818—Edmund Henley app. adm. of Abel Pearson, dec'd.

Nov. 2, 1818—Reuben Baxter app. guar. to Henry Bagley in place of Sampson Lane.

Nov. 2, 1818—Tempy Manly, relict of Daniel Manly, asks for child's part, which is within 12 months of his decease.

Nov. 2, 1818—Nancy Carter, late relict of Isaac J. Barrett, now wife of Micajah Carter, claims a child's part.

Jan. 4, 1819—Mary White app. guar. of orphans and heirs of William White: City(?), Freeman, and Richard White.

Jan. 4, 1819—Kitty Bryan, orphan of Eli Bryan, bound to Sterling Chandler.

Micajah Carter app. guard. of Judge Middleton, William Madison, and Eli H., minor children of Isaac J. Barrett.

March 1, 1819—Petition of Obadiah Ayers, assignee of William Smith.

March 1, 1819—Oliver Russell bound to Joseph McIntire.

July 5, 1819—Joshua Dorsey, orphan of Basil Dorsey, chose Henry Parks, Jr., as his guardian.

July 5, 1819—Thomas Lenore, adm. and guar. of orphans of Sam'l Hollingsworth, asks to be dismissed.

July 5, 1819—Citation to Joseph Watters and Polly Davis, formerly Polly Watters, admrs. of est. of John Watters.

Nov. 1, 1819—Jesse Aron app. adm. of James Flood, dec'd.

Nov. 1820—Zedeiah Ayers app. admr. of David Ayers, dec'd.

Nov. 1820—John Chambers app. comm. in and for Denis Duncan, dec'd.

Nov. 1820—Richard C. Bond app. com. in and for Joshua Hearon, retired.

Nov. 1820—Hannah Tate and Samuel Powers app. admrs. of William Tate.

Nov. 1820—Lucy Grissem and Amos Ozburn, orphans of Daniel Osburn, bound to John Burton.

Nov. 1820—John L. Flood, orphan of James Flood, bound to John Hamby.

Jan. 1820—Dempsey Connally app. guar. to Angeline George Connally.

March 5, 1821—John C. Christian app. adm. of Mary Christian.

March 5, 1821—John Silman, Jr., and John Dorsey app. admrs. of Wm. Smith.

March 5, 1821—Thomas Payne, Sr., and Middleton Payne, app. admrs. of William Payne.

May 7, 1821—James Purcell released from poll tax.

July 2, 1821—Disa Ayers, widow of David Ayers, takes a child's part.

July 2, 1821—Edy Holbrooks allowed $30 for support of Mary Holbrooks, an old person.

Nov. 5, 1821—Katy Payne, late wife of William Payne, takes child's part.

Nov. 5, 1821—William Flood, minor son of James Flood, bound to James Donahoo.

Sept. 1822—Catherine and Tallen Walker app. admrs. of Jonathan Walker.

Nov. 1822—Sanford Gohen (Gwinn?) app. guar. John Clark Gohen.

Jan. 1823—John Dean app. adm. of William Dean.

Sept. 1823—Ordered that Bennet Jones have 400 acres in his own and family headrights.

Sept. 10, 1823—Vouchers of the legatees of William Ishem; Abraham and John Ishem, Wm. Holcomb, (spelt Holnm). Tuition for youngest, Jinney, to Francis Satterwhite. John Baugh also a legatee.

July 1820—Distribution of negroes to Wm. Gilmore, Margaret and Elizabeth McCracken, heirs of est. of William McCracken.

May 1, 1822—Heirs of Stephen Westbrook; Barsheba (widow), Hudson, William, Thomas B., Rhoda and Mary. (The latter may be the widow—it is not clear.)

July 1818—Estate of Henry Brazziele Dr. to Washington Weems.

July 1819—Distribution of est. of James Chandler; to David and Martin Anthony in right of their wives, both names being given as "Elizabeth." To Lewis and Wyatt Chandler. David Anthony app. guar. of James and Stephen Chandler.

Feb. 1819—Reuben Baxter and Polly Bagley, admrs. of Henry Bagley. Sampson Lane is app. guar. to Henry Bagley, minor.

Nov. 10, 1820—Legatees of John Lowery; Allen Cook, Polly and James Lowery, admrs. Received of Fanny, formerly Tate, now wife of William Wilkerson, my full part of estate of Thomas Tate, Jr., dec'd. Charles Cauthon relinquishes all claim to Jas. Wilkerson, Fanny Nelms, and Orpha Tate.

July 1823—Marriage of Charles Cauthon to Rhoda Cauthon, heir of William Payne Cauthon, is mentioned.

May 1815—Receipt of Thomas and Betsy Webb, legatees of Richard Bellamy, dec'd.

May 1815—Receipt of Polly Martin, Jesse Webb, Susannah Webb, and John Bellamy.

May 1812—Heirs of William Cauthon dec'd: Larkin, Elizabeth, Chesley, and Rutha Cauthon; William and Philip Payne.

May 1812—Signal Meredith dr. to William H. Hall, guardian, to half expenses to Va. to settle an estate of Signal Abernathy, being equally interested with Meredith.

May 1812—Heirs or legatees of Benjamin Brewer: David Rice, George Good, John, Nancy, Randol and Benjamin Brewer.

May 1812—Legatees of John Wilson: William Wilson guar. of sister Polly, William Penn, husband of Abigail Wilson, Samuel Poe, wife Polly Wilson, Samuel Holbrook, wife Hannah Wilson, and Jeremiah Payne.

1814-1816—Lucy Meredith, wife of William H. Hall was sister of Signal Meredith.

1814-1816—Heirs of Philip Prewett: Bedford Roland, wife Patsey. Samuel Prewett guar. for Philip and Tilman Prewett.

March 1818—Legatees of James Chandler: David Anthony in right of his wife Elizabeth Richardson, Allen and Wiet Chandler.

1818—James Hooper is discharged as guar. for following minors: William S., Obadiah, Jr., Elizabeth, Amelia, and James, children of Obadiah Hooper of Alabama, who is app. their guar. in place of James Hooper. These chil. are heirs of Moses Sanders.

Sample for regiments—

Short Brest, one row of buttons. Four on each cuff right straight on the top. Two Buttons half from Coct Hat Blank, Cape to stand up short behind. Two large butons on Coct side with Dead Buttonholes, Buttons for Appls. as usual. (Epaulettes?)

Loose Papers: Jury for Feb. 1801.

William Little	Moses Saunders	Moses Braswell
Daniel Manly	Nathan Reed	Thomas Cothams
Obadiah Hooper	William Hall	George Garner
Henry Strickland	Robert Morris	Francis Saunders
Jesse Shumate	William Jones	Ely Rentshaw
George Pierce	William Birt	Peter Hudson
John Lowery	Harris Wiley	Joseph Chandler
Charles Walker	Thomas Meadows	Champness Payne

Joseph Pullim
James Reed

Benjamin Thrasher
Moses Trimble

Daniel Bush
Jacob Burton

Inferior Court—May 3, 1790. Larkin Cleveland, Peter Williamson, Wm. Cauthon, Esqrs., Moses Witt, Sheriff, presents jury list.

Cleyborn Cawthon
Aaron Campbell
Charles Gilbert
Baker Ayers, Jr.
Daniel Ayers
Thomas Carter

James McCann
Joseph Sinclair
Moses Watters
Peter Jones
Wyatt Langford
William Harper

William Payne
John Payne, Sr.
Baker Ayers, Sr.
William Harden
William Lewis
Obadiah Wright

Aug. 15, 1790. Nathan Coffee, Alex. Calwell, Joseph Humphries, appointed Constables. Jurors:

Thomas Crews
Lewis Bobo
John Herrington
John Lain

Thomas Sparks
William Swift
Jere Sparks
William Jones

Robert Williamson
George Clark
Patrick Vanse
Samuel Porter

Nov. 15, 1790. Jurors:

Joel Crain
John Payne, Jr.
John Cleveland
Warren Philpot
John Redding
Daniel Ayers

John Mullin, Sr.
Thomas Cox
John Bryant
John Stonecypher
James Hunt
Charles Gilbert

Martin Williams
Wm. Wilburn
Cleyburn Cawthon
William Bridges
Daniel Ayers, Foreman
Geo. Fleming, Dept. Sher.

February 1, 1791. Jurors:

John Lain
Obadiah Wright
John Clarke
John Cleveland
Joseph Edwards

William Trammell
John Harrington
Joseph Sinclair
John Watters
Peter Watters

John Payne, Jr.
Abner Franklin
Thomas Crews
William Jones

August, 1791. Jurors:

Benjamin Gates
Jacob Pennington
William Tuggle
Benedick White
Jesse Gough
Jesse LeGrand

Daniel Ayers
Benjamin Watson
Dickson Naylor
Joseph Box
Joseph Payne
William Black

Moses Guest
William Asher
Robt. Williamson
William Quillian
Joseph Gunnolds
Joseph Terrell

May 3, 1790—Orphan Mary Price living with John Moulton, Sr., bound to John Stonecypher until she is 18.

Owen and Wilson Griffin, orphans, bound to John Smith until 21.

WILLS, APPRAISEMENTS AND ADMINISTRATIONS.

Franklin Co., Ga., 1790—1812.

Will of Thomas Payne, jun.—beloved brother Nathaniel Payne, land granted to William Payne. Brothers Moses, Champens, Shrewsbury, Zebediah, Poyndexter, and Cleveland Payne. Sister Ruth Payne, negro due from Col. Benj. Cleveland. In case my beloved father should die before my beloved mother Yannaky Payne to be divided between brothers, step-brothers and sisters. Friends John Gorham, William Cawthorn and Richard White. May 15, 1786—June 1, 1787.

Wit: John Watters, Mathew McBee, Claborn Cawthon.

Inventory of estate of John Morgain, dec'd. John Williams, Wm. Gough, John Mullins. Proven accts. Jan. 10, 1798, against appraisers of said estate: John Payne, Benjamin Echols, Peter Williamson, James McBee, Ambrose Down, George Sherrell, William Daniel, Moses Perkins, Larkin Cleveland paid for grants, besides other expenses to Louisville and back in 1796. To George Sherrell (on oath), taxes for several years for orphans, Jan. 10, 1798.

Will of Jesse Walton—wife Mary and my children when son George becomes 21. Having given son Walker Walton lands and negroes previously. Exr.: wife Mary and friend Larkin Cleveland. June 13, 1789—Aug. 10, 1790. He died Aug. 10. Wit: Abner Franklin and Jesse Bond.

Accts. paid Dec. 1, 1793. Dr. Gilbert Hay judgment obtained by Chas. King vs. Jesse Walton in N. C.

Bond of James Maderson(?), Nathaniel Payne, Coller Rusel, Jeremiah Cleveland, T. C., James Bryant, Hugh Montgomery, William Brock, Benjamin Cleveland, James R. Whiting, T. C., Samuel Blackburn, Thomas Harkins and Edward Watts of Elbert Co., to Nathaniel Payne, Register of Probate for Franklin Co., Oct. 12, 1793, for Mary Bobo, Exr. of Lewis Bobo, dec'd. Bond for 1,000 lbs. Wit: John Montgomery.

Notes against Abner Ponder, Nimrod House, Moses Halkin, Ephraim Ledbetter, Robert Lamb, Chas. Hutcherson, Jeptha Rush. Appraisers: James Megomery, Edward Watts, Thomas Hooker.

Aug. 25, 1801—Inventory of est. of Conmack Haggins. Appraisers: Stephen Westbrook, William Gober, Obadiah Hooper.

*****

Inventory of est. of Joseph Brown.—Appraisers: Shrewsbury Payne, Joel Crain, Evans Todhunter. Aug. 25, 1801.

*****

Abner Vaughan dismissed as adm. of John Murphy. Oct. 3, 1801.

*****

Clement Wilkins granted letters of adm. on est. of Peter Thompson, October 3, 1801.

Will of Mary Walton—daus. Mary Carter, Rachel Williamson. Sons William Walker, Walton and Jesse. To son Killis Walton my part of a legacy left to us by Henry Mullins of Virginia. Dec'd son George. Wit: David Humphreys, Jesse Bond, Milby Sparks. Nov. 8, 1800—Oct. 6, 1801.

*****

Ordered that John Howard and Mary Woodward, now Mary Barrett, be granted letters testamentary on est. of Thomas Woodward, dec'd. March, 1802.

*****

At same time that Arnsted Barry and Kesiah Barry be granted letters on est. of Andrew Barry.
*****

At same time letters of adm. to Joseph Terrell on est. of William Watkins.

At same time letters of adm. to John Sandridge and John Gatewood on est. of William Stephens.

At same time Robert Watters and Reuben Payne on est. of Benjamin Thrasher, dec'd.
*****

Court Term, Aug. 6, 1802. Edmund Hendley adm. on est of John Gorham, dec'd.

Court Term Aug. 6, 1802. Jacob and Mary Hollingsworth on est. of Sam'l Hollingsworth.

Will of William Stephenson—Wife Martha. Daus: Elizabeth and Rebecca. Son Moore Stevenson. To Mary Stephenson. Exrs: John Sandridge and John Gatewood. Nov. 2, 1801. Date of probate not given. Wit: Susannah Sandridge, David Montgomery.
*****

Court Term, Feb. 16, 1803—

To Hannah and John Right letters on est. of Obadiah Right.

To Catherine Cleveland and Bedney Franklin on est. of John Cleveland.

To Christopher Baker and Eleanor Forester on est. of Owen Forester.

Letters of Guardianship to John and Julia Neal for the six children of Joseph Neal, dec'd, the children now of the wife of Burwell Whitehead. Namely, Jacon, Alexander, Kesiah, Judith, Obadiah, and Tabia.
*****

William Christian letters on est. of Elijah Christian, dec'd.
*****

Daniel Beall and Amos Bratcher on est. of Amos Bratcher, dec'd.

Court Term, April 12, 1803.

Letters to Elizabeth and Samuel McKie on est. of John McKie, dec'd.

*****

James Hooper, Wm. Bullock, Christopher Baker, appraisers est. of Amos Bratcher, dec'd.

*****

Inventory of est. of Andrew Berry, dec'd. No date.

Will of Charles Clayton—Wife Nancy and son Charles Colyer Clayton, Exrs. Wit: William Martin Hardin. "All my children." May 30, 1800—

Court Term, Feb. 11, 1803.

Will of William Robertson, proved.

*****

Ann Payne and Poindexter Payne letters on est. of John Payne, dec'd.

*****

Elizabeth McKie and Henry Parks letters on est. of John McKie, dec'd.

*****

Tignal Jones on est. of Arthur Jones, dec'd.

*****

Will of Richard Davis proved by James Montgomery, witness.

*****

Will of William Robertson—Wife Geen, Jesse Armstrong, and Abner Franklin Exrs. Daus: Elizabeth, Margret, Sarah, Rebecca, and Rhoda. Sons William and Samuel. Son Benjamin to enjoy the land he now lives on. Children to receive portions as they become of age. March 3, 1803— Wit: Sam'l Mackie, Benj. Jackson.

*****

Will of Richard Davis—Wife Elizabeth all property in fee simple. She is made joint excr. with Joshua McConnwell. Wit: John Parish, James Montgomery. Feb. 23, 1803.

Joel Youwell, Joseph Martin and John Blackwell, app. est. of J. Cleveland.

Court Term, Feb. 1804.

Wills of George Prickett and Adam Liner proven.
*****

Order in favor of Burwell Whitehead for $50, as guardian of Joseph Neal, dec'd.
*****

Arthur Jones gave bond for title in his lifetime to land to James Jarter, who asks that it be confirmed.
*****

Will of George Prickett—Exrs: Wife Mary and son Joel. Eldest son Israel, daus: Ann Knight, Mary Young, Sarah Williamson, and Elizabeth Weems. Sons: George, John, Josiah and Jacob. Wit: Redburn Weems and George Prickett, Jr. Sep. 12, 1803—
*****

Will of Adam Lyner—wife Betsy—"all my children." Honored father Henry Lyner. Wit: Andrew Betesbet and William Black. July 19, 1803.
*****

Court Term, Aug. 3, 1804. John Evans letters on est. of William Iram.
*****

June 6, 1790. Elizabeth Morgain and Nath. Hunt bond to Nathaniel Payne, Reg. of Probate, 500 lbs. as adms. of est. of John Morgain.
*****

Court Term Aug. 1802. Petition of Samuel Lockhart shows that Peter Thompson late of Wilkes Co., made bond July 1, 1785, to a certain tract of land in Franklin Co., a bounty warrant containing 287 1-2 acres. Lockhart prays that admrs. make title to same.
*****

August Court, 1803. William Christian letters on est. of Elijah Christian.

August Court, 1803. Daniel Beall and Amos Bratcher on est. of Amos Bratcher, dec'd. With James Hooper, William Bullock and Christopher Baker appraisers.
*****

Will of Charles Clayton—wife Nancy, son Charles Colyer Clayton "all my children." Wit: William and Martin Hardin. May 30, 1800.
*****

John Baugh, Samuel Jackson, Jesse Blackwell, appraisers of est. of Wm. Isom. April 1804.
*****

Sept. 14, 1804. Jas. Hargroves, Benj. Gates, Isaac Strickland appraisers of est. of Jacob Strickland.
*****

Inventory of est. of Samuel Whitaker. Appraisers: William Williamson, Anday Williamson, John Williamson. Feb. 18, 1805.
*****

Inventory of Isaac Whitaker, dec'd. Appraisers: Joseph Terrell, Thomas Covington, Epps Chatham. Feb. 16, 1805.
*****

Court Term July 10, 1805. Wills of Isaac Hendricks and John Holebrook, proven.

Court Term July 10, 1805. Mary Payne app. adm. of est. of Champness Payne, and she is made guardian of Patsey C. Payne, orphan of Champness Payne.

At same time William Wilson app. guar. of Mary, orphan of John Wilson.
*****

Will of Henry Lyner,—wife Margarette—dau. Margarette. Son Christopher and heirs of dec'd son Adam. Remainder to daus. Catherine Eve and Mary. Wit: And. B. Nesbit, John Black. Sept. 20, 1805.

Will of Jacob Hendricks—Wife—sons: Isaac, Joseph, and Moses, unmarried. Daus: Nancy and Annis. Eldest sons James and Andrew Hendricks and Finnell Wilson,

Exrs. Wit: William Jackson and Jesse Holland. Aug. 25, 1803.

*****

Will of John Holbrook—son Caleb land on N. Fork of Broad River; John, son of Caleb and Jincy dau. of Caleb. Son Jacob to give to my gr. son John Baker, son of William Baker; to John Baker son of Benjamin Baker; to John Baker son of Charles Baker. To John Holbrook son of William Holbrook; to John Holbrook, son of Rachel Holbrook. Daughter Nelly. Exrs: sons Jacob and William. Wit: John Smith and Martin Sims. Aug. 15, 1804. Apprs. John Gatewood, Chr. Baker, Chas. Ingram.

*****

Aug. 2, 1805. Appraisers of est. of Champness Payne; Dudley Jones, Asa Allen and Benjamin Baker.

Same time: Reuben Shotwell, Thomas Thornton and Jesse Holland, appraisers of estate of Isaac Hendricks.

*****

Feb. 11, 1806. James Galloway qualified as Excr. of est. of Charles C. Martin.

Feb. 11, 1806. Thomas Lyner app. guar. of 5 minor children of Samuel Hollingsworth.

Feb. 11, 1806. William Malone app. guard. Richard S. Harrington, orp. of Richard dec'd.

Feb. 11, 1806. Robert Williamson app. guard. of John, minor orp. of Peter Williamson.

Feb. 11, 1806. Thomas Geordean app. Adm. of est. of Joseph Gorden.

Feb. 11, 1806. Ordered that Hezekiah Terrell, Esq., and his deputy Oliver Cleveland be fined $5 for not attending this court.

Court Term, Jan. 5, 1807. Sarah app. admr. of William Williamson.

Court Term, Jan. 5, 1807. John Holland app. admr. of John Burke.

Court Term, Jan. 5, 1807. Sarah Howell and Lewis Williams on est. of Mathew Howell.

Court Term, Jan. 5, 1807. Augustus Brown applies for letters on est. of — — Brown.

Court Term, Jan. 5, 1807. Ed. Loyd Thomas and Elizabeth C. Thomas on est. of Philip Thomas.

Court Term, Jan. 5, 1807. Robt. and Sarah Carlton apply for letters on est. of Jacob Carlton.

Court Term, Jan. 5, 1807. Edmund Henby (or Henly) app. guar. of Peter Griffin Williamson, son of Peter Williamson, dec'd.

Will of Charles S. Morton—Daughter Olympia Muse Morton 4 slaves, cattle, household goods, etc., she to remain in the care of Francis Callaway and Sally his wife to be reared in the nurture and admonition of the Lord. To Francis Gallaway 250 acres of land, for him and my daughter the crop of cotton to be taken to Charleston and sold for cash. Exrs: James Lawson, Joseph Chandler, Esq. and William Calloway, Francis Calloway, and Rev. John Cleveland. Wit: Isaac Hancock, Gideon S., and Henry Smith. Jan. 3, 1806. (Francis called Gallaway, once.)

Will of Daniel Molder—wife Catherine—My children: Abraham, Mary Mitchell Lewis, Catherine Mitchell, Anne Mitchell, Daniel, Jacob, Elizabeth and Sarah. Exrs.: Wife and son in law James Mitchell. Wit: Wm. Malone, Robert Malone, and Abner Farrar. Feb. 17, 1807.

Will of Ninian Barrett—wife Mary:—Children: Isaac, Nancy Howard, Elizabeth Robinson, Patsey Kidd, Keziah Whitney, Ninian, Delilah, Polly and Harriett. Exrs: Isaac Barrett and Ninian Barrett Jr. Wit: Farley Thompson, Joseph Howard. Dec. 1806.
*****

Court Term May 4, 1807. Will of Benjamin Vaughan proven. Samuel Winningham, Exr. fails to appear.

At same time: Sam'l Prewett app. guard. of Philip, Patsy, Tillman and Zech. Prewett.

Will of Benjamin Vaughan—Wife Martha. Sons Abner and Benjamin $1 each. To the rest of my legal born children an equal part''. Exrs. Wife Martha and Samuel Winningham. Wit: Isaac Strickland, George Christian, Berry Vaughan. Aug. 5, 1806.

Appraisers of est. of Jacob Carlton: A. Williamson, Jas. and Wm. Mitchell. 1807.

Court Term Sept. 7, 1807. Jas. H. Little and John Westbrook Admrs. of est. of James Little.

Court Term Sept. 7, 1807. Lewis Williams app. adm. on est. of Mathew Howell.

Court Term Sept. 7, 1807. Silby Connally, Wm. Christian, David Morgan, est. of John Connally.

Court Term Jan. 6, 1807. John, And., and Thos. Williamson, app. est. Wm. Wm. son. Wife Sarah.

Court Term, Feb. 25, 1807. Moses Sanders, Michael Box, Thos. Lenoir—est. Mathew Hall.

Court Term May 18, 1807. Martin and Mark Hardin, Farlen Thompson—est. Ninian Barrett.

Court Term July 25, 1807. S. Simmonds, Jas. Freeman, Saml. Everett. Appr. est. of Benj. Reaves.

Will of Bassel Dorsey—Son Andrew. Exrs: John Dorsey and Elias Baker. Wit: John R. Brown and William Berry. Apprs. John and Zach. Tabor, Joseph Penn. June 16, 1806—Sept. 1807.

Feb. Term, 1804. Agreeable to order of court, guardians of orphans of Joseph Nail are directed to pay Burwell Whitehead $150.

Debtors to estate of William Stephenson, dec'd, 1802.

William Garner, William Bowers, James Flood, Peter Brown, William McGee, Charles Henly, Daniel Manly, Haines Keeling, David Nelams (Nelms?), Robert McLeod, Rial Bryan, James Turman, William Barnhill, William Burt, Meredith Brown, James Phelps, Jacob Hill, Jacob Key, John Wood, Joseph Burt, Isaac Allbritton, Lewis Graddy, Charles Dean, Henry Crittenten, Claiborn Sandridge, John Scull, William Phelps, William Woodson, Eli Bryan, Elisha Bryan, James Nettles, John M. Allbritton, Jeremiah Fowler, Thomas Harrington, Wil-

liam McGee, Mark Fowler, Richard Allbritton, John Scott
Robert Skilton, Joshua Hearn, Henning Greenwood, Eliz-
abeth Manly, Meredith Brown, Robert Lowerymore, John
Sandridge, Joseph Parker, Lambert King, Thomas Gaby,
John Allbritton, Henry Burroughs.

Debtors to the estate of Andrew Berry—
Thomas Harrison, John Caer, John Mullins, Micajah
Smithers, Feb. 11, 1803.

Sales: William Robertson's estate, Nov. 20, 1803—
To Benjamin Jackson, Edward Ryles, Jr., Wm. Boswell,
Joshua Hudson, Daniel Vineyard, Samuel Hollingsworth,
Michael Box, Thomas Wafer, John Henderson, Johnson
Randall, Abram Brown, Wm. Fleming, John Savall, Rob-
ert Fleming, Mathew Cox, Adonijah Hulsey, David San-
ders, Joel Maybry, Baily Brook (or Brock), Lemuel Bean,
John Bricksey, John Macken, John Garrison, Thomas
Munn, Barnabas Strickland, Edward Level, Isaac Dal-
rumple, Thomas Little, Benj. Jackson, Richard Dodd, Wil-
liam Cook, Jeptha Harrington, Samuel Jackson, Patrick
Maybry, Isaac Hodge, Robert Bean, Caleb Garrison,
George Gober, Zebular Garrison, Watson Cook, Wm.
Jackson, Wm. Mackee, Elizabeth Mackee.

Will of John Lowery—Wife Ellender—son James,
Exrs. "Wife and children." Wit: Daniel and William
Lowery, John Parks, Sept. 13, 1807.

Court Term Jan. 4, 1808. Justices: James Hooper, Asa
Allen, Saml. Shannon, Henry Parks, app. guar. of Patsey
Roxanna Mackee, orphan of John McKee. James Brock,
James Montgomery, John Collins, Apprs. of est. of Cor-
nelius Cooper.

Court Term March 7, 1808. John Sandridge app. guar.
of Rebecca and Polly Stephenson, heirs of the est. of William Stephenson.

At same court Thomas Hollingsworth app. guar. of
John, minor son of Saml. Hollingsworth.

Court Term May 2, 1808. Jeremiah and Ann Sparks
admrs. of est. of James Sparks.

Court Term May 2, 1808. Zebediah Payne admr. of est. of Cleveland Payne.

Court Term May 2, 1808. William Christian adm. of est. of John Christian.

Court Term May 2, 1808. Jonathan Baw app. adm. of est. of David Baw.

Court Term July 4, 1808. Sampson Lane app. adm. of est. of Isaiah Beasom.

Court Term July 4, 1808. Elizabeth Taylor app. adm. of est. of Richard Taylor.

Will of Martin Dye—Wife Catherine and sons Prettyman and Randall Exrs. Sons Beckham, John, Martin, Randolph, George, Benjamin, and Stephen Mayfield Dye. Daughters: Catherine, wife of Edmund Mayfield, Mary wife of Wyche Jackson, Rebecca, wife of Joel Smith. Wit: Saml. Shannon, John Mayfield, J. R. Brown. Nov. 24, 1807—Jan. 4, 1808.

Notes due the estate of James Sparks—

James Spurger, Robert Earwood, John Hill, Fleming Echols, James Blair. Appraisers:

July 19, 1808, Joel Yowell, Jere Sparks, Joseph Martin.

Oct. 13, 1807: Drewery Christian, Joel Hunt, Henry Black, Zebulon Garrison, appraisers of estate of John Connally.

May 24, 1808: Appraisers of est. of David Baugh: John Baugh, Jesse Blackwell, John Walraven.

Court Term Sept. 5, 1808. Ann and Joshua Hudson admrs. of est. of Joseph Hudson.

Court Term Sept. 5, 1808. David Perryman, minor orphan of David Perryman, now 14, asks that David Cleveland be appointed his guardian, and of his brother Anthony Major Perryman.

Oct. 15, 1808. Henry Parks, John Prickett, Ephraim Dixon, Apprs. est. of Joakim Hudson.

Nov. 6, 1808, William Rich appointed admr. of est. of Richard Taylor. In July 8, 1806, Richard Taylor had given bond for land in Baldwin Co., now Morgan, to William Tolbert, assignee of Thomas Jenkins, Sr. This bond is now confirmed.

Will of Joseph Johnson wife Rebeccah and Benjamin Tucker, Exrs. "All my children." Wit: James H. Little, William Blackwell, John Covington. March 24, 1808 —Jan. 1809.

Will of Cornelius Cooper—Exrs., sons Benjamin and Cornelius Cooper. Other children: Billy, George, Sally York, Betty Keeton, Milly Woodluf, Savary Allen. Wit: John Collins. Aug. 1, 1805—Dec. 20, 1808(?).

Court Term March 1809. John D. Terrell guar. of Patsy, dau. of Harry Terrell (S. C.).

Court Term May 1, 1809. Mary Willis app. admr. est. of William Willis.

Court Term May 1, 1809. Elizabeth and Joseph Chandler admrs. of est. James Chandler.

Court Term Aug. 7, 1809. John Dorsey app. guar. of Adrew Dorsey.

Will of Isaac Edwards—to Hannah Haite, $500, Sons William and Joseph, Exrs. Wit: Sterling Harris, Absalom Dunnomy, John R. Brown. July 2, 1809—Aug. 7, 1809.

June 9, 1809. William Phelps, John Holcomb, Able White, est. of Wm. Wheeler.

May 18, 1808. Silas McGrady, Bennett Ware, Bartholomew Lawrence, est. of Jas. Chandler.

Aug. 9, 1809. John Neal, John Mullen, M. Wilcox, apprs. of est. of Isaac Edwards.

Jan. 1, 1810. John Easley released as guar. orphans of Daniel Bush.

John R. Brown, Edmund Henly, Benjamin King, Esqrs. present.

Caswell Co., N. C., Court of Pleas and Quarter Sessions. Sept. Term, 1809. Thomas Connally appointed guardian for Polly, Charles and Aquilla Connally orphans of John Connally, dec'd. late of the state of Georgia, Franklin Co. George Connally and Amasy Smith, bondsmen. Jesse Carter, James Yancey and Michael Montgomery, Esqrs. being the Court then sitting.

Certified by Archibald Murphy, Clerk of Court, Caswell Co. William Rainey, chairman of Caswell Co. certifies that Archibald Murphy is Clerk of Court.

Court of Ordinary, March 5, 1810—

Abda Christian makes returns Estate of John Christian.

At same time William Robbins gives receipt to Thomas Lenoir as guardian of orphans of Samuel Hollingsworth.

Also, Thomas Storey and John Chalmers app. admrs. of est. of James Brock.

"A LITTLE NONSENSE, NOW AND THEN."

The following lines were found on the back of a loose court record, and were, no doubt, indited amidst the stress of affairs of state and country. It is illustrative of the fact that there are no bounds to the expression of genius, and that its budding does not depend upon environment, season nor place.

Written, as it was, in that restless period following the Revolution, it is indicative of the spirit of those days, aided and abetted, no doubt by other "spirits," which were also those of pre-Volstead days.

PERSEVERANCE IN LOVE.

A woman sometimes frowns what best contents her:
Send her another; never give over,
For scorn at first, makes after love the more.
If she do frown 'tis not in hate of you,
But rather to beget more love in you.
If she do chide 'tis not to have you gone,
For why?—the fools are mad if left alone.
Take no repulse whatever she doth say;
For "get you gone" she doth not mean "away."
Flatter and praise, commend, extol their graces,

Tho' never so black, say they have angel faces.
That man that hath a tongue, I say, is no man,
If with his tongue he cannot gain a woman.
                    —Bedney Franklin. (About 1803-1804.)

Some further effusion had been written on the bottom of the sheet, but a cruel fate had, with ruthless fingers, torn away all but the beginnings of the epic, the capital letters alone showing its poetic intent.
Hic Jacet.

Georgia, Lincoln Co.:
In obedience to a Commission from the Honorable the Superior Court of Franklin Co., to us directed, personally came and appeared before us
Benjamin Brown of the said county, and being duly sworn on the Holy Gospel of God to the best of his knowledge to answer to the Interrogatorys Questions annexed to the said Commission on the part and behalf of the Admrs. of Amos Bratcher dec'd. app. 1, versus John Westbrook and Stephen Westbrook Respt.
1. I know Daniel Beall, one of the parties the others I do not.
2. I new David Burks formerly of Wilkes County for eleven or twelve years. I marryed his Daughter, he is dead, died the sixth of Oct. 1804.
3. I hope to put David Burks in his Coffin also hope Bury him.   Benjamin Brown.
The answers to the above Interrogatories taken sworn to and subscribed before us this 7th April, 1807.
        P. Fleming, J. P.
        Thomas Moffett,   } Commissioners.
        Reuben Carpenter,   }

FRANKLIN COUNTY.

1827—Estate of Levi Stokes, wife Sarah, children Matilda, Jeremiah, John Franklin, Seaborn, Elizabeth, Pleasant, William.

1824—James Miller, wife Adeania "all my children."

1827—John Mays, wife Margaret, sons: Edward, Robert, Newton, Harvey, Thomas. Daughters: Malinda and Syntha. Son-in-law Wm. Turk.

1811—Nancy, widow of John Tucker—other heirs, Samuel, Joseph and John.

Signature to Deeds:

1795—Leroy Pope, wife Judith.

1794—Daniel Ayers, wife Nancy.

1806—Wm. E. Scott, wife Polly.

1809—John Black, wife Margaret.

1809—Thos. P. Carnes, wife Susan.

1809—Wm. Askew, wife Mary.

1809—Wm. Graham, wife Dicey.

1809—Philip Mulkey, wife Fannie.

1809—Jeremiah Sparks, wife Nancy.

1811—Allen Harris, wife Patsey.

1811—James Garner, wife Sarah.

1803—Richard Davis, wife Elizabeth.

1813—Groves Yarborough, adm. est. of Jas. Yarborough.

1822—James Tully, Tax Collector.

1811—John Temples, witness.

1818—Mary Wheeler, wid. adm. est. of Wm. Wheeler.

1798—Edward Rice, wife Sarah.

1809—Zachariah Thompson, wife Susannah.

1809—Gabriel Martin, justice of the peace.

1809—Wm. Jackson, wife Nancy.

1809—Eli Langford, wife Sarah.

1809—John Sandage, wife Susannah.

1809—Jeremiah Taylor, wife Leah.

1809—Abner Cleveland, wife Elizabeth.

1809—Daniel Brown, wife Rhoda.

1809—James Cook, wife Susannah.

1809—Peter B. Terrell, wife Penelope.

1808—David Hillhouse, wife Sarah.

1811—Wm. E. Scott, wife Polly.

1811—Benj. Baker, wife Mary.

1809—Wm. C. Whitney, wife Ruth.

1805—Wm. Shields, wife Mary.

1805—Wm. Young, wife Susannah.

1805—Stephen Hues, wife Tannac.

1805—Swift Mullen, wife Anna.

1805—Edmund Henley, wife Jane.

1805—Wm. Sansom, wife Elizabeth, Wilkes County.

1805—Moses Trimble, wife Catherine.

1805—John Morris, wife Sarah.

1805—Poyndexter Payne, wife Anny.

1805—John Owen, wife Rhoda.

1805—Wm. Black, wife Elizabeth.

1805—Roland H. Burkes, wife Sarah.

1805—Robert Bean, wife Martha.

1805—Thos. Sparks, wife Milly.

1805—Chas. Walker, wife Mary.

1805—Joel Doss, wife Mary (Elbert Co.)

1805—John Sapp, wife Elizabeth.

1805—Robert Shewmaker, wife Dicey.

1805—Geo. Cockburn, wife Elizabeth.

1805—Thos. Carr of Columbia Co., deed to Seaborn Jones of Richmond Co.

1805—Eliz. Williamson adm. est. of Peter Williamson.

1804—Wm. Davis, wife Lucy (Elbert Co.)

1804—Wm. Varnell, wife Elizabeth.

1804—Chris. Clark, wife Rebecca.

1794—James Defoor, witness.

1794—Julius Howard, wife Susannah (Elbert Co.)

1802—John Johnson, Sarah.

1785—Bounty Reserves to Wm. C. and John Williams, John and Wm. Stokes.

1798—Jas. McClain, wife Miney.

1798—Moses Payne, wife Jinney.

1798—Geo. Slevall, wife Ann.

1812—James R. Wyly, wife Sally.

SECTION III.

A list of Revolutionary Soldiers buried in North Carolina, compiled and certified by Miss Anna Blair, of N. C., State Historian of North Carolina, Daughters of the American Revolution, and presented to Mrs. Howard H. McCall, Vice-President General from Georgia by Mrs. Charles W. Tillet, State Regent of North Carolina.

Land Grants of Early Co., Ga., contributed by Gov. Peter Early Chapter.

Genealogical data, Russell and Christian (Christen) Families.

Darling Allen, born in Virginia, came to Anson 1798; killed by a slave; married Miss — — Anson Stanly Nance, who died March 9, 1855, very old.

John Auld, grave unknown.

David Allen, born 1762; died 1823; married Nancy Dawson.

Richard Braswell, born July 1755; died Aug. 20, 1839; married Oct. 1778, Penelope Blow(?); born Wayne County, N. C.

John Beverly, b. July, 1753; d. 1842; m. Frances.

Capt. Patrick Boggan, d. 1801; m. Mary Dabbs.

Isaac Carpenter, b. Halifax Co., N. C., 1764; d. July 23, 1837; m. Martha Allen, Anson County.

Capt. John De Jarnett, b. 1746; d. 1785; m. Jamima Owen.

Thomas Gaddy, b. 1753; d. 1817; m. Jane.

John Hill, m. Phoebe Jackson.

Joseph Howell, b. 1731; d. 1832; m. Sara Miller, 29 Sept. 1779.

Joseph Hull, b. 1757; d. 1835; m. Eleanor Garmon.

Thomas Huntley, b. 1745; d. 1814; m. Zilphis Meadows.

Gardner High, b. 1753, Dinwiddie Co., Va., m. Rachel Gibbs in Brunswick Co., Va.

Joseph Ingram, b. 1744; d. 22 Mar., 1825; m. Winnifred Nelme.

Col. John or Jonathan Jackson, b. 1731; d. 1794; m. Phoebe, 1757.

Maj. John Jennings, b. 1751; d. 1806; m. Elizabeth Lanier.

Edmund Lilly, b. 1738, England; d. 1815; m. 1 Sara Lightfoot, 2 Elizabeth Billingsly.

Burwell Lanier, b. 1737; d. 1812; m. Elizabeth Hill.

Capt. James Marshall, b. 1765; d. 29 Aug., 1830; m. Anne Harrison.

Kinchen Martin, b. Jan. 1672, Southampton Co., Va.; d. June 14, 1841, Anson Co., N. C., m. Chloe Hough, Northampton Co., N. C. Peter May.

Alexander McRae, b. 1729; m. Polly McRae, 1752.

Duncan McRae, b. 1743; d. 1820; m. McRae.

Capt. William Pickett, b. Carolina Co., Va.; m. 1, Mary Query(?), 2 Roberts (widow).

Philip Paul, b. 1765; d. 1825.

Judge Samuel Spencer, b. 1743, in Conn.; d. 1794, Anson; m. 1, Jerusha Brainerd; 2, Sybil Pegues Primason, 1759, came to Anson 1766.

Jehuor John Tyson, b. 1750; d. 1844; m. Pitt Co., Mildred Maye, 1773.

Richard Tomlinson, b. 1749; d. 1822.

Col. Thos. Threadkill, m. Tabitha Ingram.

Col. Theodorick Webb, b. 1733; d. 1816; m. Mary Anson. Stanley.

Col. Thomas Wade, b. 1722; d. 1786; m. Jane Boggan,

Col. Joseph White Stanley, b. 1724; d. 1802; m. Elizabeth 1753.

Capt. James Crump, b. 1758; d. 1800; m. Elizabeth Monroe, Page to George Washington.

John Crump, b. 1763; d. 1857; m. Mary Stephens.

Howell Parker, b. 5 Mar., 1757; d. Oct. 18, 1796; m. Elizabeth Loftin.

Solomon Burress, b. 1752; d. May 21, 1845; m. Judith Taylor.

Daniel Easley, b. 1754, in Va., Charlotte Co.; d. Montgomery Co., N. C., (Now Stanley). Served with Marquis de Lafayette.

Lieut. West Harris.

Lieut. Arthur Harris.

John Lilly, m. Dumas.

William Bennett, b. 1717; d. Sept. 21, 1815; m. 1, Miss Huckson of Md.; 2, Olivia Cheers.

Sherwood Harris, b. 1733; d. 1805; m. Elizabeth.

Hezekiah Hough, b. 1733; d. 1807; m. Mary.

Robert Wilson, b. Norfolk Co., Va., 1747; d. after 1833.

Jacob Braswell, Edgecomb Co., b. 1763; d. July 25, 1837; m. Nancy Colsen.

Van Swearengen, b. 1761; d. 1823; m. Mary.

MONTGOMERY COUNTY

William Bruton, b. 1744; d. 1811; m. Susan Wilson.

Henry De Berry, b. 1758; d. 1818; m. Sallie.

Joseph Parsons, b. 1760; d. Nov. 28, 1807; m. Nancy Jordon, Feb. 12, 1790.

RICHMOND COUNTY.

Lieut. Jesse Baldwin, b. 1750; d. 1825; m. Elizabeth Stringfellow.

William Leak, d. 1782; m. Judith Moseley.

Walter Leak, b. Buckingham Co., Va., Nov. 31, 1761; m. Hannah Pickett.

Capt. Edwin Ingram, b. April 17, 1751; d. May 11, 1843; m. Nancy Montgomery.

Richard Pemberton, b. 1732; d. 1791; m. Amy.

John Wall, b. 1746; d. Feb. 28, 1831; m. Martha Cole, June 21, 1821.

John Cole, d. 1802.

Stanley, Richmond, and Montgomery were originally part of Anson.

WAKE COUNTY.

Caswell-Nash.

Wiley Jones.

Capt. Samuel Pearson, buried two miles S. of Raleigh.

Col. John Hinton.

Capt. Simon Turner. Most of Col. Hinton's men who were killed are buried just south of Raleigh.

Capt. Wm. Utley.

Capt. Thomas Urial(?).

Capt. Cranford.

John Norris, Jr., b. 1750; d. 1822. Served in Wake Co. Militia.

Thomas Able. Buried in Haywood Co. (Dorcas Belle Love.)

William Allen.

George Hall.

John Henry.

Edward Hyatt.

Robert Love.

Christian Wesser.

Hugh Rogers.

Jacob Shook.

Elizabeth Montford Ashe

HALIFAX COUNTY.

Col. Willis Alston, b. 1780; m. Elizabeth.

Capt. John Alston, b. 1784.

Levi Browing, b. 1839. Private soldier.

Capt. Robert Fenning, 1816.

William Gary, b. Dec. 4, 1829. Private soldier.

Lieut. Col. Whitmel Hill, b. Sept. 12, 1797.

Maj. Chappell Heath, b. 1899.

William Powell, b. Sept. 9, 1814. Private soldier.

Capt. George Jollicoffer, b. 1813.

NORTHAMPTON COUNTY.

Col. Jeptha Atherton, b. 1787.

Maj. Drewry Gee, b. Jan., 1786. Also lieutenant and colonel.

Capt. Robert Peebles, b. Nov. 1795.

William Richards, b. 1820. Private soldier.

Joseph Taylor, b. Dec., 1788.

UNION COUNTY.

John Foster, b. Jan. 22, 1821. Aged 72 years. Emigrated John Foster from Ireland, 1765.

Abraham Moses.

Edward Richardson. Buried at Bethlehem Church.

Richard Griffin. Wounded at Cowpens 1781. Buried in Lanes Creek Township.

Capt. John Cuthbertson. Buried in Goose Creek Township.

Capt. Charles Pol. Buried in Goose Creek Township.

Jeremiah Clontz. Buried in Goose Creek Township.

William Pyron. Buried in Goose Creek Township.

William Simpson. Buried in Goose Creek Township.

John Wentz. Was wounded by sabre cut on head; was found by a woman in Rocky River and hidden in her chest from Tarlton's Scouts.

William Lemmond. Buried in Goose Creek Township.

John Lemmond. Buried in Goose Creek Township.

John Pyron. Buried in Goose Creek Township.

James Bradley. Buried in Sandy Ridge Township.

Rheuben Boswell. Buried in Sandy Ridge Township.

Capt. John Secrest. Moved to Tennessee in 1820.

Stephen Bellew. Buried in Jackson Township.

William Wilson. Grandfather of Stephen Bellew and first sheriff of Union County.

George McWhirter. Jackson Township.

James Ross. Came from Martin County in 1799.

John Moore. Great grandfather of Robert L. Stewart.

Hugh McCain. Buried at Tirzah Church.

Emmanuel Stevens. Buried near Indian Trail.

Philip Wolfe. Buried near Frank Kraus' home. Enlisted from Cabarrus County.

DAVIDSON COUNTY.

Valentine Leonard, b. Sept. 13, 1718; d. Nov. 13, 1781. Gen. Wm. Davidson.

Peter Hedrick, b. Dec. 17, 1753; d. Nov. 24, 1789.

Phillip Leonard, b. 1756; d. 1828.

Wooldrich Fritz, b. 1731; d. Nov. 2, 1781.

Jacon Leonard, b. Nov. 16, 1758; d. Jan. 27, 1835.

Frederick Goss. Date of birth and death not known.

Azariah Herrill. Date of birth and death not known.

Philip Sauer or Sowers. Date of birth and death not known.

Elizabeth M. Steele. Buried in Thyatira Church.

Parents of Daniel Boone. Buried at Mocksville.

William Gaston Chapter.

Thomas Campbell, d. Oct. 10, 1787. Was in battle of Kings Mt.

Hugh Ewing, d. June 28, 1824; aged 62.

George Oliver, d. Sept. 24, 1845; aged 84.

William Rankin, b. 1761; d. 1853.

Gen. John Moore, d. 1836, aged 77.

Alexander Moore, d. Nov. 24, 1837; aged 84 yrs. 1 mo. 11 days.

Thomas Henry, d. Sept. 26, 1787. Governor owed money to him after war.

Samuel Martin. Capt. of a troop in the Rev. Served at Kings Mountain.

Capt. John Kincaid. Buried at Olney Church.

John Wilson. Buried at Olney Church.

Alexander Robinson. Buried at Olney Church.

Isaac Holland. Buried at Olney Church.

James Witherspoon. Buried at Olney Church.

Adam Baird. Buried at Olney Church.

William Wood, Captain. Buried at Farmers near High Point.

CLEVELAND COUNTY.
Alexander Martin Chapter.

Col. Frederick Hambright. Buried at Shiloh Graveyard.

Christian Mauney. Buried at Beaver Dam Graveyard.

James White. Buried at Long Creek.

FORSYTH COUNTY.
Gen. Joseph Winston Chapter.

George Hauser. Buried at Bethania.

Abthony Bitting. Buried at Nazareth Country Church.

Abel Shields. Buried at Kernersville.

Dr. Haus Kalberslahn. First physician of the colony is buried at Bethania.

Rev. Rogers. Minister to colony, with his wife, at Bethabara.

Matthew Stach. First missionary to Greenland at Bethabara.

Mr. Reuter. Early surveyor—surveyed town sites, buried at Salem.

William Marshall founder of the town of Salem, burried at Salem.

CABARRUS COUNTY.
Cabarrus Black Boys.

Lieut. Wm. Alexander. Buried at Moses Alexander Place, Cabarrus Co.

Col. George Alexander. Buried at Poplar Tent.

Hezekiah J. Balch, d. 1776. He was one of a committee of three who prepared the Dec. of Ind. and the unanimous adoption of the instrument on May 20, 1775, was due largely to his eloquence.

Richard Harris. Buried at Harris graveyard.

Martin Phifer. Buried at Phifer graveyard.

William White. Buried at Spear's graveyard.

Col. Thomas McClure. Buried at Poplar Tent graveyard.

Paul Barringer. Buried at St. John's graveyard.

Capt. Joseph Shinn. Buried at Old Presbyterian graveyard, Concord.

Alexander Patterson. Buried at Barbrick-Patterson graveyard.

Charles Harris. Buried at Harris graveyard.

Gen. Robert Smith. Buried at Old Alexander burying grounds.

MECKLENBURG COUNTY.

Mecklenburg Chapter.

John McKnight Alexander, d. July 10, 1817, aged 84 years. Buried at Hopewell Church, nine miles from Charlotte.

Gen. Wm. Davidson, d. 1781. Killed in battle of Cowan's Ford, buried near J. M. Alexander.

Gen. George Graham, d. March 29, 1826; aged 68 yrs. One of the gallant 12 who dared to attack and drive 400 British troops at McIntyre's seven miles from Charlotte.

Nathaniel Alexander. Member of House of Commons in 1779 from Mecklenburg.

Abraham Alexander, d. April 23, 1786; aged 68 years. Buried at Sugar Creek Church.

Hezekiah Alexander, d. July 1801. A member of the Provincial Congress, 1776.

Gen. Joseph Graham, d. Dec. 1836. Aged 77 years. Buried near Lincolnton.

James Wallis(?). Served Providence Presbyterian Church 1792-1819.

Adam R. Alexander, d. 1790. Aged 70 years. Capt. in Rev. War in battle of Ramseur's Mills.

Robert Erwin. Member of Provincial Congress from Mecklenburg, October, 1778.

Robert McKee, d. Aug. 19, 1775. Aged 75 years.

Alexander Craighead.

Francis Bradley, d. Nov. 14, 1780. Aged 37. Killed when driving away a marauding party.

EDGECOMBE COUNTY.

Miles Harvey Chapter.

Jones Johnson. Revolutionary hero buried in Edgecombe Co.

Thomas Hall. Member of Congress in Colonial Days. Buried three miles from Tarboro.

Louis D. Wilson. Colonel in the Mexican War. Buried in the Town Common.

Col. Henry Irwin. Killed in the battle of Germantown. Buried on battlefield, afterwards brought to family burying ground three miles from Tarboro.

Col. Micajah Petway.

CRAVEN COUNTY.

Richard Dobbs Spaight Chapter.

Abner Nash. Governor North Carolina 1779. Buried at Pembroke, near New Berne.

Richard Dobbs Spaight. Governor North Carolina 1792. Buried at Clearmont, near New Berne.

Richard Dobbs Spaight, Jr. Gov. North Carolina 1835. Buried at Clearmont, near New Berne.

Prac Guion, Surgeon 1st Regiment. Born 1740. Buried at Cedar Grove Cemetery, near New Berne.

Gen. Samuel Simpson. Buried at Ft. Barnwell, near New Berne.

Corp. James Bell, 4th Regiment, buried at Harlowe, Craven County.

James Green. Buried in Christ Church Yard (Episcopal, New Berne).

William Hancock. Buried near New Berne, Craven County.

Cull Nixon. Buried in old family burying ground near New Bern.

Gen. William Bryan. Buried at his old home near Ft. Barnwell.

Solomon Wetherington. Born Oct. 4, 1761, Lenoir Co., d. 1840, buried in Craven Co. Served under Capt. Stringer and Col. Cornwell in battle of Brier Creek.

CHATHAM COUNTY.

Thomas Hadley Chapter.

William Marsh. Buried in Chatham County, a few miles from Pittsboro.

Maj. Benjamin May. Buried in Pitt County.

Capt. Thomas Hadley, N. C. Militia, is buried at Wilson.

EDWARD BUNCOMBE CHAPTER.

Revolutionary Soldiers Buried in Buncombe County, N. C.

David Vance, Lieutenant in Col. Buncombe's Regiment, great grandfather of Zebulon Baird Vance, who was Governor of North Carolina, buried in Reems Creek Cemetery.

James Alexander, buried at Piney Grove Church, Swannanoa.

William Davidson, buried at old Davidson homestead on the Swannanoa.

Daniel Smith, Colonel of Militia, buried at Newton Academy, Asheville.

Captain William Moore, buried on Hominy Creek near Sukphur Springs, near Asheville.

Robert Henry, buried at Sand Hill on Hominy Creek. (Only man in Western North Carolina who witnessed signing of Mecklenburg Declaration of Independence.)

John Weaver, buried near Weaverville.

Henry West, private, member of Paul Jones' crew on the Bonhomme Richard, buried at Haw Creek.

William Forster, private, buried at Newton **Academy**, Asheville. City's first coroner.

Col. John Pattob, buried at Newton Academy, Asheville.

Col. Charles McDowell, buried at Asheville.

Thomas Garrison, private, buried at Flat Creek.

Samuel Patton, Presbyterian graveyard, Asheville.

Thomas Westall, private, descendant of David Crockett, buried at ――――

―――― Penland, buried at ――――.

William Whitson, private, buried in the Swannanoa section.

Capt. Edmund Sams, buried in the Swannanoa Section, seven miles from Asheville.

Thomas Forster, buried at Gap Creek, and Wm. Forster, who was Asheville's first coroner.

JOSEPH McDOWELL CHAPTER.

Hendersonville, N. C.

Elijah Williamson, born 1754 in Bertie County; died Sept. 29, 1837, and was buried at Naples in Buncombe County, six miles north of Hendersonville.

Andrew Miller, born October 1750, Ireland; died October 1808, and buried at French Broad Baptist Church yard in Buncombe County.

Yadkin River Patriots.

John Cotton and James Cotton. In the edge of Montgomery County in an old unkept graveyard near the west bank of the Uwarrie River are two old graves with this inscription on slabs of slate rock: "John and James Cotton. Fought in the Revolutionary War."

John Morgan, b. 1728. Buried in old Morgan graveyard in Western Stanly, near Rocky River.

Howell Parker and Richard Parker. These two patriots are buried in Parker graveyard near New London, Stanly County, located on the original grant to the Parker family by King George.

John Nesbit Matthews. Buried in old Fourth Creek Presbyterian Church yard. Ft. Dobbs, Iredell County.

Ninian Steele, died Dec. 30, 1813.

William Stevenson, died March 7, 1830.

Mussender Matthews, 79 years old.

James Hall, b. Aug. 28, 1744; d. July 25, 1826. Buried at Bethany Church in Iredell County, about 8 miles from Statesville.

Capt. Robt. Gracey, b. Dec. 17, 1763; d. Oct. 27, 1849

Hugh Hall.

Abraham Hill, b. Sept. 6, 1832(?) Marker dim.

Capt. William Feimster. Buried at Snow Creek church in Iredell County, 10 miles from Statesville, 1832(?).

Hugh Andrews, b. 1754, d. 1846. Buried at Bethany Church.

Maj. Sharpe. Buried at Snow Creek Church.

William Hart, b. 1756; d. 1837. Possibly in Fourth Creek Cemetery.

Alexander Osborne. Buried at Center Presbyterian Church near Mooreville. Member of Committee of Safety and fought with or against Indians in Colonial skirmishes.

Joshua Lazenby.

—— Lewis. Lewis graveyard, a country place near no church now, Iredell County.

John Nicholson, b. May 9, 1757; d. Aug. 2, 1838. Buried at Muddy Creek graveyard, near Kernersville.

Matthew Vandover.

Nicholas Gaither.

John Morrison, d. 1835. Aged 92 years.

DORCAS BELLE LOVE CHAPTER.
Waynesville, N. C.

Capt. John Henry, born in Mecklenburg County, April 4, 1757; died in Haywood County, December 29, 1833. Married Nancy Newman, who died in Haywood County

in 1835. Both died at the old homestead on upper Jonathan Creek and are buried on the home farm—only the
two graves are at that place—all the descendants are
buried near by in a family graveyard established later.
John Henry enlisted in 1777 for three months and again
in 1779 for three months. He fought in the battle of Cowpens, ———. Defeat and King's Mountain. Also against
the Creek Indians. John drew a pension which was allowed January 2, 1833, less than twelve months prior to
his death. His commanding officer was Col. William
Bratton. He fought with distinction at the Battle of Cowpens, was captured, taken in irons to Ninety-six, then to
Charleston, was in prison six months, exchanged, enlisted
again for duration of the war. He was immediately promoted to a Captaincy and served to the close of the war.
He was the son of William Henry and Isabella McKeown
of Augusta County, Virginia. William Henry and four
sons; William, Malcolm, John, and Alexander, and all
fought in the Battle of King's Mountain. Captain John
Henry is the ranking Revolutionary officer buried in
Haywood County, North Carolina, whose record has been
established and whose grave has been identified. John
Henry settled in Haywood County in the year 1802. He
came from York, South Carolina. His father, William
Henry, lived three miles from King's Mountain. The
family seat was named Henry's Knob. John Henry's son,
Malcolm Henry, was in the General Assembly in the year
1808 and helped draft and pass the bill that created Haywood County.

LAND GRANT TO LIFSEY GODLEY.

For Lot No. 411, 26th District, Early Co. Dec. 15, 1824. Book Early Co., 26th District. Page 85. Secretary of State's office.

State of Georgia:

By His Excellency George M. Troup, Governor and Commander in Chief of the Army and Navy of this State, and of the Militia thereof.

To all to whom these Presents shall come, Greeting:

Know Ye, That in pursuance of the several acts of the General Assembly of this State, passed the 15th day of December, 1818, and the 16th day of December, 1819, for making distribution of land lately acquired of the Creek and Cherokee Nations of Indians, and forming the counties of Early, Irwin, Appling, Walton, Gwinnett, Hall, Habersham and Rabun, in this State, I have given and granted, and by these presents, in the name and behalf of this State, do give and grant unto—Lifsey Godley (orphan) of McNorrells district Burke County, his heirs and assigns forever, all that Tract or Lot of Land, containing two hundred and fifty acres, situate, lying and being in the Twenty-Sixth District Early County, in the said State, which said tract or lot of land is known and distinguished in the plan of said district by the Number Four Hundred and Eleven, having such shape, form and marks as appear by a plat of the same hereunto annexed:

To have and to hold the said tract or lot of land, together with all and singular the rights, members and appurtenances thereof, whatsoever, unto the said

Lifsey Godley his heirs and assigns to his and their own proper use, benefit and behoof forever, in fee simple.

Given under my hand and the Great Seal of the said State this Fifteenth day of December in the year eighteen hundred and twenty-four, and of the Independence of the United States of America the forty-ninth.

Signed by His Excellency the Governor the 15th day of December, 1824.

Elisha Wood, S. E. D.

Printed by Grantland & Orme.

Magnetic Variation 5 degrees East.

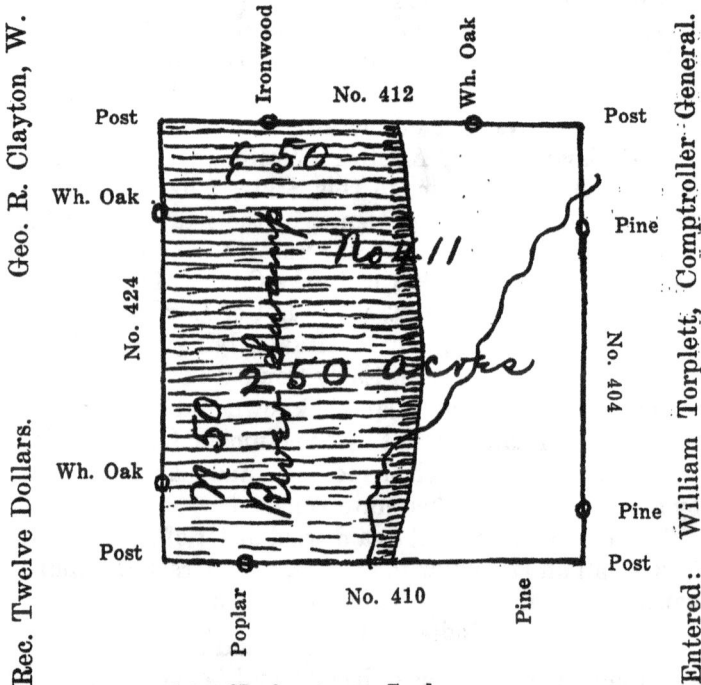

Scale of 20 Chains to an Inch.

State of Georgia:

The above plat is a representation of that Tract or Lot of Land, drawn by Lifsey Godley (orphan) ———— of McNorrells district, Burke ———— county, situate in the Twenty-Sixth district, in the county of Early, containing two hundred and fifty acres, which is known and distinguished in the plan of said district by Number 411. Surveyed on the 10th day of January, 1820.

By N. McBride, Surveyor.

Tho. Mitchell, Sur. General.

Joseph Boon, } C. C.
William Frost, }

LAND GRANT TO JOHN M. SMITH.

For lot No. 412, 26th Dist., Early Co., Ga., Nov. 6, 1821. Book Early Co., 26th District, Page 39. Secretary of State's office.

State of Georgia:

By His Excellency John Clark, Governor and Commander in Chief of the Army and Navy of this State, and of the Militia thereof.

To All to Whom These Presents Shall Come, Greeting:

Know Ye, that in pursuance of the several acts of the General Assembly of this State, passed the 15th day of December, 1818, and the 16th day of December, 1819, for making distribution of the land lately acquired of the Creek and Cherokee Nations of Indians, and forming the counties of Early, Irwin, Appling, Walton, Gwinnett, Hall, Habersham and Rabun, in this State, I Have Given and Granted, and by these presents in the name and behalf of this State, Do Give and Grant unto John N. Smith of Selman's District Morgan County, his heirs and assigns forever, all that Tract or Lot of Land containing Two hundred and fifty ...... acres, situate, lying and being in the Twenty-sixth district, Early ——— county in the said State, which said Tract or Lot of Land is known and distinguished in the plan of said district by the Number Four Hundred and Twelve having such shape, form and marks as appear by a plat of the same hereunto annexed; To Have and To Hold the said Tract or Lot of Land, together with all and singular the rights, members and appurtenances thereof, whatsoever, unto the said John N. Smith his heirs and assigns, to his and their own proper use, benefit and behoof forever in fee simple.

Given under my hand and the Great Seal of said State, this Sixth day of November in the year of our Lord eighteen hundred and twenty-one and in the forty-sixth year of American Independence.

Signed by His Excellency the Governor, the 6th day of November, 1821.

Elisha Wood, S. E. D.

Magnetic Variation 5 degrees East.

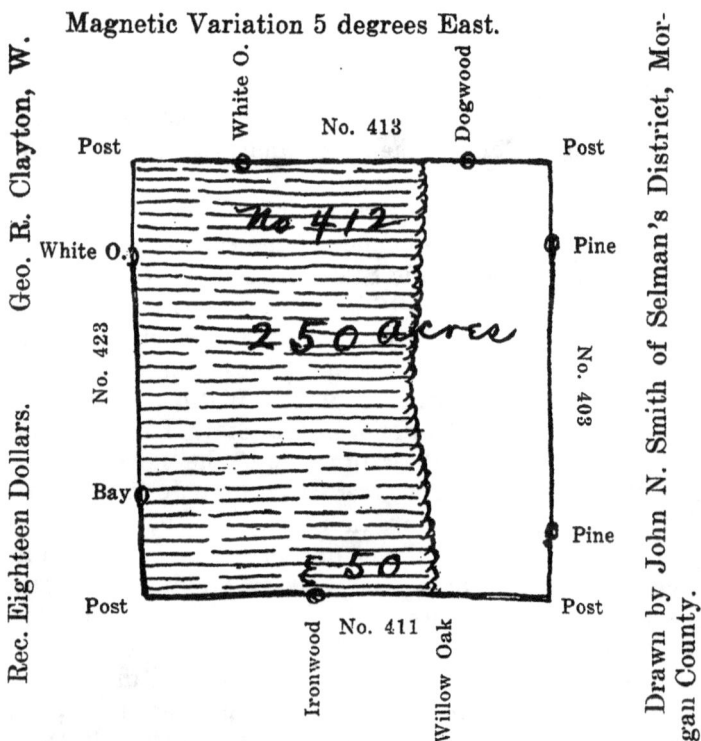

Scale of 20 Chains to an Inch.

State of Georgia:

The above plat is a representation of that tract or lot of land, situate in the Twenty-sixth district in the county of Early containing Two Hundred and fifty acres, which is known and distinguished in the plan of said district by the number 412.

Surveyed on the 10th day of January, 1820.

By N. McBryde, Surveyor.

Daniel Sturges, Sur. Genl.

Joseph Boon, }
William Frost { C. C.

GENEALOGY.

This interesting genealogy was presented to the Joseph Habersham Chapter by Mrs. Eugene Everton Smith of Atlanta, Ga. Further information in regard to these families can be obtained from Mrs. Smith, or from Selden Nelson of Knoxville, Tenn., who has written several important papers concerning these Tenn. families for the "Knoxville Sentinel Newspaper."

Gilbert Christian (Christen) Genealogy.

Gilbert Christen was born in Scotland in 1680. He removed to the Province of Ulster, North Ireland, about the year 1702. In 1703 he married Margaret Richardson. During the year 1726, Gilbert Christen and John Campbell removed with their families to America and settled near where Lancaster, Pennsylvania is now located. In the year, 1732. Gilbert Christen and John Campbell, with the Moffets, McDowell's, McClung's, Trimbles', Lockharts, Hamilton, and Russells, removed to the valley of Virginia and formed quite a colony near Stanton, Virginia.

Children of Gilbert Christen and his wife Margaret (Richardson) Christen.

John Christen.

Robert Christen married Isabella Tiffan of Winchester, Va.

William Christen married Mary Campbell.

Mary Christen mar (1) John Moffett about 1730 in Pa. She married (2) James Trimble.

William Christen [2](Gilbert)[1] was a Captain in Augusta Co., Va., militia in 2nd Regiment under Col. Wm. Byrd. He was also a member of the Council of War called by the Governor of Virginia, July, 1756, to consider at what points forts should be erected along the frontier for the protection of the inhabitants. This Council was composed of John Buchanan, David Stuart, Major John Brown, Captains Joseph Cultin, Robert Scott, Patrick Martin, William Christen, Robert Breckenridge, James Lockhart, Samuel Stalnecker, Israel Christen and Thomas Armstrong. This was during the war with the French. At the solicitation of the Indians to build a fort in the Indian Country, Col. Byrd was one of the commissioners to select a site for the fort. It was built under the instruction of Col. Lewis and named Fort London.

In 1757 Colonel (Captain) Byrd left a detatchment of troops in it.

The other forts erected by Gov. Byrd's regiment were Fort Chissel. Other forts erected and the other one was opposite the upper end of Long Island. Mention was made by Haywood that Gilbert Christen was with Col. Byrd on those excursions. Gilbert Christen son of Robert made a trip into East Tennessee in 1768.

Captain William Christen (Gilbert) (third son of Gilbert and Margaret Christen) married Mary (Molle) Campbell (the daughter of Patrick Campbell). This Patrick Campbell was the oldest son of John Campbell, who came from Ireland with Gilbert Christen, and grandfather of Gen. William Campbell, who commanded the troops at the Battle of King's Mountain.

Children of William Christen and his wife Mary Campbell.

Gilbert Christen.
Patrick Gristen married Elizabeth Robinson.
Elizabeth Gristen married David Carson.
Mary Christen married John Creely.
Margaret Christen married Andrew Russell.

Andrew Russell b. May 17, 1738, and his wife Margaret
Christian born Jan. 6, 1745, married in 1762. Their
daughter Mary Russell born Aug. 26, 1772, married Robert
Craig, their daughter Jane Craig, born Feb. 27, 1805, married May 17, 1825, to Robert Patton Martin, born Feb.
4, 1799. Their daughter, Mary Elizabeth Martin, born
March 16, 1829, married Benjamin F. Mitchell, born June,
1820, on Sept. 3, 1846. Their daughter, Mary F. Mitchell,
married Eugene Everton Smith and they have two children, viz.: Evelyn Maude Smith, married Alexander Erwin Wilson. They have three children, Alexander Erwin
Wilson, Jr.; John McKamie Wilson, and Mary Jane Wilson.

Huls Alexander Smith married Oma Carroll and they
have one child, Jane Alexander Smith.

Robert Craig of Virginia.

Robert Craig born and reared in Eastern Virginia, settled in Jefferson Co., Tenn., about 1817, married Mary
Russell (daughter of Andrew Russell and his wife Margaret Christian.)

James Craig (father of Robert Craig) was a Captain in
the Continental Army from Virginia (an engraved obit-
uary of life and death of James Craig is in the possession
of Mrs. Eugene Smith of Atlanta, Ga.)

Mary Russell Craig, wife of Robert Craig, died near
Dandridge, Tenn., Oct. 4, 1839, age 67.

Mary Campbell.

Mary Campbell, wife of William Christian was the daughter of Patrick Campbell. He was the son of John Campbell, the first immigrant to America, and traced his ancestry to Duncan Campbell and Mary McCoy, who left Scotland in 1642 and went to Ireland.

Andrew Russell of Virginia.

The Russell family traces its origin back to Normandy, and the name de Rozel seems to be the first way of spelling. The name appears as Russell in the 14th Century. The Russell family were neighbors of the Christen family and followed the fortunes of that family, leaving Scotland for Ireland and then coming to America in 1726 to Lancaster, Pennsylvania, and in 1732 to Virginia.

Revolutionary Record of Andrew Russell. Captain Andrew Russell was an officer of the 5th Virginia Regiment of the Revolutionary War. Authority for this statement is found in Stubblefield's Orderly Book, in the Virginia Historical Collection notes, page 182. The Colonel of the 5th Va. Regiment was Col. William Peacke. Also list of Va. officers by Heitman. (This record will entitle descendants of Capt. Andrew Russell to membership in the Daughters of the American Revolution. And the record of the services of Captain William Christen in Colonial Wars will entitle descendants to membership in Colonial Societies.)

Captain Andrew Russell was born in Augusta Co., Virginia, May 17, 1738. Married Margaret Christian (daughter of William and Mary (Campbell) Christen about 1762. Removed to Abingdon, Va., where some of their children were born.

They then removed to Jefferson Co., Tenn.

Both are buried at Dandridge, Tenn.

Children of Andrew Russell and Margaret (Christian) Russell:

William Russell, b. Sept. 22, 1763.
Andrew Russell, b. Nov. 30, 1765.
Elizabeth Russell, b. Jan. 6, 1769.
Mary Russell, b. Aug. 26, 1772—married Robert Craig.
Florence Russell, b. Jan. 26, 1775.
Margaret Russell, b. June 15, 1777.
Rebecca Russell, b. Jan. 26, 1780.
Gilbert Russell, b. May 18, 1782.
John Russell, b. July 18, 1785.
Sarah Russell, b. Aug. 24, 1789.

INDEX TO VOLUME I

HISTORICAL COLLECTIONS

of the Georgia Chapters

DAUGHTERS of the
AMERICAN REVOLUTION

A Memorial to Mrs. William Lawson Peel

PUBLISHED IN 1926

Compiled and edited by

MRS. J. C. GENTRY

Chairman of the Lucy Cook Peel Memorial Committee

CLEARFIELD
100 E. Eager Street
Baltimore, MD 21202

PREFACE

Volume 1, Historical Collections of the Georgia Chapters Daughters of the American Revolution, published in 1926, contains no index. Many valuable records from original documents secured at considerable cost are in this book and the need for an index being apparent, the State Regent, Mrs. Bun Wylie, authorized that an index be made. With this authority and the consent of members of the committee, Mrs. James C. Gentry compiled, edited and raised the funds to provide this complete index as her contribution to this branch of the work.

This index has been made without changing the spelling copied from the original manuscript. In many instances the same name is spelled in several different ways according to the manner of former days; in that case the various forms are given.

If this work should meet with favor and prove useful to our readers we shall feel that our effort was not in vain.

> MRS. JAMES C. GENTRY, Chairman,
> MRS. W. F. DYKES, Co-Chairman,
> MRS. HOWARD McCALL,
> MRS. JULIUS TALMADGE,
> MRS. JOHN L. DAVIDSON,
> MRS. B. A. TYLER,
> MRS. R. M. HERRON,
> MISS HELEN PRESCOTT,
> Lucy Cook Peel Memorial Committee.

GENERAL INDEX

Russell, 259; Sally, 199, 255, 257; Sarah, 237, 327; Sina, 235; Thos. A., 315; Tilman, 315; Wm., 202, 258;Wm. B., 255; Gen. Wm., 360; Zachariah, 235, 250, 291.

BUCKHANNON, Frances, 4; James, 3, 38, 49; Jane, 82; John, 370; Joseph, 78; Mary Ann, 2; Wm., 112.

BUCKHANN, Wm. F., 78.

BUCKLE, John W., 129.

BUCKNER, Chas., 85; David, 185; Mrs. Eliz., 9; Hezekiah, 209; John, 55, 85.

BUFFINGTON, Charity, 9.

BUGG, Jacob, 97.

BUGGIN, Delilah, 108.

BULL, David, 129.

BULLARD, James, 38; Jesse, 36; John, 249, 291; Lewis, 207; Sarah, 38; Wm., 41.

BULLIN, Wm., 187.

BULLMAN, John, 177.

BULLOCH, Alexander G., 71; Catherine, 59; David, 289; Hawkins S., 72; John G., 69; Polly, 95; Shadrack, 88; Spicy, 239; Wm., 239, 283, 339, 341; Wm. G., 72; Winnifred, 185.

BUNCH, Austin, 64.

BUNDLES, James, 87.

BUNKLEY, Ann Eliza, 102.

BURCH, Edward, 83.

BURDOCK, Wm., 54.

BURFORD, Amelia, 85; Solomon, 16.

BURGE, Willie, 78.

BURGER, Chas., 18.

BURGESS, Benj., 309; Effa, 214; Elias, 258, 309; Evan, 309; James, 42, 240, 309; John, 236, 238, 299, 304; John M., 211; Josiah, 85, 265, 276; Mary, 211, 240; Matilda, 204; Nancy, 214; Peggy, 309; Pleasant F., 304; Polly, 236, 238; Reuben C., 304; Sally, 82; Samuel, 309 Sarah, 304; Verlinda, 276.

BURKE—BIRKS, Chesley, 42;David, 172, 349; Eliz., 259; Isaiah, 72;James, 71; Jeremiah, 282; John, 282, 342; Jonathan, 71; Napoleon Bonaparte, 111; Nathan, 71; Roland H., 351; Sarah, 351.

BURKET, Mrs. Phereby, 111; Rhoda, 109; Wm., 109.

BURKHALTER—BUCKHALTER, Mrs. Christina, 109; Isaac, 83; Jepthy H., 114; Mary Martha, 110.

BURNAMEN, Benj., 97.

BURNEY, David, 97.

BURNHAM, Alfred, 109; Mahelia, 110.

BURNS, Andrew, 283; Aquilla, 219; John, 247; Randolph, 15; Robt.,

253; Samuel H., 242; Sarah E. H., 195; Wm., 196.

BURNSIDE, Edmund, 12; James, 12; Susanna, 12.

BURRESS—BURRICE, Elisha, 172; Matilda, 195.

BURROUGHS, Aquilla, 250; Bazel, 69; Geo. N., 317; Henry, 242, 257, 264, 266, 317, 345; James, 70; Thos., 317; Wm., 209, 299, 312, 314, 317.

BURROW, John, 35; Sally, 22.

BURSON, Isaac, 103; Sarah, 33.

BURT—BIRT, James, 85; Jesse, 85; John, 196, 280; Joseph, 344; Sarah, 196; Susannah, 195; Wm., 263, 267, 334, 344.

BURTON—BERTON, Abraham, 307; Ann, 43; Barthsheba, 307; Benj. H., 307; Elvira, 308; Hutchins, 237; Jacob, 267, 335; Jane C., 315; Jincy, 189; John, 53, 206, 210, 332; John H., 307; Martha, 194; Mary, 307; Nathaniel, 71; Patsy, 27; Peter E., 307; Polly, 200; Rachel, 242; Robt., 191, 329; Robt. Cogbil, 218; Sarah, 213.

BUSH, Abraham, 51; Bartlett, 83; Col., 177; Daniel, 200, 225, 236, 251, 252, 255, 267, 273, 303, 335, 347; Easley, 252; Edmund F., 209; Edward, 102; Eliz., 218, 225, 236, 251, 252, 255, 302; Henry, 276; Hezekiah, 242; Joicy, 305; John, 236, 251, 252, 279, 303, 321; Jonathan, 191; Judith A., 273; Judith Holland, 252; Lydia, 252; Mariah L., 201; Melissa, 197; Polly, 197; Robt., 242; Sanders, 51; Susannah Norris, 252; Thos., 218, 236, 251, 276, 279, 293, 302, 303; Wm., 185, 233, 236, 251, 279, 305, 330; Wm. F., 305.

BUSHBY, Jacob, 29.

BUSHIN, Mary, 25.

BUSHWICK, Capt., 146.

BUSSEY, Aney, 67; Dennis, 64; Hannah, 67; Hezekiah, 61; Joshua, 63; Thos., 62.

BUTLER, Amey, 68; Daniel, 169; David, 177; David B., 263; Eliz.,312; Gen., 141, 151; John, 21, 170, 171, 175, 176, 177; John M., 78; Martha, 66; Massey R., 85; Patrick R., 72; Peter, 72; Thos., 36; Zacheus, 85.

BUTT—BUTTS, Chas., 277;Eldridge, 79; John E., 80; Lewis, 2; Robt.,173; Samuel, 35; Willis, 37.

BYARS—BYERS, John, 36; Joseph, 210.

BYFORD, Fermin H., 271; John, 270; Patsy, 32; Wm., 30.

Susan, 203; Thos., 240.
CARSWELL, Alexander, 54; Gen.,
141; James A., 45.
CARTER, Abcol, 194; Absalom,
189, 233; Ann, 216; Austin, 199;
Betsy, 60; Calham, 33; Eliz.,
220, 233, 281, Farish, 2; Dr. Flour-
noy, 127; Francis, 1, 4; Henry, 83,
97; Highly, 19; Jacob, 98; James,
171, 242; Jane, 107; Jesse, 289, 290;
John, 65, 216, 218; John M., 103;
John Tilman, 193; Dr. John, 127;
Capt. John, 127; Lydia, 290; Mary,
218, 337; Micajah, 295, 317, 331;
Nancy, 218, 317, 331; Polly, 6, 330;
Rachel, 233; Richard, 39; Robt. D.,
31; Samuel, 54; Sarah, 98; Thos.,
39, 93, 180, 186, 218, 220, 230, 233,
249, 257, 273, 281; Wm., 61.
CARTLEDGE, Francis G., 63;
James, 63; John, 65; Samuel, 72.
CARTNER, James, 43.
CARUTHERS—CAROTHERS—
CARITHERS—CRUTHERS, An-
drew, 241; James, 56; Robt., 56;
Samuel M., 301; Wm., 319.
CARVER, Henry, 203.
CARY—CAREY, Ann, 55; Dudley,
16; Edward, 19; Eliza P., 24; Jesse,
58; Lucy, 17; Nancy, 210; Robt., 55,
171; Col. Robt., 171.
CASEY, Abraham, 262; James, 266;
John, 266; Nancy, 284; Stephen,
254, 284; Wm., 302.
CASH, Benj. W., 73; James, 32, 139,
142, 264; John, 103, 106, 108; Mar-
tha, 112; Patrick, 103; Peggy, 182;
Sally, 194.
CASON—CASSON, Frederick, 97;
Gabriel, 97; Sally, 105.
CASTER, Thos., 88.
CASTLEBERRY, Ann, 9; Henry,
16; John, 240; Mary, 240; Rachel,
26; Richard, 55; Wm., 73, 103.
CASWELL, Gen., 149; Matthew, 54.
CATES, John, 88, 109.
CATHY, Archibald, 16.
CATLETT, Alsa, 73; Capt., 155;
John, 206, 211; Mary, 210; Sarah,
204; Susannah, 209.
CATOE, Robt. O., 110.
CATRELL, Francis, 63.
CATTLE, John, 52.
CAUDIE, Matthew, 51.
CAUDLE, Hannah, 201; Mary, 204.
CAUSEY, Eliz., 45, 47; Ezekiel, 47;
John, 89.
CAVENAH, L. B., 45; Nicholas, 45.
CAVENESS, Nepolin, 305.

CAVIN, Alexander, 28; Forges, 28;
Mattie, 28; Wm., 30.
CAWDELL, John, 242.
CAWLEY, Catlett, 172; John, 172;
Reason, 50; Richard, 172.
CAWSWELL, Francis N., 100.
CAWTHON—CAWTHRON, Chas.,
333; Chesley, 205, 212, 233; Claiborn,
195, 241, 245, 335, 336; Eliz., 308,
333; Fanny, 199; Hannah, 241;
Orville, 20; Polly, 203; Rhoda, 256,
293, 333; Rutha, 333; Sally, 304;
Wilkinson T., 203; Thos., 283;
Wm., 53, 60, 242, 245, 256, 281, 287,
293, 335; Wm. Payne, 333.
CELLUM, Samuel, 70.
CENTERFEIT, Jesse, 59.
CERVANTES, Henry, 272.
CHAFFIN, Lemuel, 80.
CHAINES, Benj., 4.
CHAIRS, Joseph, 53.
CHALMERS, Ann, 321; Eliza, 210;
Eliz., 321; Isabella, 321; John,
253, 321, 325, 348; Wm., 260, 321, 325.
CHAMBERLAIN, Liey, 64.
CHAMBERS, John, 331, 332.
CHAMBLISS, Nancy, 7; Sarah, 5.
CHANCE, Ephraim, 52; Simpson, 52.
CHANDLER, Abram, 186; Allen,
185, 334; Ambrose, 200; Anna, 309;
Asa, 205, 206, 211; Chaffin, 296;
Daniel, 198, 203, 256, 313; Dudley,
208, 306; Edmund, 266; Eliz., 192,
194, 252, 347; Elza, 211; Frances C.,
205; Gaines, 194; Gedediah, 256;
Henry F., 307, 309; Hezekiah, 289;
James, 73, 248, 250, 252, 264, 265,
333, 334, 347; Jeremiah, 183;
Jerusha, 308; Johnson Prewett,
313; Joseph, 233, 236, 242, 249, 250,
252, 257, 259, 263, 267, 290, 309, 314,
327, 334, 343, 347; Joseph. Esq.,
279; Lewis, 199, 299, 333; Linsey,
206; Lucinda, 211; Maledda, 194;
Martha, 193, 203, 256; Mary, 197,
312; Matilda, 202, 257; Nancy, 31,
236; Peggy, 193, 256; Polly, 299,
313; Rebecca, 201; Rhoda, 197;
Robt., 257, 258; Sally, 233, 256;
Samuel, 256; Sarah, 306; Shadrack, 256, 257; Stephen, 198, 309,
333; Sterling, 103, 331; Susannah,
256, 299; Tabitha, 103; Thos., 206;
Wilkins, 313; Wm., 205, 256, 296,
298; Wyatt, 191, 309, 333, 334;
Zachariah, 202, 256.
CHANEY—CHENEY, James, 99, 109;
Thos., 25.

CHANNEL, Harman, 88.

143; Crump, 190; Ephraim, 4; Eliz., 190; Geo., 44; Henry, 45, 52; James, 72, 107; Jeremiah, 88; Jesse, 37, 56; John, 23, 73, 79, 169, 271; Joseph, 72; Leanna, 182; Mary, 223, 233; Mathew, 345; Michael, 212; Nancy, 322; Polly, 322; Rebecca, 5, 33; Richard, 17, 190; Robt. R., 187, 275; Sally, 5; Sarah, 39; Sophia, 89; Thos., 223, 233, 235, 276, 288; Wm., 248; Wylie J., 39; Zachariah, 168, 271, 289.

COYLE, Rebecca, 186.

COYNE, Phineas, 4.

CRABTREE, Littleton, 33.

CRAFT, Edward, 19; Eliz., 192; Hannah, 103; Polly, 103.

CRAFTON, Major, 139.

CRAIG, James, 371; Jane, 371; Mary Russell, 371; Robt., 53, 371; Wm., 50, 54.

CRAIGHEAD, Alexander, 359.

CRANE—CRAIN—CRAYNE, Abijah, 228; Benj., 79; Ezekiel, 89; Joel, 269, 271, 335, 337; Lewis, 16; Mary, 111, 289; Sarah, 87; Wm., 228, 287, 289.

CRANFORD, Capt., 355.

CRAVEY, David, 115; Eliz., 112; John, 110, 113; Joshua, 111; Martha E., 115; Mary, 115; Wm., 114.

CRAWFORD—CRAFFORD, Alexander, 30, 107; Augustus, 73; David, 50; Elijah, 192; Elisha, 65; Gov., 125; Hugh, 277; James, 89; John, 83, 103, 169, 195, 239, 316; Lotty, 4; Mary, 186, 239; Mathews, 242; Moses B., 215; Robt., 61; Samuel, 43; Sarah, 210; Solomon, 52; Strander, 50; Vineyard, 23; Wm., 63; Wm. H., 262.

CRAWLEY—CROWLEY, Benj., 16; Chas., 80; John, 80.

CREACH, Noah, 60.

CRENSHAW, Jarrel W., 37; Jesse, 242; Wm. H., 4.

CRESSON, Eliz., 68.

CREWS, David, 270; Ethelred, 85; Francis, 4; John, 17; Judy, 270; Susanna, 4; Thos., 265, 267, 335.

CRIDER, David, 242; John, 215; Sophia, 215; Susan, 211.

CRIM, Abraham, 109.

CRISWELL, David, 249; Samuel, 182.

CRITTENDEN—CRITTENTON, Henry, 344; John, 168; Lemuel, 86; Wm. H., 73.

CROCHET, Eliz., 107.

CROCKER, John, 201, 202.

CROCKETT, Robt., 286; Samuel, 286.

CROFTON, Lydia, 45.

CROLL, James, 35.

CROOK, Robt., 44.

CROSBY, Austin W., 206.

CROSLIN, Wm., 282.

CROSS, Ann, 38; Eliz., 192; Geo., 37; John, 37, 273, 286; Nancy, 227; Rhoda, 38.

CROSSLEY, Rachel, 53.

CROSSON, Lewis, 65.

CROUCH, Shadrack, 85.

CROW, Aaron, 18; Amos, 18; Barbary, 242; Candis, 43; James, 262, 283; John W., 209; Levi, 20; Martin, 23; Moore H., 242; Patsy, 28; Randolph, 201; Randolph C., 302; Stephen, 17; Thos. J., 208; Wm. S., 205.

CROWDER, Frank, 89.

CROXTON—CROXON, Eliz., 25; James, 17.

CRUIKSHANK, Patrick, 221.

CRUMBY—CROMBY, Abia, 33; Christian, 107; Christiana, 30.

CRUMLEY, Anthony, 97; E., 97.

CRUMLIFF, Hugh, 262.

CRUMP, Dinoelondy, 191; Eliz., Monroe, 353; Capt. James, 353; Maj., James, 157; Jane, 196; John, 353; Malissa, 186; Mary Stephens, 353; Ratha, 204; Robt., 215, 242.

CUCKSEY, Wm., 172.

CUDDY, Margaret, 45.

CULBERTSON, Isaac M., 73; Polly, 24; Capt. Robt., 158.

CULBREATH, Anguish, 73; John, 65.

CULLIFER, Henry, 85; Polly, 90.

CULLY, Nancy, 96.

CULPEPPER, Joseph, 103; Sampson, 58.

CULTIN, Capt. Joseph, 370.

CULVERSON, Samuel, 35.

CUMMERFORD, John, 49.

CUMMINGS, JAMES, 73; John, 50; Lucretia, 113; Wiley, 110.

CUNNINGHAM, Ann, 220, 239; David, 73; James, 16, 21, 34, 173; John, 15, 220, 239, 249; J. T., 103; Mary, 103; Robt. Eve, 44, 45.

CURDON, Martha, 103.

CURETAN, Andrew, 103; Ansel, 103; Eliz., 103; Polly, 107; Wm., 103.

CURRY, Augusta, 107; Cary, 1; Carvey, 4; Caty, 31; Dacan, 101; Daniel J., 100; Eliza, 108; Jacob, 171; Polly, 85; Susan, 107; Thos., 63, 65, 89.

GILBERT, Charity, 81; Chas., 222, 335; C., 248; Edward, 246; Eliz., 184, 235, 246; Felix, 232, 265; Frances, 86; Hannah, 216, 222; Isaac, 72, 246; James, 72, 246, 330; John, 103, 222, 226, 246, 248, 280, 281, 287; Mary, 226, 246, 280, 281; Nancy, 246, 328, 330; Nancy W., 33; Patsy, 93; Polly, 235; Priscilla, 191; Sarah, 222; Thos., 216, 222, 235; Wm., 191, 232, 246.

GILES, James, 90; Minna, 88; Polly, 23, 88; Thos., 85.

GILFORD, Isaac, 98; John, 97.

GILHAM—GILLAM—GILLUM, Ann 79; Chas., 79; Peter, 62; Capt. Robt., 148; Unity, 68; Wm., 54, 66, 72.

GILL, David, 112; Days, 2; Dusilla, 111; Eliz., 25; Fanny, 110; John, 80; Nielky, 26.

GILLESPIE, Eliz., 224; Esther, 108; James, 204; Jane, 224; Lowry, 224, 277; Margaret, 224; Mathew, 224; Pickens, 207; Sarah, 268.

GILLISON, Joshua, 171; Peter, 171.

GILMER, Wm., 297.

GILMORE, Ann, 26; Hugh, 54; James, 90; John, 90; Ruthy, 65; Samuel, 66; Sarah H., 93; Solomon, 27; Wm., 82, 200, 203, 333.

GILREATH, Capt., 151.

GILSON, David, 79.

GILSTRAP, Jeremiah, 84.

GILSUM, Francis, 56.

GIMMELS, Nancy, 305; Nathan, 305.

GINGLE, Polly, 64.

GIRTMAN, Benj. F., 113; Eliz., 110.

GITTENS, John, 367.

GITUIS, Richard, 98.

GLADDIN, James, 2.

GLASS, Eliz., 42; Joel, 321; Joshua, 180; Nancy, 193.

GLAWSON, Mary, 24.

GLAZE, Aaron, 34; Cidney N., 68; Mary, 63; Patrick, 27; Susanna, 63; Thos., 61, 63.

GLAZIER, Adam, 39; Chas. R., 208; Clarissa Ann, 40.

GLEESON—GLISSON, Eliz., 102; Polly N., 25.

GLENN—GLEEN, Andrew, 265; Daniel, 289; David, 265, 281; Edward, 252; Eliz., 211, 275; Franklin, 203; James, 103; John, 252; John A., 72; Joseph, 252, 253, 330; Mathew Hopson, 252; Nancy, 252; Otway, 5; Samuel, 250, 281, 301; Simmondon Goslander, 252;

Simon, 252; Thornton T., 252; Wm., 98, 187.

GLOWER, James M., 309; Jane, 214; Jesse, 51; John, 90; Wm., 138, 145, 154, 182, 263.

GOBER, Betsy, 198; Craddock, 275; Daniel, 183; Dolly, 189; Eliz., 185, 205; Geo., 230, 276, 279, 311, 345; Hiram, 198; Jinny, 196; John, 207, 230, 279, 312; Lewis, 230, 279; Margaret, 200, 228, 240; Maria, 197; Mary, 204; Nancy, 192, 276; Richard, 191; Sarah, 312; Thos., 277; Wesley A., 315; Wm., 228, 230, 240, 271, 279, 304, 337; Wm. H., 315; Wm. Jackson, 317.

GOBERT, Benj., 54.

GODARD, Simon, 56.

GODLEY, Lifsey, 365.

GODOWN, Jacob, 50.

GOFF, Catherine Jinny, 8.

GOHEN, John Clark, 332; Sanford, 332.

GOITMAN, Catherine, 47.

GOLDEN—GOULDEN—GOULD-ING, Allen, 66; Benj., 66; Eliz., 69.

GOLDMAN—GOULDMAN, Frances 63; Mary, 68; Peggy, 68.

GOLDSMITH, Eliz., 93.

GOLSON, Ann, 216; John, 216.

GOODE, Daniel, 211; Geo., 339; Jesse, 39; John, 13; John C., 86; Sarah, 13; Starling, 36; Theophilus, 37; Wm., 35, 36.

GOODGAME, Alexander, 53; John, 51.

GOODLET, James, 246; Nancy, 246.

GOODMAN, Henry, 58; James, 11; John T., 103.

GOODSON, Arthur, 85; Frankey, 91; Patsy, 209.

GOODWIN, Anna, 281; Asa, 18; Eliz., 277; Jesse, 238, 277; Nancy, 190; "Ru B.," 1; Shadrack, 56; John, 219, 249, 260, 266.

GOODY, Frances, 294, 296, 327; Geo., 294, 327.

GOOLSBY—GOULSBY, Jeremiah, 72; Job, 72; John, 38; John Geo., 296; Mrs. Rebecca, 67; Richard, 281; Wm., 36, 252.

GORDON, Alexander, 45; Ambrose, 173; Col. Ambrose, 122, 146, 155; C. F., 86; Eliz., 100; Gaven, 55; Henry, 280, 281; Isaac, 29; Jesse, 171; John, 80; Joseph, 342; Julian, 122; Kenneth, 85; Nancy, 56; Nanney, 87; R. C., 243; Samuel, 45; Serena, 87; Tabitha, 256; Thos., 264; Vincent, 72.

GORHAM—GORAHAM, John, 169, 177, 182, 248, 273, 336, 338; Thos., 183, 250, 256, 260, 295.
GORLEY, Ayers, 173.
GOSS, Frederick, 35.
GOSSETT, Jacob, 175; John W., 72.
GOUAD, Lizzy, 94.
GOUGH, Jesse, 335; Judith, 289; Wm., 289, 336.
GOVE, Elisha, 50.
GOWDY, Frederick, 190.
GOWER, James M., 103; Reuben, 72.
GRACE, James, 98; John, 98; Mary, 102.
GRACEY, Capt. Robt., 363.
GRADY—GRADDY, Eliz., 213; Lewis, 344; Wm., 186.
GRAHAM, Alex., 310; Dicey, 240, 350; Duncan B., 114; Effie, 110; Flora, 111; Gen. Geo., 359; Green G., 84; Henry, 72; Isabella, 113; Jabez, 72; James, 72, 69; John, 287; Jonathan, 202; Joseph, 72; Gen. Joseph, 359; Josiah, 72; Mary B., 111; Rachel, 111; Wm., 70, 240, 350; Wm. R., 212.
GRAMPELL, Israel, 90.
GRANBERRY, Geo., 45, 52; Sarah, 45.
GRANT, Phebee, 53; Thos., 299.
GRANTHAM, Nathan, 59.
GRANTLAND, Sarah, 5; Seaton, 2.
GRAVES—GRIEVES, Francis, 267; H., 248; James, 61; Jane, 43; John, 86, 266, 279; Sally, 28; Samuel, 268; Robt., 54; Wm., 247.
GRAY, Ann, 22; Anna, 16; Betsy, 94; Eliz., 43, 65, 95, 190; Faby, 43; Garrett, 202, 294, 297; Geo. T., 100; Isaac, 63, 297; James, 63; John B., 297; John M., 182; Johnson, 207; Johnston, 197; Joseph, 90; Letty, 297; Lucinda, 91; Mary, 297; Nelly, 297; Polly, 92; Priscilla, 1; Richard, 177, 256, 322; Sally, 297; Susan, 5; Susannah, 297; Thos., 86; Zachariah, 1, 54.
GRAYBILL, Henry, 175.
GRAYSON, John, 66.
GREEN—GREENE, Allen, 56; Ann, 6; Basley, 90; Benj., 47, 53; Betsy, 34; Burril, 38; Daniel, 5; Edmond, 19; Edney, 60; Eliz., 2, 59; Gen., 138, 141, 158; Henry, 171; James, 360; James N., 113; Jenny, 8; John, 14, 53, 103, 208; John A., 295; Larkin, 33; M'Keen, 98; Mary, 86; Mary P., 9; Mary Ann, 31; Ma-

tilda, 33; Miles, 5; Nancy, 211, 295; Nelly, 60; Patsy, 9; Peggy, 28; Philip, 11; Rachel, 45; Rice, 332; Sutton, 250; Tandy H., 198; Thos. J., 98, 180; Wm., 174; Winnefred, 102.
GREENLEAF, James, 267.
GREENLEE, James, 261; John, 261; Samuel, 1.
GREENWOOD, Henning, 345; Hugh B., 253; John, 248; Mary, 23.
GREER—GRIER, David, 180, 229; Delilah, 18; Eliz., 107; Gray Geo., 15; Hannah, 229; James, 15, 17; John, 54; Priscilla, 24; Thos., 15, 79; Wm., 182.
GREGG—GRAGG, Anna, 284; Elinor, 106; Henry, 265; Lewis, 37; Thos., 281, 283, 284.
GREGORY, Hardy, 86; Harriet E., 87; Mariah K., 93; Sallie, 109.
GRESHAM, Edmund, 34; Eliza, 68; Eliz., 19; Jeremiah, 63; Joseph, 295; Young, 16, 262.
GRICE, Nancy, 101; Wm., 100.
GRIFFIN, Anna, 59; Asa, 98, 194; Buckner, 66; Chas., 90; Drewry, 66; Elijah, 314; Emily, 305; Gheta, 43; James, 90; John, 273; Lewis, 98; Lucy, 59; Nancy, 3; Nathan, 90; Owen, 306; Richard, 61, 306; Sally, 90; Wm., 90; Wilson, 336.
GRIFFITH, Benj., 33; James, 70; James L., 72; James R., 72; John, 72; Robt., 70; Thos. D., 72.
GRIGGS—GRIG, Jerry, 90; John, 86; Rachel, 31; Robt., 86.
GRIGSBERRY, Arch, 173.
GRIGSBY, Bathsheba, 55.
GRIMAGE, Joshua, 62.
GRIMES, Abraham, 170; Bailey, 170; John, 211, 170, 287; John P., 72; Polly, 60; Thos. M., 69; Washington, 72.
GRIMMEN, Sarah, 41.
GRIMMETT, J., 248; Wm., 38.
GRIMSLEY, Eleanor, 65.
GRINER, Esther, 98; Mathew, 14; Phil., 98.
GRISSEM, Lucy, 332.
GRIZZARD, Milly, 91.
GRIZZLE, Abigail, 240; Elam, 240; Grigsby, 55; Jesse, 30; Polly, 33; Samuel, 240.
GROCE—GROSE—GROOS, Ellison, 90; Sarah, 203; Shepherd, 62.
GROOM—GROOMS, Betsy, 94; Council, 90; John, 99; Peter, 101.
GROOVER—GRUVER, Charley, 12; D. R., 14; John, 184; S. E., 14.

GROVE—GROVES, Jared, 61; Samuel, 70; Stephen, 159.
GROVER, L. H., 63; Milly, 203; Peter, 164.
GRUBBS, Wm. F. M., 102.
GUDDER, Geo., 66.
GUEST—GESS, David, 215, 243; Linna, 215; Mary, 215; Moses, 152, 154, 183, 335; Capt. Moses, 144; Wm. P., 101.
GUICE, Nancy, 65; Peter, 63.
GUINN, Angel C. R., 115; Franklin, 39.
GUION, Dr. Prac, 360.
GUITON, Moses, 269.
GULLAT, Polly, 66.
GULLEDGE, Malleciah, 40.
GULLEY, Wm., 183.
GUMBY, Wm., 63.
GUNN, Gabriel, 35.
GUNNELLS—GUNNOLDS, Avis, 203; Joseph, 226, 335; Nathan, 204, 306, 312, 394; Nicholas, 171, 172.
GUNTER, Gideon, 33; Morgan, 282; Wm., 282.
GUNTRY, Delilah, 272; Tirey, 272.
GUSKINS, Jane, 109.
GUTMAN, Bartholomew, 53; Daniel, 53; David, 53.
GUTTERY, Francis, 262.
GUY, John, 177; Wm., 274.
HAAS, John, 2.
HABERSHAM, James, 137; John, 167, 168, 172; Joseph, 175, 180; J., 173, 181.
HACKETT, Anna, 278; Eliza, 205; Robt., 278, 326; Wm., 238, 248, 277, 322, 326.
HACKNY, Nathan, 79.
HADDAWAY, Rebecca, 5.
HADDEN—HADDING, Eliz., 46; James, 181; Mary, 47; Wm., 45, 47, 51, 54, 181.
HADEN, Lydia, 236.
HADLEY, Capt. Thos., 361.
HAGAN, Edward, 16, 19; Honor, 60; James, 13; Margaret, 13; Solomon, 13; Wm., 86.
HAGERTY, Joshua, 39.
HAGGARD, Anna, 323; Frances, 106; James, 29, 270, 276, 278, 287; John, 225, 283; Jonathan, 276; Samuel, 103, 107; Trench, 299.
HAGGINS—HEGGENS—HEGGONS, Burwell, 182; Charity, 182; Conmack, 251, 337; Daniel, 19; Enoch, 192; Polly, 192; Reuben, 187; Thos., 195.
HAGLER, John, 21.

HAGOOD, Fanny, 23; James, 21; Sally, 20; Wm., 26.
HAITE, Hannah, 347.
HALE—HAILE, Betsy, 21; Edward Gortney, 168; David, 283; Hannah, 233; Hosea, 17; James, 79; John, 72; Jonas, 72; Josey, 36; Saletheal M., 73; Sally, 19.
HALEY—HAILEY, Eliz., 268; Isaiah, 248; James, 199, 268; James R., 311; Joel, 73, 311; John W., 243; Lewdeary, 189; Mark, 264, 282, 289; Nancy, 213; Thos., 283; Wm., 264, 278.
HAILING, Nelly, 188.
HALKIN, Moses, 337.
HALL, Amanda M., 115; Amey, 110; Ann, 326; Mrs. Ann, 47; Benj., 2; Betsy, 59; Dempsey, 47, 53; Elisha, 40; Eliz., 95, 213, 284, 299, 326; Geo., 198, 355; Hudson, 49; Hugh, 363; James, 53, 363; Jane, 234; Jean, 225; Jeremiah, 70; John, 37, 73, 284, 302; Joseph, 53; Judah, 194; Julia, 197; Lewis, 97; Lidy, 189; Lucy Meredith, 334; Lupina, 111; Mary, 258; Polly, 3, 88; Pool, 46; Rebecca, 107; Redding, 53; Robt., 73; Robt. H., 198; Rodney, 326; Sally, 32; Sarah A., 15; Seaborn, 195; Selena, 112; Thos., 360; V. G., 12; Wm., 26, 97, 160, 188, 225, 234, 263, 284, 329; Wm. H., 190, 259, 334.
HALLEKIT, Sarah Anderson, 19.
HALLEY, Polly, 185.
HALSTEAD, Eliza. M., 6; Jonathan, 55.
HAM, John, 149; Theophilus, 73; Wm., 111.
HAMBLEN, Thos., 253.
HAMBRICK, Chas., 62; James, 21; John, 62; Lousey, 21; Nimrod, 31.
HAMBRIGHT, Col. Frederick, 358.
HAMBY, Absalom, 40; John, 332; Levi, 197; Samuel, 24.
HAMILTON—HAMBLETON, Andrew, 107; Barton, 17; John, 108; Mordeca Stringer, 186; Robt., 78; Wm., 83, 84, 251; Winny, 36.
HAMLET, John, 73.
HAMLIN, John, 55; Richard, 55.
HAMMETT, James, 1, 203; Wm., 39.
HAMMOCK, Jesse, 23, 52; John, 53, 66; Littleton, 102; Raney, 21; Samuel, 53, 61, 62; Willoby, 15, 249.
HAMMOND—HAMMONS, Abner, 2; Daniel, 6; Floda, 310; Jacob, 61; Job., 203, 204; John, 66; Susanna, 4; Teresa C., 215; Thos., 80.

HEINEMAN, F. W., 166.
HEMPHILL, Andrew, 250; Caroline, 214; Eliz., 80; Henrietta, 302; Isabella, 258; John, 34; Margaret, 258, 268, 277; Pleasant, 73; Riddy, 294; Robt., 201, 294; Robt. I., 73; Samuel, 79, 241; Thos., 62, 73; Wm., 268, 277.
HENBY, Edmund, 343; John, 177; Mary, 250; Wm., 250.
HENDERSON, A. H., 104; Betsy, 270; Capt., 148; Daby, 169; David, 103; Eliz., 182, 189; Gen., 140; Hannah, 106; James, 85; James D., 104; John, 36, 91, 270, 273, 290, 300, 345; John G., 104; Capt. John, 141; Joseph, 192; Josiah, 103; Mary, 90; Nancy, 193; Samuel, 103; Sinah, 193; Wm., 91; Zach., 172, 180.
HENDON, Isham, 16; Noris, 23; Patience, 21.
HENDRICKS—HENDRIX, Andrew, 341; Annis, 341; Barnett, 243; Daniel, 12; David, 10; Finnel, 104; Gilford E., 211; Griffin, 11; Isaac, 341, 342; Jack, 254; Jacob, 341; James, 11, 13, 34; Jemima, 13; Jenidran, 188; Jeremiah, 210; John, 13, 53, 203, 310; Joseph, 341; Moses, 341; Nancy, 27, 190, 341; Nimrod, 253, 260; Polly, 105, 299; Sarah, 40; Susan, 91; Wm., 59.
HENLEY—HENDLEY—HANLEY, Anny, 194; Chas., 344; Darby, 257; Dennis, 181; Edmund, 188, 225, 227, 262, 263, 266, 280, 331, 338, 347, 357; Francis, 279; Freeman, 14; Jane, 227, 351; Janet Gorham, 262; Mary, 225, 226, 279, 282; Sally, 193; Sarah, 225, Wm., 84, 225, 226, 262, 279, 282.
HENNING, Geo., 261, 262; John, 22; Micajah, 5; Wm., 280.
HENRY, Alexander, 364; Benson, 234; Isabella McKeown, 364; James, 50; John, 355, 364; Capt. John, 363; Jinny, 91; Kesiah, 234; Malcolm, 364; Polly, 96; Robt., 361; Thos., 357; Wm., 364.
HENSLEE, David S., 194; Macksfield, 288.
HENSON, Alsey, 204; James, 112, 178; Joanna, 203; Joel, 198; Sally, 83; Sarah, 210; Wm., 213.
HEPBURN, Joseph S., 1.
HERBERT, Isaac, 303.
HEROD, John, 52; Nathan, 52.
HERRILL, Azariah, 357.

HERRING—HERRIN, Betsy, 23; Elbert, 295; Geo., 5; Isaiah, 295; Margaret, 196; Martha, 20; Nancy, 20; Polly, 25, 295; Sally, 25; Susanna, 26; Wm., 16, 26, 54, 195; Zacheus, 295.
HERRINGTON, Harvey, 52; John, 52, 230, 335; Nancy, 3; Polly, 185; Silas, 46; Thos., 230.
HERSEY, Martha, 114.
HERSTON, Lemuel, 238; Nancy, 238.
HERTFORD, Wm., 178.
HESTER, Eliz., 18; Frances, 68; James, 61; Lucinda, 67; Rachel, 60; Rebecca, 58; Samuel, 17; Sarah, 24; Stephen, 17; Thos., 25; Wm., 25; Zachariah, 57.
HEWELL, John, 188.
HEWETT—HUITT, John, 266, 290; Wm., 250, 272, 284.
HICKENBOTHAM—HICKUMBOTHAM, Barsheba, 82; Eliz., 90; Francis, 198.
HICKMAN, Jacob, 28; John, 6; Joseph, 16; Lemuel, 51; Wm., 103.
HICKS, Abner, 60; Daniel, 16; Eliz., 321; James, 40; Jincy, 22; Joel, 265; John, 53; John J., 79; Joseph, 4, 36, 37; Mary, 187; Mathew, 43; Matilda, 215; Nancy, 23, 69; Nathaniel, 321; Polly, 65; Stephen F., 72; Solomon, 264; Susanna, 20; Thos. R. D., 323.
HICKSON, Thos., 41.
HIGDON, Robt., 59.
HIGGENBOTHAM, Capt., 138; Jacob, 37; Joseph, 37; Nelson, 72; Rachel, 200; Robt., 37; Samuel, 72.
HIGGINS, Eliz., 191; Henry, 238; Judith, 30, 31; Mary, 238; Susanna, 29.
HIGGS, John, 97.
HIGH, Fielding, 63; Gardner, 352; John, 80; Rachel Gibbs, 352.
HIGHLAND, Ezekiel, 179.
HIGHSMITH, Daniel, 97; James, 99; Wm. B., 113.
HIGHTOWER, Amelia, 218; Rebecca, 91; Wm., 218.
HILBURN, N. E., 215.
HILL, Abraham, 363; Benj. R., 214; Caleb, 206; Cinthia, 89; Col., 160; Eleanor Garmon, 352; Eliz., 21, 216; Geo., 85; Capt. Green, 161; Isaac, 17, 38, 39; Jacob, 344; James, 15, 37, 172, 180, 217; Jeptha, 5; Jeremiah, 22; Jesse, 233, 237, 239; John, 86, 113, 256, 346, 352; Joseph,

277, 286, 351; Tanner, 351; Thos., 35, 62, 98; Wm., 54, 212.
HUGHLETT—HULETT, Allen, 113; Wm., 291.
HUGULY, Geo., 62.
HULN, Sarah, 197.
HULL, Gen. Wm., 117.
HULSEY, Adonijah, 345; Anny, 191; Edmund, 183; James, 282; John, 193; Pleasant, 184; Wm. 182, 184.
HUMBLE, Geo., 289, Sarah, 289.
HUMPHRIES — HUMPHREYS, David, 246, 337; Eliz., 205; Geo., 198; Geo. W., 209; Hannah, 222; James, 114, 194; John, 70; Jonathan, 294, 297; Joseph, 103, 218, 222, 248, 335; Rebekah, 218; Uriah, 16; Wm. C., 2.
HUNGLING, Caty, 88.
HUNNICUT — HONYCUT, Elisha, 91; Joseph, 271; Patsy, 298; Wm., 91; Wilson F., 213.
HUNT, Alexander J., 57; Betsy G., 322; Chloe, 50; Eliz., 193, 202; Esley, 211; Fitz. M., 283; James, 226, 335; Joel, 346; Mary, 197; Nathaniel, 226, 280, 340; Olive, 7; Richardson, 180; Sarah, 6, 283; Thos., 352; Wm., 73; Wm. H., 26; Winnie, 7; Zilpha Meadows, 352.
HUNTER, Benj. T., 114; Edward, 173; Eleander, 68; Hardy, 66; Jesse, 168; Job, 61; Col. John, 139; Sally, 23; Samuel, 61; Sarah, 66.
HURD, Jincy, 21.
HURT, Chas. S., 86; Sarah, 86.
HURTARD, Henry, 91.
HUTCHINS—HUTCHINGS, Burwell, 108; Drury, 238, 327; Eliz., 46; Frances, 215; John, 233; Margaret, 111; Nancy, 59; Redmond, 27; Robt., 57; Sarah, 238.
HUTCHINSON — HUTCHERSON, Abisha, 197; Adam, 128; Alexander, 128; Ann, 196; Chas., 337; Eliz., 128; James, 98; John, 128; Richard, 231; Wm., 6.
HUTH, Rebecca, 93.
HUTSON, Caty, 16; Esther, 20; Hall, 50; Henry, 31; Peter, 250.
HUTTO, Ann, 61; Elas, 59; Henry, 59; John, 58.
HUXHAM, Wm., 253.
HYATT, Edward, 355; Eliz., 213; Hezekiah, 262.
HYDE, Sally, 203.
HYLTON, Thos., 12.
HYMER, Rev. Samuel, 139, 142, 147, 149.

HYNES, Lewis, 107.
IBALINE, Miss, 112.
INGLAND, Daniel, 195.
INGLE, Paulser, 271.
INGRAM, Benj., 229; Chas., 224, 226, 229, 232, 278, 342; Capt. Edwin, 354; Eliz., 229, 278; Geo., 46, 53; Hugh, 51; Isaac, 62; James, 51; John, 46, 53, 226; Joseph, 352; Mary Ann, 226; Martin, 193; Nancy Montgomery, 354; Wm., 46, 51, 74, 226; Winnifred Nelms, 352; Thos., 226.
ILEY, Barbary, 207; Cynthia, 209.
INLOW, Peter, 167; Sevastin, 216.
INNES, Andrew, 282; John M., 111.
IRAM, Wm., 340.
IRBY, Winny, 91.
IRONS, Wm., 91.
IRVIN, Cynthia, 6.
IRWIN, Benj., 40; Col. Henry, 360; James, 79; Gov. Jared, 272; John, 51, 91; Sally, 85; Samuel, 46.
ISAAC—ISAACS, Eliz., 191; Mrs. Eliz., 129; Col., 145, 153; Ralph, 129; Samuel, 263, 289.
ISAM—ISOM, Christian, 79; James, 184; Wm., 246, 341.
ISBELL—ISBEL, Allen, 213; Capt., 143; Clarkey, 214; Col., 143; James, 243, 300; John, 213; Pendleton, 217; Robt. G., 311, 315; Sarah, 205, 217, 307; W. F., 315.
ISHAM—ISHEM, Abraham, 333; James, 50; Jincy, 333; John, 193, 333; Wm., 333.
ISLER, Wm., 84.
IVEY—IVEY—IVIE, Anderson, 280; Isaac, 31; John, 43, 193; Lott, 35, 284; Marion, 64; Patsy, 27; Polly 41; Robt., 2.
IVINS, John, 193.
JACK, Mrs. Kitty, 118; John, 283; Lettis, 283; Samuel, 174, 179; Capt. Samuel, 118; Wm., 108.
JACKSON, Absalom, 168; Mrs. Anne, 118; Benj., 108, 266, 268, 339, 345; Betsy, 22; Charity, 110; Chas. C., 19; Daniel, 170; David, 32, 85; Drecy, 209; Drucilla, 9; Drury, 1; Eliza, D., 8; Eliz., 88, 105; Frederick, 98; G., 14; Henry, 17; Hugh, 109; Isaac, 91, 107, 176, 177; Mrs. J. Hardwick, 124; James, 98, 264, 265, 312; James Lander, 118; Jesse, 46; Joel, 91; John, 20, 36, 173, 176; Col. John (or Jonathan), 353; Joseph, 46, 53, 312, 315; Katrin, 22; Kirza, 83; Lev, 52; Lucy, 297; Martha, 186; Mary,

243, 294, 303, 316, 321; Sally, 323; Stephen, 38; Tandy, 83, 104, 105; Talbird, 294; Talbot, 214; Winney, 28.

KIDD, John W., 228; Martin, 228.

KILBY, Wm., 37.

KILCREAS, Edmund, 67.

KILGO, Wm., 91.

KILGORE, Col. Benj., 140, 149, 157; Eliz., 21; Mathew, 23; Nancy, 66; Peter, 16; Polly, 67; Robt. 67; Simeon, 37; Solomon, 24; Thos., 92; Wm., 15.

KILLBEE, Christopher, 98.

KILLEBREW, Robt., 86.

KILPATRICK, Thos., 92.

KIMBAL, Gideon, 20.

KIMBRO, Wm., 25.

KIMBROUGH, Bradley, 91; Shadrack, 180; Thos., 86.

KINARD, Martin, 42.

KINCAID, Capt. John, 357.

KINDA, David, 64.

KING, Augusta W., 315; Benj., 182, 269, 347; Besof F., 315; Berry, 198; Carson, 70; Chas., 46, 336; David, 52; Edmund, 67, 231, 233, 264, 279, 286, 329, 330; Elijah, 21; Eliz., 41, 231; Geo., 188, 257, 269; Grace Sterling, 127; Hannah, 315; James, 212, 327; John, 1, 34, 91, 104, 221, 290; John B., 74; John C., 207; John M., 36; Joseph, 50; Joseph B., 315; Lambert, 345; Lewis, 91; Littleberry, 55; Louisa Woodward, 128; Margaret, 2, 86; Martha, 315; Mary, 315; Melia, 189; Milisa, 315; Nancy, 221; Polly, 225; Sarah, 4; Susan, 316; Thos., 147, 166, 200, 201, 294, 296, 303, 308, 315, 327; Thos. D., 46; Thos. M., 201; Wm., 212, 225, 300; Wm. P., 243, 315.

KINGSTON, Polly, 33.

KINMAN, Thos., 91.

KINNEBREW, Jacob, 67; Wm., 62.

KINNEY—KENNY, Betsy, 31; Chaney, 19; James, 67; Jesse, 23; Sally, 18, 24.

KINNINGS, Edward, 246; Eliz., 246; Mary, 246.

KINSEY, Peter, 288.

KIRBO, James, 29.

KIRBY—KERBY, Arthur, 13, 14; Hannah, 14; Henry, 67; James G., 13, 14; James J., 15; Jesse, 80; Mary, 14; Rosanna, 14.

KIRK—KERK, John, 57; Nancy, 210; Sarah, 214.

KIRKLAND, A. L., 14; John, 14;

Richard, 10, 11; Samuel, 58; Sion C., 46.

KIRKLEY—KERKLEY, Charlotte, 1; Eliza, 29.

KIRKPATRICK, Capt., 166; James, 232; Samuel, 1.

KIRKSEY, Isaac, 98.

KIRKWOOD, Sally, 21.

KISER, Joseph, 229, 275.

KITCHEN—KITCHENS, Geo., 198; Samuel, 97; Wm., 57.

KITH, Jeremiah, 91.

KNIGHT, Ann, 340; Eliz., 59; Holley Ann, 100; James, 39; John, 91.

KNOWLES—KNOLLS, Dennis, 42; Ira, 111; Nathaniel, 52; Parker, 41; Wm. P., 110.

KNOWLING, Martha, 113.

KNOX, Anny, 105; Cynthia, 33; E. M., 310; Geo., 289; John, 192; John G., 64; Samuel, 30, 104, 204, 211, 310, 315.

KOEL, Thos., 30.

KOGER, Darkis, 241; Nicholas, 241.

KOLB—KOLBE, Agnes, 32; Jonathan, 104; Wilds, 80.

KORNEGAY, Geo., 84.

KRAUS, Frank, 356.

KUNAM—KUNUM, James, 22; Patsy, 26; Polly, 22; Suckey, 25.

KYLE, Robt., 260.

LACY, Delilah, 3; Jordan, 265; Nancy, 55; Stephen, 39; Sylvania, 209.

LAFAVOR—LAFEVER, Abraham, 46, 50.

LAIR, Rev. Mr. 320.

LAIRD, Robt., 17.

LAMAR, Alasannah, 219; Basil, 62, 168, 221, 241; Betsy, 221; Jacob, 62; James, 174, 219; Jeremiah, 6; John, 57, 221; LaFayette, 64; Mary, 66, 221, 241; Thos., 169, 174; Zachariah, 2, 17, 54.

LAMB, Isaac, 46; Robt., 337.

LAMBER, Edwin, 83.

LAMBERT—LAMBERTH, Eliz., 19; Joel, 20; John, 104; Minna, 89; Noel, 58; Thos., 17; Wm., 80, 92.

LAMPKIN, Robt., 92.

LANCASTER, Eliz., 68, 238; John, 237, 238; Joseph, 237; Richard, 237; Sarah, 63; Wm., 62, 237, 238.

LAND, Eleanor, 298; John, 53.

LANDERS—LANDER, Eliz., 63; Francis, 118; James, 74; Dr. James, 118; John, 64; Lewis, 74; Samuel, 74; Wm., 74.

LANDRUM, Joseph, 104; Thos., 35.

LANE—LAIN, Benj., 92; Henry, 20; John, 10, 265, 274, 335; Jonathan,

MATTOX—MATTOCK, Aaron, 101; Elijah H., 100; Emaly, 101; Hannah, 89; Hardage, 80; John, 100; John A., 102; Julia A. H., 103; Louisa A., 100; Mary, 100; Michael, 97; Pleasant W., 102; Stephen, 102.
MAULDEN—MAULDING—MALDIN, Absalom, 67; Andrew, 230; Egis, 300; Eliz., 207, 300; Nancy, 202; Richard, 281, 300, 321; Virginia, 213.
MAULENS, Sally, 214.
MAUNEY, Christian, 358.
MAY, Maj. Benj., 361; Eliz., 65; Francis, 52; Martha, 112; Peter, 353.
MAYFIELD, Catherine, 346; Edmund, 346; Edward W., 306, 317, 324, 326; John, 230, 270, 275; Martha, 199; Mary D., 326; Pilly, 298.
MAYLAY, Isabel B., 113.
MAYO—MAYHOE, Nancy, 190; Temperance, 84; Wm., 84.
MAYS—MAYES, A. N., 243, 306; Benj., 53, 104; Betsy, 304; Charlotte, 190; Edward, 293, 350; Ellender, 42; Harmon, 53; Harriett, 304; Harvey, 214, 350; James, 192; Jane, 192; Jean, 304; Jenny, 69; Joel, 304; John, 293; Jonas, 53; Malinda, 293, 296, 350; Margarette, 293; Martha, 304; Matilda, 206; Nancy, 304; Newton, 293, 304, 350; Peggy, 304; Permelia, 304; Polly, 304; Robt., 293, 350; Samuel, 46, 53; Syntha, 350; Thos., 193, 258, 293, 304, 350; Wm., 190, 293.
MAXEY, Ann, 20.
MAXWELL, Felix, 52; James, 75.
MEACHUM, Henry, 2.
MEAD, Edward, 80.
MEADOWS — MEADORS — MEADERS—MEDDERS, Berry G., 75; Christopher, 203; Duren H., 75; Esther, 213; John, 281; Noah W., 75; Sally, 210; Thos., 263, 267, 334; Zedediah, 200.
MEANS, Margaret, 219; Robt., 219.
MEARS, Henry, 46; Meshack, 46.
MEDDIS, Susanna, 25.
MEDFORD, Geo., 82.
MEDICI, Lieut., 150.
MEDKIFF—MEDKEFF, Aditha, 34; Patsy, 106.
MEDLOCK, Eliz., 192; Isome, 320.
MEEKS, John, 189; Littleton, 184, 185, 204, 209, Martha, 192; Martin, 209; Milly, 297; Nacy, 210, 256, 260, 274; Susan, 197.
MEGAROY, Edward, 279.

MEGNIS, John, 306.
MELEAR, Robt., 41.
MELLVILLE, Thos., 50.
MELTON, Jonathan, 15; Joseph, 6; Timothy, 36.
MERCER, Betsy, 26; Dorcas, 218; Eliz., 42, 258; Henry F., 64; Jacob, 39; James, 258; John, 258; Malachi, 15; Robt., 258, 281; Silas, 218.
MEREDITH, David, 329; Polly, 18; Signal, 259, 334; Tignal, 196, 299.
MERIDA, Lucy, 190.
MERIWETHER, David, 17; Geo. M., 39; James, 46; Judith, 22; Thos., 46, 54.
MERON, Geo., 50.
MERONY, Eve, 95; John, 74; Wm., 74.
MERRELL, B. T., 204; Eliz., 185; John, 274; Mary F., 208.
MERRIAN, Daniel, 53.
MERRITT, Mary, 111; Thos., 42.
MESSER, Jane, 185; Joseph, 36; Norah, 57; Sarah, 57, 316.
METHVIN, Richard, 7.
METTS—METT, Mary, 113; Samuel T., 242.
MEYERS, Eliz., 246; Priscilla, 246.
MICHAEL—MICHEL, Frederick, 178; Joseph, 179.
MICHOLDS, Ann, 194.
MICKLEJOHN, Geo., 54.
MICKLEROY, Thompson, 74.
MICHUM, John, 266.
MIDDLEBROOKS, Fanne, 24; Isaac, 11, 16, 79; Lucy, 25; Thos., 57; Wm. S., 57.
MIDDLETON, Eliz., 225; John, 83; Owen, 7; Polly, 19; Robt., 24, 173, 174, 225, 284.
MIFLIN, Rhoda, 4.
MIKELL—MIKEL, Allen, 13; David, 14; James, 12, 94; Seaborn, 13.
MILBURN, John I., 81.
MILDER, Geo., 171.
MILES, John, 1; Lucy, 3; Mary, 8; Wm., 67.
MILHAM, Henry, 75.
MILLEN, James I., 318.
MILLER, Adene, 215; Adenia, 293; 350; Andrew, 362; Asariel, 193; Benj., 10; David H., 30; Dicey, 196; Ebenezer, 27, 108; Eliz., 27, 108; Gade S., 102; Geo., 57, 67, 172; James, 14, 92, 281, 350; James J., 13, 15; James M., 293; John, 104, 191; John Adam, 232, 277; Lance E., 214; Mary, 193, 211; Oliver C., 207; Prudence, 198; Rebecca, 65; Rhoda, 29; Robt., 193; Sally,

PARSONS—PERSONS, Ann, 47; John, 47, 54; Joseph, 354; Josiah, 7; Nancy Jordan, 354; Thos., 47, 50; Wm., 47, 54.

PARTEE, Benj., 7.

PARTIN—PARTAIN—PARTEN, Eliz., 99; Hugh G., 100; John, 216; John G., 101; Peter, 55; Robt., 98; Sary, 216.

PASCHAL—PASKIL, Harriet, 203; Samuel, 36, 79; Wm., 64.

PASKINS, Hugh, 171.

PASNER, Joseph Gabriel, 47.

PASS, Mourning, 89.

PASSMORE, Rhoda, 109.

PASSONS, Patsy, 40.

PATE, Chas., 32; Cloey, 48; Peterson, 93; Phebe, 66; Wm., 39.

PATILLO, David, 78; James, 52; Major James, 47; Patience, 83.

PATRICK, Alex., 249; David, 272; Hannah, 28, 107; John C., 39, 43; John H., 150, 195, 243; Mary, 272; Solomon, 39; Wm., 181, 262.

PATTERSON, Alexander, 224, 359; Calvin W., 212; Eliza, 311; Hampton, 214; Isaac, 173; Jesse, 259; John, 75; Mary, 48; Milly, 207; Nancy, 20, 212; Peggy, 82; Polly, 157; Rachel, 28, 185; Robt., 47, 49; Robt. M., 7; Sarah, 43; Thos., 47; Tryon, 157, 229, 262, 276; Willie, 57.

PATTON—PATTEN, Arcada, 218; Caty, 108; Charity, 108; Elijah, 75; Frances, 32; James, 75, 224; Jane, 16; John, 75; Col. John, 362; Robt., 32; Samuel, 75, 104, 362; Thos., 218; Wm., 250.

PAUL, Moses, 67; Philip, 353.

PAULETT, David, 46, 51; Eliz., 47; Harvey, 54; John, 54; Mary, 47.

PAULK, Geo., 110; Micajah, 49.

PAXTON, Thos., 176; Wm., 176.

PAYNE, Absalom E., 98; Ambrose, 210; Ann, 298, 300, 339; Ann Poyndexter, 280; Anny, 227, 351; Asa, 191, 199, 201, 207, 299; Atena, 214; Benedick, 297; Bennett, 301; Champneys, 219, 244, 263, 267, 268, 334, 336, 346; Chas., 247; Chas. S. M., 299; Cleveland, 244, 255, 256, 278, 336, 346; Daniel, 97, 98; David, 189, 259, 298, 301, 308; Edward, 19, 263, 266; Edy, 193; Elijah, 97; Eliz., 234, 298, 301, 308; Geo., 58; Harrison, 325; Irene, 202; James W., 306; Jane, 288; Jenny, 219; Jeremiah, 334; Jinny, 351; John, 21, 39, 194, 219, 232, 247, 255, 265, 288, 298, 299, 317, 336, 339; John E.,

314; John H., 308; John M., 209, 296, 299; John W., 197; Jonathan, 232; Joseph, 227, 281, 320, 335; Katy, 332; Kesiah, 198; Malinda, 208; Malisa, 212; Martin, 198; Mary, 227, 281, 341; Maxfield H., 200, 204, 298, 301, 308, 317, 319, 325, 327, 328; Middleton, 332; Milly, 24, 225, 235; Moses, 219, 261, 281, 288, 336, 351; Nancy, 219, 243, 301; Nathaniel, 219, 244, 245, 265, 336, 337, 340; Nelly, 33; Oliver T., 308; Patsy C., 341; Philip, 235, 333; Polly, 109, 190, 268, 299; Poyndexter, 227, 239, 244, 268, 336, 339, 351; Reuben, 232, 270 297; Rhoda, 194; Ruth, 183, 219, 244, 336; Rutha, 256; Samuel, 287, 298, 301, 325; Samuel T. 206; Sarah, 238, 243; Sarah Williamson, 327; Shrewsberry, 219, 244, 285, 336, 337; Thos., 1, 24, 175, 188, 190, 206, 210, 219, 225, 232, 243, 244, 245, 248, 255, 278, 287, 296, 299 301, 308, 317, 325, 327; Wm., 38, 219, 223, 244, 285, 308, 325, 332, 335; Yanaky, 229, 245, 278, 336; Zachariah, 98; Zebediah, 244, 253, 255, 278, 308, 346; Zedediah, 237, 301.

PAYTON, Howard, 75; Randolph, 75.

PEACOCK, Abraham, 52; Arthur, 52; Daniel, 38; Eli, 52; John, 38.

PEAD, John, 68.

PEALMAN, Eliz., 64.

PEARSON, Abel, 331; Ben., 13; Benazae, 110; Samuel, 355.

PEAVY, Lucinda, 95; Prudence, 25.

PECK, Ruth, 27.

PEDAN, James, 195.

PEEBLES—PEEBIES, PEOBIES, Ephraim, 49, 267; Capt. Robt., 356; Thos., 54.

PEEK—PEAK, David, 81; Leonard C., 113; Lucy, 201; Nancy, 193; Peggy, 106.

PEEL, John, 46, 50; Mary, 49, 59; Richard, 47, 49; Wm., 49.

PEET, Wm., 193.

PEMBERTON, Amy, 354; Richard, 354.

PENDALL, Sarah, 62.

PENDERGRASS, Edwin, 104.

PENDLETON, Coleman, 93; Eliz., 93; Jacob, 307; Wm., 52.

PENICK, Joseph P., 81; Robt., 79, 82.

PENN, Abigail Wilson, 334; Maj. Gabriel, 138; Joseph, 236, 246, 344; Richard T., 75; Wm., 190, 334.

PENNINGTON, Abram, 106; Jacob, 291, 335; John, 108; Sion, 47;

PONCE, Dimos, 131; Isabella, 131; Sturges, 131.
POND, Capt. Samuel, 156.
PONDER, Abner, 337; Ephraim, 46; Jamima, 24; John H., 81.
POOLE, Aaron, 47, 50; Eliz., 47; G. W., 306; James, 194; Joseph, 50; Polly, 28; Rebecca, 187; Samuel, 104; Walter, 243; Wm., 243, 284; Wm. R., 213.
POOR, David, 260; Wm., 42.
POPE, Burwell, 17, 249, 291; Cary W., 41; Fleet, 58, 59; Henry N., 20; John, 180, 181; Judith, 239, 350; Leroy, 239, 350; Louis, 249; Michael, 109; Priscilla, 291; Wilie, 167; Wiley H., 81; Villis, 32.
POPPEL, Sarah Ann, 103.
PORCH, Henry, 93, Wm., 52.
PORTER, Aves, 209; Bartholomew, 75; Benj., 179, 217; Douglas M., 79; Eliz., 37, 81; Jedathan, 243, 304; John, 81; Lawson, 93; Patsy Claborn, 217; Sampson, 171; Samuel, 335; Thos., 180; Capt. Thos., 175.
PORTERFIELD, James, 70.
POSEY, Casy, 106; Chester, 93; John, 94, 109; John H., 86; Louisa, 114; Mary Ann, 109; Matilda, 95; Tabitha, 65.
POTTER, Capt. Abram, 141; Brig. Gen., 158; Patsy, 227, 281; Plumber, 75; Solomon, 227, 264, 280, 281.
POTTS, Col., 141; Geo., 227, 281; Henry, 104; Judy, 227, 281; Stephen, 38, 39, 178; Wm., 104.
POU, James, 39.
POUND, Merryman, 86; Sally, 96.
POURNALL, Geo. W., 110.
POWELL—POWL, Abram, 102; Abraham, 110; Almond, 260; Ann D., 48; Chas., 16; Cynthia, 99; Eliz., 24; Francis, 67; Hearly, 19; James, 47; Jason, 47; John, 21, 40, 52; Dr. John, 47; Katherine, 24; Lewis, 23, 172; Mrs. Margaret, 111; Millenton, 93; Moses, 36; Olive, 294; Oliver C., 75; Patience, 34; Reuben, 47, 52; Richard, 53; Sarah, 4; Stephen, 47, 53; Theophilus, 47; Tillman, 260; Wm., 26, 36, 355; Zacheus, 35, 40.
POWER, Chas. T., 75; David, 70, 75; Francis, 70; James, 70; James M., 75; John M., 75; Samuel, 332; Wm., 41, 70, 75, 102; Wm. G., 75; Wm. W., 70, 75.
PRATHER, Wm., 68.
PRATOR, Jennet, 79.
PRATT, John, 7; Polly, 41.

PREGNALLS, Absalom, 236; Nancy, 236.
PREPWOOD, Robt., 7.
PRESCOT, Ephraim, 31.
PRESLEY, Jincy, 95; Wm., 93.
PRESTON, Thos., 17.
PRESTIDGE, Elcy, 230; Eliz., 230; John, 223; Joshua, 230; Larkin, 223, 230, 266; Thos., 223.
PREVATT, Bathsheba, 102; Peter, 98.
PREWETT—PRUITT—PRUET, Anna, 235, 239, 268; Behethland, 5; Benj., 230, 278; Berryman, 319; Daniel, 213; Eli, 311; Eliz., 311; Emeline, 105; Hezekiah, 311, 313; James, 20; Japeth, 247, 280; Jeremiah, 311; John M., 298; John W., 299, 313; Johnson, 313; Joseph, 299, 311, 313, 319; Kesia, 313; Mary, 4, 230, 278; Philip, 235, 239, 268, 334, 343; Patsy, 343; Polly, 199; Robt., 303, 311, 319; Robt. W., 204, 313; Samuel, 235, 247, 298, 319, 328, 329, 334; Samuel Riley, 313; Samuel W., 313; Tillman, 334, 343; Wilkins, 313; Wm. A., 311; Zech, 343.
PRICE, Catherine, 96; Chas., 293; James, 17; John, 16, 63; Mary, 282, 336; Peter, 171; Rial, 225; Stephen, 16; Zemelia, 86.
PRICKETT, David, 68; Edward, 283; Geo., 225, 279, 318, 340; Israel, 340; Jacob, 340; Jesse, 189; Joel, 183, 340; John, 37, 340, 346; Josiah, 194, 340; Mary, 185, 227, 340; Naomi, 197; Patsy, 258, 318; Sarah, 184, 225, 279.
PRIDE, John, 7.
PRIDGEN, Mack, 97.
PRIMING, Joseph, 23.
PRINCE, Edward, 240; Oliver H., 68, 232; Mary, 51.
PRINE, Joseph, 267.
PRITCHARD—PRICHARD, Lavoice, 6; Presley, 86; Sion B., 207.
PRITCHETT, Geo., 259; Israel, 228; Jacob, 75; Josiah, 250; Patsy, 250, 259; Sarah, 228.
PRITCHFORD, Judy, 275; Nathan, 275; Wm., 275.
PROCTOR, Delilah, 4; Susanna, 106.
PROPHET, James, 22.
PRUAL, Rebecca, 95.
PRYOR—PRIOR, Absalom, 50; Eliz., H. C., 81; John, 79; Martin L., 1; Robt., 46, 50; Wm., 7.
PUCKETT, Edmond, 94; Edmond D., 201; Martin, 81; Sally, 95.
PUGH, Elijah, 34; Miriam, 107; Rachel, 41; Regin, 105.
PUGSLEY, John, 54.

Margaret, 202; Martha E., 109; Milly, 32; Osborn, 23; Patience, 30; Rev., 358; Rhoda, 202; Susan Ann Bailey, 111; Timothy, 8; Thos., 51, 181; Unity, 29; Uriah, 99; Wiley, 8, 240; Wm., 172; Wm. D., 101; Wm. L., 113; Willy, 8; Wyley, 232.
ROLAND, Bedford, 330, 334; Drury, 188; Robt., 325, 330.
ROLLINS, James W., 112.
ROLLS, Robinson, 86.
RONALDSON, Wm., 53.
RONEY, Celia M., 91.
ROOK, Richard, 68; Wm., 75, 272.
ROOT, Eveline, 2.
ROPER, Geo., 7; Lydia, 213.
ROQUEMORE, Peter, 170; Thos., 85.
ROSE, Anny, 206; Col., 138; Drury, 228; Hardy, 204; Henry, 216, 228, 271; Jesse, 192; John, 216; Mehaly, 96; Susannah, 57; Thos., 187, 216.
ROSS, A. W., 205; David, 290; Isham, 53; James, 356; James J., 39; Lany, 88; Richard, 186; Sally, 106; Sarah, 42; Wiley, 106; Wm., 287.
ROSSER, David, 86; Geo., 85; Sarah, 86.
ROUNDTON, Eliza, 112.
ROUSSEAU, Wm., 85.
ROUZ, Martin, 208.
ROWDEN, Beddy, 33; Rachel, 105.
ROWE, Martin, 75; Sally, 87.
ROWELL, Edward, 98; Eliz., 93; G., 98; Jesse, 292; Richard, 2.
ROWLAND, Mrs. C. A., 124; Drury, 242; John, 51, 58; Levina, 60; Rosey, 31.
ROYSTER, Wesley, 212.
ROYSTON, Richard, 303; Robt., 16.
ROZIER—ROSER, Adam, 170; Amos, 170; Darby, 171, 175; Isham, 68; John, 50, 84.
RUCKER, Catherine, 240, 320; Cinthia, 198; Eliz., 320; Frances, 320; Geo., 240, 243, 287, 320; Indey, 320; Martin, 39; Mary, 320; Nancy, 193, 320; Simeon, 320; Susannah, 320.
RUDD, Nancy, 207; Rebecca, 206; Thos., 181.
RUSH, Jeptha, 263, 337; Isaac, 328.
RUSHIN, Briant, 18.
RUSKIN, Caroline, 112.
RUSSELL, Ailsey, 218; Andrew, 371, 373; Capt. Andrew, 372; Burnett, 79; Clareann, 63; Collier, 337; David, 37; Eliz., 69, 373; Florence, 373; Gilbert, 373; Hiram, 206; James, 63, 171, 193; Jenny, 41; John, 75, 105, 373; Joseph Martin, 218, 286; Luisa, 60; Margaret, 29, 206, 373;

Martha, 6; Martin, 2, 183; Mary, 371, 373; Mary Jane, 8; Nancy, 305; Oliver, 331; Rebecca, 373; Sallie,190; Sarah, 373; Washington, 68; Wm., 8, 62, 172, 180, 373.
RUSON, James, 94.
RUST, Robt. W., 243.
RUTHERFORD, David, 28; Gen., 144, 145, 151; John, 2; Nancy, 2; Robt., 8.
RUTLEDGE, Capt., 153; Eliz., 19; James, 85; Kioh, 8; Mary, 82; Rutha, 123; Thos., 289.
RYALS—RIALS, Henry, 100; Maria L., 115; Mary Ann, 114; Owen, 110; Rebecca, 10, 102; Siphia, 58; Wm.,113.
RYAN, Edward, 52; Harris, 174, 179; Hiram, 42; John P., 82; Joseph, 168; Obedience, 104; Philip, 104.
SABELLAH, Candace, 304; Jane,304; Sarah, 304.
SABIN, Resolved, 36.
SAFFOLD, Adam G., 81; Daniel, 223; Eliz., 223; Seaborn J., 81.
SAILORS, Wm., 33.
SALE, Peyton W., 64.
SALTER, James, 59; Simon, 179.
SAMMONS, Benj., 51; Nancy, 49.
SAMPLE, Nathaniel, 57; Sarah, 7; Thos. B., 34; Wm., 28.
SAMPSON—SAMSON—SANSOM, Archibald, 36; Eliz., 227, 351; James, 40, 41; John, 21; Polly, 40; Robt.,40; Sally, 41; Wm., 8, 227, 351.
SAMS, Capt. Edmund, 362.
SAMUEL, Ann, 69; Benj., 64; Capt., 139; Edmund, 63; Eliz., 64; Lucy, 68.
SANDERS—SAUNDERS,Aaron, 182, 243, 321, 330; Betsy, 82; Calvin, 198; Catherine, 94; Daniel, 94, 321; David, 268, 321, 330; E. E., 313; Elias, 233; Eliz., 18, 313; Frances, 267; Frances Emely Amelia, 110; Hambleton, 321; Hardy T., 76; Harris, 300; Henry, 236; James, 70; James H., 75; James M., 84; Jane, 236; Jesse, 8; Joel, 243, 321; John, 68, 94, 176, 189, 313, 321; Jonathan, 76; Jones, 321; Josiah, 179; Lewis, 198; Marter, 321; Martha, 313; Mary, 205, 233; Mary A., 37; Menyard, 305, 313; Moses, 228, 246, 267, 268, 313, 321, 330, 334, 344; Nancy, 91, 193, 222, 313, 321; Nathaniel, 321, 330; Patience, 214; Polly, 313, 321; Rachel, 92, 202; Robt., 62; Sally, 189, 321, 330; Samuel, 203; Sarah, 313; Silas, 76; Simeon, 76; Starke, 222; Stephen, 311, 313; Tully, 76; Wm., 26; Wm. T., 243; Wingard, 311.

SANDFORD—SANFORD, Adeline, 204; Benj., 53; Caswell, 53; Frederick, 8; Henry, 53; Jesse, 2; John,53; Presley, 40; Samuel, 53; Sarah S., 87; Thos., 53; Thornton, 8; Wm., 2.
SANDIFER, John, 47; Priscilla, 47.
SANDIFORD, John, 52.
SANDRIDGE—SANDIDGE—SANDAGE, Claiborn, 344; Eliza C., 207; Garrett L., 169, 189, 205, 276, 325; John, 202, 231, 239, 294, 338, 345, 350; Rev. John, 148, 155; Susanna, 231, 239, 338, 350; Wm., 190.
SANDS, James J., 101; John, 97.
SANDWICH, Thos. K., 68.
SAPP, Eliz., 229, 351; Howell, 99;Jackson, 102; John, 229, 266, 351; Lemuel, 115; Sarah, 102; Wm., 101; Winny, 99.
SARTAIN—SARTIN, Elijah, 205; James, 263, 267, 270, 271; John, 197, 211; Rachel, 299; Tapley, 202.
SASSER, Howell, 99.
SATERWHITE, Francis, 333; Paul,24.
SAUER, Philip, 357.
SAULS, Abram, 97.
SAVAGE, John, 310; Zebulon, 265.
SAVALL, John, 345.
SAWERS, Peggy, 18.
SAWYER, Eliz., 92; Jonathan, 54; Prissa, 3; Simpson, 8.
SAXON, Alex, 275; Francis, 243; H., 248; James, 211; Mary, 275; Lieut. Samuel, 148; Solomon, 104.
SAYRE—SAYER—SAYE, Asena, 20; Francis, 2; Ichabod, 207; Wm. H., 76.
SCAGGS, Eliz., 87; John, 94.
SCALES—SCALEZ, Eliz., 302; Sary, 312; Thos., 25; Willis, 243, 312.
SCARBOROUGH, Allen, 84; Frederick, 40, 70, 76; Silas, 14; Wm., 76.
SCHLEY, Michael, 54; Thos., 54.
SCOFIELD, Liza, 65.
SCOTT, Abram, 33; Agrippa, 207; Allen, 213; Alexander, 178; Andrew, 76; Anny, 107; Aquilla, 248; Archer, 241; Archibald, 327; Asa, 208; Col. Chas., 137; David, 61; Eliz., 218; Francis, 87; James, 2, 76, 249, 250; Joel, 215; John, 171, 345; Joseph, 79, 104; Joseph J., 28; Lucinda, 213; Malinda, 210; Martha, 92; Mary, 47, 48; Patrick, 76, 283; Philip, 47, 54; Polly, 232, 350, 351; Capt. Robt., 370; Samuel, 176; Sarah, 241, 297; Susannah H., 307; Thos., 218, 243; Thos. B., 261; Wm., 38, 39, 186, 232, 322; Wm. E., 351.
SCROGGIN—SCOGGIN, Chatton, 15; David, 314; Martha, 214; Pamelia,

3; Smith, 2.
SCULL, John, 344.
SCOURLOCK, Joshua, 2; Kitty, 88; Winny, 8.
SCOURRY, Richardson Owen, 8.
SEAGRAVES, Alford, 76; Noah, 76.
SEALE, Cynthia, 67;Robt., 63;Thos., 94.
SEALWAY, Thos., 94.
SEATS, Thos., 81.
SEAY—SAY, Phoebe, 218; Richard, 259; Wm., 218.
SEEREST, Capt. John, 356.
SEGARS—SEEGAR, Harriet, 308; Mary, 313; Susanna, 209; Winney, 208.
SELBY, Alcey, 4.
SELF, Joseph. 22; Tabitha, 89.
SELLERS, Mary, 98; Polly, 30; Samuel, 98.
SEMLER, John, 312.
SENTERFILT, Henry, 53.
SESSIONS, Daniel, 82; John, 95; Robt. F., 83.
SEWELL—SEWALL—SOWELL, Abyhugh, 40; Ann, 185; Asa, 206; Col. Ben, 150; Christian, 319;Comfort, 196; Deborah, 196; Eliz., 201; 202; Francis, 213; Greenberry, 186; Green B., 206, 208; Guilroy, 322; Henry, 250, 262; Isaac, 319, 329; James, 254, 258, 319, 329; James A., 210; Jane, 208; Jinny, 198; John, 273, 294, 319; Johnson T., 202; Joseph, 265; Joshua, 204; Justina, 317;Lewis, 224, 241, 272, 286;Matilda, 206; Mary, 188, 294, 319; Samuel, 194, 195, 279, 280, 319, 329; Smith, 202; Washington, 253; Wm., 76.
SEXTON, Eliz., 9.
SEYMOUR, R. A., 87.
SHACKLEFORD, John, 79, 262;Wm., 215.
SHAHAN, Nancy, 25; Tapley, 25.
SHALLEEN, James, 194.
SHANKLE—SHANKEE, Abraham, 231; Betsy, 231; Eli, 104, 231; James W., 104, 309; John, 231.
SHANNON, Daniel, 197; David, 169, 243; Dicey, 243; Eliz., 205; John H., 316; Leonard, 313; Mary, 215; Moses, 192; Sally, 320; Samuel, 243, 273, 274, 296, 317, 318, 320, 321, 324, 326, 329, 346; Sarah, 320; Sophia, 204; Thos., 168, 169; Thos. M., 203, 305.
SHARBER, Martha, 111; Nancy, 112; Providence, 110; Rebecca, 111.
SHARMON, Wm., 63.
SHARP, Eliz., 30; Grover, 98; James, 38, 39; John, 63, 97, 98; Maj., 363;

P., 316; Mildred, 90; Nancy, 296;
Penelope, 100; Peter, 85; Polly P.,
203; Sarah, 93; Sarah T., 209; Thos.,
94; Thos. P., 316; Wm. W., 316.
STUDSTILL, Eliz., 114; Hustus, 111;
John, 171, 177; Lydia, 115; Nancy,
110; Zachariah, 113.
STURDEVANT, Denny, 95; Eliz., 5;
James, 8; Jincy, 95; John, 39, 86;
Mathew, 62; Polly, 7; Susannah, 92.
STURGES, Daniel, 369; David, 54.
SUDDUTH, Agnes, 65; Elijah, 63;
James, 62; John, 62; Lawrence, 63;
Lettice, 68; Spencer, 68; Willis, 68.
SUILLY, John, 98; Nicholas, 98;
Samuel, 98.
SULLIVAN, Gen., 158; James, 305;
Thos., 168.
SULTER—SOULTER, John, 172,
179.
SUMMERELL, J., 248.
SUMMERFIELD, Thos., 51.
SUMMERHILL, Philip, 172.
SUMMERLIN, Thos., 88.
SUMMERS, Dancy, 171; Eliz., 26;
John, 172; Joseph, 57; Maj., 162;
Nancy, 23; Richard, 53.
SUMTER, Gen., 140, 142, 146.
SURRENCY, Jacob, 99; James, 100;
Penelope, 101; Robt., 101.
SUTLEY, David, 199; Mary, 201;
Michael, 197; Susan, 184.
SUTTON, Abner, 253; Francis S., 64;
Jacob, 53; Joel, 253; Moses, 84;
Sarah, 87.
SWAIN, Betsy, 108; Martha, 112; Wm.,
186.
SWAN, Caty, 195.
SWANSEY, Nathaniel, 51.
SWANSON, Francis, 87; John, 81.
SWANTROUTER, Lieut., 150.
SWARDS, Edward E., 275.
SWEARENGEN, Mary, 354; Van, 354.
SWEATMAN, Augustine, 235; John
James, 235; Polly, 235; Wm., 235.
SWENDLE, Solomon, 76; Thos., 76.
SWIFT, Elias, 79; Flower, 231, 284,
326; John, 276, 284, 326; John D.,
81; Katherine, 81; Lucy, 228, 278;
Mary Ann, 211; Thos., 81; Tyre, 197,
326; Tyrus, 265; Wm., 79, 228, 278,
326, 335.
SWILLY—SUILLY, John, 97, 98;
Nicholas, 98; Samuel, 98; Sarah, 8.
SWINNY, Samuel H., 25.
SWINSON, Thos., 60.
SWISHER, Eliz., 67.
SWORDS, Susan, 64.
SYBERT, John H., 64.
SYKES, Arthur, 98; Charlotte, 101;

Frances, 108; Josiah, 98; Samuel,
110.
TABOR—TABER, Adkinson, 327;
Eliz., 232, 297; Francis W., 297;
Isaac, 196, 297; James, 297; John,
232, 245, 257, 260, 297, 344; Milly, 201;
Pardon T., 273; Susan, 207; Susan-
na, 297; Zachariah, 245, 344.
TACKETT, Wm., 266.
TAILOR, Geo., 189.
TALBOT—TALBERT, John, 169,179;
Mathew, 284; Matilda, 182; Peggy,
187; Suckey, 26; Thos., 282; Wm., 15,
346.
TALLEY, Joannah, 187; Page, 54.
TALLENT, Sally, 32.
TALLIAFERRO, John, 9; Richard,
9; Sally, 3.
TANIN, Geo., 53.
TANKERSLEY, Fountain, 19; Whin-
ney, 19.
TANNER, Abram, 68; Elviney, 101;
Polly, 64.
TANNEY, Miss E., 22.
TAPLEY, Adam, 51; Joel, 83.
TAPP, Curtis, 210; Willis, 198.
TARRANTS, John, 28.
TARVER, Bird, 53; John F. M., 47;
Samuel, 47; Tabitha, 81; Wm., 47.
TATE—TAIT, Ann, 241, 319; Ann C.,
319; Anna Victory, 319; Catherine
K., 319; Chas., 226, 261; Cooper B.,
204; Eliza C., 199, 319; Eliz., 194, 203;
Frances C., 319; Hannah, 332;
James, 104, 226, 240, 264, 266, 269,
270, 275, 276, 297, 319; Jiny, 23; John,
158, 241, 287; Lucinda, 210; Mary,
213; Ospah, 295, 333; Rebecca, 223,
240; Richard, 171; Robt. L., 70; Sam-
uel, 319; Capt. Samuel, 277; Sarah,
203; Solomon, 197; Thos., 333; Thos.
S., 319; Wm., 332; Wm. B., 319; Wm.
H., 226.
TATOM—TATUM, Abel, 62; Abner,
268; Absalom, 68, 268; Avarilla, 65;
Fanny, 68; Isaac, 62; James, 68;
Jane, 62; John, 62, 63, 228, 271,290;
John N., 102; Joseph R., 288; Mary,
J., 206; Nancy, 66; Wm., 189.
TAYLOR—TALER, Anna, 37, 258;
Betsy, 258; Chas., 258, 259; Col.,155;
Daniel, 77; David S., 295; Edmond
W., 19; Edmund, 287; Eliz., 33, 60,
184, 271, 346; Eliz. B., 192; Geo., 69,
255, 258; Grant, 169, 283; Grant R.,
77; Hannah, 92; Hiram, 196; James,
81; James M., 84; Jeremiah, 228, 260,
350; Jesse, 172; John, 79, 122; John
Van, 113; Joseph, 17, 295, 356;
Joseph G., 56; Josiah, 20; Laura,

YARBROUGH, Celia, 60; Eliz., 204; Graves, 243, 259, 327, 350; James, 21, 96, 259, 272, 287, 350; Japeth, 275; Jeremiah, 21, 238; John, 272; Katherine, 212; Nancy, 201; Thos., 15; Wm., 173.
YATES, James, 60; Joseph, 258.
YEARGIN, Samuel, 325.
YEARLAW, Eliz., 194.
YEATES, John, 59.
YERBY, Abraham, 51; Mary, 49; Wm., 78.
YORK, Asa, 215, 314; Betsy, 33; James, 69; John, 253; John G., 206, 299; Nancy, 296; Ruth, 194; Singleton, 69; Wm., 166, 205, 206, 296.
YOUMANS, Nancy, 100.
YOUNG, Chas., 224; David, 50, 117; Delphia, 27; Gad, 261; Geo., 49; Isham, 168; James, 14, 50, 76, 257, 281, 287, 288; John, 172, 173; Mary, 340; Owen W., 58, 59; Rebecca, 82, 113; Richard, 50; Shadrack, 114; Susannah, 236, 357; Thos., 3; Wm., 78, 120, 170, 236, 264, 265, 361; Wm. A., 313.
YOW, John Wm., 189; Thos. A., 243.
YOWELL, Joel, 227, 237, 263, 280, 340; Joshua, 280; Lucy, 227, 280.
ZACHARY—ZACHRY, Abner, 81; Asa C., 81; Clementina R., 81; James, 10; Jesse, 96; John, 57.
ZARA, Williamson, 96.
ZELLERS, Jacob, 63.
ZELNER, Geo., 63.
ZIMMERMAN, Philip, 62.
ZUBER, Jacob, 85; John, 96.

www.ingramcontent.com/pod-product-compliance
Lightning Source LLC
Chambersburg PA
CBHW050555270326
41926CB00012B/2068